Praise for *The Art of Insight*

Data visualization books don't typically transport you to new worlds. Alberto Cairo's *The Art of Insight* delves into the lives of numerous designers and what has shaped them. Each chapter showcases stunning examples, but also life stories and the motivations that informed choices. I laughed, I cried, I cheered, but perhaps most importantly, I caught glimpses of myself and my own story. **—Bridget Cogley, co-author of *Functional Aesthetics for Data Visualization* and chief visualization officer at Versalytix**

Practitioners of data visualization and storytelling hope to get people to see, understand, and feel differently about data. *The Art of Insight* has me thinking differently about the field of data visualization and storytelling itself. Cairo's intimate and caring interviews and commentary are revealing, thought-provoking, and most of all, inspiring. **—Steve Wexler, professional chart looker-atter and co-author of *The Big Book of Dashboards*, and Author of *The Big Picture***

This book is a breath of fresh air following the exhaustion of the pandemic! Written in dialogue with numerous data artists, designers, and illustrators, Cairo has crafted a pragmatic, inspiring reflection on the process and purpose of contemporary data visualization. **—Catherine D'Ignazio, associate professor and director of the Data + Feminism Lab, MIT, and co-author of *Data Feminism***

In today's frenetic life, it's common to quickly consume, scan, and scroll, rarely giving a data graphic we encounter more than a few seconds of our time and attention. In *The Art of Insight*, Alberto Cairo slows down the pace for us and takes us on a much deeper dive into the rich narratives, human emotions, and profound motivations behind the data. The way he weaves his own illuminating thoughts and observations together with the words and stories of the creators themselves will leave you feeling both informed and inspired. This book is a much needed demonstration of the opposite of superficial critique, and the data visualization world will be better off for it. **—Ben Jones, co-founder and CEO of Data Literacy**

The concept of "data visualization" means so many different things for many different people. With *The Art of Insight*, Alberto Cairo brings us along on his exploration of the new and different ways designers are visualizing our world. It's an uplifting journey to get a glimpse into the perspectives and processes of these creative data artists. **—Randy Krum, visualization designer, author of *Cool Infographics: Effective Communication with Data Visualization and Design*, and founder of InfoNewt**

The world of data visualization is a beautiful mess, and we are lucky to have Alberto Cairo as such an experienced, empathetic and curious guide to show us around. Tying the seminal data visualization works covered in the book to intimate conversations on the biographies and thoughts of the creators behind them paints a rich and multi-faceted portrait of this ever-evolving field. This book allows us to see the world of data visualization through many different eyes, offering plenty of opportunities to find personal connections and inspiration to aspiring practitioners and seasoned professionals alike. Bravo! **—Moritz Stefaner, independent data visualization expert at Truth & Beauty**

I've been a fan of Alberto Cairo's work for years, and his new book, *The Art of Insight,* is a delightful addition to his body of work. I enjoyed his conversations with designers from around the world about their histories, their evolution as artists and artisans, and their insights about their work in visualization. Examples ranged from the humorous to the tragic. I'm grateful to Alberto for sharing his conversations with these brilliant visualization designers and for the inspiration for all of us who share the goal of creating visualizations that carry meaning to an audience. **—A. John Bailer, Professor Emeritus of Statistics at Miami University, past president of the International Statistical Institute, podcast host of Stats+Stories, and author *Statistics Behind the Headlines***

This is a terrific idea for a book. It takes us directly into the minds of information designers. Alberto has wisely and generously given them a platform to describe—in their own words—how they work, and how their often quite personal data pieces led to real-world visualizations. **—Nigel Holmes, designer and author of *Joyful Infographics: A Friendly, Human Approach to Data***

Visualization stretches beyond reports and sterile charts to uses more tightly coupled with real life, which is full of beauty, complexity, and stories. With *The Art of Insight*, Alberto Cairo places the full field on display. Learn the design and analysis processes of those in less traditional visualization roles, alongside Alberto's unique perspective, and your own data work will benefit, wherever that may be. **—Nathan Yau, statistician, FlowingData.com**

The creative process can often seem like a black box, a mysterious contraption of levers to get to a final solution. In his latest book, Cairo unpacks this mysterious activity, unveiling the story behind incredible data visualization and information design pieces, and in the process, revealing the human behind the data. **—Manuel Lima, author of *The New Designer: Rejecting Myths, Embracing Change***

The Art of Insight is an inspiring collection of tales of forms and shapes. Not the forms and shapes that make up beautiful art and visualisation but the journeys that formed and shaped the visualization artists behind them. In Cairo's book, visualization artists reflect on their diverse backgrounds, inspirational sources, and haphazard career paths. They share insights into their thought processes, their sources of inspiration, and both the little and big things in life that influence them. The book provides wonderful insights into the conscious and sometimes unconscious steps that preceded the artists' creations. By providing a lens into how these artists were formed, the reader is left feeling encouraged to embrace their own journey into visualization. **—Claus Thorn Ekstrøm, professor of Biostatistics at the Department of Public Health, University of Copenhagen**

Another amazing book by Alberto Cairo. It presents a broad overview of contemporary visualization practices through a plurality of voices that are diverse and culturally rich. Conversations with key visualizers from around the globe are interwoven with insights and acuity from Cairo's deep and vast knowledge of the field. The book is a must for practitioners and students alike as we are introduced to a variety of approaches to representing data, including first-hand experiences guided by the author's generous views. What a joy! **—Isabel Meirelles, professor, OCAD University, and author of *Design for Information***

What a treat to get a glimpse into the thought processes and motivations of world-class data visualization designers! It's hard to quantify the amount of inspiration to be drawn from the stories behind the powerful images in this book. The sheer variety of visualizations shown also serve as an important reminder of the huge array of purposes that data visualization can serve. Many chart creators (including myself) fall into the trap of thinking of "charts" as just being of the particular type that they tend to design (data art, business reporting, infographics, etc.). Seeing so many effective visualizations serving so many different purposes is an instant cure for this myopic view. **—Nick Desbarats, educator and author of *Practical Charts***

Alberto Cairo's books to date have been about encouraging us to better understand, read, and make data visualizations. *The Art of Insight* seeks to do what many ask about but which is often intangible: What is it that makes great visual designers able to come up with their magic? He achieves this through essays crafted in conversation with people who pull back the curtains on some of their work.

Visualization is about communication, language and syntax, and about the multiple small decisions taken. However, more than anything, it's about the love that is poured into the work. Love is the hardest emotion to define, though we recognize it when we see it, and yearn for its warm embrace. Love is sometimes conventional, sometimes unexplained, and this book is a wonderful exploration of both Alberto's, and his interviewees' love of their craft. There are great examples of technique, and discussion on how to elevate it through best practice or by breaking so-called "rules." This book goes behind the scenes of this brilliant work, and it expresses deep reflections on the foundations of the craft, and how we might do the same to find our own way.

Of course we all have our own opinions but Alberto teaches us to converse with what we see, and also with its creators. This is a wonderfully freeing principle to better understand data visualizations, and to do so critically, but with empathy.

Finally, any book that includes a quote from Black Sabbath gets my unconditional love.

—Ken Field, researcher, cartographer, and author of *Cartography* and *Thematic Mapping*

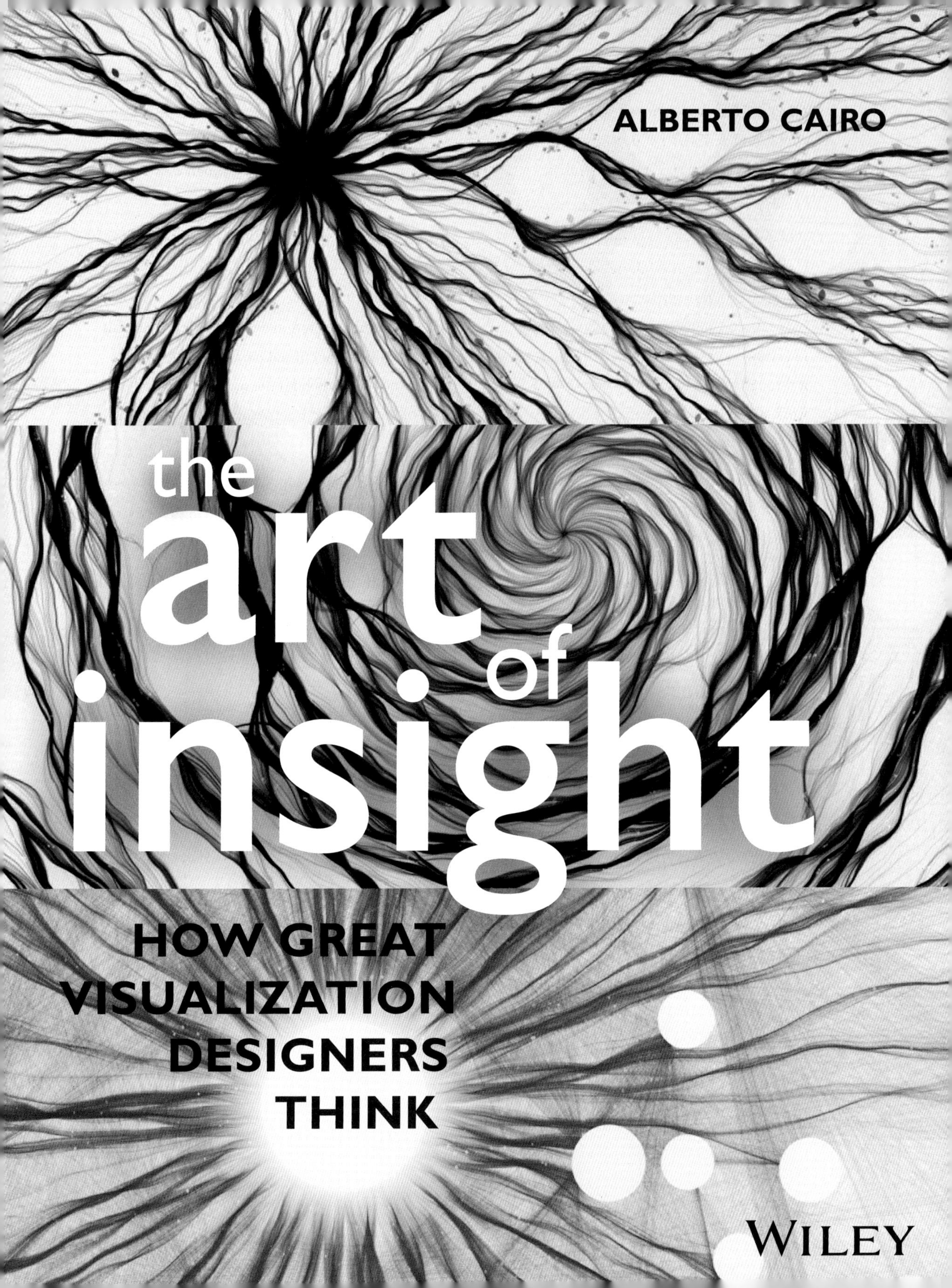
ALBERTO CAIRO
the art of insight
HOW GREAT VISUALIZATION DESIGNERS THINK
WILEY

Published by John Wiley & Sons, Inc., Hoboken, New Jersey.
Published simultaneously in Canada.

For general information on our other products and services or for technical support, please contact our Customer Care Department within the United States at (800) 762-2974, outside the United States at (317) 572-3993 or fax (317) 572-4002.

Wiley also publishes its books in a variety of electronic formats. Some content that appears in print may not be available in electronic formats. For more information about Wiley products, visit our web site at www.wiley.com.

Library of Congress Cataloging-in-Publication Data is Available:

ISBN 9781119797395 (Paperback)
ISBN 9781119797241 (ePDF)
ISBN 9781119797234 (ePub)

Cover Design: Alberto Cairo and Wiley
Cover Image: © Nadieh Bremer | Visual Cinnamon

SKY10056021_092223

For Alex,

lover of darkness, dragons, and dreams

I have sought only reasons to transcend our darkest nihilism. Not, I would add, through virtue, nor because of some rare elevation of the spirit, but from an instinctive fidelity to a light in which I was born, and in which for thousands of years men have learned to welcome life even in suffering.
Albert Camus

Take advice to ditch all adverbs lightly.
Ursula K. Le Guin

Enjoy and have others enjoy, without doing harm to yourself or anyone else; that is all there is to morality.
Nicolas Chamfort

Being a person is not a goal that can be achieved but a purpose to be sustained.
Martin Hägglund

It is not doctrines that console us in the end, but people: their example, their singularity, their courage and steadfastness, their being with us when we need them the most. In dark times, nothing so abstract as faith in History, Progress, Salvation, or Revolution will do us much good. These are doctrines. It is people we need, people whose examples show us what it means to go on, to keep going, despite everything.
Michael Ignatieff

The lover of life's not a sinner.
Black Sabbath

CONTENTS

About the Author

Alberto Cairo is the Knight Chair in Visual Journalism at the School of Communication of the University of Miami (UM). He's also the director of visualization at UM's Institute for Data Science and Computing.

Cairo is the author of the books *The Functional Art: An Introduction to Information Graphics and Visualization* (2013), *The Truthful Art: Data, Charts, and Maps for Communication* (2016), and *How Charts Lie: Getting Smarter about Visual Information* (2019).

Cairo is a journalist and a designer with a long career in the news industry. He has been the director of online information graphics at the Spanish newspaper *El Mundo*, and director of graphics and multimedia for the magazines of Editora Globo, in Brazil. Since the early 2000s he has worked as a designer and educator in more than 30 countries.

Besides teaching, Cairo regularly designs visualizations and consults for technology companies, governmental agencies, educational institutions, and international organizations.

A Note on Typography

This book contains numerous and extensive quotes. I'm using two main type styles. The one in this paragraph indicates that I'm the person who is writing.

> This other style—smaller font, different color—indicates a quote from either a book, an article, or the words of one of my many interlocutors.

"One Amongst Many," a physical, interactive data installation of women in computing.

"Young women entering fields dominated by men often feel like there is no history of people like them in their field. We know now that this is an issue of storytelling, not of history. Women have been contributing to every field, however invisibly, since the beginning of time. One Amongst Many attempts to illuminate the histories of women in computing that have been diminished or erased. It is a data installation where each woman is arranged in a field by the year of her greatest achievement, and the height of the orb correlated to her renown. Every orb starts dimmed, and gets brighter each time another person reads about them, literally shedding light on the woman's accomplishments."

By Christina Dacanay, Tina Rungsawang, and Shirley Wu: https://oneamongstmany.com/

Photos by Nok Jangkamolkulchai.

Introduction

On Magic

with Shirley Wu

To live well is to cope with the ways in which life is hard while finding enough in one's life worth wanting.

—Kieran Setiya

One early morning in November of 2021, Alex, my youngest son, questioned me about the apparent meaninglessness of life. "What are we humans here for anyway?" he asked.

Alex has been a precocious old soul since he learned to talk. The week I was working on this preamble, he wrote an autobiographical poem that contains a haunting alliteration to define who he is: "I'm a lover of darkness, dragons, and dreams."

At the time of our conversation we were both coming to terms with that darkness: healing, mustering our dragons for battle, and rebuilding our dreams. The pandemic years had been tough.

I remember myself thinking in silence for a moment. We were on our morning commute. Alex, sitting in the back of the car, was looking out at parents and kids passing by on their way to school. He was in a somber mood, and I guess he wasn't expecting a quick answer from Dad, who's usually so aloof and introverted.

But my answer poured out like a torrent. Life, I said, is indeed meaningless in itself. Meaning isn't a predetermined thing that exists beyond ourselves and our connections to others, or that we receive from higher powers. Meaning is something that we build by living through the myriad of little but immensely relevant events that cross our paths. It emerges from paying deep attention to the joys and beauty offered by the objects, creatures, and people whom we love, and by sharing back with them. That's all there is to a good life brimming with magic.

Alex's reply was a soft murmur.

I parked at school and noticed that my son was staring at a fence next to us. There was movement on it.

Alex suddenly yelled, his voice a mixture of excitement and wonderment: "Dad, look, songbirds!" Indeed, there they were, two merry critters standing on the wire, chirping at each other while ignoring the multitude below.

I smiled. "See? That's what I meant. That's the magic."

~ ~ ~

This is a book about such magic. To write it, I spoke with many magicians, visualization designers who build meaning as a tribute to themselves or as an aid to others. They make things, they enjoy the process and, by sharing its results, they brighten the world.

Some of these designers are old friends; others are people whose work I've found fascinating more recently. They are data scientists, engineers, analysts, humanists, artists, journalists, and educators, each with their own views about the practice.

My sample for this book isn't representative of anything outside of my head. The designers you're about to meet are the first who came to my mind when I felt the need to rekindle my love for the design of information, the craft to which I've devoted my professional life. A half-joking alternative title I entertained was *On the Consolation of Visualization*, as a nod to Boethius's famous *On the Consolation of Philosophy.* The list of people whose work I find interesting, inspiring, or intriguing is much longer, though; should I have more pages and time, I'd have reached out to many more designers to seek solace.

This is also a book about insight. Not in the sense of data-driven analytical insight; there are plenty of books in the market about that, including some I've written myself. This book is different. I use the term *insight* in the sense of exploring who the designers I spoke with are and how they see themselves. I'm interested in how they shape their craft, how the craft shapes them in return, and how that interaction creates an ethos.

Finally, I envision this book as one link in the broader chain of historical conversations about information design and visualization. It's the result of the interplay between what my interlocutors told me, past readings that were brought back to memory during our chats, and my reflections about both. I've ended up writing an essay in the literal sense of the term: a way to *essay* ideas, to contemplate them in a nonjudgmental manner with no expectation of reaching conclusions, of inferring overarching lessons, or—gods forbid the hubris—of developing a coherent system of thought. The philosopher Joan-Carles Mèlich calls this approach to thinking and writing "the wisdom of the uncertain."

This *The Art of Insight* is, then, a wandering, and not a solitary one.

I'll begin it with my friend and occasional collaborator **Shirley Wu**, and to the one-night show that she hosted at EV Gallery (New York City) in the fall of 2022. It was titled "~~wonder~~ & *hope*" (**Figure I.1**).

Figure I.1: "~~wonder~~ & *hope*" Tuan Huang /

https://www.wonder-and-hope.art/ / last accessed Febuary 16, 2023

~ ~ ~

'~~wonder~~ & *hope*' was a data-driven reflection on loss, grief, and healing:

> Until the beginning of the COVID-19 pandemic, I had always loved being outdoors. There was a sense of wonder about it: the blue sky, seeing flowers blooming, and birds chirping. I used to take many photographs whenever I went outside or visited a different city for work.
>
> And then the pandemic happened. We all had to isolate. My husband and I started reading report after report of anti-Asian hate crimes across the United States, especially in New York and San Francisco (where we used to live), and I stopped going out by myself. When we moved to New York City a year later for me to start grad school, I often had to walk outside by myself, and I was paralyzed with fear. I realized that I had stopped looking up. I'd keep my eyes firmly on the ground because I had read that making eye contact could be a trigger for hate crimes. I had lost all joy of being outside.
>
> I wanted to tell that story somehow. I've always used data to tell stories about others, but could I use my own data to explain and understand myself? I started thinking about how to quantify the joy I used to feel, and realized that I used to love taking photos outside. So I gathered four years of my photos, from March 2018 to March 2022, and processed their dates, primary colors, and geotagged coordinates. And just for fun, I went through all 20,000 or so photos by hand to categorize them into food, flower, and art photos.

The first half of Shirley's 2022 show, "~~wonder~~," consisted of a series of concentric diagrams, the first two corresponding to March and April of 2018 (**Figure I.2**).

In these visualizations, each symbol corresponds to a photograph out of large database. Symbols are colored and arranged according to each photograph's most common color. Symbols closer to the center, enclosed by a thick line, are photographs taken inside Shirley's home in Tokyo, where she lived during the spring of 2018. Shirley loves flowers and food, therefore the predominance of photos about them:

> I start the show with March 2018, which is one of my favorite months, because I got to see the cherry blossoms in Tokyo. That's reflected in the data and denoted in the visualization with a flower symbol. The next month, I got to visit China and Amsterdam, so those photos are marked by dots and flowers further from the center. The same happens in May 2019, when I was in Spain and Germany (**Figure I.3**). But in February 2020, the dots shrink back into the center. It was right before the lockdowns, so we stopped going out as much. At the same time, we were cooking a lot more at home, hence all the food photos, denoted by double rings—they look like plates!

On March 16, 2020, the city of San Francisco issued a stay-at-home order, which would end in May. The plates corresponding to April, May, and June of that year, shown in mar 2018 — tokyo

Pre-pandemic, I used to love being outside. I loved looking up at a bright blue sky and feeling the wind on my skin and the sun on my face. I'd see the flowers blooming or hear the birds chirping and be overcome with a sense of wonder.

When I moved to Tokyo for three months in March 2018, I spent a whole month chasing cherry blossoms. I have fond memories of growing up in Japan and seeing the streets lined with pink every spring—and to be able to see that again for the first time in two decades, my heart burst with joy and nostalgia.

how to read this visualization

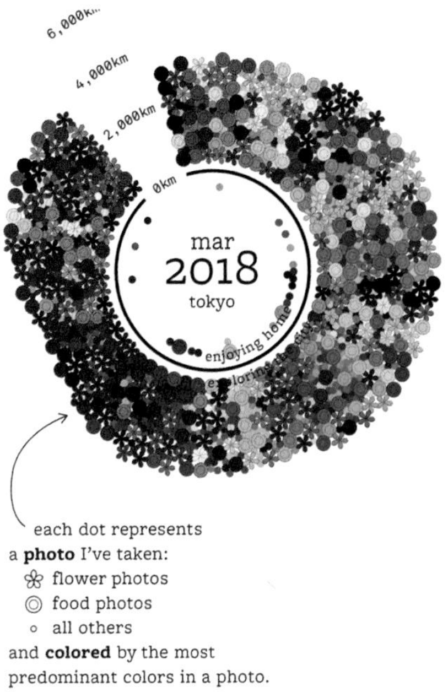

apr 2018 — tokyo

I also used to love traveling. I'd tack on a few days (or weeks) before or after a conference and explore the area. And in April 2018, I got to spend a whole week traveling through southern China with my mom and grandparents. They were 81 and 82, but they hiked to waterfalls and hotels with little help. And in every place we stopped, my grandpa would proudly tell anyone who'd listen: "这是我孙女，她特意从美国回来陪我的! (My granddaughter came back all the way from America to travel with me!)".

(omg I cry.)

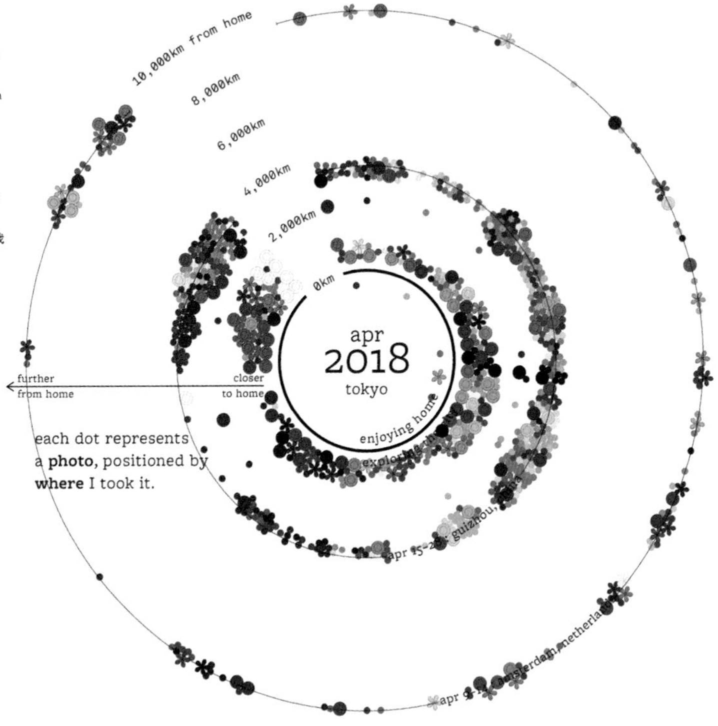

Figure I.2: "~~wonder~~ & *hope*" March and April of 2018

In May 2019, I was able to fulfill a years-long dream to create a physical data visualization. I collaborated with my super talented then-studiomate Alice Lee to create a data-driven window display of 30 women Nobel Laureates. It was a series of firsts: buying wood panels, figuring out the laser-cutter, inviting friends over to paint the laser-cut flowers, being part of my very first art show.

That show gave me the courage to create "One Amongst Many"—a physical data installation of sixteen women in computing—with Tina Rungsawang and Christina Dacanay during my artist residency at NYU ITP. I will never forget the story of an older woman from the university's computer science department, who said the installation made her hopeful that *maybe one day someone would honor her work in this way.*

Each dot represents a photo I've taken between 2018 and 2022.

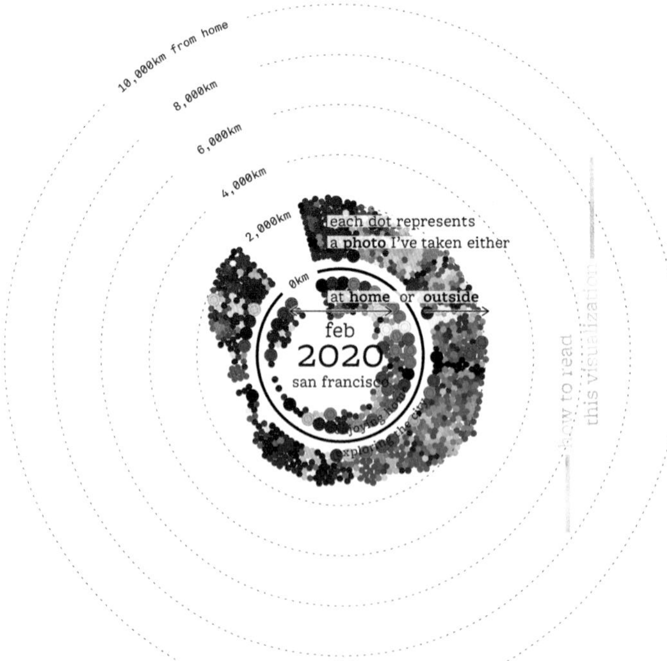

During my three-month residency at ITP, I had Airbnb'd a single bedroom in Brooklyn and ate out most of the time. So it was a relief to get back home to our own kitchen in San Francisco and cook for ourselves (which is reflected in the photos, hehe). At the same time, we were becoming increasingly aware of a new epidemic making its way across the Pacific and after one last Napa trip in mid-February, we hunkered down at home—hoping for the best but preparing for the worst.

feb 2020 san francisco

Figure I.3: "~~wonder~~ & *hope*" May of 2019 and February of 2020 a three-dimensional array on **Figure I.4**, reveal a striking reduction of the number of photographs. Shirley would only resume taking outdoor photos almost a year later, in the Spring of 2022:

> We moved to Brooklyn in August of 2021, and I had a daily commute. That's when you start to see more photographs outdoors again. But I realized that I lost all sense of wonder about being outside.

Shirley's joy had vanished. That's noticeable on the graphic corresponding to March of 2022 (**Figure I.5**). There aren't photographs of flowers, and just a handful of food. Her sense of the passage of time also got distorted. As part of the '~~wonder~~' portion of the show was a bowl where the circular diagrams were projected chronologically. Above this bowl, a solenoid valve—a device controlled programmatically to open and close at varying intervals—released water (**Figure I.6**):

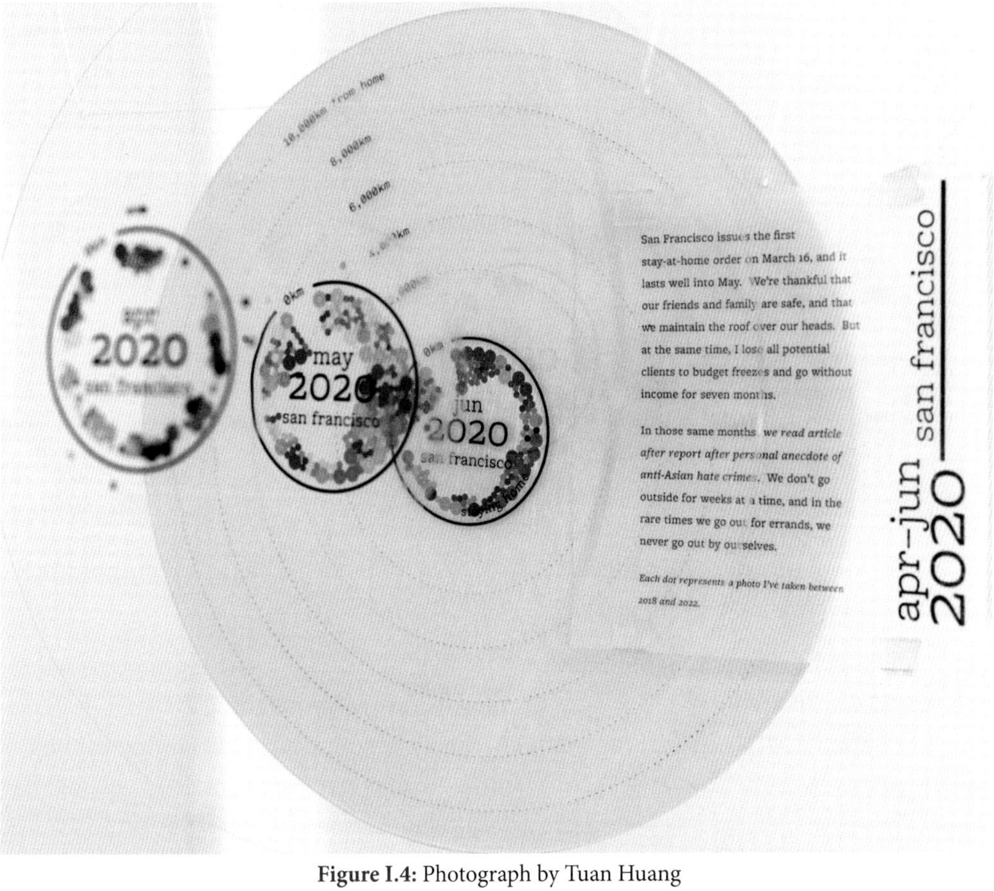

Figure I.4: Photograph by Tuan Huang

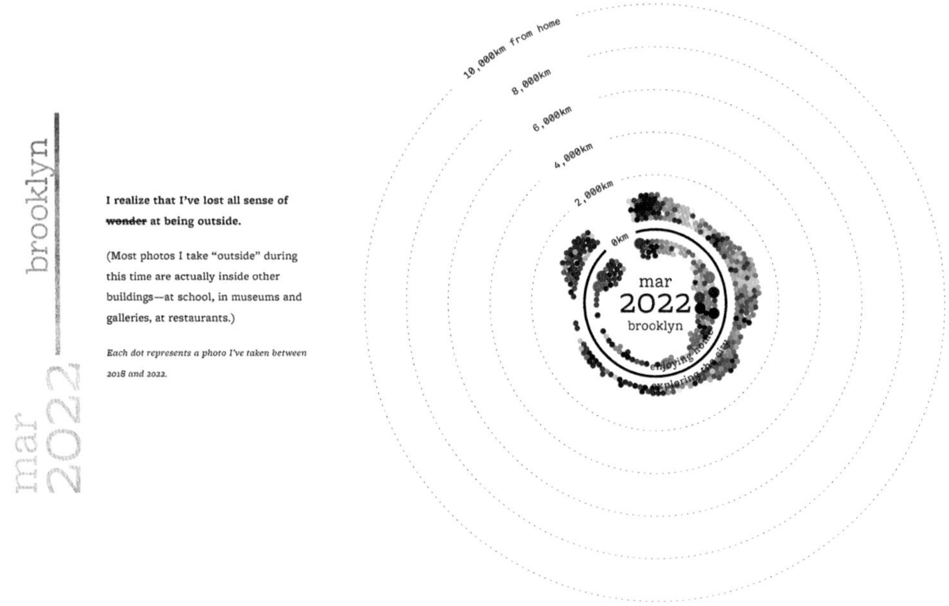

Figure I.5: "~~wonder~~ & *hope*" March of 2022

> The speed of the water drip corresponds to the number of COVID deaths each week. I wanted the water drip to distort the graphics, symbolizing what I felt during the pandemic: a warping of time and of reality itself. I was in constant fear and worry, and this felt like the best way to convey it.

Shirley then explained a marvelous design accident:

> The solenoid valve, because it was mechanical, had this really loud clicking noise. Do you hear a click, click, click sound?

I told Shirley I did. She continued:

> There was one person who told me something really beautiful. She thought that the water drips were tears. I really liked that interpretation.

I then told Shirley about a theme I'll return to later in this book: the types of visualizations that I design are intended to "communicate," to "carry meaning" from a designer (me) to an audience (you). The way that I've usually taught this process is that (a) I have a message that I wish to convey—a "story," should you prefer that term; (b) I encode that message using shapes, colors, and other visual attributes paired with textual annotations; and then (c) I show the result to an audience to decode and interpret.

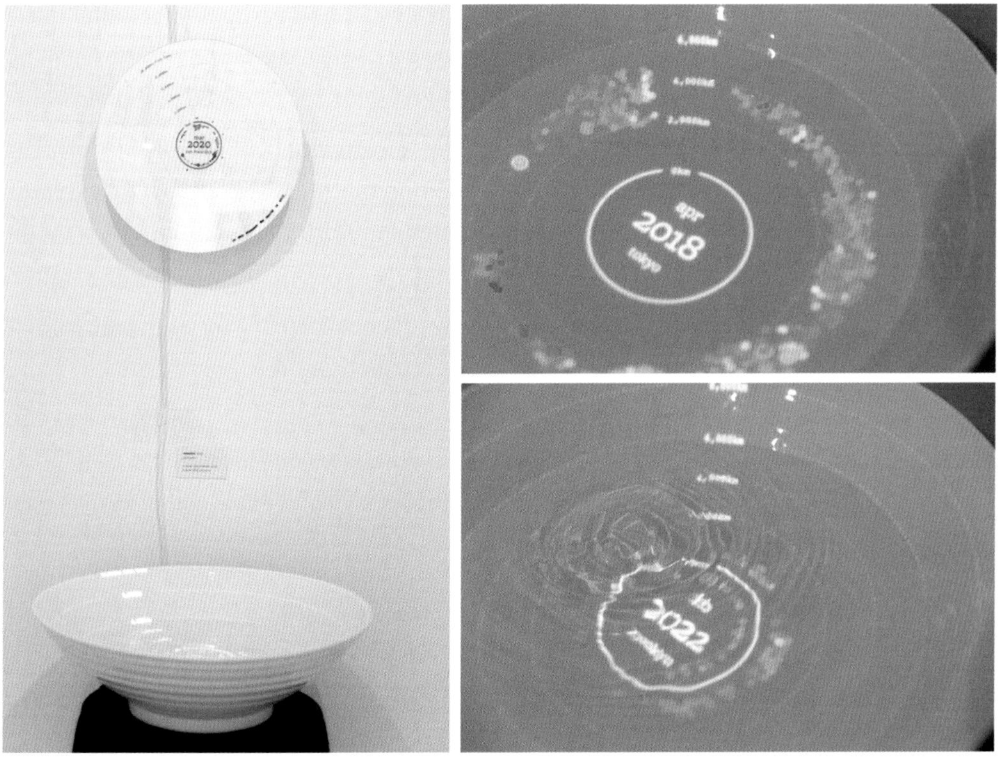

Figure I.6: Photographs by Tuan Huang

The challenge to this way of conceiving data visualization is that it's naive. We can control what happens on our end, but we might lose sight of what happens on the other, the reader's. A reader's interpretation can be very different to what we intended:

> There's a part of this project that I don't consider data visualization, but art. In data visualization we try to communicate; sometimes we succeed, sometimes we don't. But the artistic part of my project is that it gave people enough space to relate to its content, and come up with very personal interpretations and make the project their own. Visitors saw themselves in the diagrams that I had designed. They projected their own lived experiences. So, the story in these graphics is very personal, but it's also not personal at all. It's a shared experience.
>
> Let me go back to the water drip. I purposely didn't add a label to explain that the speed of the water drip was based on COVID data. I got a lot of questions about it, and when I explained the meaning behind it, everyone appreciated the answer. Even before they asked, they told me that the clicking sound caused a certain anxiety within them. They intuitively grasped that the emotion I wanted to elicit was related to my experience through the pandemic, and they felt it too.

> Because I didn't explain everything, and instead offered viewers space, it led to beautiful interpretations, like the tears. The push and pull, the tension between giving enough and then pulling some things back—that's one of the most relevant things I think I've learned in this past year.

In my book *How Charts Lie* (2019) I wrote that the information that we put in a visualization is sometimes less revealing than the information that we leave out. By not explaining her designs, by leaving the door open to ambiguity, Shirley allowed visitors to walk into her visuals and see themselves in them.

The second part of Shirley's exhibit was titled '*hope*'. It consisted of a series of white flowers (**Figure I.7**):

> ~~wonder~~ is about my experiences leading up to March 2022, when I first realized what I had lost. After that, I forced myself to look up and around more when walking outside. For a month, I kept feeling dread. Things that used to excite me before the pandemic, like beautiful architecture, would mean nothing to me.

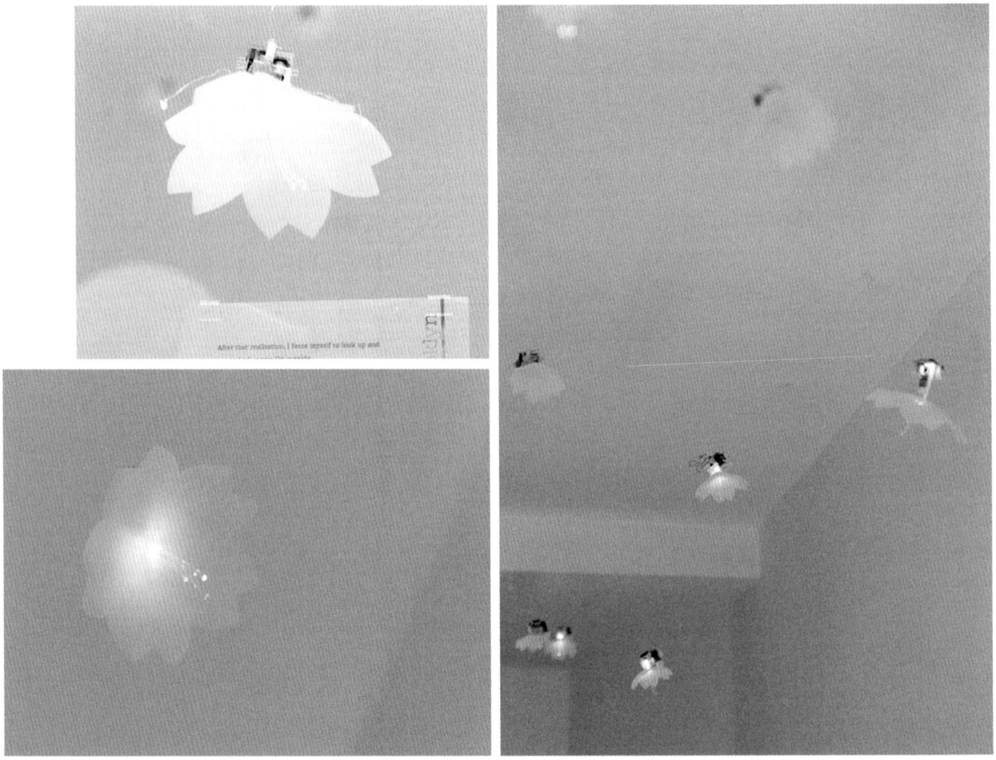

Figure I.7: Photograph by Tuan Huang

> Then one day in April, I looked up and saw a tree with its first blooms. I immediately thought, "Oh, that's really beautiful," and in that moment I felt hope again. That's why the flowers in my show are suspended above everyone's line of sight. I wanted visitors to notice only after they've gone through the whole story, the whole journey with me. I wanted it so that when they finally looked up, they'd see the flowers, the hope.
>
> Each flower corresponds to a week between 2018 and 2022. Their size is proportional to the number of photos of flowers I took during those seven days. When people walked past them, a motion detector made each flower gently light up.

The metaphor is straightforward. Flowers had disappeared from Shirley's photographs during the pandemic as a result of her life becoming grayer, duller, sadder. Their blooming, and their lighting up in the show are expressions of Shirley's healing. In hindsight, Shirley sees her show at EV Gallery as a culmination of a process of reflection, self-discovery, and the value of community, both professional and personal:

> I realized how my identity was intertwined with the show. As a child, I was a Chinese girl growing up in the Japanese countryside. Then, my family moved to the United States and I was a Chinese girl in America. Later, I became a professional and I was a Chinese-American woman working in software engineering in Silicon Valley. All of these different cultures have implicitly told me in one way or another that I should be obedient, quiet, and humble, that I shouldn't take up space.

Shirley says that her upbringing and career led her to struggle to be "socially acceptable": too many times she heard people say that she was too loud, opinionated, and intimidating. She felt pressure to conform to patriarchal social norms and she adopted a habit of belittling herself:

> This show has meant so much to me because I've spent most of my life making myself small. It's been healing to be able to take up actual physical space with my work. I've also always had a hard time asking for help. Why would anyone want to help me with such a personal project? But with this show, I was forced to ask for help; it was on a much bigger scale than I could handle by myself, and I'm glad I did. So many friends volunteered, helping with the design of the room, with the fabrication, with the install—and the install alone took more than twenty hours!
>
> And then there were all the people that showed up in person. That was amazing to see. I had so many friends and family drop by, but also so many people I didn't know, who came because they liked my previous digital work and wanted to offer support. That gives me courage and confidence, it shows that what I do matters—that *I* matter.

Later in the conversation, Shirley zoomed out from the "~~wonder~~ & *hope*" show:

> When I first started with data visualization, I didn't take myself that seriously. That's reflected in one of my earliest (and favorite) projects, the 2016 "An Interactive Visualization of Every Line

in Hamilton" (**Figure I.8**). I was obsessed with the musical. A year later, when working with my friend Nadieh Bremer on an article about homelessness in the U.S. that was published by *The Guardian*, I realized that I could use visualization for more serious topics that I also cared about.

"Legends" (**Figure I.9**), launched in 2018, is my most pivotal project; it changed the way I view my work. While working on it I realized the huge discrepancy between the number of women Nobel laureates (51 at the time) and their male counterparts (853). I was incensed. That's when I remembered how rarely I saw women's names in history and science textbooks, and in that moment I realized how small I had made myself—because I had subconsciously internalized that women couldn't be legacy-worthy.

That's when I promised myself that I'd pursue my lifelong dream of being an artist. That year (2019), I was able to land an artist residency at NYU ITP, a master's program for art and technology. There, I collaborated with two of the students, Christina Dacanay and Tina Rungsawang, on a physical data installation of 16 women in computing—my first project that took up space. The experience was so inspiring that I decided to go back to ITP as a grad student.

In the last two years, I've explored what my art could look like, experimenting with data visualization within the context of that art, and taking the time to work on myself, instead of what my clients want me to work on. That's how I got to "~~wonder~~ & *hope*."

My conversation with Shirley foreshadows many of the themes of this book: visualization as a language; the plurality of goals that such language can pursue; its power to not only enlighten an audience, but also its creators; the relevance of community; or the tricky balance that all designers negotiate in their own way between conventionality and uniqueness, norm and transgression, tradition and innovation, the impersonal and the authored, the prosaic and the poetic.

When we were about to wrap up, I asked Shirley: "Have you truly recovered your sense of wonder, then?"

"I have hope," she replied, a subtle smile illuminating her face.

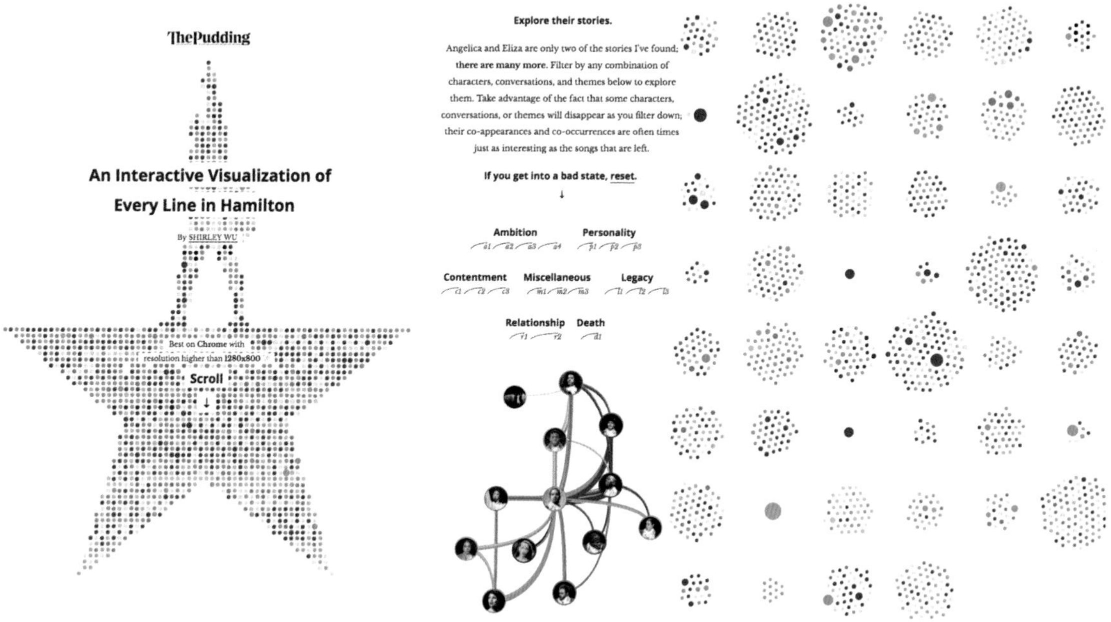

Figure I.8: "An Interactive Visualization of Every Line in Hamilton"

https://pudding.cool/2017/03/hamilton/

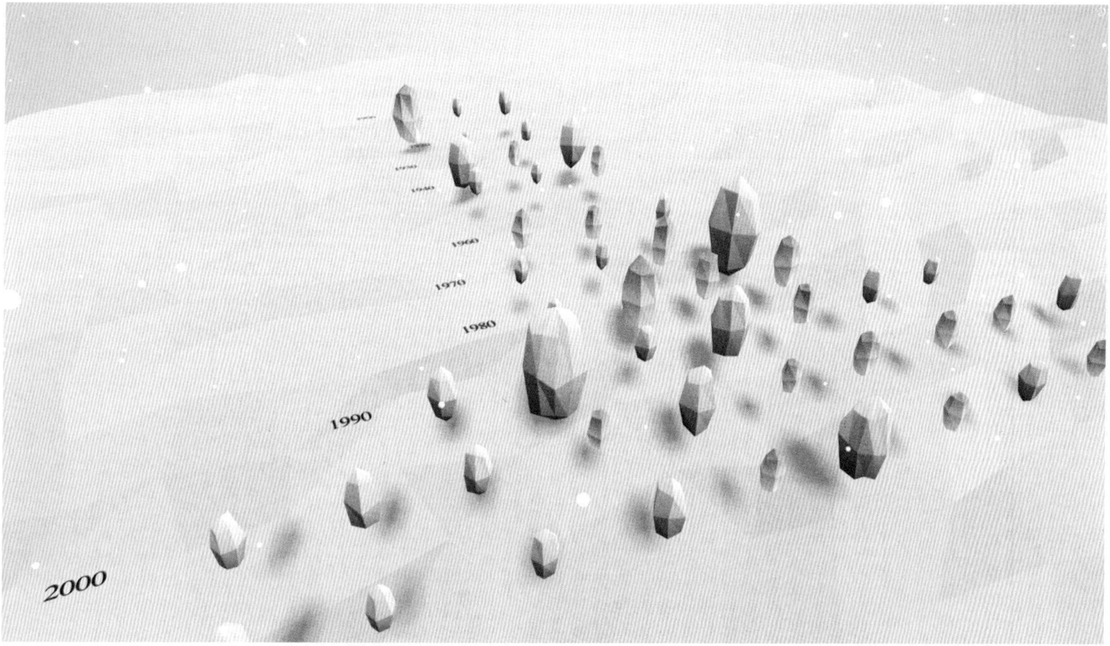

Figure I.9: "Legends"

http://shirleywu.studio/legends/ / last accessed February 16, 2023

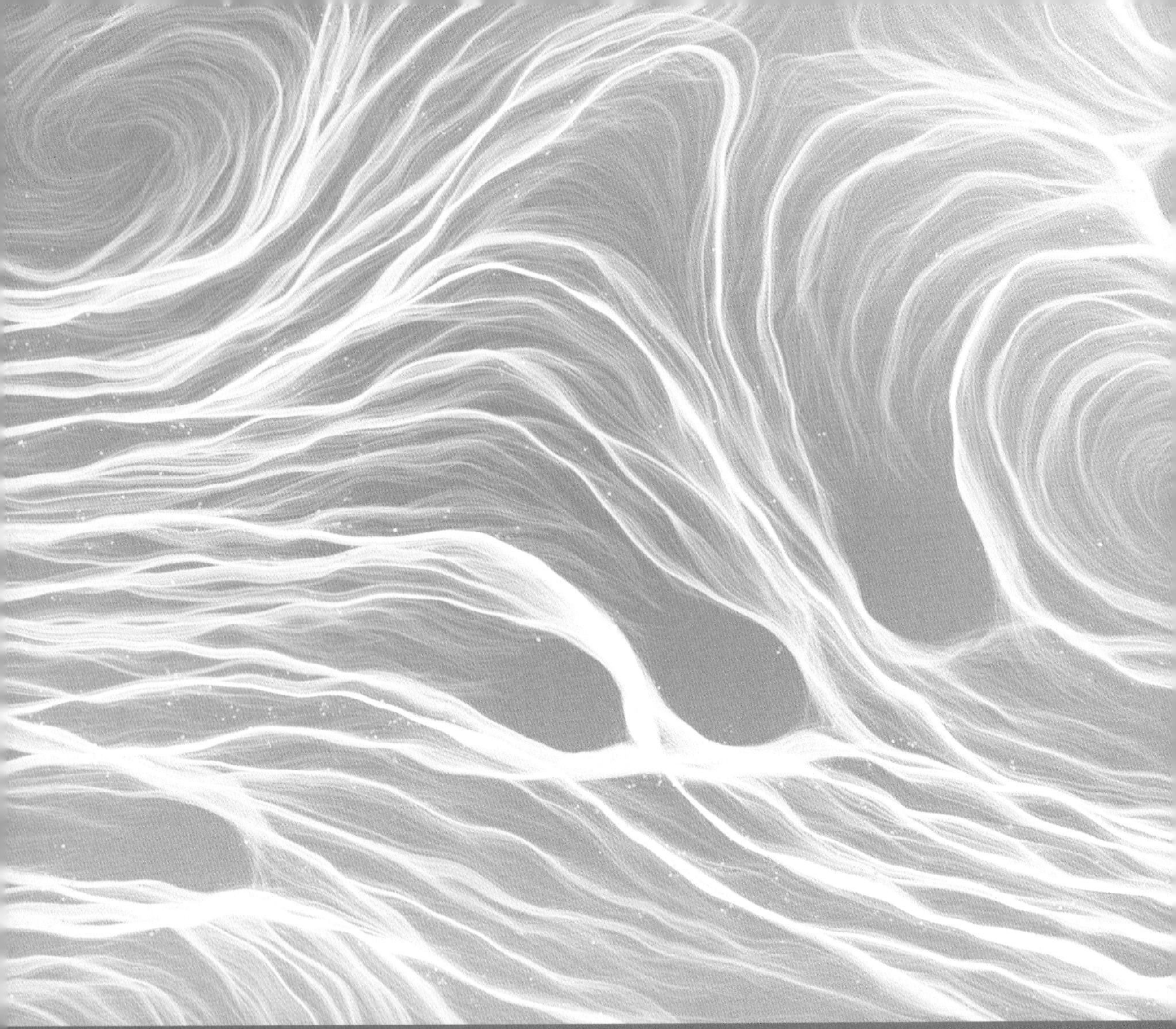

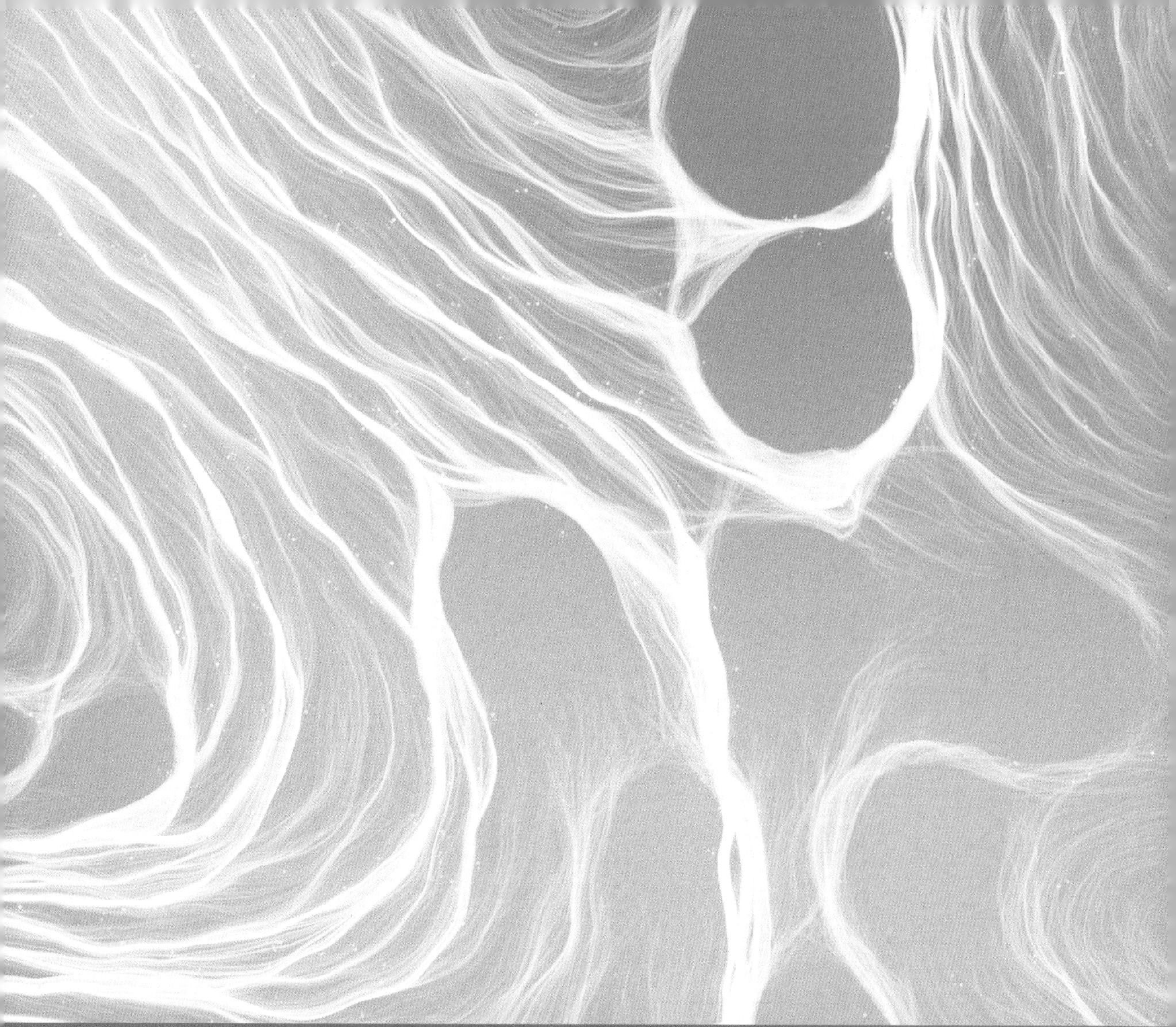

PART I

pragmatists

Figure 1.1: Ellie Highwood's global warming blanket

Elliehighwood / https://elliehighwood.com/2017/06/12/climatechangecrochet-the-global-warming-blanket/ / last accessed Febuary 16, 2023

Chapter 1
with Ed Hawkins

Unruly Stripes

There are no absolute truths, there is nothing Good, Bad, True, Beautiful, or Just in itself, but only relatively, evaluated according to a clear and distinct plan [...] Think in terms of action, and base your actions on the effects they will have.

—Michel Onfray

On June 10, 2017, Ellie Highwood, then a climate physics professor and Dean of Diversity and Inclusion at the University of Reading (UK), tweeted out an image of a blanket she had been working on over weekends: "Ok so I am a crochet addict. This is my 'global warming blanket' -stripes coloured according to last 100 years T anomaly" (**Figure 1.1**).

"Anomalies" are departures from a common baseline, which in this case was the mean world temperature between the years 1900 and 2000. In Highwood's blanket, which encompasses the 1916–2016 period, blue and green hues represent years when the mean world temperature was below the average of the 20th century, while pink, yellow, and red stripes correspond to years when temperature was above that average. Read from top to bottom, the blanket reveals a pattern of constant warming. **Figure 1.2** is based on a similar data set.

Two days later, surprised by the popularity of her tweet, Highwood acknowledged in her blog many other crocheters who had been making blankets and clothing based on climate, weather or even sky-color data. She also mentioned a charming metaphor: "global warming is often explained as greenhouse gases acting like a blanket, trapping infrared radiation and keeping the Earth warm. So that seemed like an interesting link."

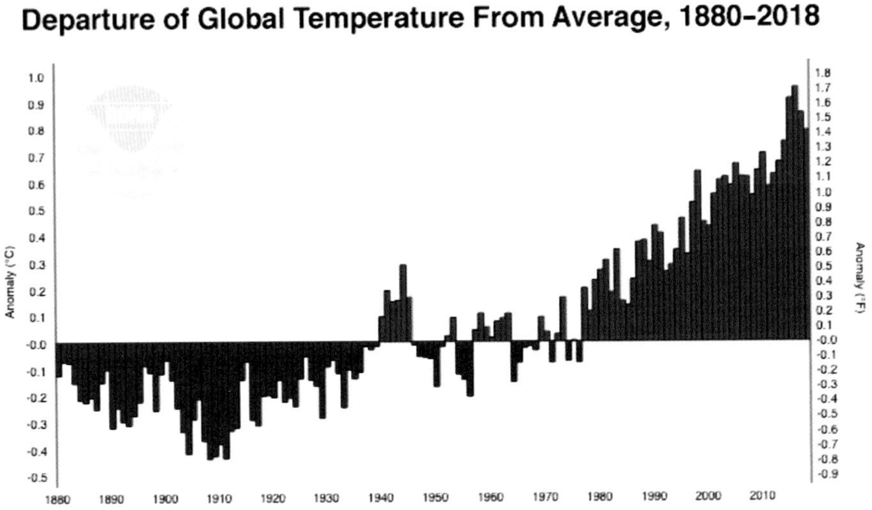

Figure 1.2: Temperature anomalies year (NOAA)

Source: NOAA National Centers for Environmental information, Climate at a Glance: Global Time Series, published May 2023, retrieved on June 3, 2023 from https://www.ncei.noaa.gov/access/monitoring/climate-at-a-glance/global/time-series

Interesting to many, including to **Ed Hawkins**, also a climate scientist at the University of Reading, who told me: "Ellie showed me the blanket in 2017 and that kick-started a thought process for me."

Before the conversation with Ellie Highwood, Hawkins had been interested in "representing climate data as simply as possible to the general public." In 2016 he designed an animated visualization that became part of the opening ceremony of the Olympic Games in Rio de Janeiro (**Figure 1.3**). Since then, Hawkins has created several variations of this spiral graphic, including one in three dimensions that looks like a tornado.

The popularity of Hawkins' spiral would pale in comparison to his next creation. Here's how he explained the genesis of what he'd call the "Warming Stripes" (**Figure 1.4**), for which he used a more vibrant color palette than Highwood's original blanket (according to Hawkins, she had to use the wool that she had available):

> In early 2018 I was invited to give a presentation at the Hay Festival of Literature & Arts, a famous literary event in the tiny little village of Hay-on-Wye, on the Welsh-English border. The Hay Festival is iconic in the book world, but that year the organization decided to put on events around the edges of their normal program. Three of those events, organized in partnership with the UK's environmental academic community, were about climate science, and paired scientists with authors and artists.
>
> My partner was [author and zoologist] Nicola Davies, who writes children's books and poetry, often about environmental issues and wildlife. During the planning for the joint event, it became

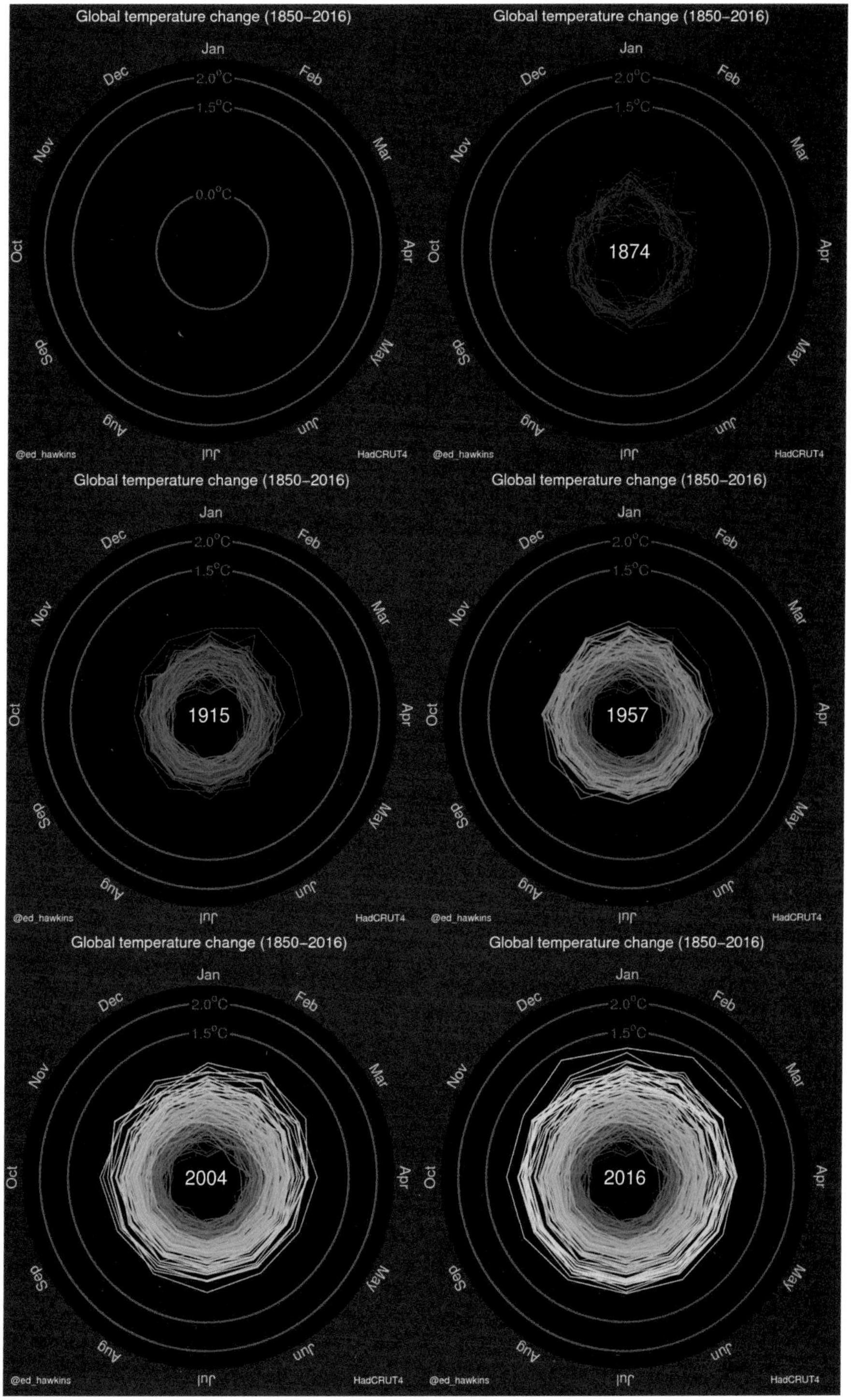

Figure 1.3: Animated climate spiral by Ed Hawkins
https://www.climate-lab-book.ac.uk/spirals/

Figure 1.4: "Warming Stripes"
https://showyourstripes.info/

clear quickly that we both wanted a visual to pair with a couple of Nicola's poems that touch upon climate science and with my own short explanation of that science.

I decided that the visual would be a very simple representation of climate change. Because this was an event attended mainly by people who are interested in books, but not necessarily people who would go to a scientific talk, I didn't want to show any traditional graphs.

I asked Hawkins whether by "traditional graphs" he was referring to visuals such as the "hockey stick" chart (**Figure 1.5**), which I've discussed at length in previous books:

Exactly. That wouldn't have worked. I decided to do something simple just with colors. A bit before Hay, in May of 2018, I had used global temperature data to produce the global version of the stripes, the first version. I put it online and got very popular very quickly. I realized that this graphic was useful as a concept.

However, I also wanted to make it more relevant to people attending the Hay Festival, because the notion of global temperature is too abstract; it doesn't mean anything to anybody, as no one experiences global temperature change directly. We experience the climate and weather where we live. That's why I got data for the town of Hay, which goes back to the late 1800s, and I produced a version of the graphic representing the *local* change in temperature. It was projected behind us while Nicola and I talked (**Figure 1.6**).

This version uses the same colors but it focuses just on the location where we were sitting. It was very powerful, I think. As soon as I put it on the screen and talked about it, you could see the audience going, "Oh, I get it!" We all often hear about climate change and global temperature

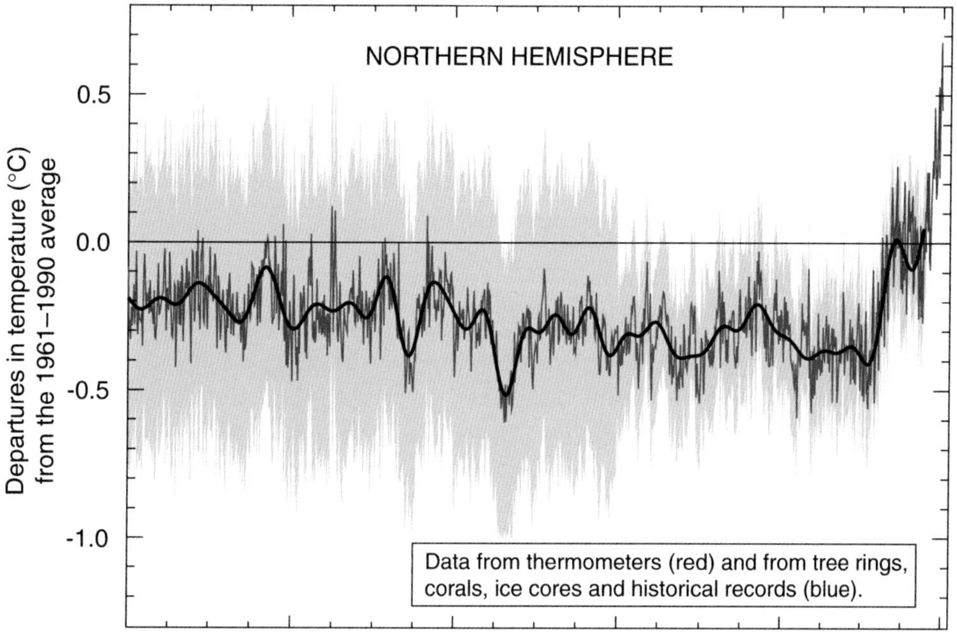

Figure 1.5: The "hockey stick chart" by Michael E. Mann, Raymond S. Bradley, and Malcolm K. Hughes. It appeared in the "Summary for Policymakers" of the *2001 Third Assessment Report of the Intergovernmental Panel on Climate Change.*

Figure 1.6: Nicola Davies and Ed Hawkins presenting at the Hay Festival of Literature & Arts

Ed Hawkins / Twitter, Inc. / https://twitter.com/ed_hawkins/status/1539249299804065793/photo/1 / last accessed Febuary 16, 2023

> heating up, but putting the pieces together to make the public attending the festival realize that their local area was changing—that was a missing piece in the puzzle.

Later, Hawkins would produce a website, https://showyourstripes.info, where readers can see visualizations of the entire world, or of their own regions. Hawkins believes that the success of these graphics is due in part to readers being able to see themselves in them, but also to the clear message they convey:

> It has to be, to my mind, the simplicity of it. You can take one glance at it and if someone tells you this is the warming climate, that's all you need to know. It goes from blue to red, so you've automatically got the representation of cold to hot. That's built into the graphic, and it's striking. The colors change so rapidly toward the end that the graphic tells that story about what's happening even if you don't know any of the details. It draws people into the discussion. You show the graphic and they go, "Oh, wow, things are changing!"
>
> That's when you can start the conversation about why climate change is happening. What are the details about it? How much has the world warmed? Where has it warmed the most? What are the consequences? You've drawn someone into that conversation by making the basis of it very simple to understand.

The stripes didn't just lead to conversations about global warming at the Hay Festival of Literature & Arts. It did it at a global level. Since it was published, it has appeared in many demonstrations against climate change, on the covers of newspapers, magazines, and books, on clothing items—and even on electric cars (**Figure 1.7**).

Responses weren't always enthusiastic, though. Hawkins told me he got some puzzled reactions from members of the visualization community:

> I remember an interview for a data visualization podcast. The host told me, we have all these rules with data visualizations and these are the things that you must or mustn't do about creating successful information graphics. You've broken many of those rules. Why did you choose to break them?
>
> And my answer was, well, I didn't know the rules because I'm not a professional data visualization designer. I think that surprised them. But I think that's a really interesting point, that the rules are there for good reasons, I suspect, for making effective data visualization. But breaking rules is often really important in pushing boundaries.

The podcast Hawkins referred to, which I can't recommend enough, is *Data Stories*, by Enrico Bertini, a professor at Northeastern University, and Moritz Stefaner, a famous visualization designer. I listened to their interview with Hawkins, and its tone is friendly and constructive, although it's true that they joked about how "Warming Stripes" broke certain rules.

Figure 1.7: Mark Hanson's car
Mark Hanson / https://www.netzeromn.com/blog/mr-musk-please-meet-professor-hawkins / last accessed Febuary 16, 2023

The *Data Stories* episode reminded me of my own first reaction to Hawkins' graphic; I was wary. "A time-series heat map without a legend or labels?" I remember asking myself. "How am I supposed to read it? What years do these stripes correspond to? What temperature ranges do these shades of color represent?" I later realized that I was asking questions that were beside the point.

"Warming Stripes" employs the language of data visualization—the encoding of data through the variation of certain attributes of objects, such as height, length, position, area, color, and the like—not merely to reveal patterns or trends. It's not intended to enable exploration and analysis or to weave a narrative, like the data visualizations and infographics that I have designed throughout my career. Hawkins' sole purpose was to create an iconic data-driven image to get conversations started. Judged by that goal, his visualization was a success.

ৡ ৡ ৡ

My conversation with Ed Hawkins made me reflect on the ways that visualization professionals and scholars talk about what we do and why we do it. I also remembered a question that I'm asked often: **What are the rules of data visualization?**

I was born in Galicia, Spain. We Galicians are known for replying to questions *with even more questions,* so I often ask in return: **What are the rules of writing?**

I find such questions puzzling. I think of visualization as a technology that humans have devised to engage with the world. It's a form of speech whose syntax consists of mapping data onto symbols. In this sense it isn't that different from writing. In writing, beyond a loose observance of the vocabulary and grammar of the language we employ, there are no universal rules that are applicable to *all* its varieties regardless of purpose or audience.

This misconception about the existence of universal rules in visualization is in part due to the inheritance—and also to a slight misreading, I'd say—of what I call "the Tuftean consensus," after Edward Tufte, author of several influential books, the best among them being *The Visual Display of Quantitative Information* (1983).

In *The Infographic: A History of Data Graphics in News and Communications* (2020), Murray Dick, a journalism professor at Newcastle University, describes various discourses in visualization, which are ways to think and talk about the craft. The first is the functionalist-idealist discourse. Tufte is the most popular exponent of it, although Murray cites several other statisticians and cartographers, such as Jacques Bertin, author of the foundational *Semiology of Graphics* (*Sémiologie Graphique. Les diagrammes, les réseaux, les cartes*, 1967.)

The functionalist-idealist discourse, Dick explains, has been dominant for decades. It conceives of visualizations "first and foremost as a scientific methodology" and as a form of "visual logic [based on] the rigorous application of a monosemic system that depends on a priori rules (present in standards, and in conventions, such as the use of grid lines, legends, labels, etc.) These provide a means by which signs may be used to connect propositions in a logical sequence."

According to Dick, to someone who favors the functionalist-idealist discourse "graphics necessarily deal in complex, multivariate ideas and they must explain clearly and efficiently, telling the truth about the data." Then he adds a key sentence: "The notion that designer and audience may not share a common and irreducible understanding of what 'the truth' means is not countenanced." To the functionalist-idealist discourse, the quality of a graphic depends largely on the nature of the information presented and on the decisions that its designer makes about it within existing norms.

That's why Tufte has written that "if your statistics are boring, you've got the wrong numbers" or "the only worse design than a pie chart is several pie charts." However, being boring—or clear or efficient—isn't a property of things, but of the relationship between those things and the people who experience them. The best statistics *can* be boring, and the clearest and most efficient graphic *to you* can be confusing and inefficient *to others*. Pie charts are often misused, but this is also true of any other chart type. No graphic form is good or bad in essence.

Designers who favor a functionalist-idealist discourse often come up with comprehensive and coherent systems of thought and action—sometimes involving transcendentals such as truth, goodness, or beauty—derive rules from them, and use them to judge whatever they see. Tufte doesn't employ the term *rules* in his books, but he has defined a series of uppercase "Principles of Graphical Excellence."

I've seen people try to apply these principles to their work too strictly—and fail. The reason is that they should be taken instead as sensible guidance whose pertinence depends on many considerations. Tufte himself is subtler than his most devoted fans, as he usually adds the caveat "within reason" to soften his otherwise strongly worded recommendations. For instance, he suggests maximizing "the share of a graphic's ink devoted to data [...] within reason." These last two words shall remain undefined.

Murray Dick's discourses aren't mutually exclusive; the same person can use different ones. I've employed a functionalist-idealist discourse myself, but *The Infographic* says that my predominant discourse is pragmatist.

Such a label encapsulates my ideas well. I respect the functionalist-idealist discourse, as I've learned a great deal from those who favor it. However, I've come to think, teach, and talk about visualization not as a series of allegedly universal principles, but in terms of ad hoc reasoning. This reasoning is informed by aims, constraints, conventions, trade-offs, likely outcomes, culture, personal experience and taste, and by an ever-imperfect but ever-evolving body of scientific knowledge.

I don't deny the possibility of norms, but I don't understand them as rules that can be given, top-down, by supposed leaders in the field. Instead, norms are tacit patterns of behavior that emerge, bottom-up, from the ongoing historical dialogue between those who practice the craft. Because of this, norms can and should always be subject to examination.

It's for this reason that, instead of a hierarchical professional landscape where authoritative figures assemble lists of principles, I prefer to foster a level field where conversations among kind peers flourish. *Kind* not in the sense of being *nice*, but of being welcoming, helpful, and constructive. My most cherished mentors, colleagues, and critics were and are kind, but not all mince their words.

Finally, I also believe that a central goal of visualization is to benefit an audience somehow—and that this audience could be the designer alone. *Benefitting*, by the way, doesn't always mean "getting the most information in as little time as possible." That's just one of the many purposes that a visualization may have.

Therefore, my discourse isn't just pragmatic. It's also pluralistic—if visualization is a language, many *dialects* are possible—and even a tad hedonistic.*

* I'll break my self-imposed goal of avoiding footnotes to clarify what I mean by *hedonistic*. Hedonism has nothing to do with the contemporary vulgarization of the term, meaning sensory excess. Hedonism is a set of philosophical schools with ancient roots that, in broad terms, agree that *pleasure*—roughly equivalent to welfare and the diminishing of suffering—is a moral good (for some schools it's *the key* moral good.) Whatever contributes to pleasant lives is generally considered more desirable than what doesn't.

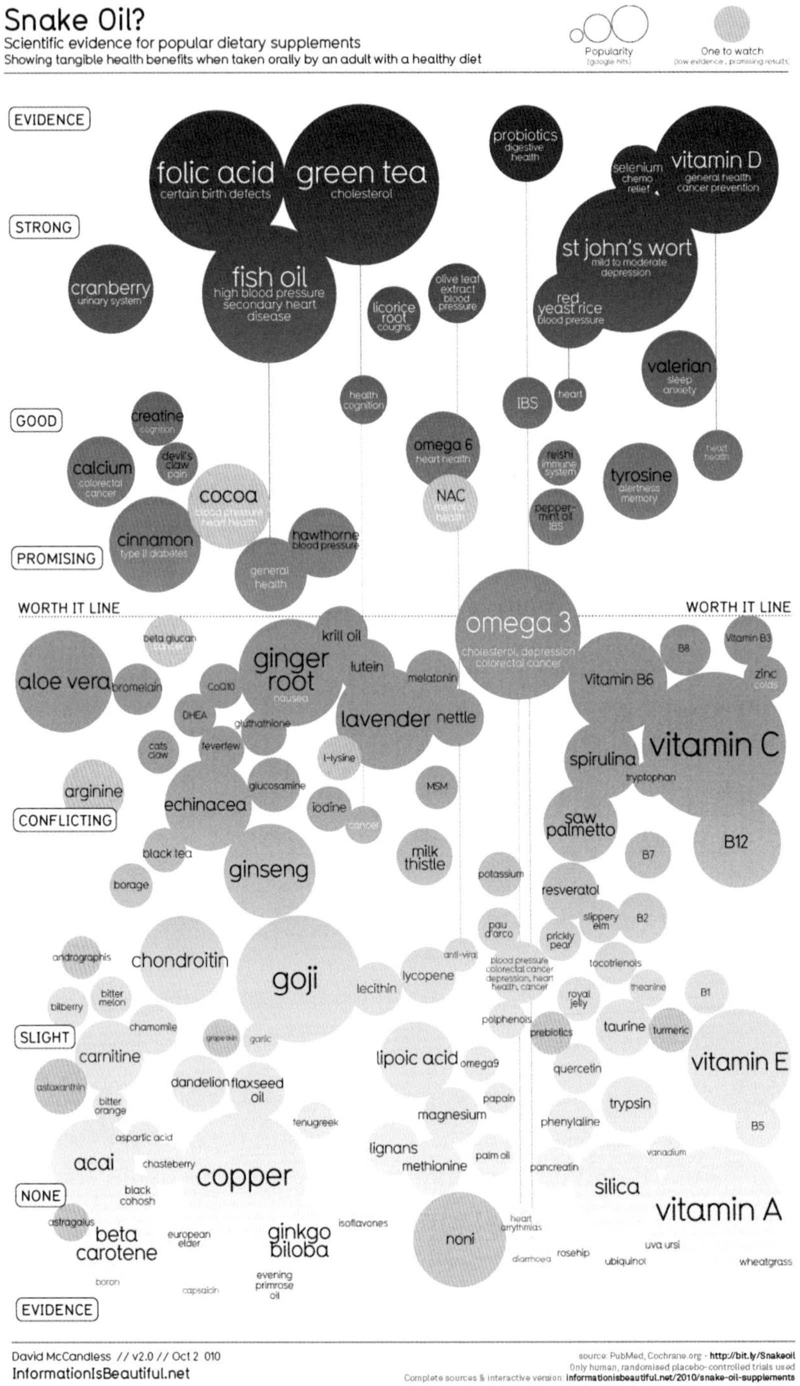

Figure 2.1: "Snake Oil Supplements? Scientific evidence for popular health supplements"

http://tinyurl.com/4dvpuu59

Chapter 2

A World of Conversation

The experienced person is always undogmatic.

—Joan-Carles Mèlich

Besides the functionalist-idealist and the pragmatist discourses, Murray Dick's *The Infographic* identifies two others in the academic and professional literature about visualization: the didactic-persuasive and the expressionist-aesthete. The former discourse, which Dick exemplifies with Otto Neurath, Marie Reidemeister, and Gerd Arntz's Isotype picture language, emphasizes visualization as an educational instrument for social change.

Dick explains the expressionist-aesthete discourse referring to the work of designer and author David McCandless (**Figure 2.1**). This discourse "is bound up in expressive experimentalism, with a premium on aesthetics and an emphasis on the importance of play and fun."

Visualization discourses will keep appearing, as people from increasingly diverse cultural and professional backgrounds embrace the language. For example, I think that we can already acknowledge a critical, intersectional feminist discourse, whose most salient exponent is Catherine D'Ignazio and Lauren Klein's *Data Feminism* (2020). This discourse analyzes hierarchies, privilege, and power in visualization not just related to sex and gender, but also to race, ethnicity, and economic inequality. D'Ignazio and Klein wrote:

> Those who wield power are disproportionately elite, straight, white, able-bodied, cisgender men from the Global North. The work of data feminism is first to tune into how standard practices

> in data science serve to reinforce these existing inequalities and second to use data science to challenge and change the distribution of power. Underlying data feminism is a belief in and commitment to co-liberation: the idea that oppressive systems of power harm all of us, that they undermine the quality and validity of our work, and that they hinder us from creating true and lasting social impact with data science.

I also see the seeds of what could become a disability-accessibility discourse, focused on equal access to information and data not only through vision, but also through our other senses. We can encode data into objects, but why do these objects need to be just visual? Why not tactile? Or auditory? Or olfactory? In their book, D'Ignazio and Klein themselves discuss this physicalization, called sometimes "data visceralization," and mention some of its proponents, such as Kelly Dobson, founder of the Data Visceralization Research Group at the Rhode Island School of Design (RISD).

Interest in visualization accessibility is picking up. While I write these lines, I have next to me a paper presented at the 2022 Eurographics Conference on Visualization (EuroVis) titled "How accessible is my visualization? Evaluating visualization accessibility with Chartability." Its authors, Carnegie Mellon University's Frank Elavsky, Cynthia Bennett, and Dominik Moritz, summarize a growing body of scholarly literature.

The paper also introduces Chartability, the first attempt anyone has made to collect resources and give guidance on more than just visual disability for visualization. It's a set of testable questions "to evaluate data-driven visualizations and interfaces for visual, motor, vestibular, neurological, and cognitive accessibility."

A recent article by Niklas Elmqvist, a professor at the University of Maryland, titled "Visualization for the Blind" makes the compelling case that visualization isn't really *visual*, but *spatial* and that, therefore, "visual reasoning does not require vision." Visualization isn't something that happens on paper or on screen, but in the brain: "The general approach is known as *sensory substitution* in accessibility research, and enables, for example, a blind person to use touch to 'feel' a chart, or a deaf person to read subtitles on a screen in lieu of hearing the words spoken."

The coexistence of various ways of thinking about visualization and practicing it is a sign of a pluralistic craft. By pluralistic I mean that visualization discourses are in constant dialogue, but may not be reducible to one another.

Nonetheless, people who favor one discourse—or one dialect—over others may be prone to attempting such folly. They may even confuse the increasing pluralism of visualization with relativism or cacophony. I myself have been seduced by this hubristic impulse, thinking that I was entitled to apply my own pragmatic way of reasoning to projects designed under different standards. At times, I've failed to see the absurdity of trying to judge, say, a business dashboard using journalistic design conventions. The common language of visualization will always spawn new dialects, and using the peculiarities of one dialect to evaluate another is misguided.

If taken to the extreme and deprived of a healthy and ironic skepticism about their own postulates, all discourses can degenerate into monistic and tyrannical versions of themselves. They may claim an unmerited monopoly over truth, or a right to define what is right or wrong and to demand from others to conform to such judgments.

As seductive as reductionism is, it ought to be resisted. As long as none of the discourses claims an unwarranted hegemony, they will become strands intertwining to form a more robust rope.

~ ~ ~

Murray Dick's visualization discourses in his *The Infographic* reminded me of a beautiful essay by political theorist Michael Oakeshott titled "The voice of poetry in the conversation of mankind" (1959):

> There are philosophers who assure us that all human utterance is in one mode. They recognize a certain variety of expression, they are able to distinguish different tones of utterance, but they hear only one authentic voice [...] The view dies hard that Babel was the occasion of a curse being laid upon mankind from which is the business of philosophers to deliver us, and a disposition remains to impose a singe character upon significant human speech.

Oakeshott's voices are modes of interpretation and expression of human experience. There are countless voices, but Oakeshott's essay focuses on the most common ones: the practical voice, which deals with the activity of *contriving*; the scientific voice, focused on the activity of *knowing*; and the poetic voice, interested in the activity of *contemplating*.

Voices evolve over time, and the interaction between those who use them may lead to the emergence of norms, conventions, and heuristics. Voices are also prone to *superbia*, "an exclusive concern with their own utterances." Oakeshott warned against it. Every voice ought to learn to recognize itself "as a voice among voices" participating in an endless conversation that, like all good conversations, has no predefined limits, aims, or destinations, and no uniform notion of excellence or perfection.

Like visualization discourses, Oakeshott argues that voices in conversation should behave like friends lost in the enjoyment of each other's company. Friends don't demand change or improvement from one another. They might slowly change due to mutual influence and gentle persuasion, but that's just a possible side effect of their dialogue, not its goal. To Oakeshott, conversation is "an unrehearsed intellectual adventure," and who doesn't love an adventure?

What is my discourse? A rather practical one with very little of Oakeshott's poetry, I'm afraid. I practice and teach visualization design as a process that considers purpose, audience, means, constraints, personal preferences, and whatever evidence may exist, and then tries to make reasonable choices based on them. I envision the design process also as a conversation, sometimes just with myself, sometimes with others.

Such conversation can be casual, but there are cases when it requires a higher rigor. Since 2017 I've been part of a research group attempting to devise new types of graphics to inform the public about possible impacts of extreme weather events, such as hurricanes and tropical storms. Our team, which has ties to organizations such as the National Weather Service and the National Hurricane Center (NHC), includes atmospheric scientists, social scientists, visual designers, and experts in user experience research.

We have evidence that many people misinterpret graphics such as the NHC's Track Forecast Cone, also known as the "cone of uncertainty" (**Figure 2.2**). They read it as saying, "If I'm inside of the cone, I'm in danger; if I'm outside of it, I'll likely be fine." In reality, the cone is a probabilistic depiction of where the storm center may be in the following few days, and the effects of a hurricane can be felt many miles away from the cone's boundary.

When seeing the cone it's useful to imagine hundreds or thousands of lines, each corresponding to a possible track of the storm center, quickly appearing and disappearing. Most of them will be within the boundaries of the cone, but some will run outside of it. This is the language that the NHC uses to explain this:

> The cone represents the probable track of the center of a tropical cyclone, and is formed by enclosing the area swept out by a set of circles (not shown) along the forecast track [...] The size of each circle is set so that two-thirds of historical official forecast errors over a 5-year sample fall within the circle [...] The entire track of the tropical cyclone can be expected to remain within the cone roughly 60-70% of the time.

Error in this context doesn't mean *mistake*. It's the quantified difference between estimates and reality, between forecasted tracks and the actual path of the storm's center.

Any of our team's graphic prototypes begins with meetings and focus groups to identify the needs of regular people whose lives, families, or property could be threatened by extreme weather. Common questions are: What information do they need to protect themselves?

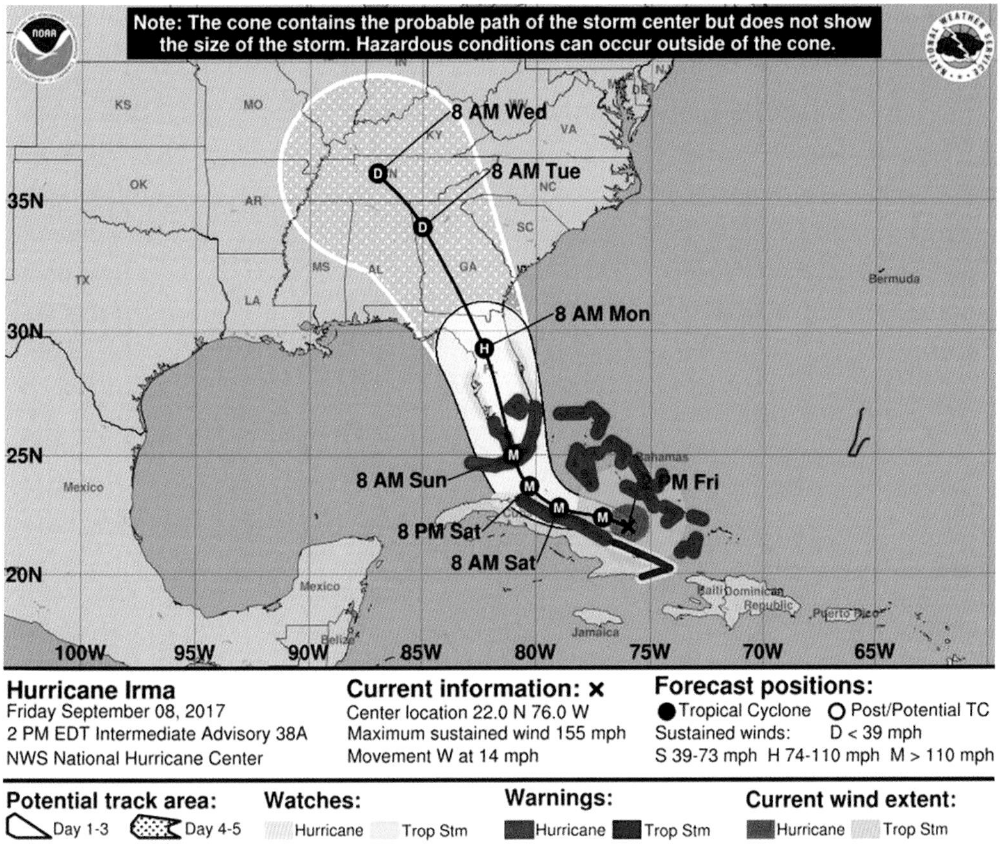

Figure 2.2: The NHC's Track Forecast Cone
https://www.nhc.noaa.gov/aboutcone.shtml
More information about our research group at https://interactive.miami.edu/hurakan/

Do existing graphics provide such information? Can readers understand those graphics? If not, what do they think would work better? And many others.

The data collected in these meetings is then codified and used to guide the design of new prototypes. These are brought back to community members and tested for comprehension by my University of Miami colleague Barbara Millet, an expert in user experience and human-computer interaction, and her graduate students.

❧ ❧ ❧

I grew up in the world of daily news, so most graphics I've created in my career had to be finished in a matter of hours, not weeks or months; there wasn't a chance for formal evaluation. In fact, I claim no expertise in such matters. If you're interested in testing methods for visualization, books such as *Functional Aesthetics for Data Visualization* (2023) by Vidya Setlur and Bridget Cogley, or Tamara Munzner's *Visualization Analysis and Design*

(2014)—in my opinion the most important book about visualization in the last decade at least—are good starting points.

My own process, and the process followed by several of the designers you'll soon meet in this book, is based on guesswork informed by inherited practices, tacit knowledge, and some awareness of research. It's a subjective process: even when working with the same information and pursuing the same purpose, every designer will end up with a different visualization simply because we all have our biases and styles. However, *subjective* doesn't mean *arbitrary*. It's advisable that the decisions that we make are deliberate, and that they can be reasoned about, discussed, and justified.

When teaching visualization, I've found it useful not only to deconstruct my own graphics—my previous books contain some examples—but also to encourage students to reverse-engineer visualizations made by others. Whenever you see a visualization that you love, I tell them, try to put yourselves in the shoes of its designer and ask, "What steps would I have taken to reach these same results, which I like so much?" What follows is an example of such an exercise.

The Pudding, one of my favorite reads, is a digital magazine that publishes essays based on data and infographics about topics that are ignored or not properly treated by traditional news organizations.

These topics are sometimes weighty—minority representation in the media, abortion, access to healthcare—and sometimes a bit whimsical, but informative and engaging nonetheless. A few examples include "We couldn't get an artificial intelligence program to win the New Yorker Caption Contest," "The Sounds of CDMX: How informal street vendors define the sonic landscape of Mexico's capital," and an article on how we often misspell celebrities' names (**Figure 2.3.**)

A particularly compelling Pudding essay, written and designed by Jan Diehm amd Amber Thomas, addresses a common complaint: on average, women's pants pockets are smaller than men's (**Figure 2.4.**) This project is a lovely combination of narration and interaction, and a good example of how to merge the pictorial with the data-driven.

The Pudding has a commercial side, Polygraph (https://polygraph.cool/), a design firm that produces work for clients. In 2018 Polygraph partnered with the Google News Initiative and the American Society of News Editors (ASNE) to visualize the results of its annual Newspaper Diversity Survey. Most newspapers that participated in the survey are more male and white than the communities they serve.

Figure 2.3: "The Gyllenhaal Experiment"

THE PUDDING / https://pudding.cool/2019/02/gyllenhaal/ / last accessed Febuary 16, 2023

Polygraph's interactive visualization contains many charts: tables, scatter plots, dot plots, and the beeswarm plot in **Figure 2.5**. This one uses a dot's position on the horizontal scale to display employees' gender breakdown, while the area of the bubbles represents the size of the staff of each newspaper. When I saw this graphic, I realized that, if I had been hired to design it, I'd probably have come up with something similar.*

In their classic 2011 paper "On the role of design in information visualization," Andrew Vande Moere and Helen Purchase explained that visualization design consists of balancing

*In the following pages I'll focus just on design, not on the quality of the data. If this were a real project, though, I'd ask ASNE a few questions. For example, the survey doesn't have a non-binary option for people to report their gender. (ASNE solved this in 2019.) Questions about data are beyond what I intend for this book so I'd recommend consulting the growing literature critical of data science, such as Cathy O'Neil's *Weapons of Math Destruction* (2017), Safiya Noble's *Algorithms of Oppression* (2018), Justin Joque's *Revolutionary Mathematics* (2022), Jer Thorp's *Living in Data* (2022), or Heather Krause's "We All Count" (https://weallcount.com/).

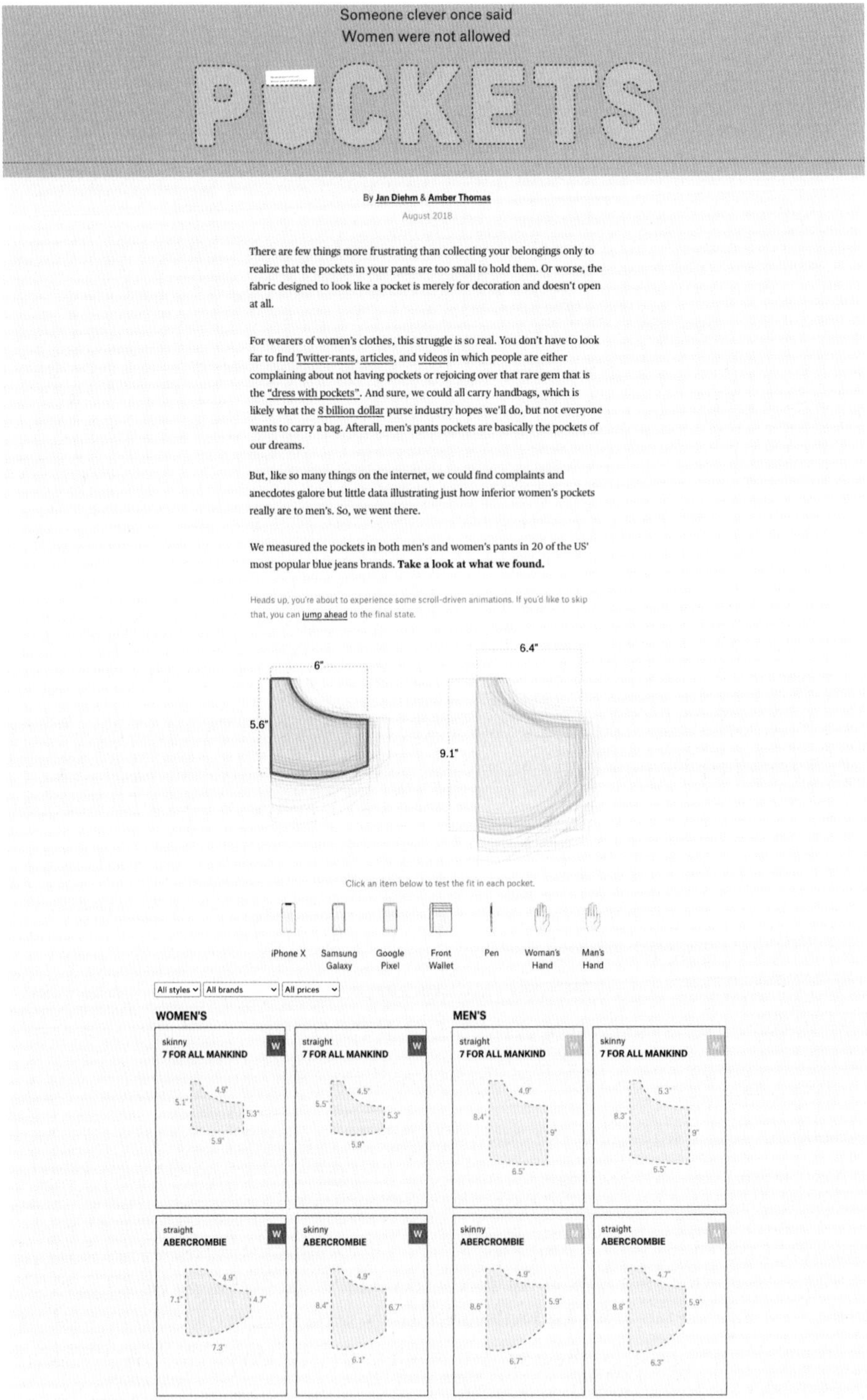

Someone clever once said
Women were not allowed

POCKETS

By Jan Diehm & Amber Thomas

August 2018

There are few things more frustrating than collecting your belongings only to realize that the pockets in your pants are too small to hold them. Or worse, the fabric designed to look like a pocket is merely for decoration and doesn't open at all.

For wearers of women's clothes, this struggle is so real. You don't have to look far to find Twitter-rants, articles, and videos in which people are either complaining about not having pockets or rejoicing over that rare gem that is the "dress with pockets". And sure, we could all carry handbags, which is likely what the 8 billion dollar purse industry hopes we'll do, but not everyone wants to carry a bag. Afterall, men's pants pockets are basically the pockets of our dreams.

But, like so many things on the internet, we could find complaints and anecdotes galore but little data illustrating just how inferior women's pockets really are to men's. So, we went there.

We measured the pockets in both men's and women's pants in 20 of the US' most popular blue jeans brands. **Take a look at what we found.**

Heads up, you're about to experience some scroll-driven animations. If you'd like to skip that, you can jump ahead to the final state.

Figure 2.4: "Someone clever once said women were not allowed pockets"

https://pudding.cool/2018/08/pockets/

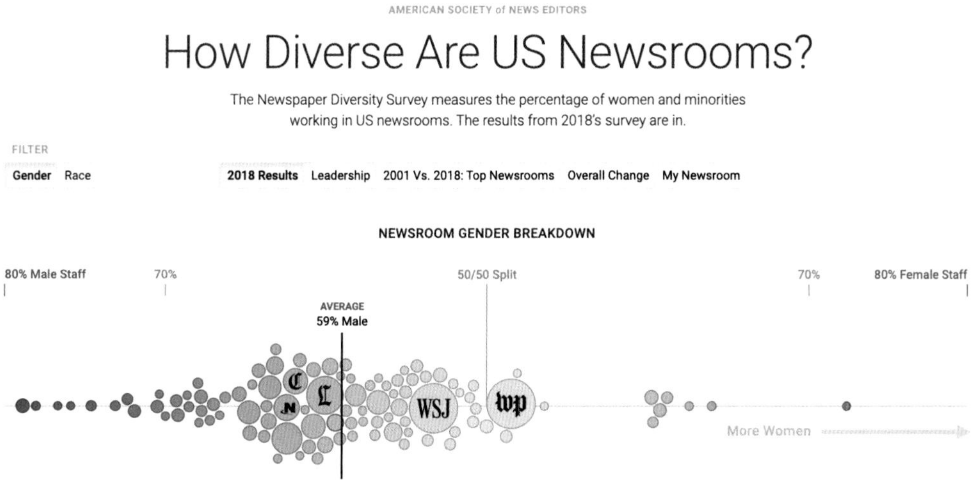

Figure 2.5: "How Diverse Are US Newsrooms?"

https://googletrends.github.io/asne/

three requirements: *utility*, *soundness*, and *attractiveness*. These are inspired by architectural theory, particularly by Roman architect and engineer Vitruvius (1st century BC.)

Utility is related to the effectiveness, efficiency, functionality, usability, and usefulness of a graphic. ***Soundness*** has to do with the graphic's reliability and robustness. An interactive visualization that doesn't crash is sound, and so are familiar and well-tested graphic forms (think of bar graphs or line graphs), regardless of whether they are static or interactive.

As for ***attractiveness***:

> Attractiveness refers to what we have [called] "aesthetics": the appeal or beauty of a given solution. Aesthetics does not limit itself to the visual form, but also includes fuzzy aspects such as originality, innovation and novelty, and other subjective factors comprising the user experience. Furthermore, aesthetics can apply to more than the designed artefact, for example to the methodology or structure of the solution itself.

I find this simple framework useful to this day. Perhaps due to my journalistic inheritance, my inner conversation while designing the newsroom diversity visualization would begin by focusing on *utility*: What is the point of this graphic? Who are its intended readers? What is it that I want them to see? The core message of the graphic goes like this: In society, roughly 50 percent of the population identifies as male or female but, according to the survey, the average newspaper newsroom is 59 percent male.

Just reporting those numbers is valuable, but I don't think it is enough. I want readers to see not only highly aggregated statistics such as averages, but also the distribution of values. How many newsrooms are close to the 50/50 split? How many are clustered around the 59 percent average? How many are on the extremes, being more than 70 percent female or male?

There are many ways to visualize the shape of a distribution and the concentration or dispersion of its values: box-and-whisker plots, histograms, density curves, violin plots, and others. In this case, I'd like to show every newsroom as an individual symbol. Therefore, a strip lot may be an appropriate choice:

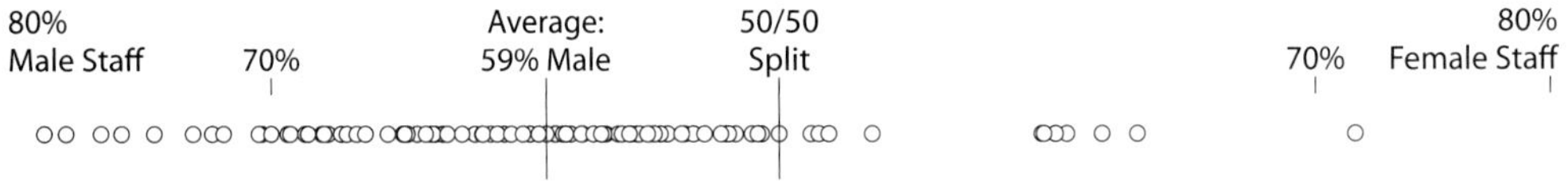

Why do I think a strip plot appropriate, you may ask? We can appeal to *utility*: research suggests that position over a common scale—the encoding in a strip plot—is appropriate when the purpose of a visualization is to enable readers to make accurate estimates about the data represented.

We can also justify the choice of the strip plot by appealing to its *soundness*: it's a relatively simple and common graphic form based on familiar conventions: an X-axis, tick marks or gridlines, axis labels, and so on.

Our current chart looks too bare, though. What if we color the dots blue or red depending on whether the newsrooms they correspond to have more men or women on staff?

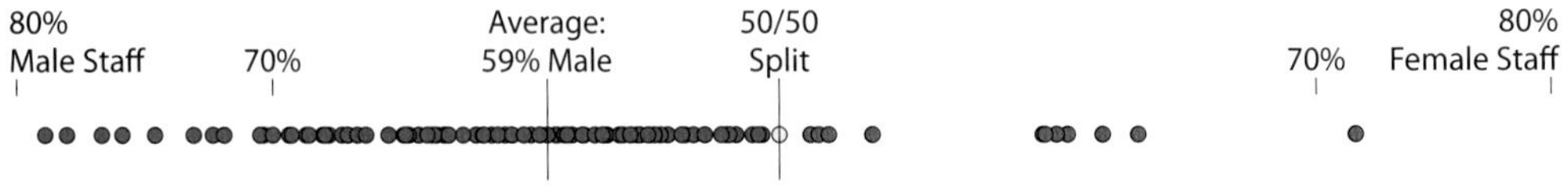

We can play not just with color hue, but also with shade, making dots *bluer* or *redder*:

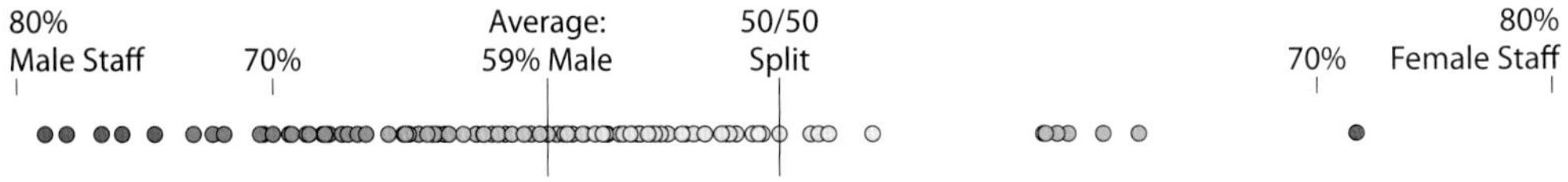

Why add color hue and color shade as encodings, when position on the X-axis seems to be enough to reveal the skewness of the gender distribution? Isn't that redundant? I can offer several reasons, some related to *utility*, some to *attractiveness.*

As for utility, I'd mention redundancy. Redundancy has an undeserved bad name in certain circles, but in this case it helps *emphasize* the gender imbalance. It's of course possible to notice it in the black-and-white strip plot, as it's obvious that most dots are to the left of the 50/50 divide. However, it's not far-fetched to guess that some readers might miss the point of the chart, and that color can call their attention to it.

A second reason for the seemingly gratuitous hue and shade encodings is aesthetics. In visualization design, personal stylistic taste derived from practical experience matters. I believe that the graphic looks better with color than without it, and my conjecture is that this new version is likely to get the attention of more readers than the first. They'll also enjoy it more.

Here's a little secret that visualization professionals don't disclose often enough to beginners: We make plenty of decisions because their results please us, and sometimes we are tempted to pass off personal opinions as norms. For instance, here's one of Edward Tufte's Principles of Graphical Excellence: "Graphical excellence is that which gives the viewer the greatest number of ideas in the shortest time with the least ink in the smallest space."

I wouldn't dare to call that a principle, even less a universal one. It's a worthy recommendation applicable just to a subset of visualizations. It's also grounded on a personal worldview that, being inspired by certain Western schools of philosophy, design, and the arts, prioritizes efficiency as a value. However, other values are possible.

One limitation of the charts I've designed so far is that they make all newsrooms look the same size. However, in the distribution we have big newspapers such as *The Wall Street Journal* or *The Washington Post*, and much smaller ones, such as the *Corpus Christi Caller-Times* or the *Statesmen Journal* (in Salem, Oregon). Let's add another encoding: area, representing staff size:

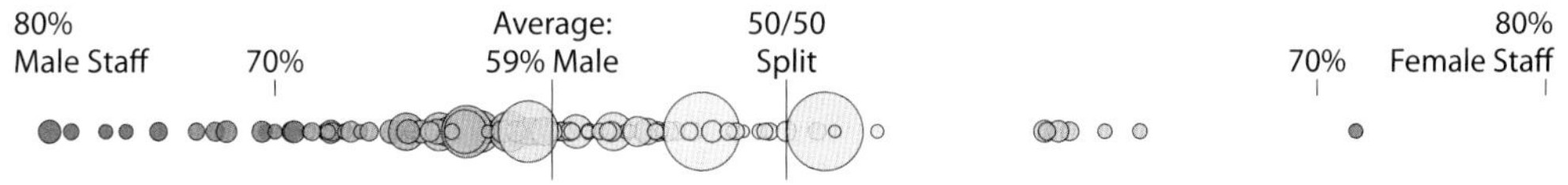

Overlap has become a problem; bubbles obscure each other. This makes reading the graphic harder than it should. I'd then tell myself to vary the position of the bubbles on the vertical axis, even if such variation doesn't encode any data. The result is the original beeswarm plot:

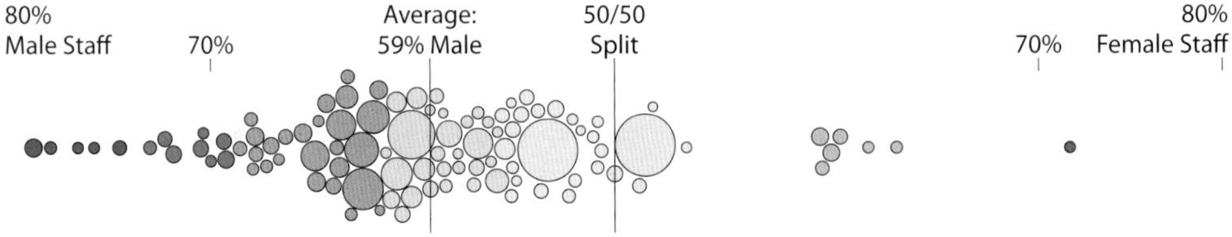

Area is a tricky encoding. Research has repeatedly shown that we are better at estimating lengths, heights, or positions measured over common baselines than we are at comparing areas. That's a *utility* reason *not* to use area as an encoding if comparing newsroom sizes were the primary purpose of the chart. But *it isn't.*

Rather, my primary purpose is to reveal the gender imbalance, for which I used position as encoding. Newsroom sizes are secondary to that and, therefore, I don't think that it's essential that readers are able to compare them accurately. I could also offer an *attractiveness* reason: the graphic looks organic, unique, and even playful.

The final touches to the graphic would involve arranging its layout and its annotation layer, the textual elements that introduce the chart's main point, emphasize it, or provide some context. This includes headlines, subtitles, footnotes, and the like. On **Figure 2.6** there's a diagram summarizing the steps leading to the final design with some references to the thinking behind them.

All reasons I've given myself in my inner conversation—or that I'd offer in a conversation with others, should I be part of a team working for a publication or client—can be justified with varying degrees of rigor or informality, from "past research about graphics like this suggests that...," down to "based on my experience, this might work," or "I have the hunch that readers will find the graphic attractive if it's designed this way."

All these reasons are open to question, a few of them could even be *operationalized*—strictly defined to make them measurable—in a scientific experiment, if we had the time to conduct it. These reasons could be proven misguided or wrong, but none is arbitrary.

This exercise reveals that the way I think about visualization tends to be orthodox and conventional. That's the weight of inherited practice. Journalism, my main profession, is suspicious of novelty, innovation, or originality, and reluctant to evolve.

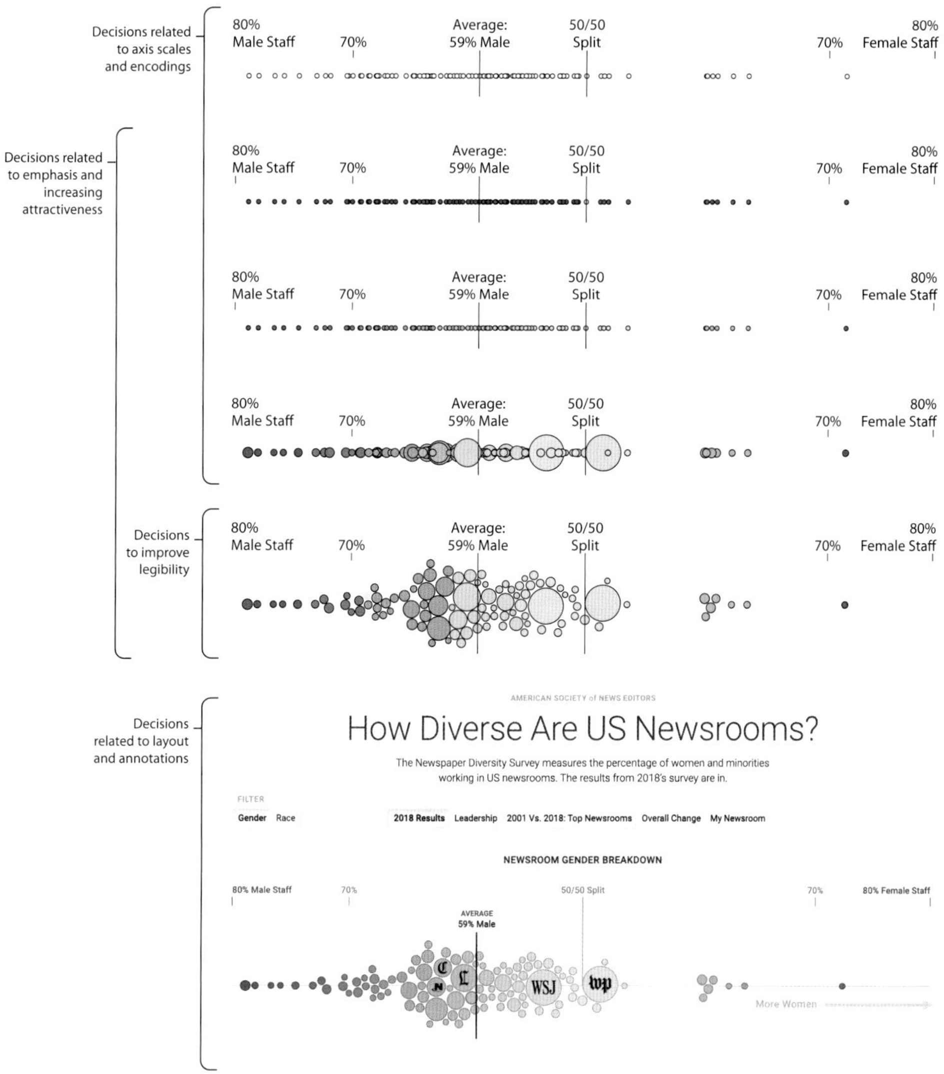

Figure 2.6: All steps in the reverse-engineering exercise

However, this doesn't mean that visual journalists like me aren't curious about alternative worlds or that we don't grasp that there might be myriad ways of being a good professional. This is why my wandering turns now to visualization designers whose motivations, opinions, and tastes are most different to mine, as their main goal isn't always clarity or effective communication, but experimentation or self-expression. French anthropologist David Le Breton once wrote, "Like Ulysses, sometimes we need to travel around the world and lose ourselves in a thousand follies before returning to Ithaca." It remains to be seen whether I'll return, but I shall enjoy the journey nonetheless.

PART II

eccentrics

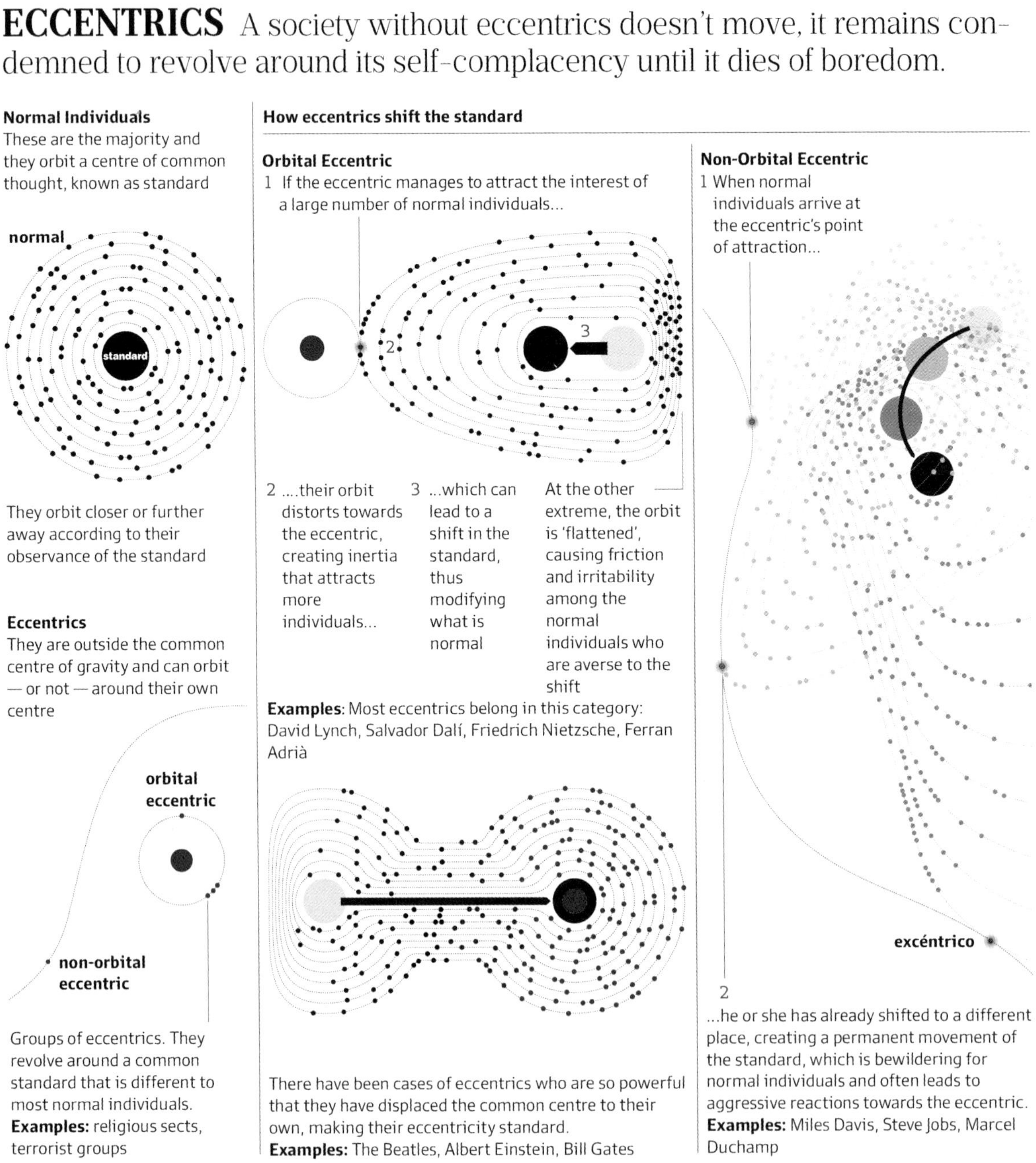

Figure 3.1: "Eccentrics"

https://www.archivosjaimeserra.com/archivos/excentricos

Chapter 3
with Jaime Serra

The Eternal Wanderer

The word [normal] *uses a power as old as Aristotle to bridge the fact/value distinction,whispering in your ear that what is normal is also right.*

—Ian Hacking

Whenever I think about rules, norms, conventions, or leaders in information design and visualization—about their influence or their evolution—I return to a diagram designed by **Jaime Serra** titled "Excéntricos," ("Eccentrics"). It has a static (**Figure 3.1**) and an animated version.

Jaime's graphic depicts how orthodoxy and heterodoxy interact in any human realm: society, culture, the arts, or the sciences. In the first step of his graphic, all individuals, represented by dots, orbit around a central black circle that corresponds to a norm or an influential thinker. Some dots are closer to the circle—those are the individuals who try to stick to the norm strictly—while others are far from it.

Some individuals, the eccentrics—the big red circles in the graphic—don't orbit around the common norm. They fly away from it. If the gravitational force of an eccentric is strong enough, it may make the orbit around the common norm bulge in its direction (**Figure 3.2**). Some individuals around the norm will approach the eccentric with curiosity; others will be reluctant.

Sometimes, the gravitational pull of eccentrics can be so powerful that they become new centers of gravity (**Figure 3.3**). And what would happen if this pet universe had multiple

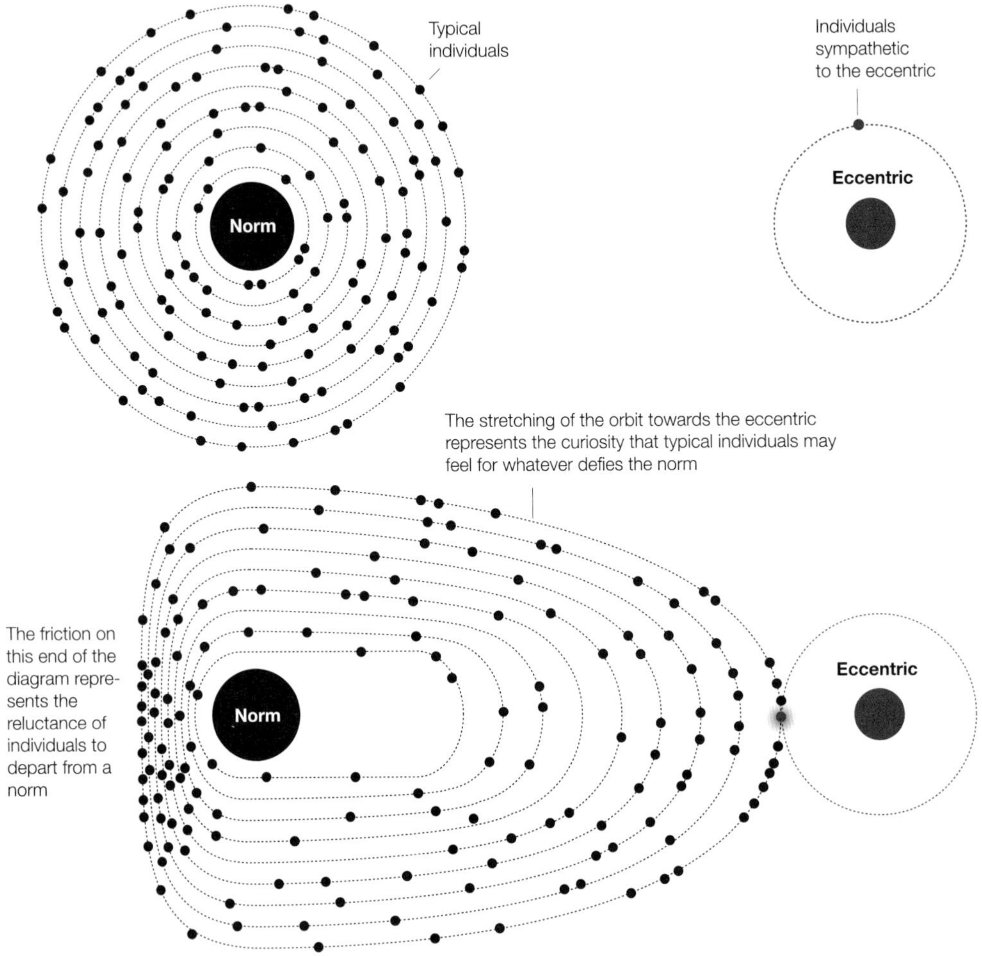

Figure 3.2: Two frames of the animated version of "Eccentrics"

eccentrics, with gravity fields overlapping each other, I wonder? Who knows; perhaps individuals may navigate from one orbit to another, in a dance of happy anarchy.

❧ ❧ ❧

The Catalan designer and journalist Jaime Serra has always been a splendid eccentric. He began designing information graphics for newspapers in the mid-1980s. I became familiar with his work in the late 1990s, when he was already a trend setter in the field. Like so many others in this book, he became a graphics designer due to a chain of coincidences:

> I discovered news infographics by happenstance in 1986. I was 21 at the time, taking my first steps as a professional commercial illustrator. One of the agencies I worked for had *Periódico de*

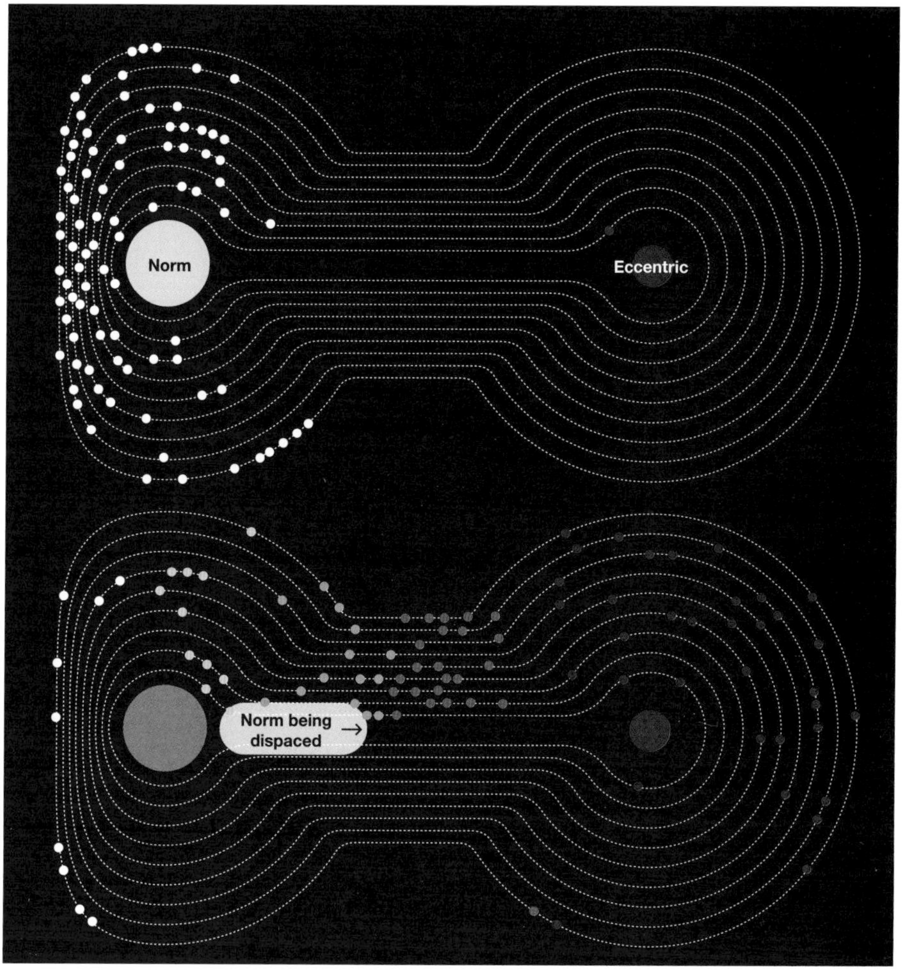

Figure 3.3: Two frames of the animated version of "Eccentrics"

Cataluña, a premier newspaper in Catalonia, Spain, as a client. *Periódico* was building an infographics department. I had a conversation with its art director, and he asked me whether I knew any "infographics designer."

I didn't know what he was talking about. I had never heard of "infographics" before. Graphics weren't common in Spanish newspapers at the time, so I was at a loss for words. But then I noticed that the art department that he directed owned one of the first Apple Macintosh. Computers were very expensive at the time, and I was interested in learning to use them, so I proposed myself for the job.

That hasty decision became a pattern in Jaime's life. Journalism was a perfect match for his wandering personality, as it was for mine. I also began my career in daily newspapers a decade later than Jaime. I could make his words mine:

> Journalism allowed me to explore multiple topics, jumping from one to the next, always finding something interesting to do every day. I fell in love with the culture of breaking news, of having to create explanation graphics in a matter of a few hours, seeing them published, and move on to new projects the day after.

Jaime told me that he was inspired by our common friend Nigel Holmes—a famous graphics designer and journalist who used to integrate data visualizations with vector illustrations—and by *USA Today*, a newspaper recognized as pioneer in news graphics:

> My graphics at the time were rudimentary, and also pretty standard. They were mostly small maps, charts, and explanatory illustrations. But I was lucky; as there were very few people in Spain working in news graphics, I was able to be promoted rather quickly. In just five years I moved from being a junior designer to becoming the head of the graphics department.

In the early 1990s, Jaime reached an impasse, and his restless temperament took over:

> I believe in boredom as a factor that prompts you to keep improving, and I got bored. I had reached a point when I felt that I had learned everything I could learn at *Periódico de Cataluña*. I started fantasizing about moving elsewhere and doing other things. A former colleague of mine was working as a design consultant at one of the main newspapers in Argentina, *Clarín*, and I was offered to lead their burgeoning graphics department.
>
> I hadn't visited Buenos Aires before, but I made the decision in seconds. I was ready to move on.

Jaime spent seven years at *Clarín*, where he revolutionized news graphics by showing a generation of designers worldwide how to experiment with the form and expand the boundaries of what was acceptable:

> *Clarín* was in a process of rapid transformation, incorporating new technologies, color printing, and launching a weekly magazine. There wasn't an established culture of news graphics in Argentina. There weren't many settled standards, so I was able to try new things without much interference. I could create something new almost from scratch.
>
> Before going to Argentina I had already tried to make infographics by hand, incorporating illustrations and physical objects. The computer is great as a tool for editing, but design software was very limiting. I took this to a new level at *Clarín*. For instance, years after the Rwandan genocide of 1994, I designed a map of the country locating refugee camps and places, carving a piece of plaster, framing it, photographing it, and then adding labels and annotations in the computer (**Figure 3.4**). I also designed my most famous graphic, about southern right whale sightings in the coast of Argentina (**Figure 3.5**).

Jaime's graphics for *Clarín* may not look that innovative today, in the early 2020s, when so many designers are bringing to the craft influences from the visual arts and other fields, but their impact on the small world of news graphics in the 1990s was tremendous. Here you had a designer unwilling to surrender to the strictures of computer software—the crude first versions of Macromedia Freehand or Adobe Illustrator—and

Figure 3.4: Map of Rwanda

https://www.johngrimwade.com/blog/2016/10/17/jaime-serras-game-changer/

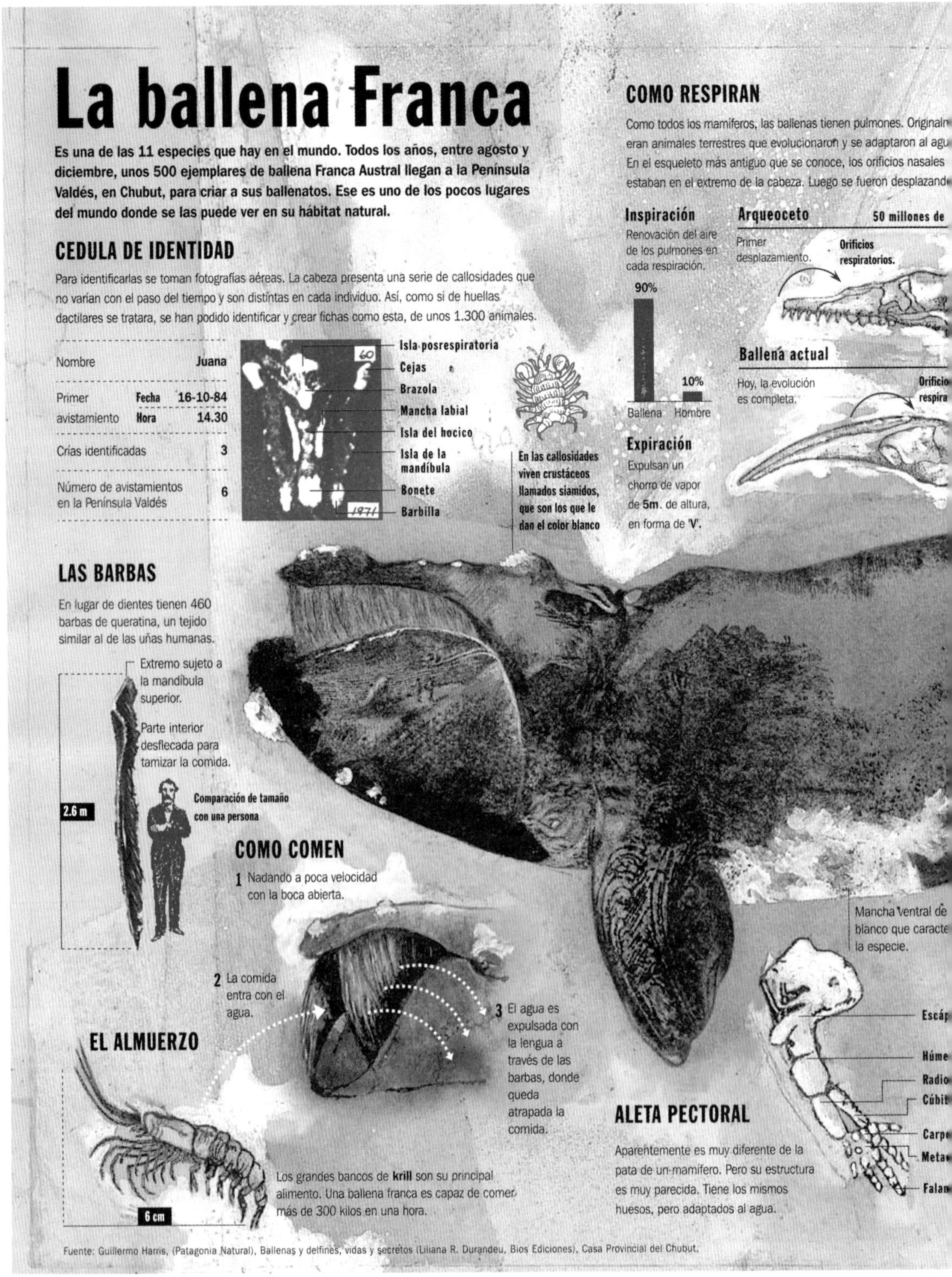

Figure 3.5: "The southern right whale"

Jaime Serra Palou / https://www.archivosjaimeserra.com/archivos/ballenafranca / last accessed Febuary 16, 2023

CICLO VITAL

allenas se reproducen en
no en aguas cálidas. Durante
ano viajan para alimentarse
juas frías. Tienen una cría
tres años.

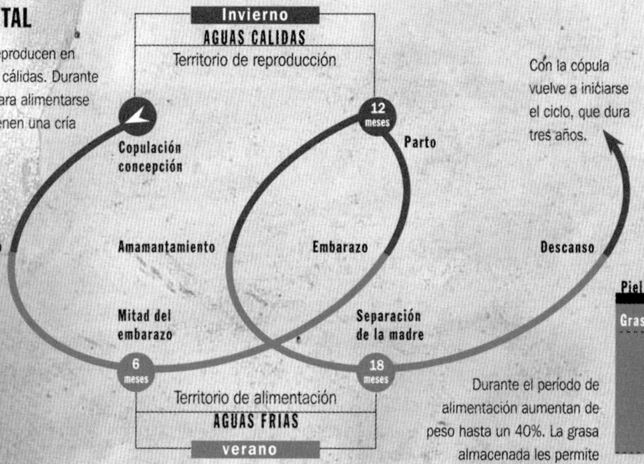

Con la cópula vuelve a iniciarse el ciclo, que dura tres años.

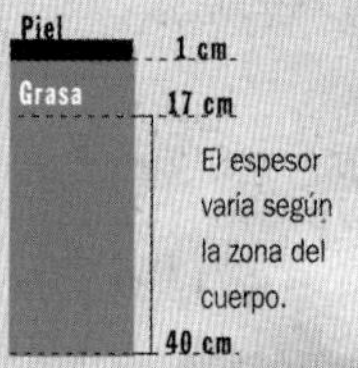

Durante el período de alimentación aumentan de peso hasta un 40%. La grasa almacenada les permite sobrevivir a los inviernos, cuando ayunan, y sirve como aislante térmico.

Ni tan grande ni tan pequeña

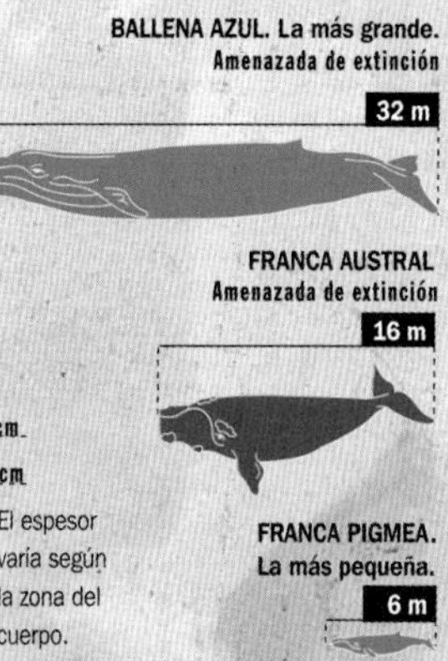

Datos generales

Longitud	Machos	14 m
	Hembras	16 m
	Al nacer	5 m
Aleta caudal		5 m
Peso de un adulto		40 tn

El equivalente a 10 elefantes

Peso al nacer	2,5 tn
Tiempo de vida	60 años
Velocidad	30 kms/h
Profundidad de descenso	300 m

Comparación del tamaño de una ballena con una persona

Restos de huesos pelvianos. En embriones de 2 cms se pueden apreciar adosados a la columna. Luego, cuando crece, se desprende.

¿ A DONDE EMIGRAN ?

Las zonas donde viven en verano siguen siendo un misterio. Sin embargo, las áreas donde fueron cazadas, hasta su prohibición, permiten suponer que viven entre los paralelos 20 y 60.

● Registros de captura. 1785-1913

Una lenta recuperación

En todo el mundo

En este período fueron cazadas hasta casi su extinción

En la Península Valdés

La población se duplica cada diez años. Cada temporada crece un **7%**

Según distintas estimaciones

Infografía: JAIME SERRA

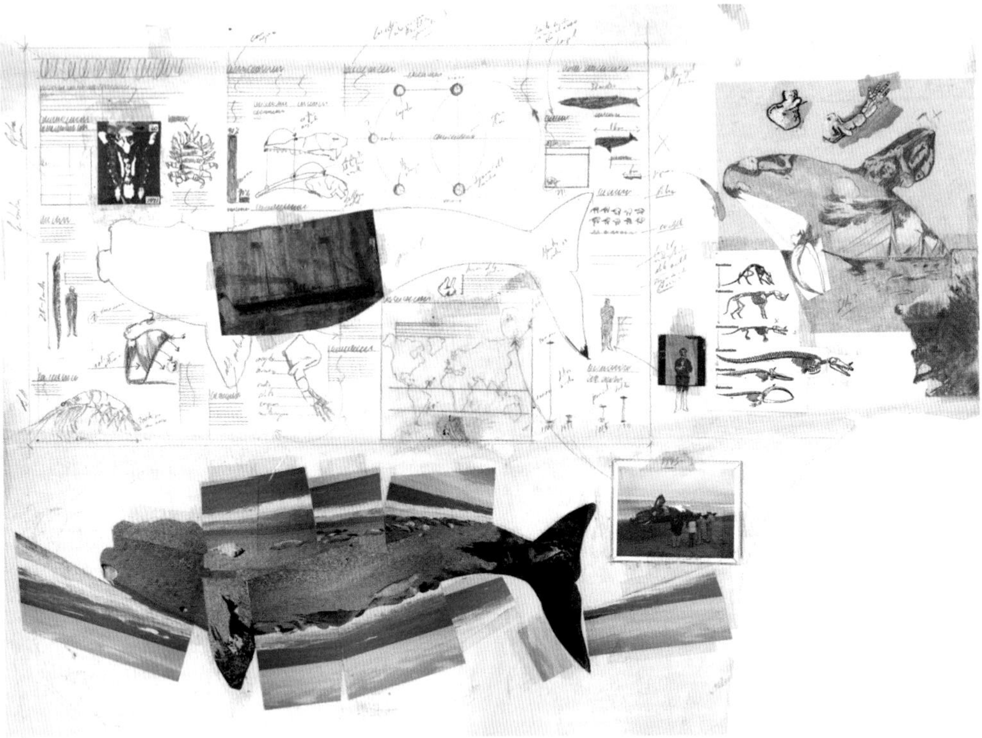

Figure 3.6: Draft and early notes for "The southern right whale" infographic

who understood that the sanitized style that vector design software prompted designers to adopt was inadequate to portrait the real world, with all its imperfections.

Jaime's southern right whale graphic made a big impression on me when I discovered it. I inquired about its inception. It turns out that the way this project came to be is also reflective of Jaime's deepest motivations:

> At *Clarín* I created a culture that is common in modern newsrooms. At the time, news graphics designers were passive; they waited for reporters and editors to make "requests." They didn't do any reporting themselves. I changed that. I wanted my department to be proactive. We pitched projects; we investigated them. The southern right whale infographic was one of those.
>
> Being new to Argentina, I didn't know that one of the best places in the world to see whales is the Valdés Peninsula, in the Chubut province. I really wanted to go there and see whales, so I proposed to cover it. The response from my editors was: "But we've covered whale sightings at Valdés for ages. Why would we do it again?" My response was: "Sure, but you've never done it with a big infographic!"

And so he did. Jaime traveled to the Valdés Peninsula with a reporter and a photographer. When he came back, he designed a graphic full of information and rich detail in which every element was deliberately chosen:

> The main illustration of the whale is made of allegorical images of the sea. Look closely: there are dolphins, ships, a stranded whale, the profile of a sailor... I played with positive and negative spaces, and surrounded the main illustration with information about the anatomy and behavior of this species. None of this information was new to readers at the time, but it had never been presented this way in a newspaper. The response was very positive.

Jaime eventually moved back to Spain and after trying to become an independent consultant and designer, he landed a job at *La Vanguardia*, the main competitor of the newspaper where he had began his career, *El Periódico de Cataluña*.

Besides leading the graphics desk at *La Vanguardia*, he became a columnist. Not any kind of columnist, though, but a *visual* opinion writer. In fact, "Eccentrics," the piece that opens up this chapter, was originally published as an opinion article.

Being a columnist allowed Jaime to pursue his interest in merging the language of news graphics with his love for the visual and performative arts:

> Once the department that I created started functioning without close supervision, I felt bored again. But I was older. I was not going to leave Spain again. I thought that maybe I could explore my interest in art in the newspaper. So I proposed a Sunday opinion column to use it as a place for experimentation. I ran it for five years. Not all the columns I designed and wrote are great, but there are around a dozen that I still feel proud of, and that ended up in art galleries.

I drink a lot of coffee, so I love Jaime's column about his own coffee-drinking habits, illustrated with a physical visualization (**Figure 3.7**). Each of the 12 paper sheets in it represents a month, Jaime folded them repeatedly to make them look like pages of a calendar. Whenever he drank a cup of coffee, he left a stain on the corresponding paper sheet.

I remember staring at this visualization and making up stories: "Look, in May (fifth sheet) Jaime was probably very stressed, so he drank a lot of coffee, but in December he was probably on vacation; there's almost no coffee at all." Jaime told me that this is exactly the reaction he wanted readers to have:

> The intention of my opinion columns and visualizations was to be a space to connect with readers through empathy. That's why I touched upon quotidian themes, such as drinking coffee, or topics that are intrinsic to the human condition, such as childhood, romantic love, or family life.

I asked Jaime why he thought newspaper readers and people who visited the art galleries where he showed some of the visualizations from his opinion columns found them so interesting. Were they learning anything through them?

> I don't believe in the idea of "communication" in the traditional sense of a designer having some information to convey, encoding it, and then passing it on to readers to decode. It's not that

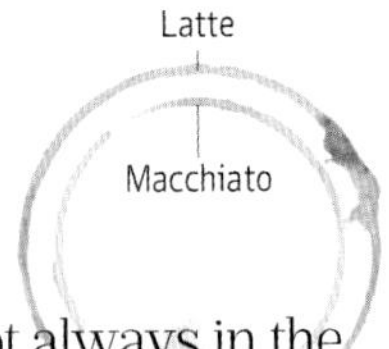

DAILY COFFEE Time can be measured in many ways. Not always in the same manner as a clock, where each second is identical but in other nonconstant, noncontinuous ways, just as it is in reality. Yesterday was a short day: one coffee; today feels eternal: six coffees; and the day before yesterday didn't exist.

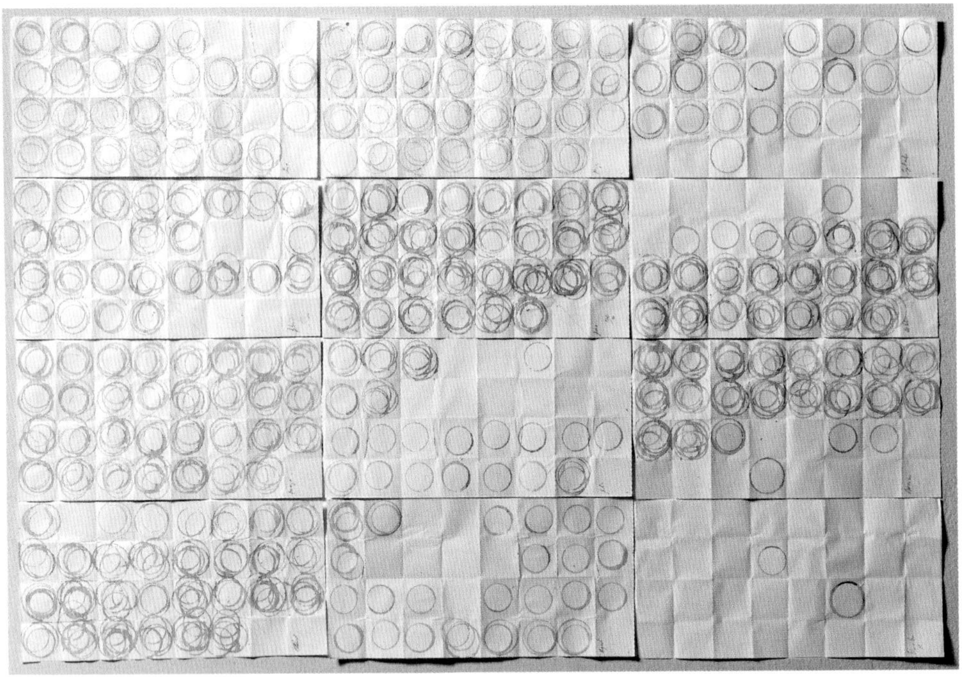

Over the period of a year, I recorded the coffee I consumed, printing the coffee cup mark on a piece of paper. I used two sizes, as I took them: latte or macchiato.

The twelve pieces of paper that create this visualisation correspond to the twelve months of the year, from top to bottom and from left to right.

The size of the pieces of paper (25 cm by 50 cm) is not random: folded in half five times and then unfolded they create thirty-two squares measuring 6 cm each.

This size, slightly larger than the bottom of a latte cup, allowed me to carry the bits of paper around with me everywhere I went and use them as a coaster.

Like a calendar, each square represents one day, with the last square empty to write down the month and other notes.

Figure 3.7: "A Daily Coffee"

Jaime Serra Palou / https://www.archivosjaimeserra.com/cafediario / last accessed Febuary 16, 2023 simple. We humans see what we want to see when reading a visualization. We often just see ourselves in the data.

The data I used in many of these pieces is irrelevant *per se*, as it's simply the result of quantifying a certain aspect of my personal life. Who cares about me, or about what I drink, eat, or do? But we all drink, eat, have sex, etc. And we like to see ourselves in others. That's the connection. Readers look at these visualizations and they somehow see themselves, filling in the gaps.

Jaime likes to defy expectations and taboos not just with design choices, but also with the topics he covers. One of the most famous visualizations he designed for *La Vanguardia* mapped his sexual life over a year (**Figure 3.8**).

The graphic consists of 365 black stripes stacked vertically, each corresponding to a day. Each stripe is subdivided into several thin lines representing whether the partners reached an orgasm or whether they practiced certain sexual activities. A color legend identifies them. A black line means sex was absent.

I showed this piece at several art galleries and listened to people looking at it. They were connecting and imagining: "Look, there's a gap here; maybe she had cystitis, or he was travelling." Visitors were bringing their own experience to the visualization. I also created an interactive version of this graphic where people could input their own data anonymously and compare the results to my data or other visitors' data.

Jaime has also visualized his least healthy habits:

In 2009 I decided to quit smoking. My memories of many important events in my life are associated with smoking. I said goodbye to my old friend, the cigarette, with a 42-day trip across the United States, from Hibbing, Minnesota, to New Orleans, Louisiana.

I consumed 729 cigarettes during the trip. I carried a map with me and, using a GPS to locate the points where I was smoking, I left a cigarette burn on each. When I came back to Spain, I published a column with a photograph of the map and an image of the burns colored in red (Figure 3.9).

It was a temporary goodbye, though. As the wanderer that he's always been, Jaime was destined to eventually return to his "old friend". He continues smoking to this day—albeit in a classically hedonistic manner: thoughtfully and moderately.

Figure 3.8: "The Sex Life of a Stable Couple"

Jaime Serra Palou / Domestika / https://www.domestika.org/en/projects/519345-vida-sexual-de-una-pareja-estable / last accessed Febuary 16, 2023

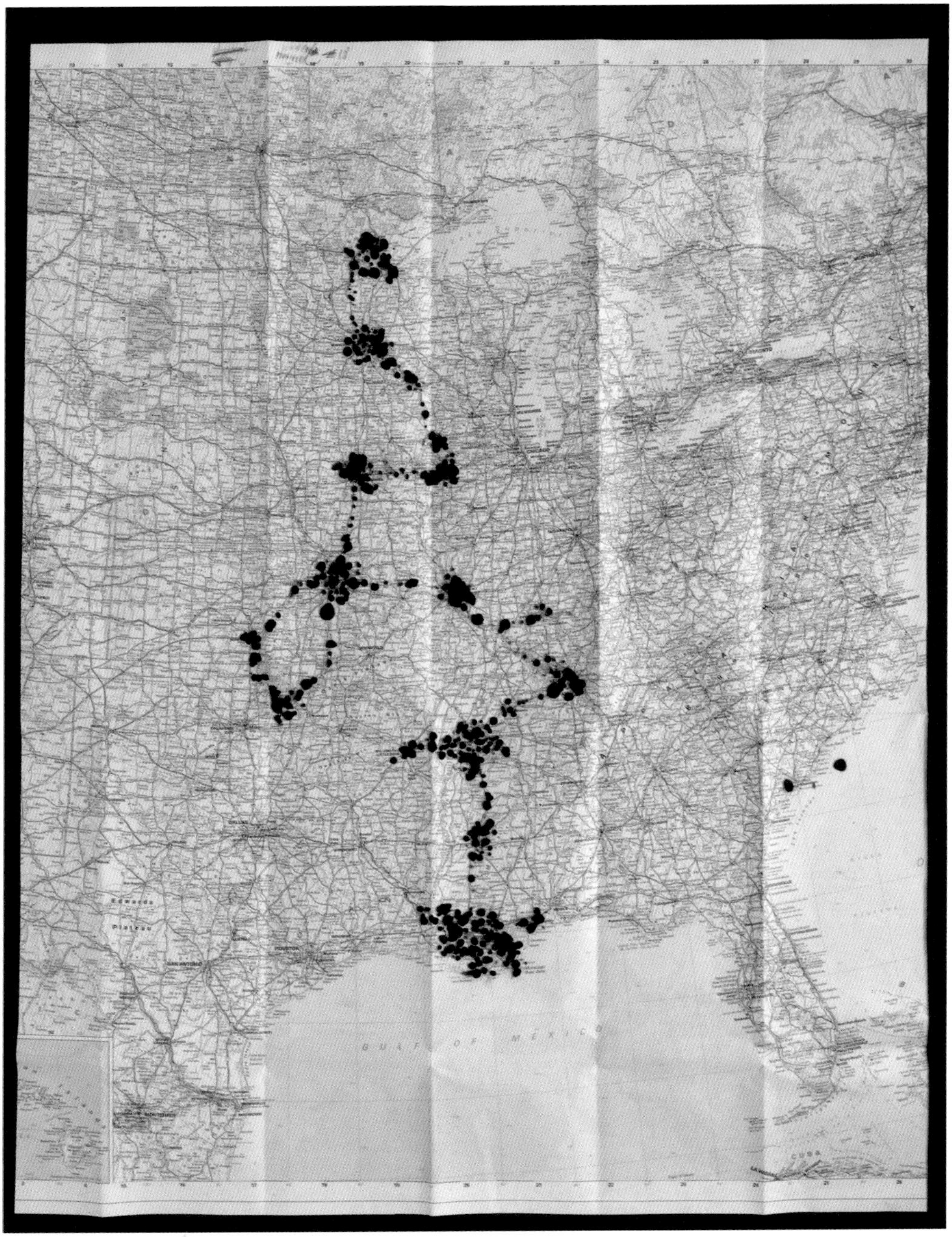

Figure 3.9: "To an Old Friend"

Jaime Serra Palou / Domestika / https://www.domestika.org/es/projects/520033-a-un-viejo-amigo / last accessed Febuary 16, 2023

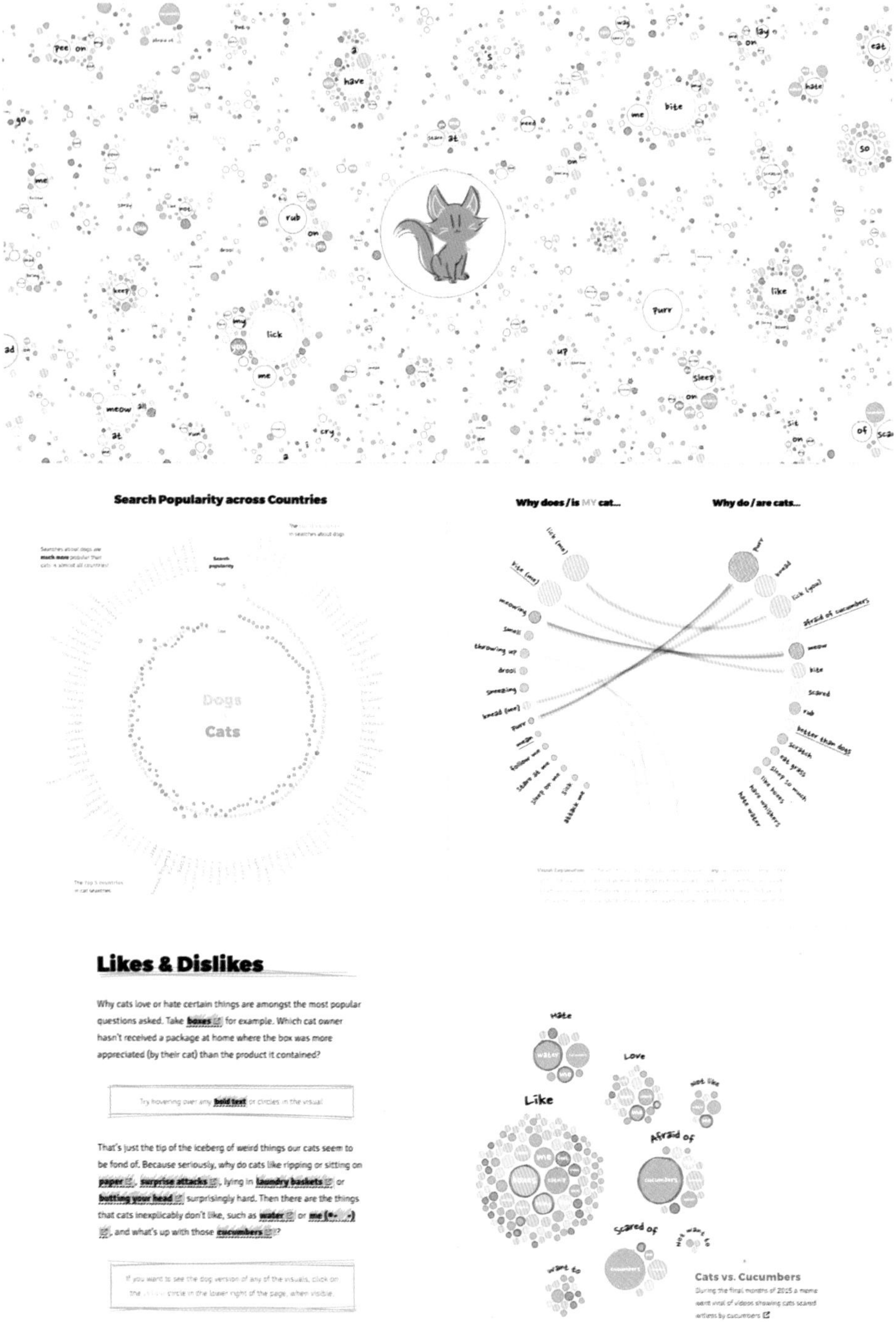

Figure 4.1: "Why Do Cats and Dogs?"

https://whydocatsanddogs.com/

Chapter 4
with Nadieh Bremer

A Certain Inner Light

> *[There's a] difference between defining beauty and defining what beauty does in the body. The latter question belongs to the realm of aesthetics, the study of bodies in proximity to beauty.*
>
> *—Chloé Cooper Jones*

Nadieh Bremer's visualizations bring me joy. I can't think of better praise.

Years ago Nadieh and I collaborated on a few projects for Google. The best one is "Why Do Cats and Dogs?" (**Figure 4.1**). It shows the most common questions people pose to Google Search about their beloved pets.

If you are a dog person—I am—it won't be surprising that the most common dog-related search by far is "Why is my dog licking...?" But you might not guess what comes next: "legs and feet." "Why is my dog eating...?" is another typical search, followed by both "grass" and "poop."

Working with Nadieh was delightful not only because I got to enjoy her beautiful sketches (**Figure 4.2**) before she made them public on her website, or because I was lucky to witness a brilliant mind at work—but also because we laughed a lot whenever we chatted. I've come to believe that Nadieh's intricate, colorful, and playful designs are an expression of a certain inner light she possesses.

Nadieh inhabits many worlds. She's worked for news organizations and companies, visualizing their data in straightforward ways—bar graphs, line graphs, data maps—but

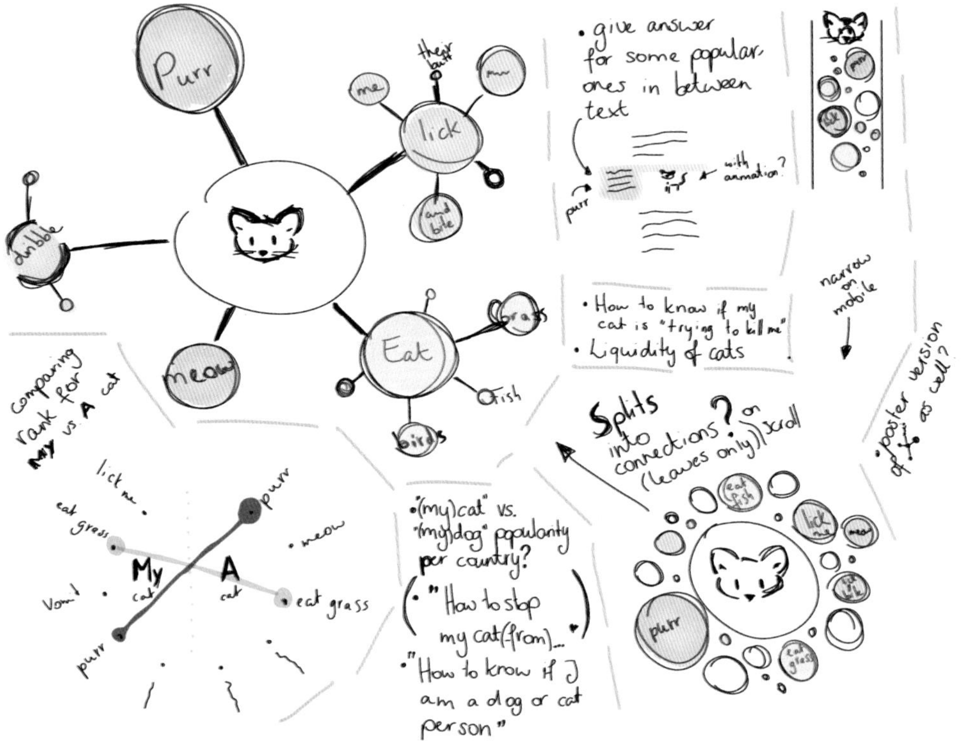

Figure 4.2: Early sketch for "Why Do Cats and Dogs?"

she's also produced work, like her projects for Google, that is much more experimental and heterodox.

That plurality of approaches and styles matches her multidisciplinary background, which combines the scientific and the analytical on one hand, with the humanistic and the artistic on the other:

> I graduated as an astronomer in 2011. After that I decided that I didn't want to pursue a career in academia, so I became an analytics consultant for Deloitte. At first, I deeply enjoyed my job, but after four years and doing my *n*th predictive model and customer segmentation, I realized that the honeymoon phase was over.
>
> At the time I was already playing around with D3.js [a data visualization library], but it was always in service to being a data analyst first and designing the visualization second.

Most people I know in visualization, including me, didn't plan for a career in the field. Instead, we stumbled upon visualization by happenstance and fell in love with it. Nadieh isn't an exception:

> I had an epiphany when I attended a talk by Mike Freeman, a data scientist and visualization developer. His first slide mentioned "data visualization specialist." I remember asking myself: "Wait, is this a separate thing from data analysis? Is it an actual career one can pursue? Sign me up!" From that point on I knew that's what I wanted for myself, so I invested all free time I could in learning about it.

However, pretty often the seeds are already planted in a designer's mind for that sort of epiphany to happen:

> Art runs in my family. My grandfather, who died before I was born, was a painter. I grew up loving his work. My father was also very artistic and I guess that I inherited a bit of that. As a child, I would paint, cross stitch, do origami, and whatnot in my free time. I've always had this urgent need to create stuff.
>
> When I stumbled upon data visualization, I discovered a perfect mesh of two things I love, science and art. Visualization would allow me to work with data, math, and analysis, trying to figure out what insights to communicate, what stories to build and tell—and I could also be creative and design beautiful objects.
>
> And there's something else to visualization. It gives me the opportunity to explore subjects I suddenly get interested in. I love learning and I love to bring other people along on the journey.

I told Nadieh that this is a common impulse among those who pursue careers in journalism. When I worked in newsrooms, I certainly enjoyed giving readers information that could make their lives better, but what I enjoyed the most was the freedom to learn something myself and, as I mentioned in the previous chapter, the opportunity to jump from one subject to the next without a roadmap.

This is the spirit that fueled Nadieh's most famous project, "Data Sketches," a collaboration with Shirley Wu, whom you met in the introduction:

> Shirley and I first met in a small Slack channel about visualization. She and I had been invited to be speakers at the 2016 Open Viz conference; we had lunch before the event and became friends. One day we were talking about the Information is Beautiful Awards [an international visualization competition] and we both realized we hadn't designed graphics worth submitting. Shirley proposed that we force ourselves to design a series of visualizations, and we later agreed to work on the same topics.

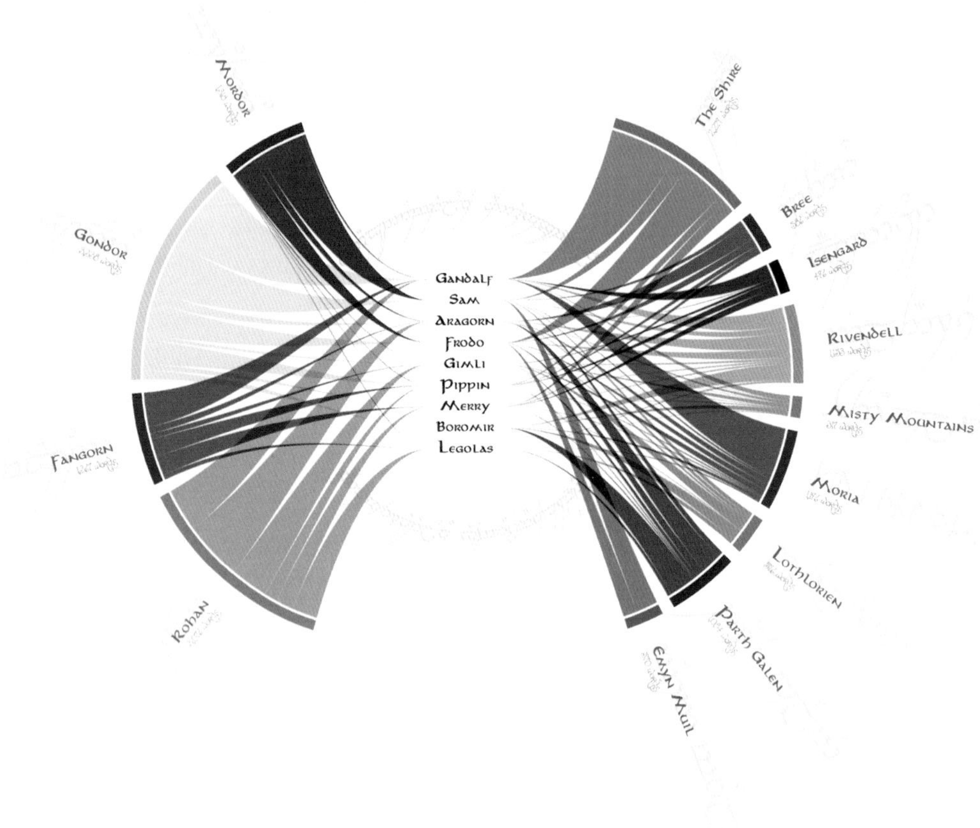

Figure 4.3: "The Words of *The Lord of the Rings*." Data Sketches https://www.datasketch.es/

Every semester, as part of my job of educating students in the craft of visualization, I encourage them to challenge themselves, to develop a work discipline and a regular schedule, and to hold themselves accountable. For most people it's hard to accomplish all these on their own.

Nadieh and Shirley did it together. Each month for a year they would agree on a broad theme—travel, books, music, nostalgia, and so on. After that, each would choose a story to tell within that theme. For instance, in the "nostalgia" month Nadieh focused on the anime series *Dragon Ball Z*. In the "movies" month, she visualized the more than 17,000 words spoken by the main characters of Peter Jackson's *The Lord of the Rings* movie trilogy, (**Figure 4.3**) and the locations where those words were spoken.

Shirley's and Nadieh's "Data Sketches" became a book with the same title in 2021. I wrote the prologue for it, where I said:

> Orthodoxy and eccentricity are opposing but complementary forces in any field, and data visualization isn't an exception. Periods when orthodoxy prevails over eccentricity discourage whim,

> passion, and experimentation, and favor stability and continuity. When the opposite happens, when eccentrics take over, chaos and turmoil ensue, but progress becomes more rapid, and invention—fruitful or useless—more likely. This is a book where eccentricity abounds.

Nadieh's visualizations for news publications or nongovernmental organizations are much more orthodox than the unique and often whimsical graphics in "Data Sketches":

> Sometimes a client comes to me with a large data set, and they don't know what to do it with. In such cases, I do some data exploration and try to find "stories" in the numbers, possible angles that I can pursue. If the client takes my suggestions, I begin an iterative process consisting of first designing a rough sketch to ensure that the main point, or points, that I'm trying to make are properly displayed. But I still think more like a scientist than as a journalist. It's hard for me to be extremely concise. I have this drive to try to provide as much context as possible, or to even show everything, not just the core insight.

That sounds very much like the way I think about data-driven stories. I then asked Nadieh what she finds more exciting about visualization:

> Being honest, and perhaps not surprisingly since nowadays I'm moving more and more towards data art, it's the visual aspect that personally excites me the most. A good visualization should of course provide some insights, or let the reader explore the data, or communicate something about the numbers—but what really drives me is the fact that readers would look at a visualization I created and they might be enraptured by the aesthetics of it.

Nadieh sees "Adore You" (**Figure 4.4**), which she designed for Sony Music, as a transitional project between her traditional data visualizations and her current interest in art. Based on Spotify and YouTube data, this graphic reimagines the Gold Record, one of the certification plaques given by the Recording Industry Association of America to recognize best-selling songs or albums:

> My focus on art is related to your question about what I get most enjoyment from. I enjoy creating something that I find that looks visually interesting, beautiful, maybe even something that people will want to put up on their walls.

On their walls or in other places. I loved Nadieh's 2021 series of generative art pieces "Elemental Flows" (**Figure 4.5**) so much that I decided to display them on this book's cover. They are visualization poetry:

> In July of 2021 I designed a visualization that looked at the number of trees per square kilometer compared to the size of a country. I enjoyed working with that data set, and that led me to wonder about how I could use it in a much bigger project. I began to think about how trees relate to earth, and how earth is one of the four classic elements. What if I made a visualization about trees per capita (earth), about air quality (wind), about the number of sunlight hours (fire), about rainfall (water)? And I did.

However, I didn't want to design a conventional data visualization revealing patterns in such data. Instead, I used flow field and noise algorithms, and then I adjusted the code and math to make the graphics look like the elements they represented. Therefore, earth looks like roots branching outward, water is like a whirlpool, and so on.

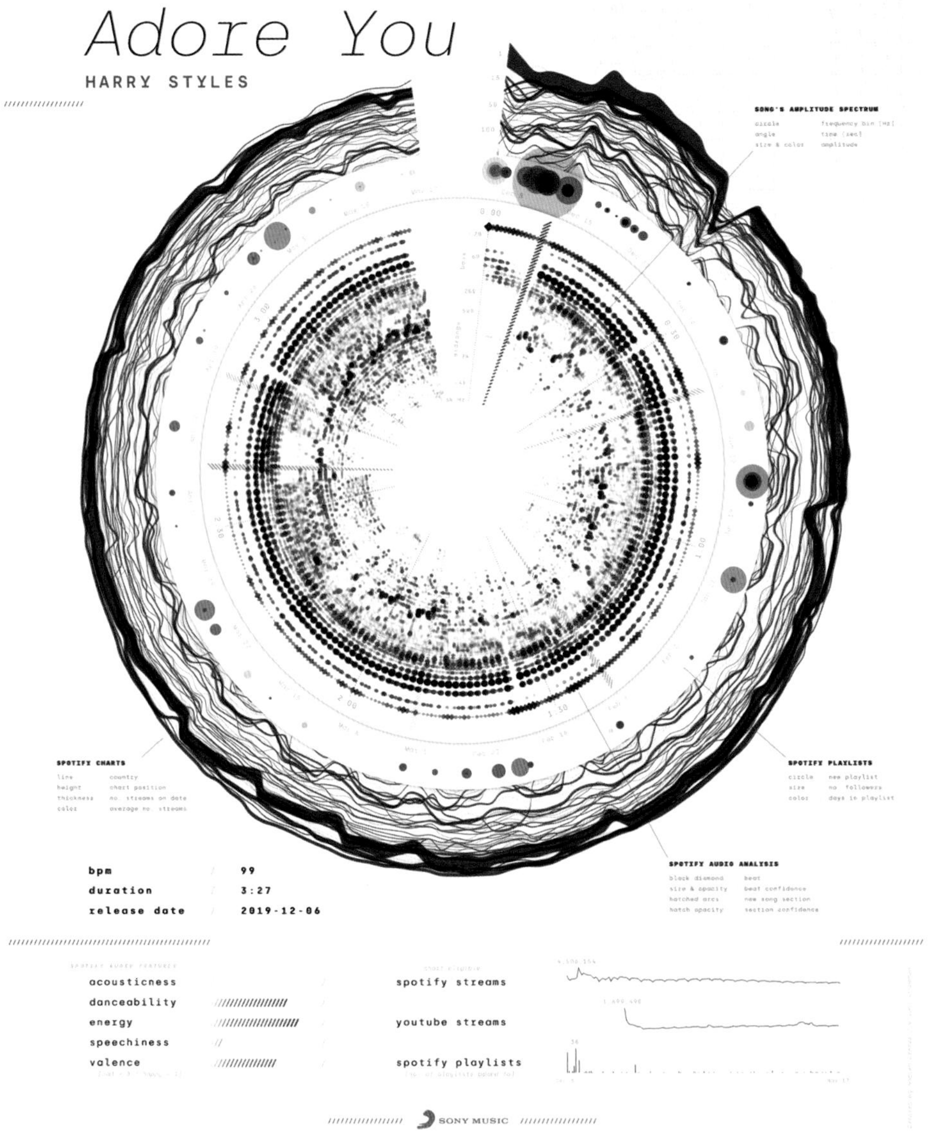

Figure 4.4: "Adore You"

https://www.visualcinnamon.com/portfolio/sony-music-data-art/

Figure 4.5: "Elemental Flows"

https://www.visualcinnamon.com/art/elemental-flows/

Figure 4.6: "Elemental Flows: Digital"

I added a fifth element, which I called digital, something we can no longer live without anymore in the modern world (**Figure 4.6**). It's made of straight lines and invisible circles. The circles are positioned around a spiral; they get bigger the farther they are from the center of the graphic.

Nadieh has designed more data-driven paintings in recent years, such as a collaboration with UNICEF which resulted in a thousand non-fungible tokens (NFTs) collectively called "Patchwork Kingdoms" (**Figure 4.7**):

I'm very proud of that project. UNICEF used those images to celebrate their 75th anniversary. The project is based on school Internet connectivity data. Each square on an image represents a school, and it contains an abstract symbol selected randomly from a gallery.

Figure 4.7: "Patchwork Kingdoms"
https://www.visualcinnamon.com/collection/patchwork-kingdoms/

The symbols inside the squares look very unique and varied. However, Nadieh didn't design a huge gallery of them, but just a few dozens that she arranged in different ways:

I designed around fifty of them by hand (**Figure 4.8**) and ended up recreating them programmatically. The complexity of these symbols is proportional to the speed of each school's Internet connection. There were some schools for which I had no data; I represented them as birds and clouds.

The squares stack to form "buildings" and, side by side, an entire "kingdom." I placed the squares of each kingdom above or below a horizontal line. This represents the digital divide. Schools above that line are connected to the Internet. They have vibrant colors and contain intricate symbols. The schools below the line are not connected; their colors are muted and faded.

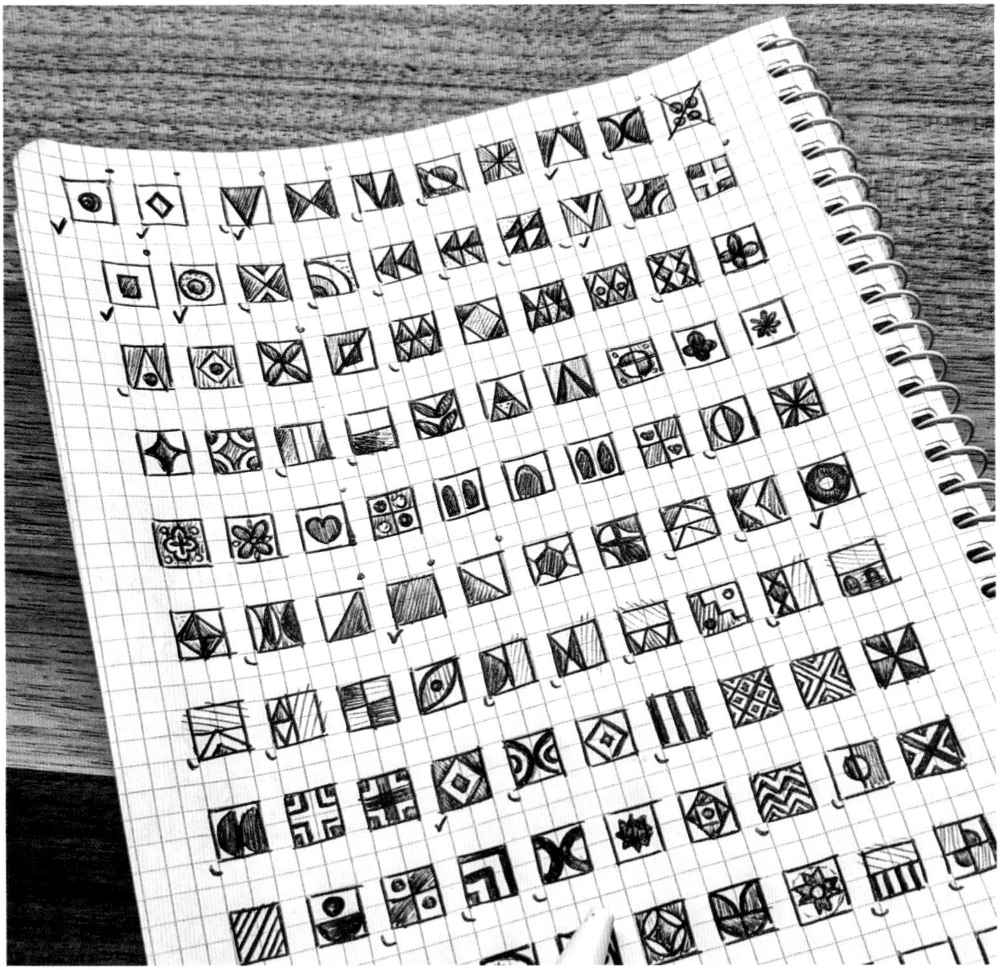

Figure 4.8: Sketch for "Patchwork Kingdoms"

Nadieh Bremer / www.visualcinnamon.com/art/patchwork-kingdoms / last accessed 8 May, 2023

> I wanted to give this project a child-like appearance. An initial inspiration were wooden block building sets—my own father had one—and the work of Mary Blair.

Mary Blair (1911–1978), was a designer famous for her work at Disney. One of her most popular creations, the one that Nadieh mentioned in our conversation, is her concept art for "It's a Small World", a popular Disneyland attraction. Coincidentally, Blair created it originally for the UNICEF pavilion at the 1964 World's Fair in New York City.

As someone who is incapable of working on more than one or two long-term projects at the same time, I'm always curious about how freelancers manage the need to focus deeply during extended periods of time with the also fundamental need to meet deadlines for several clients. Nadieh and I are similar in the way that we organize our time; we are both one-thing-at-a-time people:

> I don't know why, but I have this tendency that if I find something interesting, I just want to know everything about it, watch all YouTube videos I can find, and obsessively read as much as possible about it.
>
> This may be the reason why it's hard for me to work on different projects in a day, or even switch between projects easily. I've been in such a situation, but I try to avoid it. I prefer to focus on a single project two or three days in a row, losing myself in the work.

What Nadieh said reminded me of Mihaly Csikszentmihalyi's *Flow: The Psychology of Optimal Experience* (1990). According to Csikszentmihalyi, flow is "the state in which people are so involved in an activity that nothing else seems to matter; the experience itself is so enjoyable that people will do it even at great cost, for the sheer sake of doing it."

Meaningful and worthwhile activities performed with our full attention give us peace and joy. Such activities don't need to be work. A walk in the woods during which we quiet our stream of consciousness, and we instead engage entirely with surrounding sights, noises, or smells, can have the same effect. But they often *are* work, particularly when the work is a craft, either physical or digital.

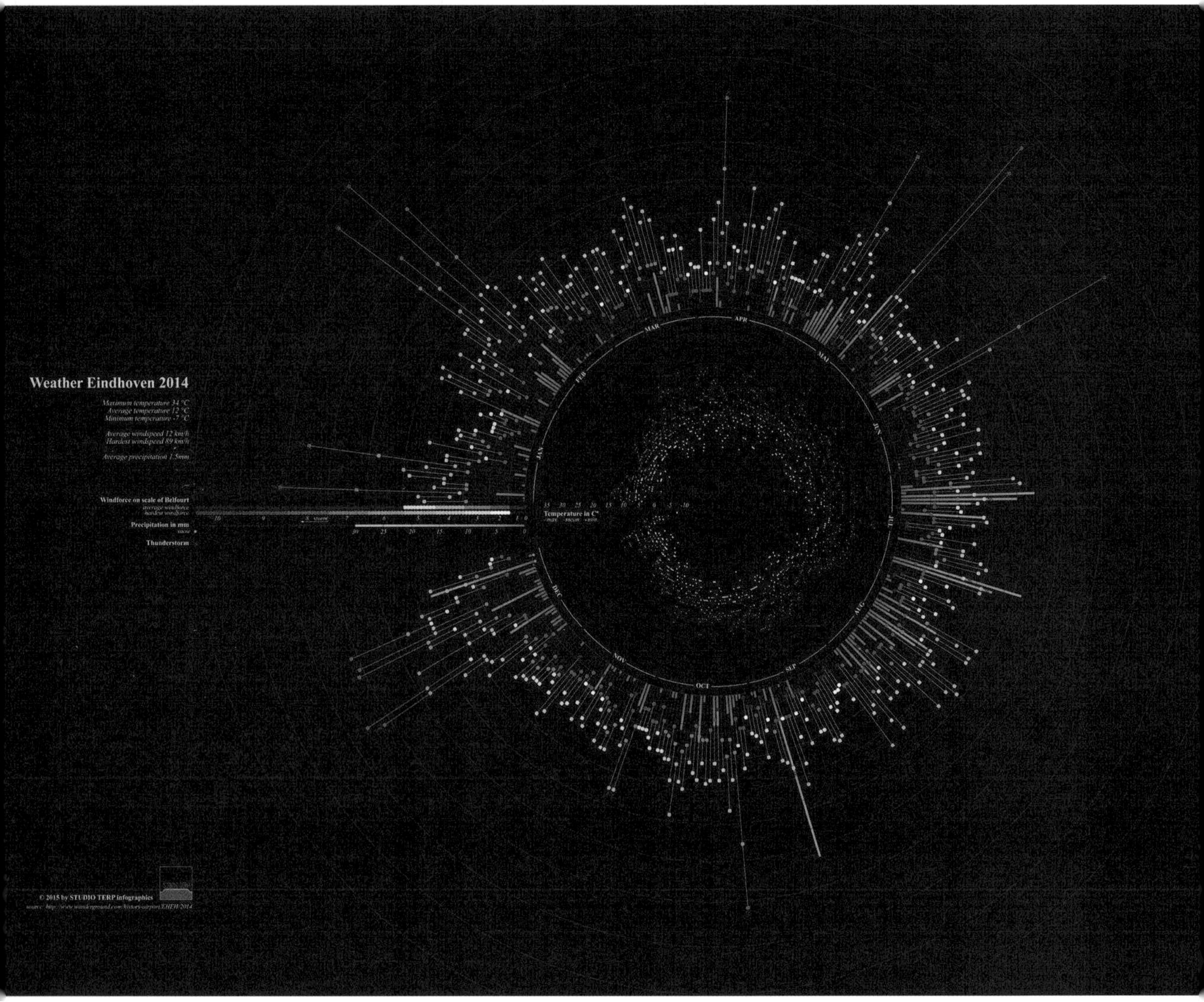

Figure 5.1: "Weather Eindhoven 2014"

http://www.studioterp.nl/weather-eindhoven-2014/

Chapter 5
with Sonja Kuijpers

A Mindful Artisan

During the making life feels uncharacteristically centered, and the calm that comes with clear intent sustains the uncertainty of creating something new.

—Mary Jane Jacob

Flow and the joy it brings about are a constant presence in books about artisanship. In *The Craftsman* (2008), Richard Sennett quotes sociologist C. Wright Mills:

> The laborer with a sense of craft becomes engaged in the work in and for itself; the satisfactions of working are their own reward.

Sennett also discusses how craft is supposed to differ from art. He explains that a common view—which he challenges as simplistic—is that we act as artisans when we work outward, toward our communities, while we become artists when we work inward, turned upon ourselves. The difference is one of intention, agency, autonomy (not being limited by expectations or conventions), and also sociological, dependent on how the work is perceived by the society where it's undertaken.

If we accept this view, are the designers I'm showcasing in this second part of the book artisans or artists? Like Sennett, I don't believe in essences, or in sharp categorical boundaries between fields so, at the risk of offending those who are knowledgeable in the philosophy of art, I'll tentatively take the pragmatic route and say these designers *are* both because they *act* as both. Their stances and decisions depend on the projects they undertake at every moment.

In the world of visualization, arguments about whether a particular data-driven graphic is data visualization or a piece of data art, or about how to demarcate those fields, have been fierce, exhausting, and boring. They reveal a crude notion of what visualization and art are. Unfortunately, they are also the reason why designers such as **Sonja Kuijpers** have decided to adopt the neutral-sounding label "data illustrators":

> It was a decision based on a certain frustration. Around 2013, a couple of years into my journey of becoming a graphics designer, I grew tired of constant back-and-forths online as to whether this or that project is a "data visualization" or "data art." Some people said about designers like me that we aren't data visualization designers, but data artists.
>
> Recently I asked myself, "Why should I care about this? I'm a settled professional. I'll just call myself a data illustrator and get on with it. Let people try to figure out what that means!" In hindsight, I think that such label is fitting. I take data and shape them into graphics, so I do illustrate data.

I find the nitpicky gatekeeping Sonja faced unsavory because territoriality repels me. Fields such as information design or data visualization can be defined strictly and narrowly, or loosely and vaguely. I prefer the latter because it's more likely to lead to open, fluid, and enriching communities that attract people with varied backgrounds:

> I studied design, and ended up working in a landscaping firm for about a decade. I did a lot of public space and interior design. I think that this experience eventually helped me with what I do today, as it required a lot of deep analytical reasoning. To design a space you need to do research on the location and the resources you have available, and then plan how to take advantage of them, almost like if you are structuring the layout of an information graphic.
>
> The economic crisis of the late 2000s impacted architecture and landscaping in the Netherlands hard. I lost my job around 2010, along with many others, and I was left with not much to do.

Sonja stumbled upon visualization thanks to the Infographics Congress, an annual conference in the Netherlands that hosted its first edition in 2011:

> I don't remember why I attended the conference. I guess that it was out of curiosity. I had a vague familiarity with graphics used to explore and explain things, and I thought, "Wow, people really do this for a living?" I was blown away. After that, I did plenty of reading online, looking for tips, resources, and inspiration. The more I read about visualization, the more I realized it was somehow connected to my previous job.
>
> At the time I was still involved in some landscaping projects as a freelancer, and I began designing visualizations on my own. I also started participating in online communities where people design graphics, share them with everybody, and then discuss them. I learned a lot, but I also had to deal with the negative vibes that sometimes appear in such spaces.

This happened with the first of my visualizations that got some notoriety (**Figure 5.1**), about the weather in the town where I live, Eindhoven, in 2013. Not everybody who saw it understood that it was a personal piece that I had designed mainly for myself. I'm not good at handling numbers mentally, and that's why something magical happens when I transform them into objects. I can understand those numbers better. The very process of designing the graphic helps me to grasp their meaning.

There's also an emotional component to this process. When I'm designing, it doesn't matter whether it is a simple bar graph or a more creative display, I need to be able to step back from the work, look at it, and say, "This looks fascinating and aesthetically pleasing. It'll probably look like this as well to other people!" Obviously, the information in the graphic needs to be correct, but its aesthetics matter a lot, as well. I know this might sound a bit egotistical, but it's the truth.

I mentioned to Sonja that most designers I know, regardless of whether they create their visualizations for analysis, communication, or other purposes, feel in a similar way. Before we can satisfy an audience, we need to be fulfilled ourselves, proud about the work we've done. We're the audience before the actual audience.

To Sonja, this is true of client work, as well. To interest others, she first needs to be interested herself. In 2017, she was hired by the German newspaper *Frankfurter Allgemeine Zeitung* for a special multipage project about the Bayreuth Festival, which honors Richard Wagner's operas (**Figure 5.2**). Wagner himself launched the event in 1876 in a theater built specially to host it, the Bayreuth Festspielhaus:

I designed visualizations for three of the five pages of the special coverage under the supervision of the newspaper's graphics team. The other two pages showcased comics by the wonderful artist Attila Futaki. The project didn't just appear in the paper, but a special edition of it was printed and given to the people attending the festival.

To me, this project was an opportunity to visualize various data related to the Wagner family, the history of the festival, Wagner's operas, and many other things—and to learn myself through the process of gathering the information, shaping it, and then structuring the layouts. As usual, I was the first reader of the graphics I was designing. That's something I find appealing about the work that we do.

One of Sonja's most famous projects is her partnership with Stefanie Posavec for *The Climate Book* (2022), authored by environmental activist Greta Thunberg. Sonja collaborated with Stefanie and many scientists in the design of the graphics for the book. When we talked, Sonja acknowledged the positive impact that this side of her career has

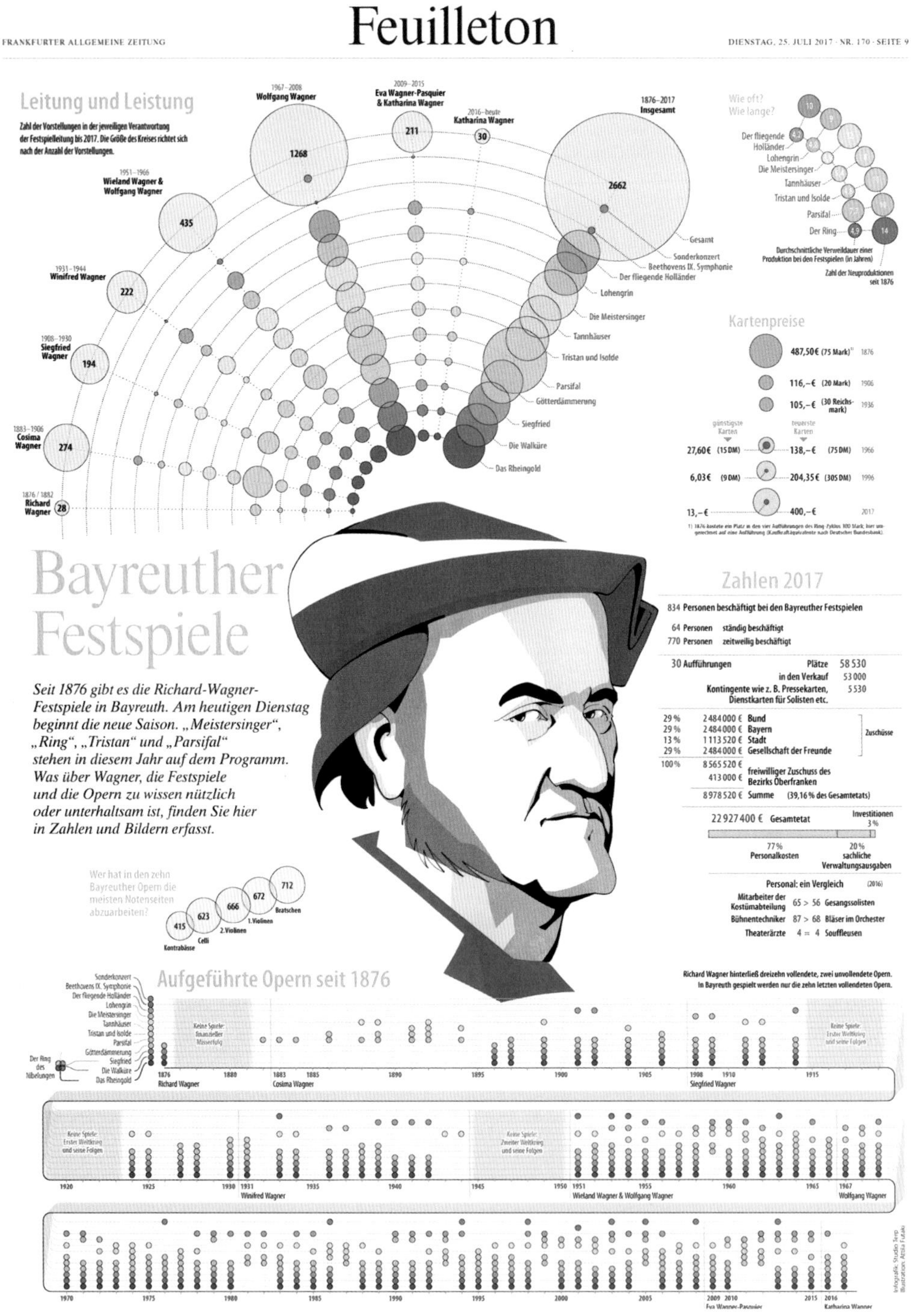

Figure 5.2: One of the pages of "The Bayreuther Festival, 2017"

http://www.studioterp.nl/datavisualization-bayreuther-festspiele-faz/

on readers but, at the same time, she sounded more enthusiastic when speaking about projects that she had initiated herself:

> I'm a fan of John Irving's novels. *The Hotel New Hampshire* (1981) is the first one I read, and it's still one of my favorites. Irving's stories are full of colorful characters who go through emotionally intense events. Why not represent them through shapes arranged in an appealing manner? That's the drive behind a project I designed a few years back (**Figure 5.3**.) It consists of twelve panels, one per chapter. I came up with an icon for each character; its size on every chapter-panel corresponds to the number of actions that character undertakes. The number of words and sounds characters utter are represented by bubbles of varying areas.

Sonja's take on Irving's novel is captivating. I find it reminiscent of Vassily Kandinsky's Bauhaus period in the 1920s and early 1930s, when the famous painter experimented with geometry and wrote several influential essays, such as *Point and Line to Plane* (1926). I asked Sonja where she had obtained the data:

> Well, there's some uncertainty to the numbers because I collected them manually. I counted every word and every action. The entire project is handcrafted—the data gathering, the design of every icon, the layout. I spent countless hours on each one of those stages in a state of deep concentration.

Visualization design leads Sonja to meditative states of awareness of the present moment. Her next words resonated deeply with me:

> As I create all my graphics by hand, I do a lot of repetitive actions such as copying, pasting, rotating, displacing. This isn't something negative, quite the contrary. At some point in the process, all my thinking quiets down, my mind frees up, and it's like I step outside of myself and my hands move on their own.

I often experience something similar, even with the most mundane of tasks. I told Sonja of the time when I designed a cartogram of Brazil by copying hundreds of little squares, each of them representing thousands of people, and then manually positioning them so they'd resemble the actual map of the country. If I had to do the same today, I'd use a mapping tool or code, but I doubt that I'd get the same inner peace I experienced then. The practice itself often brings serenity to the soul. It can even be life-saving:

> Between 2018 and 2019 I fell into a deep depression that, unfortunately, led to suicidal thoughts. My genes and certain life events led to it. It took me time, effort, and professional help to recover. During this time I also created my most personal project, "A View on Despair". (**Figure 5.4**.) It visualizes suicide statistics for the Netherlands in 2017.
>
> This project also contributed to my recovery, as it originated from my being mad with myself. Let me tell you: being mad is a powerful motivation. I told myself: "this shouldn't be the way that

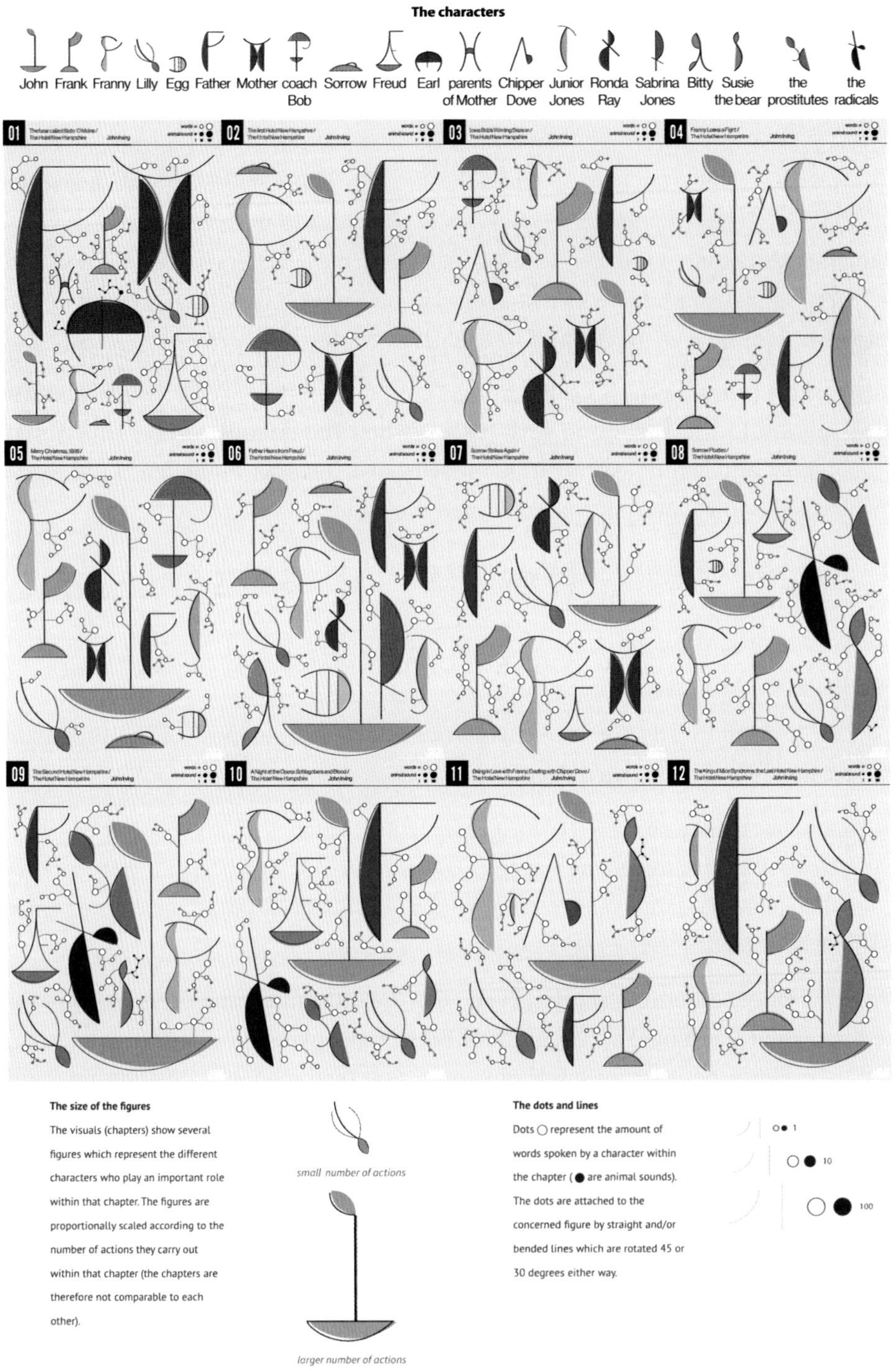

Figure 5.3: "The Hotel New Hampshire"

http://www.studioterp.nl/the-hotel-new-hampshire-a-data-art-project-by-studio-terp/

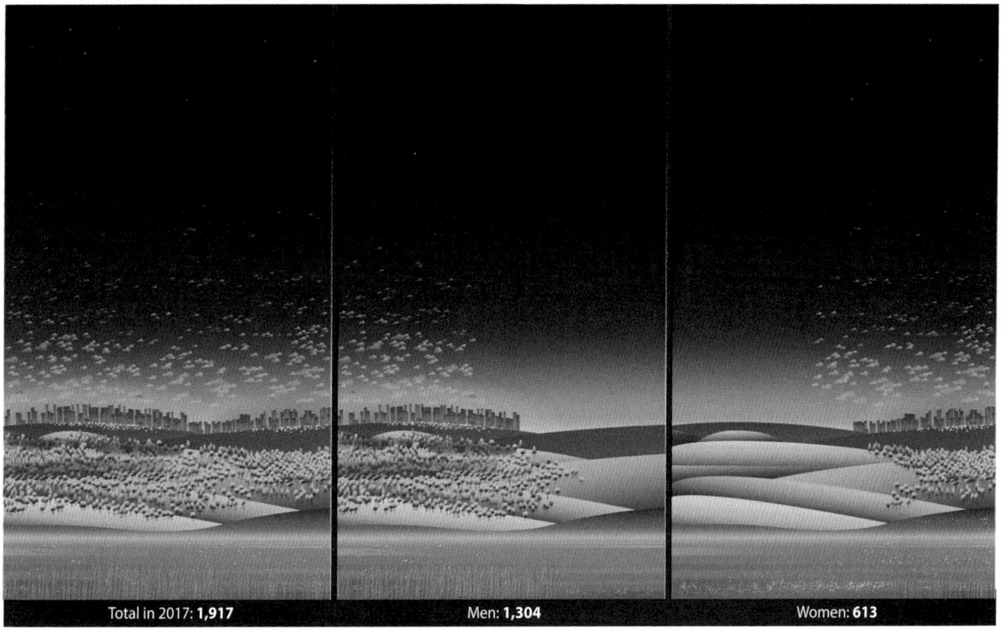

Figure 5.4: "A View on Despair"

http://www.studioterp.nl/a-view-on-despair-a-datavisualization-project-by-studio-terp/

my life is going to be like." So I got to work. Since almost this project's inception, I knew the tone that I wanted for it: not dramatic, but not overly abstract or neutral, either.

"A View on Despair" does include some traditional visualizations, such as line graphs, but its core visual element is a landscape populated with trees, buildings, clouds—each corresponding to a person. As I believe that sensitive subjects should be approached tactfully, I added a trigger warning, information about where people in emotional distress can get help, and even advice derived from my own experience: "I do recommend you get professional help. It's important to have someone with an objective and non-judgemental view to talk to. Depression is something to take very seriously. Take yourself seriously."

I won't lie, at first I was afraid of how readers would react. Isn't it dehumanizing to represent people as objects, even if they aren't geometric objects but real things such as clouds or trees? During the COVID pandemic there were similar debates in the visualization community about whether visualization is too abstract, obscuring the tragedies that it informs about.

In spite of her worries, the responses to "A View on Despair" were unanimously positive. Some readers reached out with appreciative messages. One said, "My sister would be one of your clouds up there." Sonja's reaction was to think, "That's beautiful."

Is there a higher reward for work done with attention, love, and care?

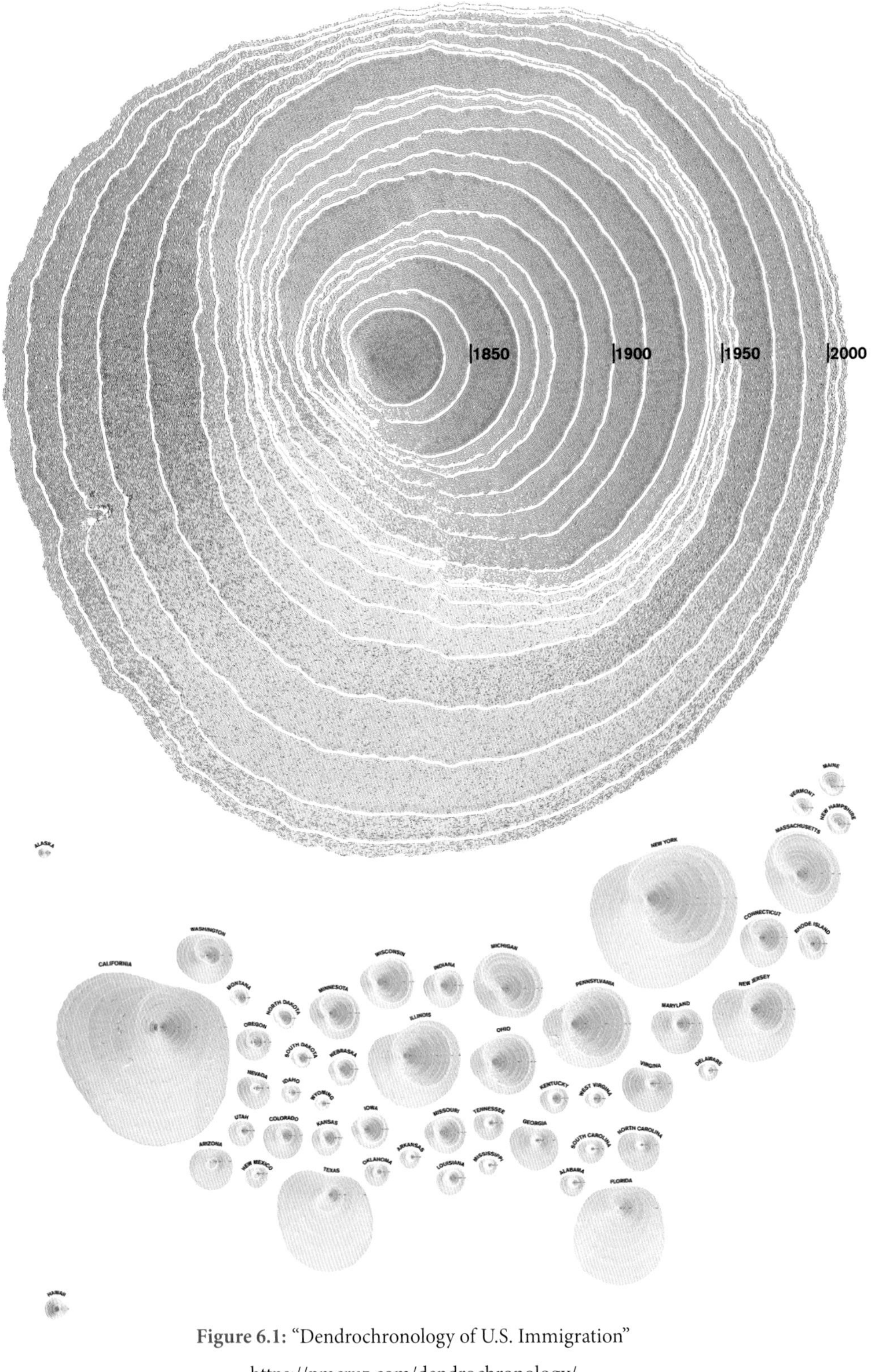

Figure 6.1: "Dendrochronology of U.S. Immigration"

https://pmcruz.com/dendrochronology/

Chapter 6
with Pedro Cruz

Living Visualization

Trees fall with spectacular crashes. But planting is silent and growth is invisible.

—Richard Powers

I connected the last words of my conversation with Sonja Kuijpers to a passage from *The Best of Two Worlds* (1953) by the naturalist and pantheist Joseph Wood Krutch:

> Order and obedience are the primary characteristics of that which is not alive. The snowflake eternally obeys its one and only law: "Be thou six pointed"; the planets their one and only: "Travel thou in an ellipse." The astronomer can tell where the North Star will be then thousand years hence; the botanist cannot tell where the dandelion will bloom tomorrow. Life is rebellious and anarchical, always testing the supposed immutability of the rules which the nonliving changelessly accepts.

Traditional visualizations are often an attempt to reveal characteristics of the living, but they do it by forcing such phenomena to conform to the lifeless perfection of geometric shapes. There are designers who rebel against such tyranny of the straight, the smooth, the sterile. Nadieh and Sonja are among them, and so are Federica Fragapane (Chapter 7) and **Pedro Cruz**, a designer and professor at Northeastern University whose most famous visualization is titled "Simulated Dendrochronology of U.S. Immigration" (**Figure 6.1**). Pedro has written about it:

> This work embodies my approach to visualization by simulating natural systems that result in familiar metaphors for the visualization of information. It shows waves of immigration into the

> United States expressed in the form of tree rings. During Donald Trump's administration, a time when anti-immigrant discourses were more apparent, this work came as a celebration of diversity, and as an ode to inclusion. The visual quality and level of resemblance with actual tree rings were made possible by an algorithm that I developed. This algorithm simulates how cells grow in a tree under the pressure exerted by the tree's bark and react probabilistically to different degrees of growth depending on environmental conditions.

In the graphic, each ring corresponds to a decade (1830–2016), and each dot represents 100 people. Their position and color depend on the country or continent where immigrants came to the United States from (**Figure 6.2**).

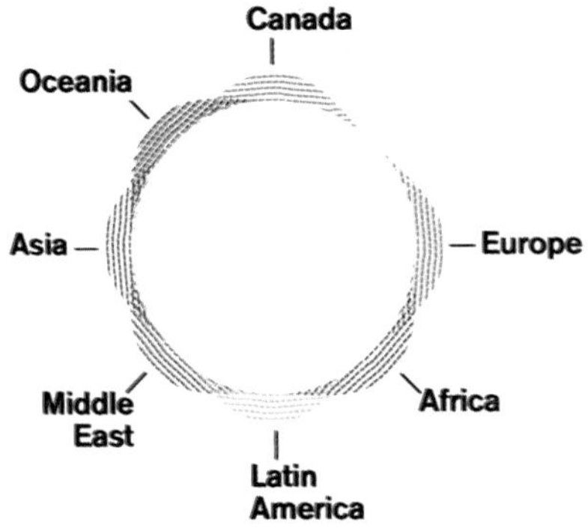

Figure 6.2: Legend of "Dendrochronology of U.S. Immigration"

Patterns become visible after some scrutiny. In the main graphic, immigration from Europe is dominant at first, but after a few decades, rings begin shifting to other regions such as Latin America and Asia. A comparison between states reveals stark differences. Historically, each received immigration from different parts of the world. Pedro told me:

> Before the dendrochronology project I hadn't worked with U.S. census data. I saw it as an opportunity. I wanted to do it in a way that preserved as much granularity as possible. I couldn't represent every individual, but I also wanted to avoid aggregating individuals too much, so I reached the compromise solution of making every dot to be equal to 100 people.
>
> There are several metaphorical layers to the dendrochronology project. It is certainly a depiction of growth but also of the resistance to that growth. Cells reproduce in between rings, and they meet the resistance of the bark, which is forced to bend to make room for the cells.

Pedro often uses his dendrochronology to explain his philosophy of design:

> My practice as a designer is centered on the exploration of metaphors for the communication of information through simulated nature-inspired systems. This practice involves computationally replicating phenomena found in nature in a way that such systems become the visualizations themselves. This way, visualizations are not only a one-way view of the data, but they can

encompass many forms, as the visualization reacts and adapts to data, rather than just being a straightforward mapping of it.

I inquired about how such philosophy developed. It began with his education in science:

I'm originally from Portugal. I studied engineering physics at the University of Lisbon for two years. I didn't know anything about graphic design, but I did learn programming, which led me to create my first visualizations during a course called computing for physics. They were interactive simulations of things such as springs and electromagnetic fields. I also got interested in communicating science to non-scientists.

Pedro changed his major to informatics engineering, a mix of computer science, software engineering, and network theory:

I wanted to be a software developer, knowing that I was fairly good at it, but for some reason I started getting interested in typography and reading a lot of books about it.

Why typography? Whenever I walked around the city I saw these posters by several design studios. They looked so simple that I thought to myself that, well, I could design something like that. But whenever I tried, it was impossible for me to come up with the organized simplicity that I so admired. I wanted to find out why those typographical posters captivated me, what the heck was in them that I couldn't see, but that made me attracted to them. Often we say that good design is invisible, right? Well, it was visible to me.

Typography was my gateway to visual design. I began perceiving that my interests in typography, design, physics, math, and algorithms were somewhat connected. In all those fields there's often a fascination with efficiency and elegant solutions.

What about visualization? How did Pedro move from general graphic design inspired by typography to what he does and teaches today?

In between finishing my bachelor's degree and beginning a master's degree, also in informatics engineering, I spent some time in Brazil taking computer science classes and designed my first project that had significant public exposure. I had just learned how to simulate soft bodies by building skeletons made of springs and how to make them collide with each other. I wanted to use that technique somehow.

I've always been fascinated by the gradual dissolution of colonial empires, the Portuguese, the Spanish, the English, or the French, so I visualized their decline with an animation that depicts them and their former colonies as cells that organically split up into smaller cells (**Figure 6.3**).

This project went through several versions. The second one won the Student Research Competition at the SIGGRAPH computer animation festival back in 2010. The animation is fun to watch, but it also has deliberate political undertones:

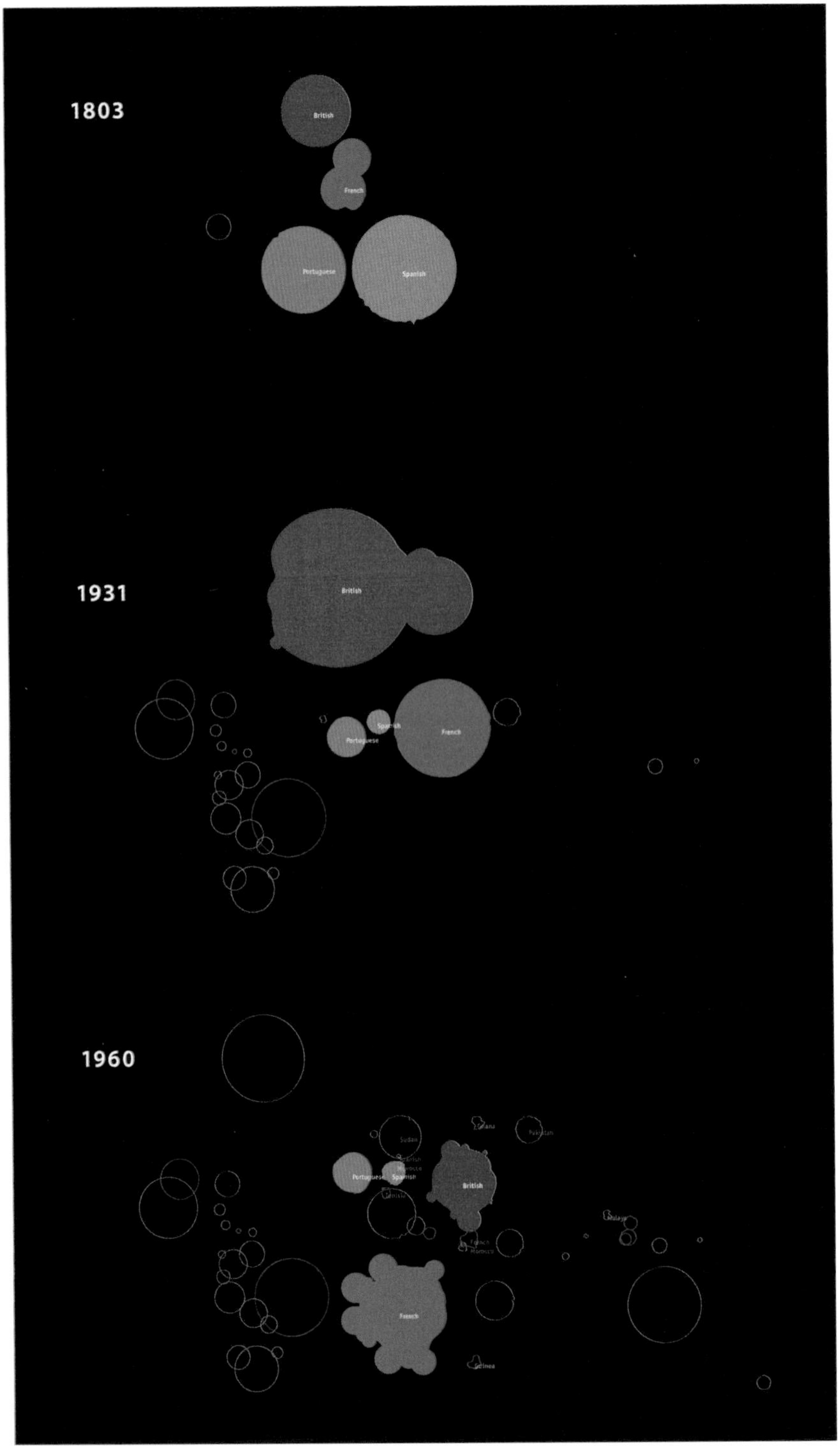

Figure 6.3: "Visualizing Empires Decline"
https://pmcruz.com/works/visualizing-empires-decline.html

It's a celebration of the demise of those empires. Some design decisions I made are related to this. For instance, I wanted to portray some sort of rejection between the former metropolis and the newly formed countries. When the smaller cells split up from the main bodies, they fly away from it quite quickly.

Pedro told me that this project combines the manual with the automated and the algorithmic:

On one hand, I spent a lot of time collecting information manually from different sources. I created the data set, and it was a headache. A key challenge was definition and demarcation. In some cases, former colonies became entirely sovereign political entities, countries, but others—particularly former territories of the British Empire, such as Canada—had a much more complex status.

Another challenge was that some places have a specific date for their independence, but others don't. Finally, the size of each cell is proportional to the land area of the empires and their former colonies. Collecting and curating all this information took tons of time. That was the manual part.

But there's also the automated part. Remember that this project is based on a physics engine that projects soft, roughly round bodies that collide and bounce off each other; the fun part of it, then, is that there's some randomness to this visualization. Every time you render it, with the former colonies being propelled from the main body of their empires, it behaves a bit differently.

Why represent empires disintegrating as cells, and not through a traditional timeline or a map?

Because this type of natural metaphor is often much more suggestive than traditional graphics. It carries messages of its own. For instance, notice that when a former colony departs from its empire, there seems to be a small explosion, and the blob flees with what appears to be a sense of urgency. That's deliberate. It indicates violence sometimes, but also the joy of liberty, of creating a new nation, expressed through something that looks like fireworks. After this project was published, somebody took it and created a new version in which they added explosion sounds.

In 2011, Pedro spent a year at the MIT's Senseable City Lab; he was also working on a PhD in information science and technology at the University of Coimbra, Portugal, where he reflected on his use of organic shapes in visualization. His dissertation, which can be found online, is *Semantic Figurative Metaphors in Information Visualization* (2016). Its prologue might sound quaint nowadays, but it looked defiant to me when it was published:

Visualization is often seen as neutral, relinquishing discussions on design choices for communication and assuming that those who produce a visualization must have no authorial intent. This

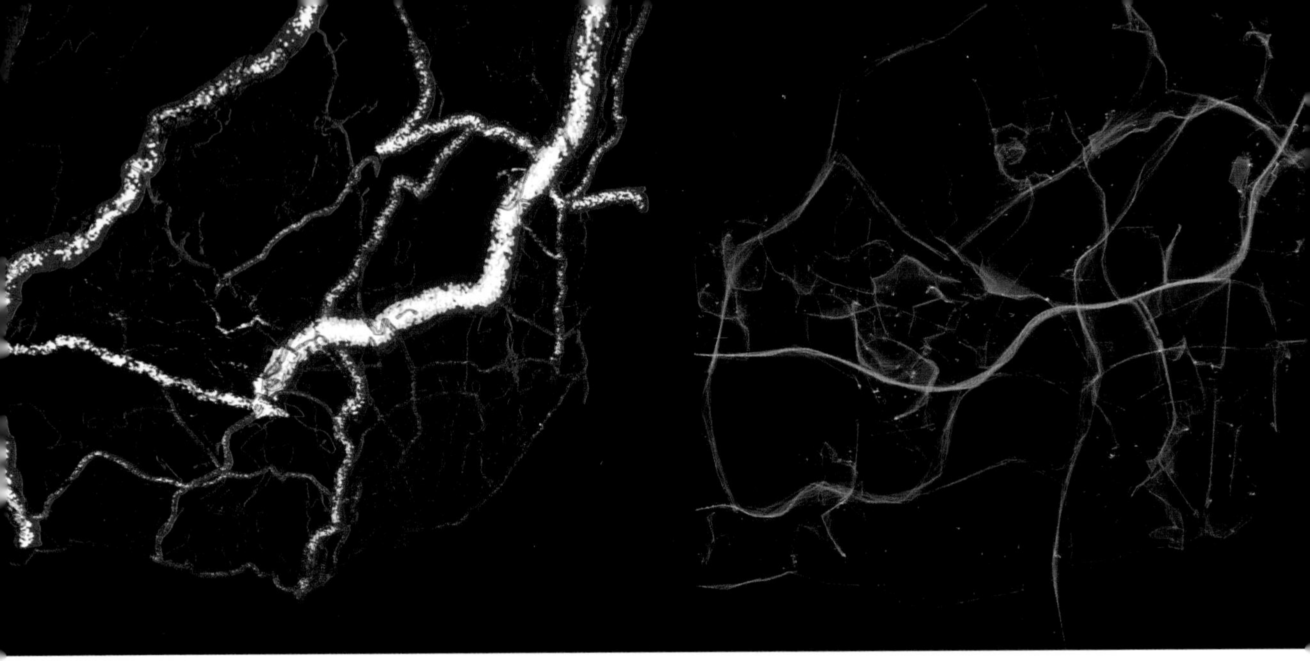

Figure 6.4: Blood vessels cartogram

Pedro Cruz / https://pmcruz.com/works/blood-vessels-cartogram.html / last accessed Febuary 16, 2023

practice of visualization research embodies a reductionist view of visualization. In this view, data are seen as "sacred," where representations should be stripped of any non-data or redundant elements. Embellishments in visualization are viewed with suspicion and as something to completely avoid.

A core part of Pedro's dissertation was an animated cartogram of vehicle traffic in Lisbon (**Figure 6.4**) that eventually became part of an exhibit at the Museum of Modern Art (MoMA) in New York. It looks like a living heart pumping:

> I titled this piece 'Blood vessels' because I wanted to convey the idea that Lisbon is an organism with circulatory problems. The cartogram expands or compresses when the city slows down or speeds up. When traffic slows down, it takes you more time to get to places, and so distances feel longer than they truly are. The opposite is also true. When there's little traffic, time and space are perceived as shorter. I played with multiple encodings. For instance, I mapped slow velocities to red and faster velocity to greens and cyans.

The second visualization discussed in Pedro's PhD dissertation, "The Ecosystem of Corporate Politicians" (**Figure 6.5**), is prodigiously funny. I also think that it demonstrates once again that visualization shouldn't be limited to presenting data as accurately or efficiently as possible. It's a language that can be used for many other purposes, including humor and satire:

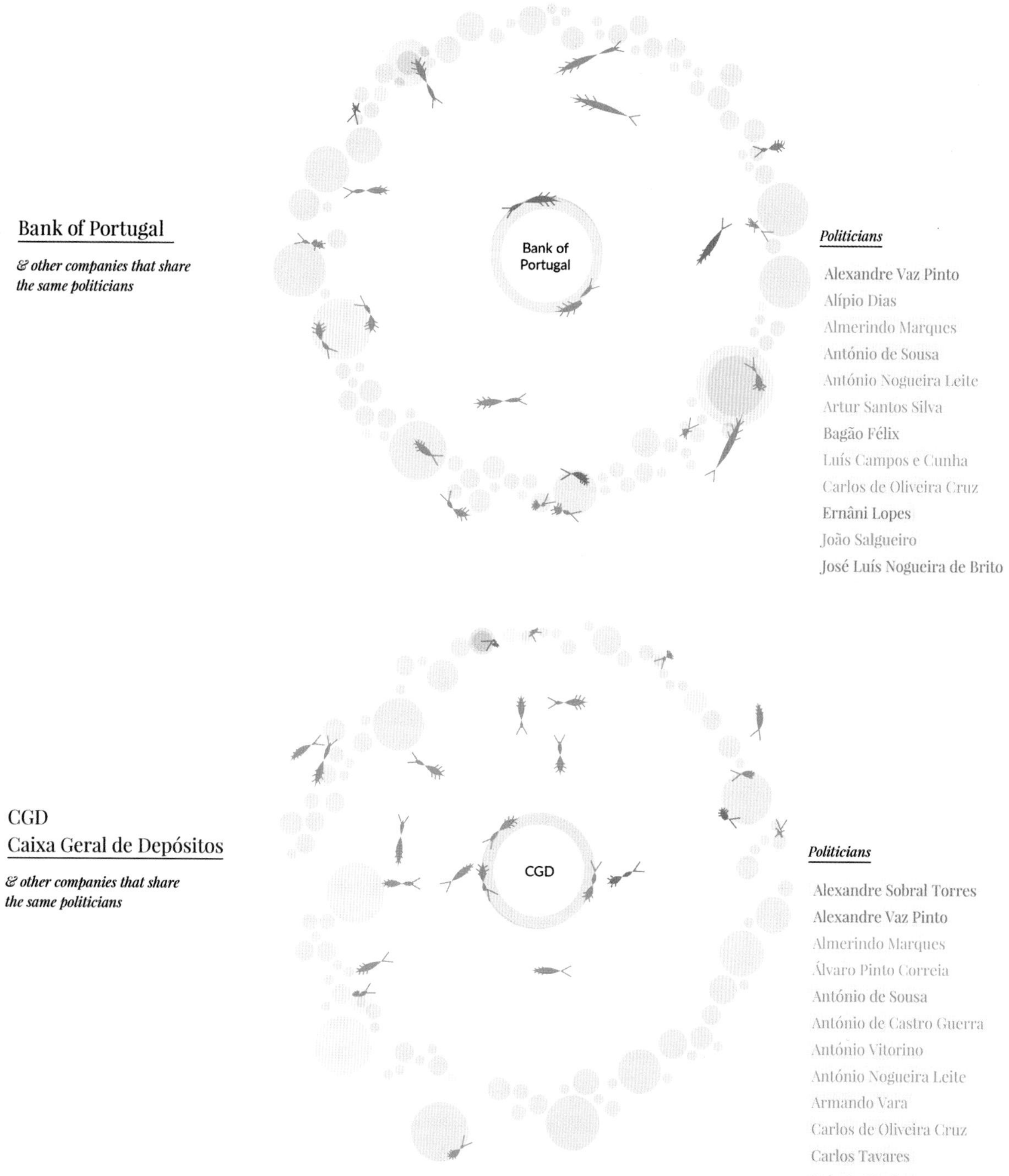

Figure 6.5: "The Ecosystem of Corporate Politicians"

https://pmcruz.com/eco/

> When I was working on my dissertation, there was a major political crisis in Portugal. It was a crisis of trust in government and in politicians because of generalized corruption. I found this book, *Os Donos de Portugal* (*The Owners of Portugal*, 2010) that listed the resumes of everyone that had ever been in government in Portugal from 1950 until the early 2000s, and it also discussed who among them held lucrative positions in big companies. I used that book as a primary source, and expanded the data set based on several more recent studies.
>
> Politicians are represented by small insects generated programmatically. They have different shapes and number of limbs depending on the number of companies they had been related to, and they are color-coded by party affiliation (blue for conservatives, orange for centrists, etc.).
>
> When insects walk into the scene, they start circling around companies, or jumping from company to company. Companies are depicted as bubbles; their size is proportional to how many politicians had a seat in their boards.
>
> The visualization is fully interactive. If you click on a bubble, it shows you what politicians were part of that company, and if you click on an insect, it shows you the companies that hired that specific politician.

The insects are autonomous agents, and their behavior isn't entirely predictable. They may take a different path on the screen whenever you refresh the visualization. The code that runs it simply tells insects which companies they need to swirl around, and the time they must remain in its orbit. This is proportional to the actual time that each politician spent at every company:

> My intent for the project, I believe, is explicit. I wanted it to be satirical, dramatic, and fun. A key inspiration for this project was Nigel Holmes, particularly his work combining statistical graphs with pictorial illustrations from the 1980s.

I'd add that it's also politically charged, a feature of Pedro's work that I find attractive. Perhaps because I was born in Spain, a country with strong historical ties and parallels to Portugal, the topics that Pedro chooses for his projects have a great appeal to me: political corruption, the inheritance of an imperial and colonial past, and immigration.

I've been an immigrant myself—once to Brazil, twice to the United States—and, like Pedro and my next guest, Federica Fragapane, I'm dismayed by the rise of hyperbolic and bigoted anti-immigration rhetoric in so many countries. Maybe visualization can play a role in combating it by debunking its roots?

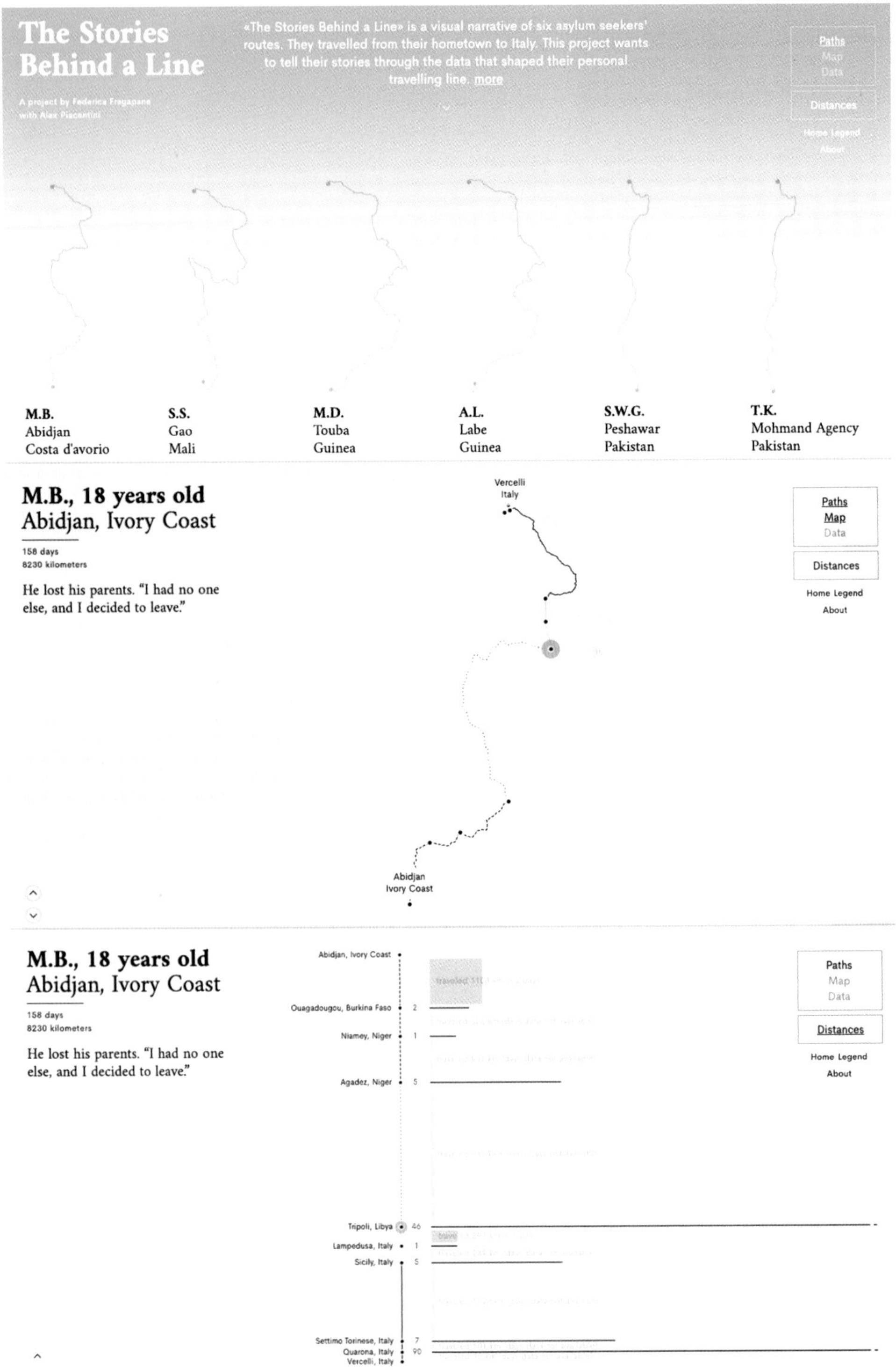

Figure 7.1: "The Stories Behind a Line" by Federica Fragapane, in collaboration with Alex Piacentini

http://www.storiesbehindaline.com/

Chapter 7
with Federica Fragapane

Data and Persons

> *We are ready to question the impersonality of a merely technical approach to data and to begin designing ways to connect numbers to what they really stand for: knowledge, behaviors, people.*
>
> *—Giorgia Lupi*

The week I was transcribing the following conversation with Italian designer **Federica Fragapane** I was also reading Helen Macdonald's luminous essay collection *Vesper Flights* (2020). In the introduction, Macdonald talks about the accelerating extinction of animals and plants:

> I think of the wood warbler, a small citrus-colored bird fast disappearing from British forests. It is one thing to show the statistical facts about this species' decline. It is another thing to communicate to people [that their experience of a forest] that is made of light and leaves and song becomes something less complex, less magical, just *less*, once the warblers are gone.

Federica's best work isn't about birds, but about people. However, the interplay between the statistical, the qualitative, and the personal is often present in her delicate designs. Her "The Stories Behind a Line" is a good example (**Figure 7.1**):

> Years ago, my boyfriend met an asylum seeker who had arrived in Italy from Somalia. He spoke about his journey, particularly about the Mediterranean sea route, the most commonly mentioned in Italian media when talking about migration from Africa to Europe.
>
> When my boyfriend mentioned this conversation to me, I began thinking about how little I knew about the vast distances that African migrants often travel before they even get to the Mediterranean sea. I began attending events at community centers in Vercelli, my hometown in Italy, to meet other asylum seekers and learn about their stories.

In one of those visits, Federica connected to a local volunteer who put her in touch with six asylum seekers willing to see their experiences reflected in a visualization:

> I didn't want to design a generic visualization. Instead, I aimed to give each individual's experience its own shape. With the help of Google maps, I reconstructed each asylum seeker's route, and the key stops in it. I asked the same questions about those stops: how many days they had traveled to get there, how long they stayed, what method of transportation they used. Manually collecting data at this micro level was a new experience for me. All my past projects were based on larger data sets that I hadn't created myself.

The landing page of "The Stories Behind a Line" consists of a title, a brief introduction, six squiggly lines labeled with the initials of each immigrant, and nothing else. Only by navigating the projects can readers obtain more context and information through maps and graphs:

> The extremely minimalistic style of this project is deliberate. When doing the reporting for it, I collected quantitative data, but also memories that these asylum seekers wished to add to their narratives. The way that they described these memories, no matter how sad or painful, was rational, calm, almost detached. I felt that I should pay homage to their discourse visually.
>
> There is another reason why I wished the design to be clear, clean, even subdued. Immigration is a hot topic in countries such as Italy, and it's often sensationalized in the media. I thought that I shouldn't contribute to that sensationalization; a presentation like this can be, at the same time, elegant, tasteful, and also emotional.

Data about distances and time provides the scaffolding and the background, but what really matters at the end is the persons behind the graphics, Federica said:

> These asylum seekers shared many precious memories and reflections about suffering and relief. At the end of our meeting, S.G., a 26-year-old immigrant from Pakistan, told me. "My mind is quiet now. I am quiet because I'm safe, and that's why I love Italy." A.L., a 17-year-old boy from Guinea who had crossed part of the Sahara Desert on foot, said, "You have a beautiful life here because you know that you are safe."

I went back to Federica's origins as a professional. She's part of a generation of designers who had their beginnings at Politecnico di Milano's Density Design Lab in the early and mid-2010s. At that time, the lab was directed by Paolo Ciuccarelli, nowadays a professor at Northeastern University, like Pedro Cruz (Chapter 6). Federica described her path:

> After graduating from high school I wasn't sure about what to study. I loved math and science, but also drawing and theater. I guess that I disappointed some of my teachers when I eventually chose to become a designer, and not a medical doctor or an engineer!

I enrolled in Politecnico di Milano and first tried to study fashion design. It wasn't for me, so I switched to communication design. I did both a BA and a master's degree. As part of the latter, I took the course offered by Density Design in 2011. It interested me because it combined the quantitative, the narrative, and the visual.

My thesis project for the M.Sc, which also was my first ambitious visualization, was an exploration of organized crime in Northern Italy intended to be used by specialists such as journalists and academics.

The process began by defining my audience and talking with some potential readers to learn what they would need to get from an exploratory tool like this. To collect the data, I got the help of the Antonio Zampolli Institute of Computational Linguistics and its ItaliaNLP Lab, which specializes in natural language processing.

The data came from annual reports by the Anti-Mafia National Office. These are very long PDF documents with information about criminals, crimes, their locations, etc. (**Figure 7.2** summarizes this process). Finally, I designed the online visualization (**Figure 7.3**), which was later tested with actual readers.

Another famous graduate from the Density Design Lab is Giorgia Lupi, a designer and author who has spoken and written extensively about humanistic approaches to data visualization. Giorgia and Federica met two years before the latter finished her master's:

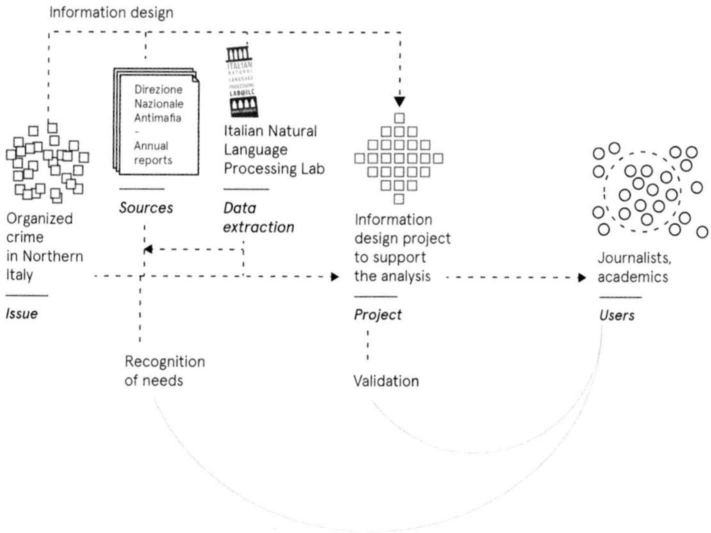

Figure 7.2: Scheme describing the creation of "Crime in Northern Italy"
https://cargocollective.com/federicafragapane/Crime-in-Northern-Italy

One of the requirements for my degree was an internship. Back in 2012, Giorgia was doing her PhD at Density Design, and we got along really well. She had just founded her famous data visualization studio, Accurat (https://accurat.it/), in Milan, and she asked me whether I wanted to join her.

And then a momentous accident happened:

A couple of weeks before I joined Accurat, I got a serious corneal infection. I was forced to stay home for more than a month. After I recovered part of my sight, I began working, but my eye was still too sensitive to light. I had to wear a patch and sunglasses in the office. The experience of almost going blind in my left eye transformed me and shaped my approach to design.

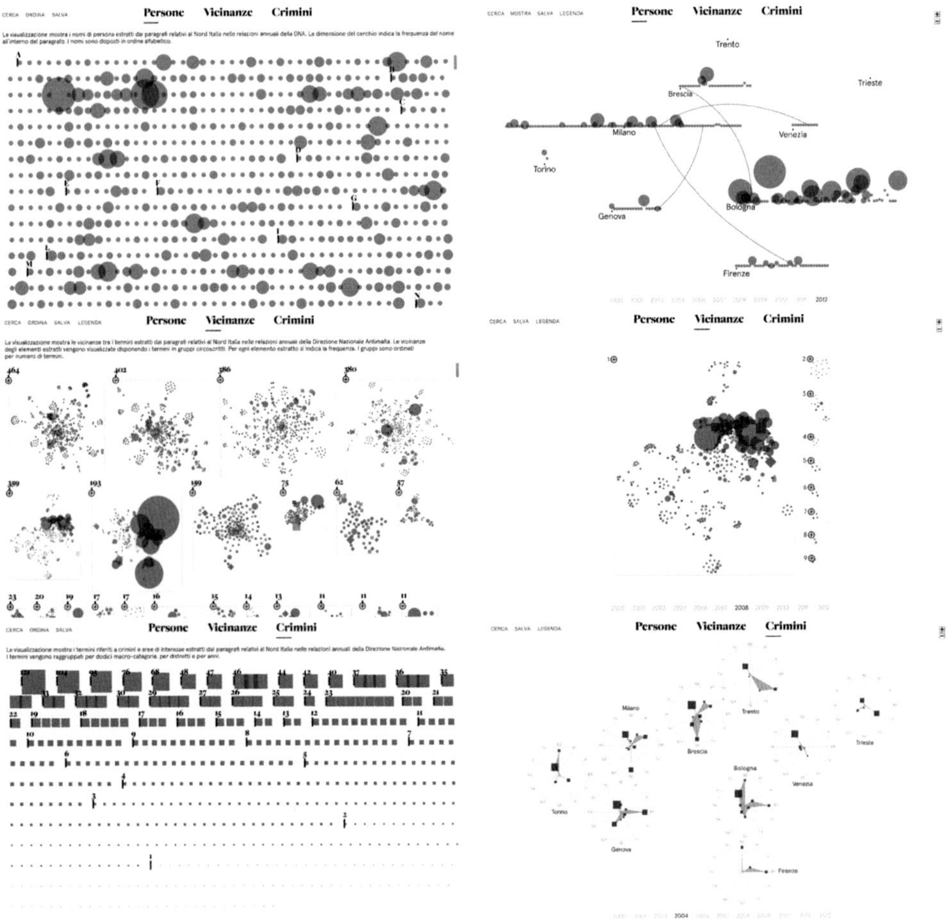

Figure 7.3: "Crime in Northern Italy"

https://cargocollective.com/federicafragapane/Crime-in-Northern-Italy

Federica gave a talk in 2018 about her illness, and also wrote an essay about it titled "I'm a Visual Designer Whose Sight Is Not Perfect Anymore." She wrote:

> I'm a visual designer whose sight is not perfect anymore and it won't ever be. But I also think that for this reason I love looking at things so much. I love paying attention to details, shapes and textures, and to examine how these visual elements can have different impacts on me. [...] My sensitiveness to visual elements particularly emerges during an important phase in my design process, the inspiration one. I usually spend a lot of time looking for visual inspirations, not only when I have to start a new project, but almost every day. And I love to pay attention to the visual elements and to understand which shapes, colors and textures could be for the readers the—hopefully pleasant—elements to hook their gaze to.

Federica's style today is reflective of such interest in the visual arts and the natural world. Her designs sometimes look like rocks, crystals, waves, feathers, plants, flowers, butterfly wings—or human clothing:

> I'm personally attracted to organic and soft shapes. Throughout the years I've created a vast collection of images that I draw inspiration from. I visit it constantly to look at textures, colors, and shapes that I enjoy, and to wonder how to use them in my work.
>
> Choosing the right words when we write can convey deep meanings. Why should it be different in visualization? In visualization, the choice of visual words matter, it's essential. If your visualization is about something that lives, that is organic, why should the shapes of your visualization look dead and inorganic?

For years Federica collaborated with *La Lettura*, the weekly cultural supplement of the Italian newspaper *Corriere della Sera*. In our conversation we used one of her intricate, poetic, handcrafted visualizations, about the early Renaissance painter Piero della Francesca (**Figure 7.4**), to discuss her approach to graphics.

Piero della Francesca is well known for being a pioneer in the use of geometry and naturalistic perspective in paintings, but another peculiarity of his work is realistic depictions of drapery:

> The visualization itself looks like drapery using colors mimicking his paintings, doesn't it? *La Lettura* wanted a visualization about Piero della Francesca, but they didn't know what data to use. I proposed to visualize the places where his most famous paintings are located, in Europe and North America.
>
> I could have designed a traditional map, but I wanted something a bit more evocative. Each city is represented by a circle sized by the number of della Francesca paintings in it. I traced lines

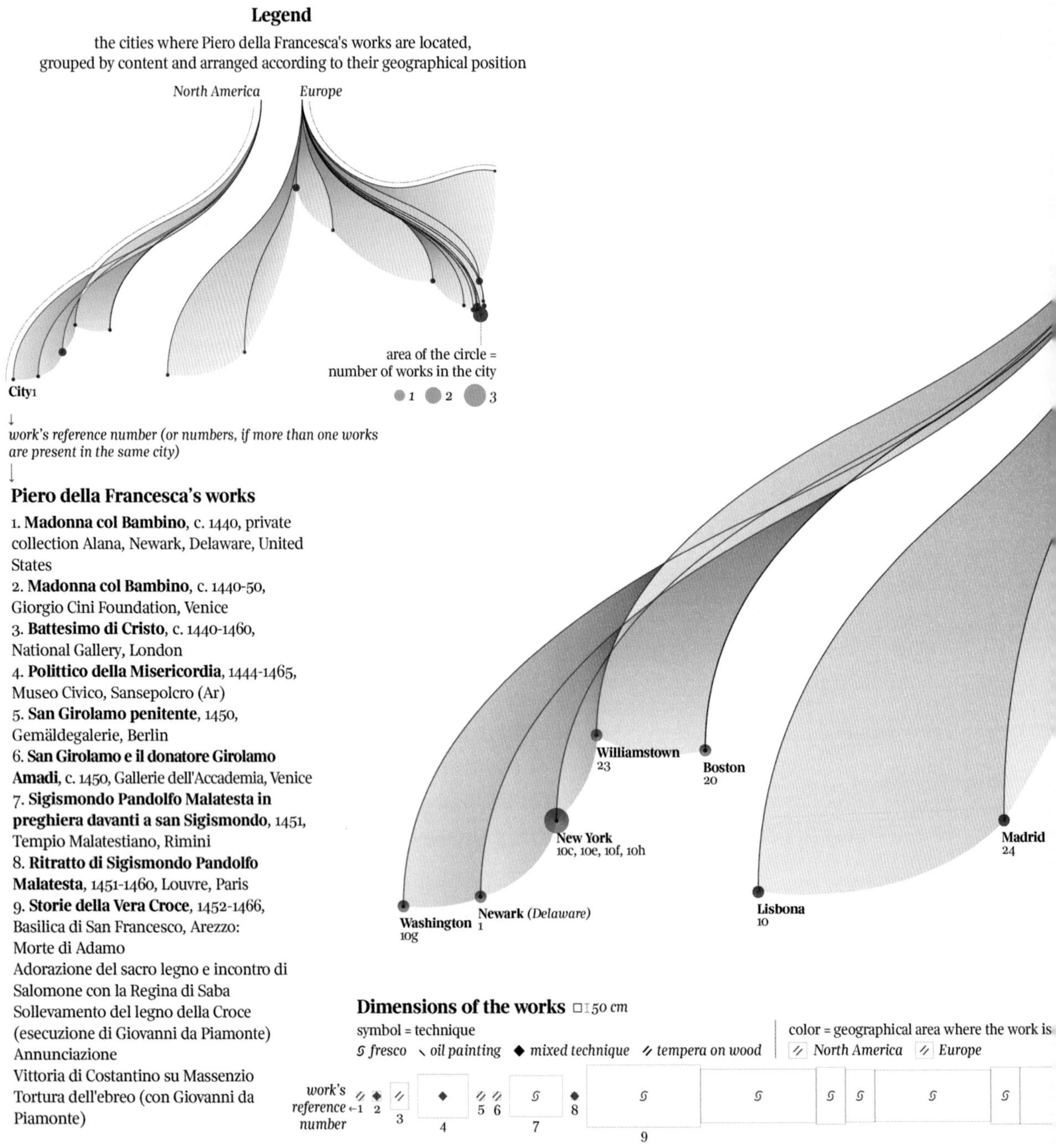

Figure 7.4: "Where is Piero?"

https://www.behance.net/gallery/135267321/Piero-della-Francescas-works

Where is Piero?

The cities hosting Piero della Francesca' masterpieces

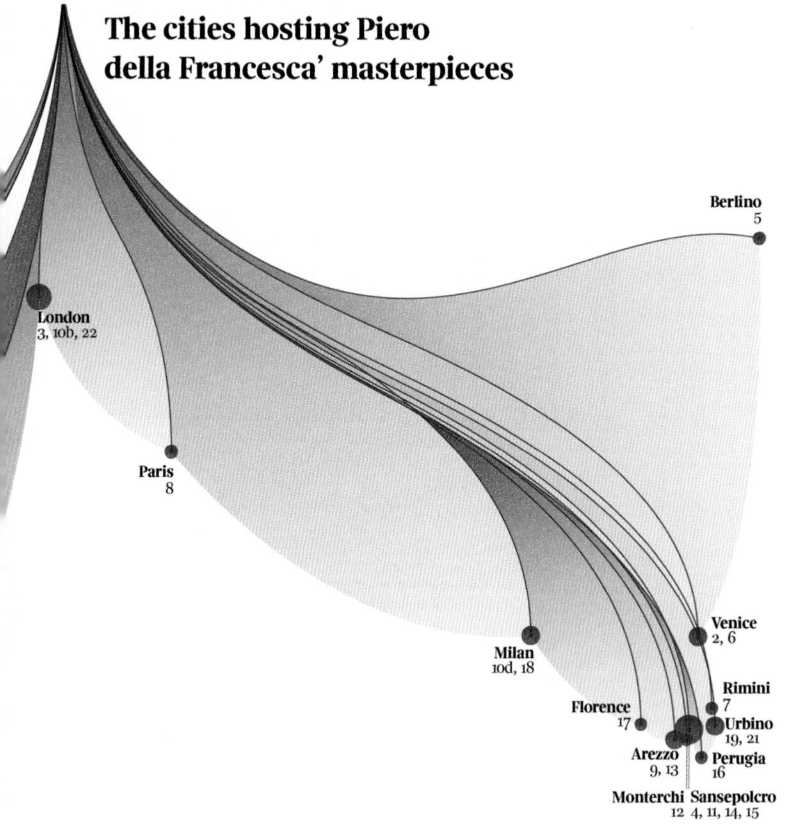

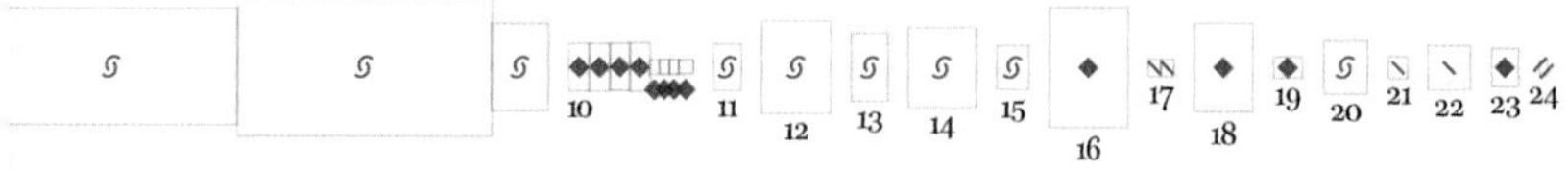

Ritrovamento e verifica della vera Croce
Battaglia di Eraclio e Cosroè
Eraclio riporta la Vera Croce a Gerusalemme
Profeta Ezechiele (esecuzione di Giovanni da Piamonte)
Profeta Geremia
Angelo, frammento
Cupido
10. **Polittico di Sant'Agostino**, 1454-1469, dismembered and partially dispersed
10a. **Sant'Agostino**, Museu Nacional de Arte Antiga, Lisbon
10b. **San Michele Arcangelo**, National Gallery, London
10c. **San Giovanni Evangelista**, Frick Collection, New York
10d. **San Nicola da Tolentino**, Museo Poldi Pezzoli, Milano
10e. **Santa Monica**, Frick Collection, New York
10f. **Santo agostiniano**, Frick Collection, New York
10g. **Sant'Apollonia**, National Gallery of Art, Washington
10h. **Crocifissione**, Frick Collection, New York
11. **San Giuliano**, 1454-1458, Museo Civico, Sansepolcro (Ar)
12. **Madonna del parto**, 1455-1465, Museo della Madonna del Parto, Monterchi (Ar)
13. **Maria Maddalena**, 1460-1466, Duomo, Arezzo
14. **Resurrezione**, 1450-1463, Museo Civico, Sansepolcro (Ar)
15. **San Ludovico di Tolosa**, 1460, Museo Civico, Sansepolcro (Ar)
16. **Polittico di Sant'Antonio**, 1460-1470, Galleria nazionale dell'Umbria, Perugia
17. **Doppio ritratto dei Duchi di Urbino**, sul verso Trionfo di Federico da Montefeltro e di Battista Sforza, c. 1473-1475, Uffizi, Firenze
18. **Pala di Brera**, 1472-1474, Pinacoteca di Brera, Milan
19. **Flagellazione di Cristo**, c. 1470, Galleria Nazionale delle Marche, Urbino
20. **Ercole**, c. 1470, Isabella Stewart-Gardner Museum, Boston
21. **Madonna di Senigallia**, 1470-1485, Galleria nazionale delle Marche, Urbino
22. **Natività**, 1470-1485, National Gallery, London
23. **Madonna col Bambino e quattro angeli**, 1475-1482, Clark Art Institute, Williamstown (Massachusetts)
24. **Ritratto di bambino** (Guidobaldo da Montefeltro?), (uncertain attribution), c. 1483, Thyssen-Bornemisza Museum, Madrid

Sources: britannica.com pierodellafrancesca.it wikipedia.org from those circles to a common origin, on top of the page, and then I drew a shape filling up the spaces between those lines. The result is something that looks like drapery. To that I added a key to reading the graphic and contextual information, such as sizes and techniques.

To me, designing visualizations like this is like writing, but using visual alphabets. I like to experiment with new visual letters, instead of sticking to traditional ones, such as bars or circles.

My time at Accurat gave me the confidence to experiment. My overall rule as a designer is to create objects that if I were a reader myself would make me think, "Oh, I really would like to have created something like that!"

Coming up with my own style wasn't intentional. It derives from my desire to work on things that I can be proud of, things that I can look at and enjoy.

Shapes in Federica's graphics, no matter how organic and intricate they are, represent data in similar ways as traditional forms in visualization—straight lines or bars—would:

When working on a project I always try to understand the information and I do use conventional graphics as a "skeleton." I layer my own shapes on top of them. I may begin with a bar graph or a radar graph, but I transform them into, say petals of a flower.

Among Federica's most cherished projects is a series that she designed for ODI, a think tank based in London that focuses on injustice and inequality. The first is "Key workers: Migrants' contribution to the COVID-19 response" (**Figure 7.5**). It maps political reforms and campaigns to support migrant essential workers all over the world during the pandemic.

The visualization is based on shapes that resemble trees. Each root corresponds to a country, the main branches are economy sectors (healthcare, agriculture, etc.) and each little dot at the tip of the branches are stories that appeared in news media:

I started working on this project in the spring of 2020, and I've been updating it to this day. The first version I designed visualized the data in a very straightforward manner, but we quickly decided that it wasn't the right approach. ODI regularly publishes reports of its research that contain tons of classical graphs and charts. This time they wanted something that they could bring outside the world of think tanks and experts, something that could be showcased in a museum, in universities, in high schools, that was beautiful and engaging to encourage interaction.

Another project for ODI was based on a data set of narratives, sentiments, and attitudes toward migrants in six European countries, Germany, Spain, the United Kingdom, Italy, France, and Sweden (**Figure 7.6**). Federica drew colorful waves to encode time-series data: migration trends, sentiments toward migration, salience of migration as a news topic, and so on.

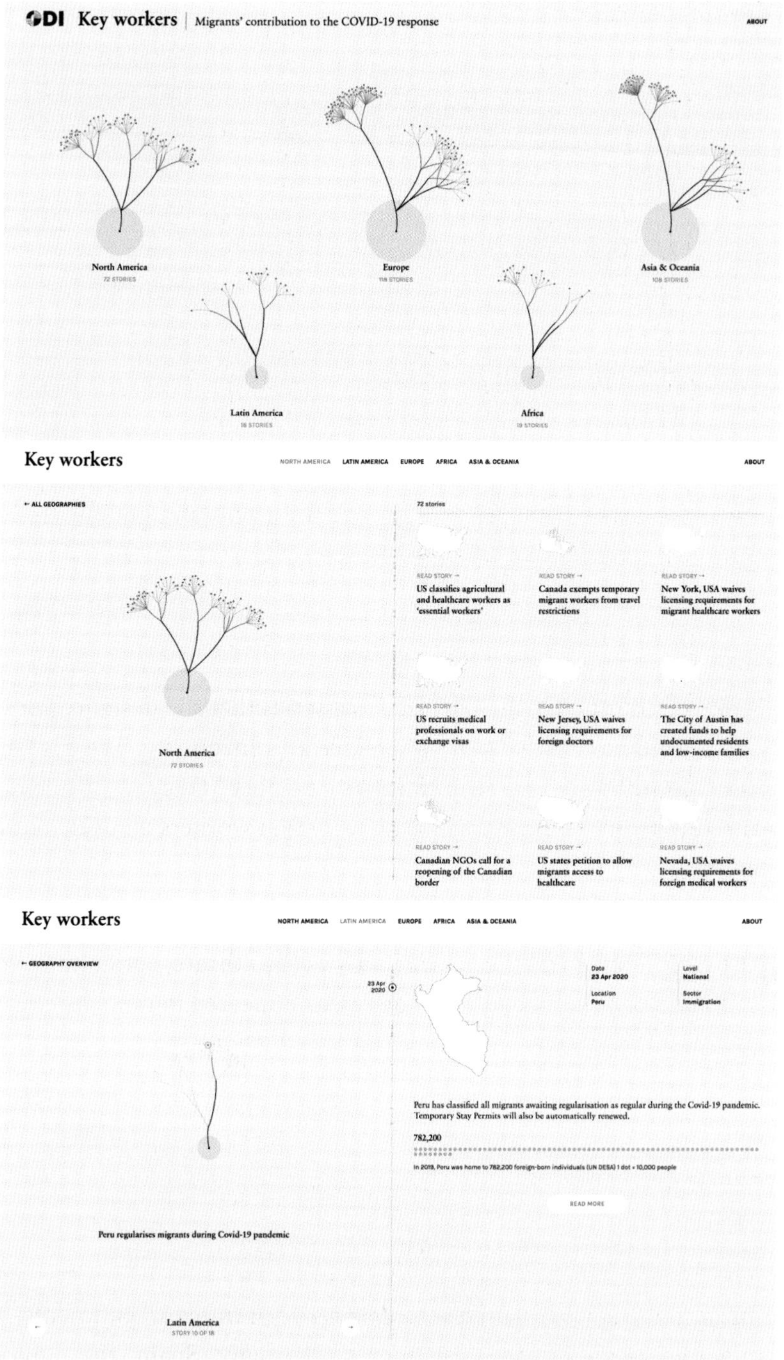

Figure 7.5: "Key workers: Migrants' contribution to the COVID-19 response," co-designed by Federica Fragapane and Alex Piacentini in collaboration with Marta Foresti and ODI

https://migrants-keyworkers-covid-19.odi.digital/

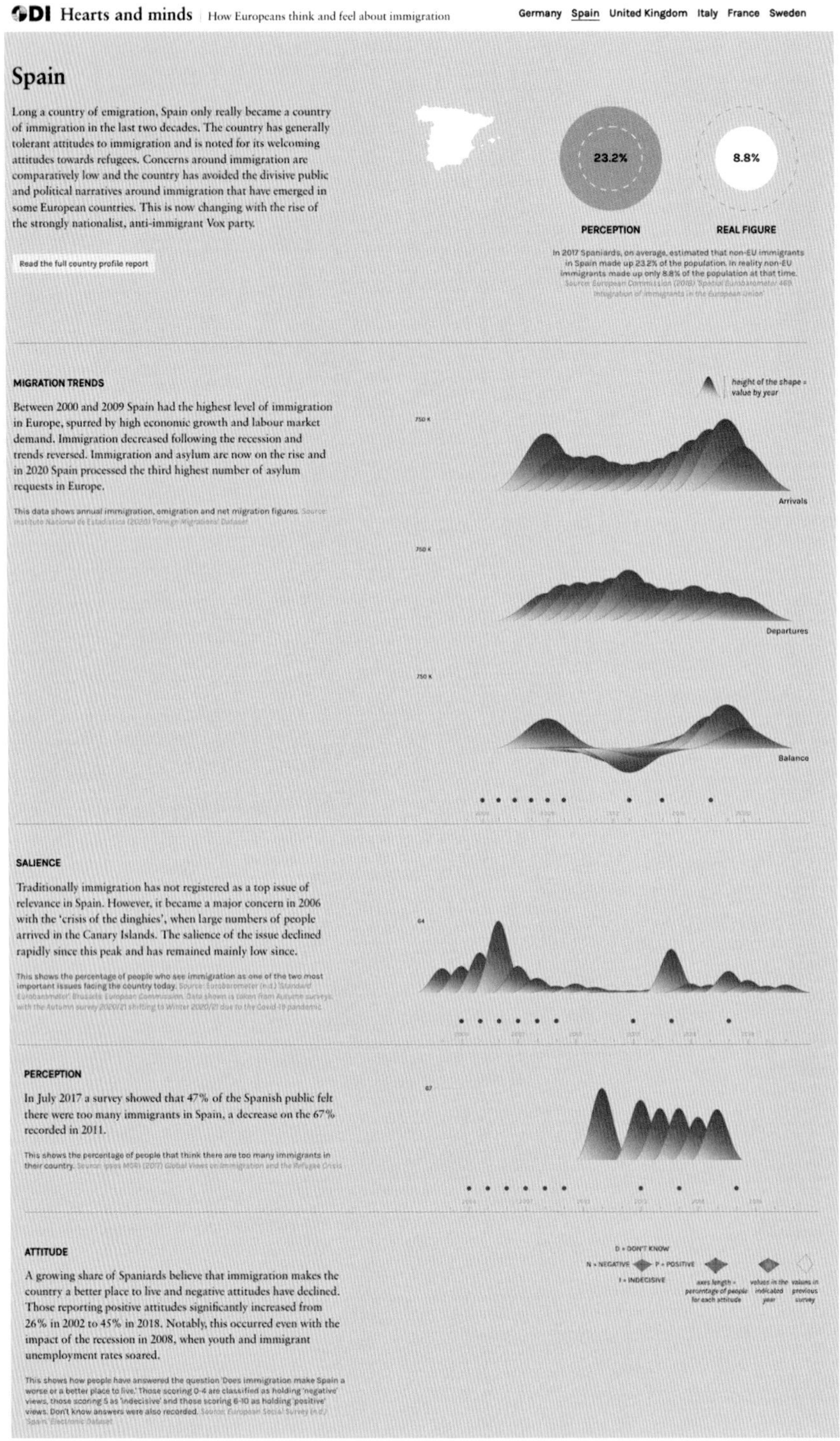

Figure 7.6: "Hearts and minds," co-designed by Federica Fragapane and Alex Piacentini in collaboration with ODI

https://heartsandminds.odi.digital/

When I visited this project, I immediately clicked on my country of origin. As the project itself explains, Spain has historically been a country that people migrated *from* not *to*. In the 19th and 20th centuries, thousands upon thousands of Spaniards, particularly from impoverished regions such as Extremadura, Asturias, or Galicia, where I was born, or those fleeing from Francisco Franco's dictatorship, after his victory in the Spanish Civil War (1936–1939), migrated to America and other parts of the world. I still have distant relatives in Argentina because of this.

This trend shifted a couple of decades ago. Spain became a country that people from Latin America and Africa migrated to. Spaniards' views on immigration are contradictory nowadays. On the one hand, a majority thinks that immigrants make the country better; on the other, according to ODI's surveys, nearly half of Spaniards also think that there are too many immigrants around.

I don't have evidence—other than many anecdotal observations—to back up the following conjecture, but I believe that this might be a reflection of the difference between opinions based on interacting with actual persons coming from other countries, and opinions derived from imagining them as abstractions.

When asked about whether immigrants make Spain better, perhaps the first impulse most people have is to invoke salient memories: your Dominican neighbor, the Ecuadorian supermarket clerk, your Colombian primary care doctor. Of course they make the country better; they make *your life* better. In this case, we are envisioning people not as *people*, but as persons, individuals.

On the other hand, a question such as "Are there too few or too many immigrants in Spain?" might nudge our brains to think not about persons, but about group or statistical aggregates. The faces and voices of your neighbor, the supermarket clerk, and your primary care doctor blur into a blob of abstraction. You don't envision individuals anymore, but an undifferentiated mass.

And it's easier to reject a mass than it is reject an individual.

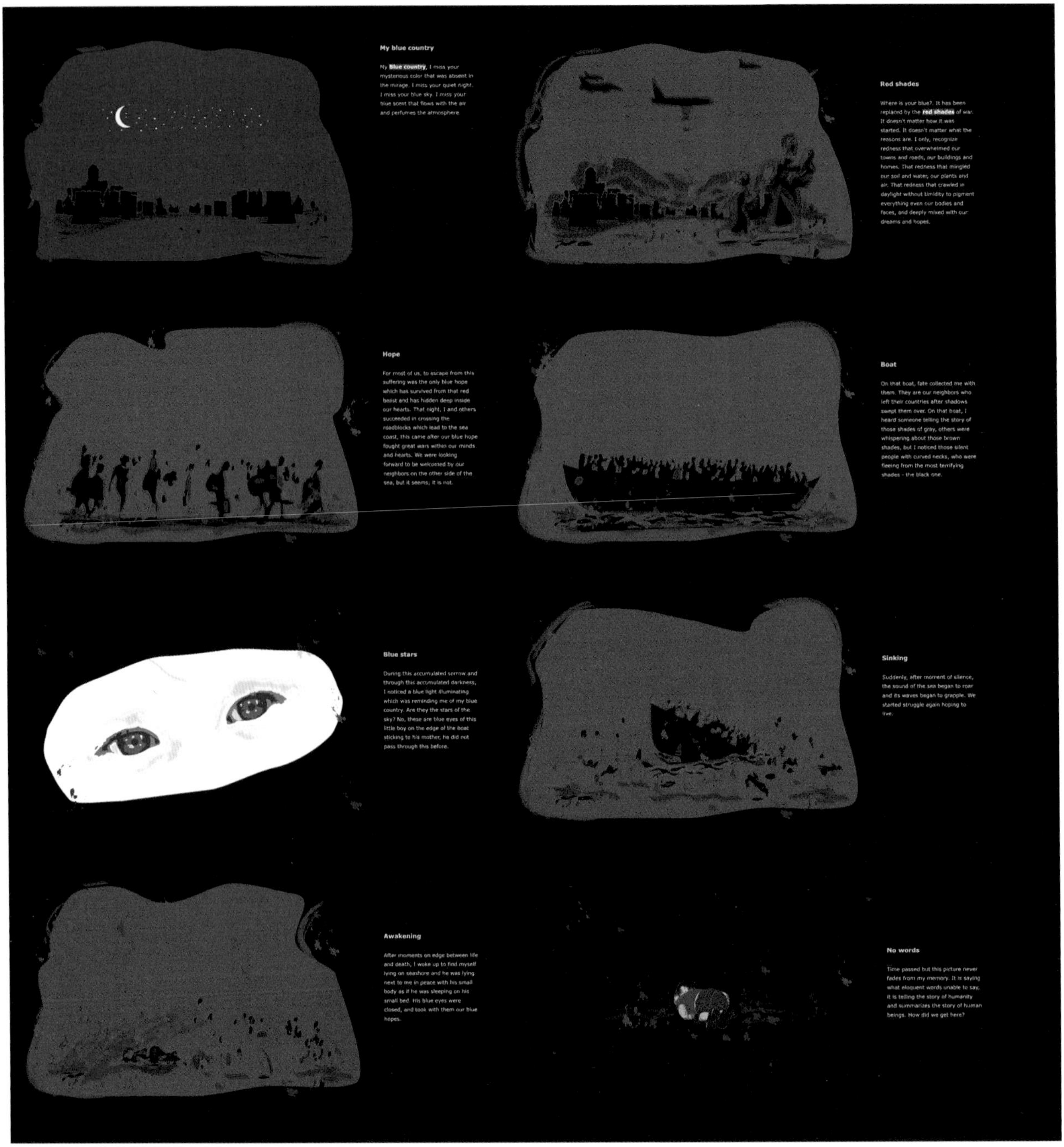

Figure 8.1: "The Unwelcomed"

https://alhadaqa.com/project/the-unwelcomed/

Chapter 8
with Mohamad Waked

Souls before Numbers

Objectivity of whatever kind is not the test of reality. It is just one way of understanding reality [...] Sometimes, in the philosophy of mind but also elsewhere, the truth is not to be found by traveling as far away from one person's perspective as possible.

—Thomas Nagel

On September 2, 2015, two boats carrying two dozen Syrian refugees capsized near Bodrum, Turkey. Half of them drowned, including two-year-old Alan Shenu and his brother. A photo of Alan lying on a Turkish beach soon appeared in social media, where it was viewed by tens of millions of people.

Alan became a symbol of the ongoing refugee humanitarian crisis in the Mediterranean, which had begun in 2011. After his death was reported in news publications worldwide, there was an outpouring of attention to the civil war in Syria. **Mohamad Waked**, a data scientist and visualization designer based in Cairo, Egypt, remembers being moved to action by Alan's photograph:

> That photograph is the origin of my "The Unwelcomed" (**Figure 8.1**). I had been reading terrible stories about refugees and immigrants desperately trying to cross the Mediterranean for a while, and Alan's photograph horrified me.

In an article published in 2017, "Iconic photographs and the ebb and flow of empathic response to humanitarian disasters," Paul Slovic, a professor of psychology at the University of Oregon, and his collaborators described the consequences of Alan's case and the difference between the death of individuals and statistical deaths:

Figure 8.2: Two images from "The Unwelcomed"

https://www.alhadaqa.com/the_unwelcomed/

> We cannot assume that the statistics of mass human crises will capture our attention or move us to take action, no matter how large the numbers. Our search data show that the world was basically asleep as the body count in Syria rose steadily into the hundreds of thousands. Perhaps this should not surprise us. A famous saying, sometimes attributed to Joseph Stalin, observed that "One man's death is a tragedy, a million deaths is a statistic." Similarly, economist Thomas Schelling wrote that "the death of a particular person evokes anxiety and sentiment, guilt and awe, responsibility and religion...[but] most of this awesomeness disappears when we deal with statistical death."

Slovic uses the term "psychic numbing" to refer to the indifference to statistical deaths, no matter how horrific the realities behind the statistics are.

We visualization designers cherish our data; they are part of the *logos* in classic rhetorical persuasion theory, our appeal to a reader's reason. However, we also know that facts are usually not enough to inform or to change minds. That's why sometimes it's appropriate to employ another rhetorical mode: *pathos*, an appeal to emotions and empathy.

There's both logos and pathos in Mohamad's "The Unwelcomed." The project combines the personal with the statistical (**Figure 8.2**). It opens up with a fictional first-person narration accompanied by haunting illustrations. The last one shows Alan, and the text that goes with it asks, "How did we get here?" Mohamad told me:

> After years of reading stories here and there about the refugee crisis and the suffering of migrants trying to cross the Mediterranean from the Middle East and North Africa, I felt prompted to look into the data. I wished to get a sense of the scope of this challenge. The personal, individual stories are important, but I believe that data can also help bring those stories to life. Data can also contribute to an increase in empathy. That's why I designed this project. We shouldn't close our eyes to this tragedy.

The most important rhetorical mode, *ethos*, is also present in Mohamad's work. Ethos consists of establishing credibility based on morality—"We shouldn't close our eyes to this tragedy"—professional expertise, and the way that communicators present information; in other words, their style.

Depending on the type of story and its intended audience, a neutral tone may be more persuasive than a strident one. A subtle detail in "The Unwelcomed" that Mohamad mentioned to me is that its dominant colors, red and blue, are the colors that Alan was wearing when he died.

About his career prior to "The Unwelcomed," Mohamad said:

> I have a background in mechanical design and production engineering. Engineering was my dream job when I was a kid. Since a young age, I loved to design things and to understand how

they work. After I graduated, I joined the automotive industry in Egypt, which is a dream job for any engineer, working in process analytics.

This was my first serious and systematic contact with data. The job consisted of studying production lines, finding bottlenecks and hurdles, all to increase efficiency. I often found myself enthralled when looking at the data we gathered. I loved exploring it, digging into it, slicing and dicing it. I also loved visualizing it. I realized that graphics were a great way to summarize insights and to communicate those stories.

I remember myself beginning with the most basic charts: bar graphs, line graphs, etc. It wasn't very innovative, but it was useful and efficient. At the time, I didn't have much awareness of visualization theory or practice, so I learned by doing. Only later, I read many books and looked for tutorials online. I even did an online specialization on data science offered by Johns Hopkins University.

These years provided the foundation for his later work as a visualization designer:

I think that you cannot be good at visualization without some foundations in data science. The steps I took in my education were essential. Every step led me to the next. But from the beginning, I could not imagine that I would be doing what I do today.

However, to me data science isn't the entire story. Since I was in school I've had an interest in art. You can notice that in all my personal projects, like in "The Unwelcomed," I include drawings.

I told Mohamad that it's unusual to find designers who are so versatile, skillful in so many things: data science, programming, visual design, storytelling, illustration, and so on.

I actually don't like coding! I enjoy drawing and designing much more. Coding is great, though; it gives me freedom to shape my personal projects in ways that off-the-shelf tools, such as PowerBI, Tableau, and others wouldn't. Those tools are amazing, don't get me wrong, but they greatly constrain what you can or can't do. To me, learning to code was similar to learning to draw: It expanded my horizons and freedom.

Mohamad speaks fondly of his personal projects, which he uses to quench his curiosity and to experiment with the form, but his day job involves designing more conventional visualizations:

I work for the Egyptian government in a role that combines project management and data science. The Ministry of Communication has a division that monitors and helps startups and tries to foster entrepreneurship, and I'm responsible for all its data projects: conducting analysis, designing dashboards, creating reports, etc. I design visualizations sometimes, but their purpose

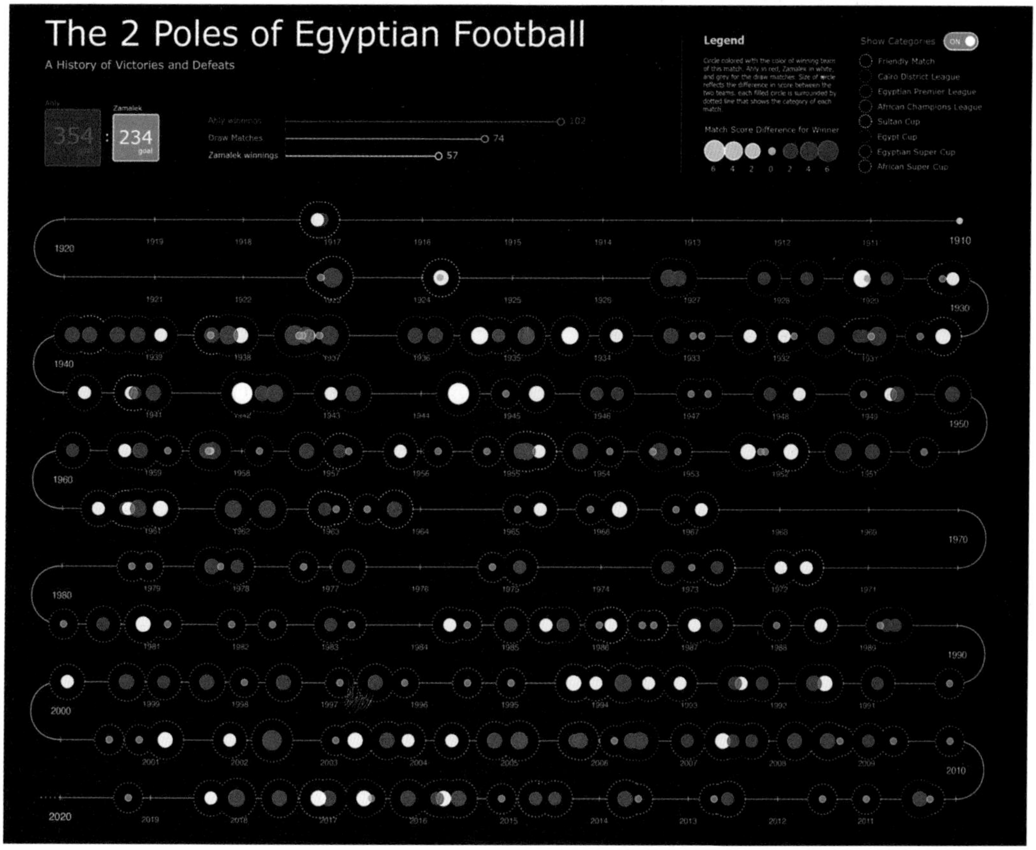

Figure 8.3: "The Two Poles of Egyptian Football"

https://alhadaqa.com/project/poles-of-egyptian-football/

is different, so I follow different standards. Those graphics cannot be as creative or artistic as the ones I design for my side projects. They need to be straightforward and traditional.

Some of Mohamad's personal projects are also straightforward, as well as lighthearted or subtly humorous. For instance, "The Two Poles of Egyptian Football" (**Figure 8.3**) combines a timeline with a bubble chart:

Soccer is big in Egypt, as it is in Spain, and people are passionate about their teams. In your country, Spain, there's a longtime rivalry between Real Madrid and Fútbol Club Barcelona, In Egypt we have a similar rivalry between Al Ahly Sporting Club (Cairo) and Zamalek Sporting Club (Giza).

Egyptian soccer fans are constantly debating which club is the best. Exchanges of opinions are often very heated, but rarely based on data, even if these two teams have been competing with

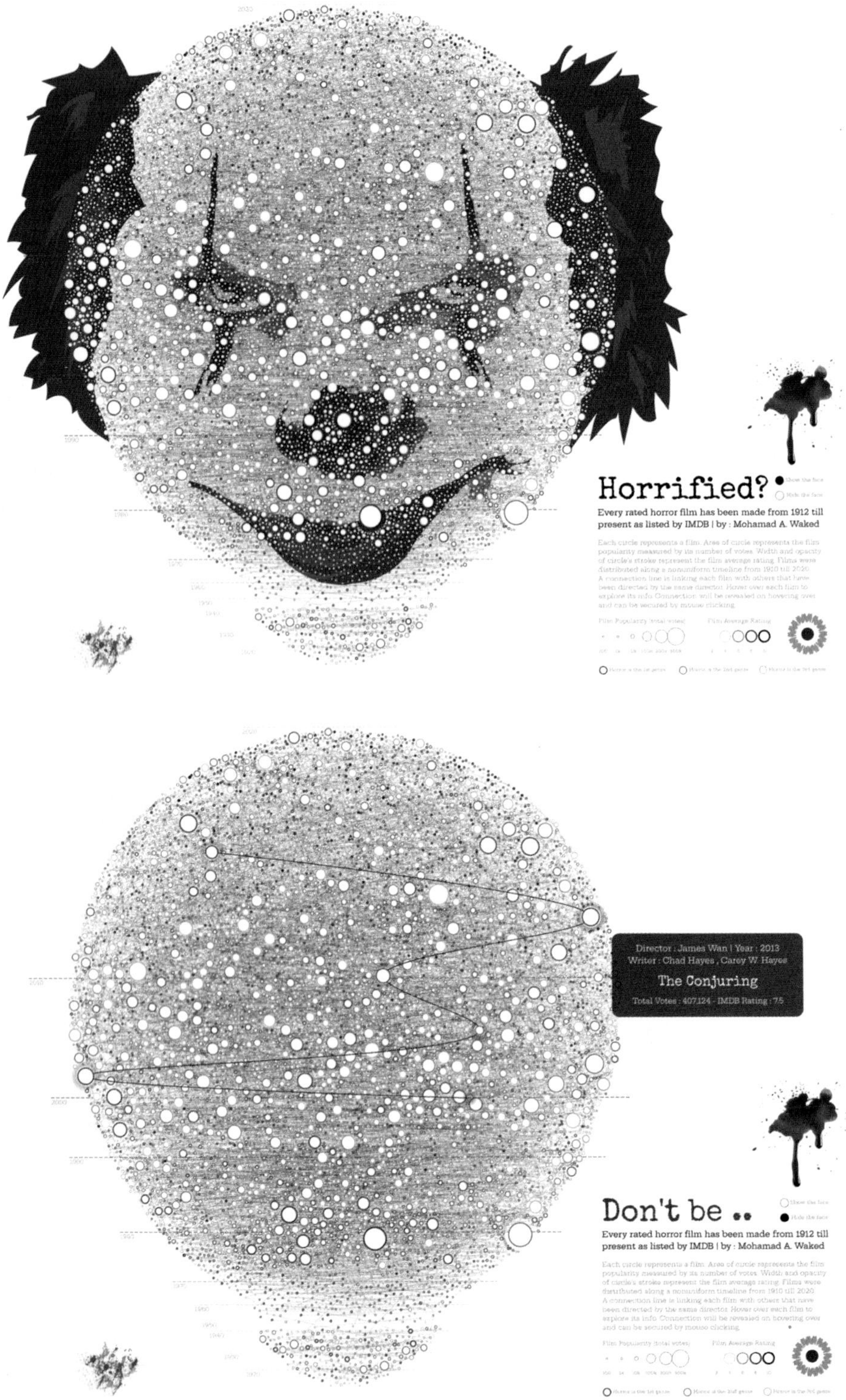

Figure 8.4: "Horrified? Don't Be..."

Mohamad Waked / https://alhadaqa.com/project/horrified/ / last accessed Febuary 16, 2023

> each other for more than one hundred years. I saw this as an opportunity. I thought to myself: Let's quantify the results of matches between the two teams. The result is that Ahly is ahead, both in terms of matches won, and in goals scored.
>
> Not surprisingly, this project got a lot of attention, and even requests from news organizations to publish it. Other personal projects of mine are much less mainstream than this one.

We talked about one of them, "Horrified? Don't Be..." (**Figure 8.4**). It visualizes historical popularity and ratings data of horror and horror-adjacent movies and movie directors extracted from the Internet Movie Database (IMDb). Movies are arranged chronologically from the bottom to the top, and the resulting baroque beeswarm plot forms the face of a creepy clown. Mohamad said:

> I'm not a fan of horror movies, but my wife is very enthusiastic about them, so we watch them together. I made this project for fun—and as a gift for her.

Mohamad sees projects about sports or popular culture as a way to make other people feel intrigued about data science and visualization:

> Data is often seen as boring, or even irrelevant. Many people have a hard time grasping that data can illuminate their own interests, no matter how seemingly trivial these interests might be. Visualizations such as my soccer project or the one about horror movies can work as gateways, opening people's eyes to visualization as a way to understand anything better.
>
> Here's something that I find puzzling: Egypt is a country of more than 100 million people, but there's not much visualization around. This is also true of the rest of North Africa and the Middle East. I don't know anyone who does it for a living. It's for this reason that I've been trying to spread the word. For instance, through my job I've been involved in the organization of hackathons to generate ideas for future startups. In some of them I was able to convince the organization to include a category of data visualization, to raise awareness and prompt participants to think about it.

A few weeks after my conversation with Mohamad, I was interviewed by Amal Mounir, a mass communication PhD student at the University of Cairo. Her dissertation is a comparative analysis between U.S. and Egyptian newspapers. Amal told me that Mohamad's assessment is accurate. Visualization is still being discovered in their country. Egyptian news media publish infographics, but they usually are illustrations or photographs surrounded by numbers written in large type.

Mohamad and Amal made me think about an impulse that many people in visualization seem to share: What's the point of loving a craft if we can't share our thoughts with others who are also able to grasp its possibilities and beauty?

Coda

In his elegant *The Grace of Great Things* (1990), a meditation on creativity, innovation, design, art, and the good life, philosopher Robert Grudin wrote:

> Our sense of beauty is generally restricted to those categories (art, music, love, nature) to which aesthetic language is applied by our culture. But independent insight in all fields involves in some way the experience of beauty. In fact, the thrill conveyed by inspiration in any field is perhaps best described as coming from a sense of participation in beauty, a momentary unity between a perceived beauty of experience and a perceiving beauty of mind.

Experience and practice are requirements for meaningful experimentation. Acquiring the skills of a craft requires effort that is often grueling and thankless, but that leads to sudden instants of joy. Grudin added:

> Having internalized method, [creative people] may allow themselves the luxury of conjecture, the thrill of intuition. Having mastered order, they are open to the chaos of discovery.

All my interlocutors in Part 2 learned through a combination of study, practice, and reflection, and alluded to the many traditional charts, graphs, and maps they designed throughout their careers. I conjecture that they have developed an understanding of the proper or conventional uses of the best-established graphic forms in the visualization vocabulary, and that this tacit knowledge of the craft enables them, as authors, to experiment, and to challenge and stretch its tenets. They can use different dialects of visualization depending on what they're working on; their styles can be, at times, prosaic, essayistic, or poetic.

Heterodoxy makes some of these designers feel uncertain and uneasy. When asked about the reasons for certain choices in their most personal designs, "I'm not sure" was a common answer. This might be why they are often self-deprecating and humorous when talking about themselves and their most eccentric work. I was again reminded of Robert Grudin, who wrote:

> Humorless people are unlikely to discover much. They are usually more concerned with their own dignity and rectitude than with anything going on around them.

Notice the last few words. Good designers are hardly solipsistic.

❧ ❧ ❧

To these designers, perceived success or failure in their experimentations are beside the point. In our conversations I got the sense that they don't play with the language of visualization because they have a conscious drive to expand its syntax, vocabulary, or style, although that might be a by-product of their activities. They don't need such motivation. They do it because it's what they feel they ought to be doing.

They seem to share an autotelic temperament. *Autotelic* is a term popularized by Mihaly Csikszentmihalyi, the theorist of flow whom I mentioned in Chapter 4. *Autós* refers to the self, and *telos* refers to goals. Autotelic people are capable of pushing themselves to engage in activities that require skill and sustained concentration for their own sake. It's the work itself that matters to an autotelic person, not so much the work's external goals or end products.

❧ ❧ ❧

Having an autotelic temperament doesn't imply that these explorers of the fringes of visualization orthodoxy are selfish or oblivious to their surroundings; on the contrary, they are attuned to their communities and to the news.

Their personal projects may spark from a sudden, seemingly capricious interest in a topic but, more often than not, such a topic will prove itself relevant to others: the prevention of depression and suicide, the predicaments of war refugees, the suffering of immigrants crossing the Mediterranean, the damage that political corruption causes. In other words, these designers are sensitive to the myriad of inequalities, sufferings, and injustices that plague the world.

Even in cases when a project is created for fun or is a bit whimsical—Mohamad Waked's horror graphic, Jaime Serra's sexual life of couples—it has a social dimension. It's designed to be shared with a partner or to allow people to engage with the information depicted, projecting their own experiences on it. Visualizations born out of individual curiosity end up enlightening or entertaining others.

In Chapter 5 I quoted Richard Sennett's *The Craftsman* (2008) on the boundaries between art and craft. A classical notion says that we engage in a craft when we work outwards, when we produce work to serve our communities, and when such work is guided and constrained by inherited principles, traditions, and conventions. We do art when we work inwards, toward ourselves, which liberates us from at least some of such constraints.

I doubt that such boundaries exist. I'm sympathetic to John Dewey's reasoning in his *Art as Experience* (1934). The venerable pragmatist explained that craft and art aren't separable. To Dewey, art consists of an elevation of the mundane. The products of any craft or other human activities can become art when they lead to heightened experience: insightful, delightful, life-changing. In fact, life itself can be artistic. Dewey wrote:

> Because experience is the fulfillment of an organism in its struggles and achievements in a world of things, it is art in germ. Even in its rudimentary forms, it contains the promise of that delightful perception which is an esthetic experience.

Art to Dewey is not something that *is*, but something that *happens* in the meeting between the intentions and acts of a creator and the perceptions of an audience:

> We have no word in the English language that unambiguously includes what is signified by the two words "artistic" and "esthetic." Since "artistic" refers primarily to the act of producing and "esthetic" to that of perception and enjoyment, the absence of a term designating the two processes taken together is unfortunate.

Something has "esthetic standing only as the work becomes an experience for a human being." It's hard for me not to relate Dewey's reflections on art to my own feelings while making or reading certain visualizations, and to what I heard from the designers that have joined me in my wandering so far. Engaging in the craft of visualization, or witnessing its products, can lead both designers and viewers to artistic experiences.

In her book *Dewey for Artists* (2018), Mary Jane Jacob reflects on the therapeutic properties of these experiences:

> Making is vitalizing, Dewey observed, because it feels vitally important and can only be understood by carrying it out. The aliveness experienced by makers in the process derives from what they truly care about. Thus the creative act is quite literally a life force.

It's a life force because a craft isn't just skill and practice. It is, above all, a way of *being* in this world. I shall return to this theme in Part IV of this book, for which I talked to the people who are the most similar to me, visual journalists.

The vitality, the love for the craft, the immersion in its processes, its evolving nature, and its products can be enjoyed in solitude only for a while. At some point there will be a need to transform the inner conversation into a conversation with others. A few of my interlocutors in this section have become professors; others organize courses and workshops; some volunteer their time to share their passion during free and public events.

There are professionals and scholars who have made spreading their love of visualization one of their core activities. They raise awareness of its beauty and power, and foster communities around the craft. They frequently become role models whose exemplarity many others aspire to imitate. I shall call them ambassadors. To them I turn now.

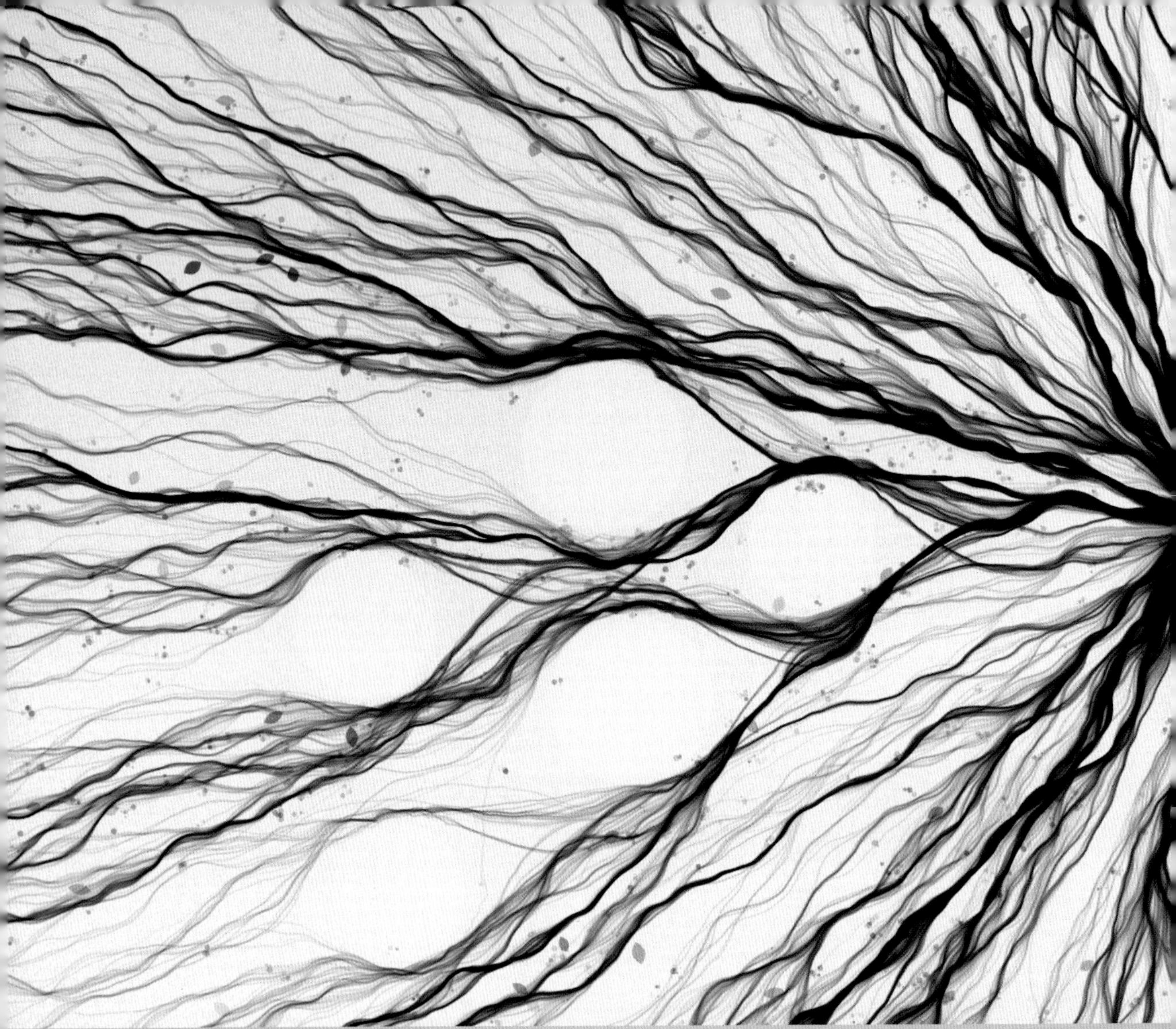

PART III
ambassadors

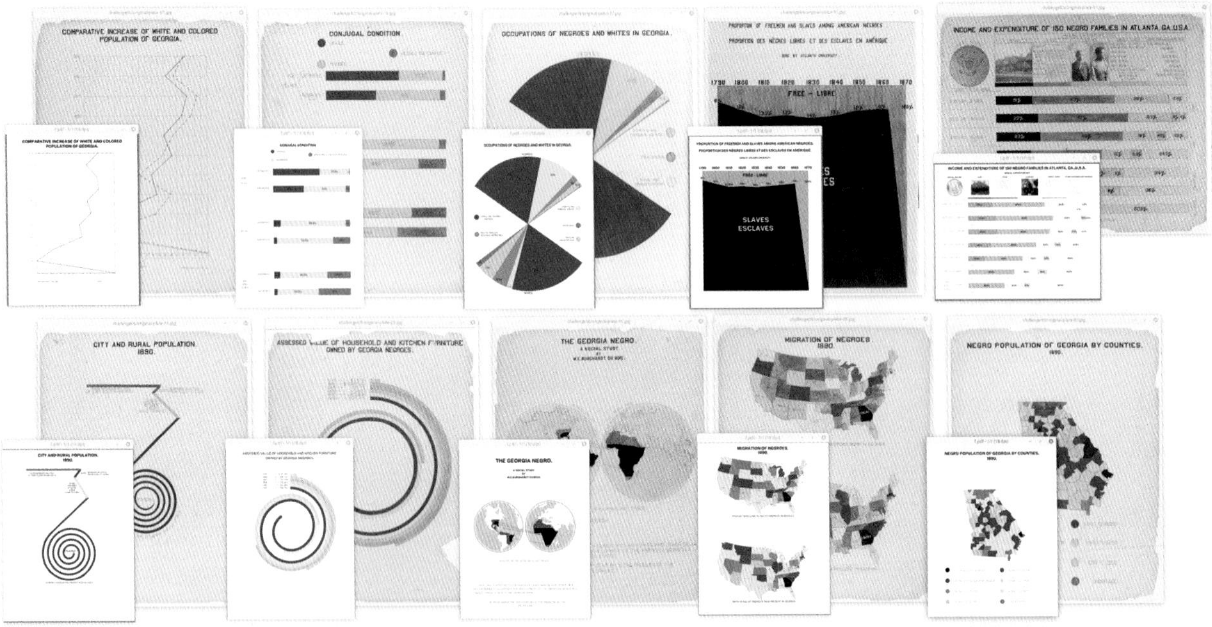

Figure 9.1: The #DuBoisChallenge has its origins in Anthony Starks' recreations of sociologist W.E.B. Du Bois' series of Data Portraits for the 1900 Paris Exposition

Data Visualization Society / https://nightingaledvs.com/the-dubois-challenge// / last accessed Febuary 16, 2023

Chapter 9
with Allen Hillery

Building Bridges

The paradox of education is [...] that as one begins to become conscious one begins to examine the society in which he is being educated [...] No society is anxious to have that kind of person around. What societies really, ideally, want is a citizenry which will simply obey the rules of society.

—James Baldwin

Conversations can help us see ourselves through the eyes of others. In the middle of my dialogue with **Allen Hillery**, I realized that I've devoted a substantial portion of my life to making connections. It's not a secret that I've used my books about visualization as excuses to muse about other matters—epistemology, literature, cognitive science, philosophy, the good life—that I believe can inform our work. I've also mentored many people and put them in touch with one another when I thought that such connections would be mutually helpful.

When these thoughts crossed my mind, I gently interrupted Allen and said, "Have you noticed that you've always been a bridge-builder, both literally and figuratively?"

It's such moments of unforeseen insight that make conversation so marvelous. Today, Allen teaches at The City College of New York, his alma mater, and at Macaulay Honors College, both part of the City University of New York. He teaches data literacy and he's organized various initiatives related to it, such as The #DuBoisChallenge (**Figure 9.1**), which we discussed at length. Allen and I first talked about bridge-building:

Today that I'm working with data, visualization, and literacy, some people joke that I picked the wrong university degree. But I chose to study civic engineering because I've always loved bridges. I wanted to build train systems and bridges!

Right out of school I worked at an engineering consultancy, where I learned SQL and database design. Then I was hired by Verizon and did e-commerce and customer behavior analysis. In the six years that I spent there I did a lot of storytelling work, getting insights from data and trying to communicate them to others. Those others could be people who weren't very fluent in data. I learned that you shouldn't overload people with numbers. The numbers are of course important, but you want to present them as part of a concise narrative.

At the same time, I realized that it was wrong to create or strengthen artificial barriers between "data people" and "non-data people." I myself didn't want to be a pure analyst or a programmer. I saw myself as an ambassador within the organization, someone who could partner up with other teams, do training on the visualizations and dashboards that we built, and so on.

Allen, who is African American, said that the gaps and barriers that he described are often the result of gender, race, or education imbalances:

When I began my career there weren't many people who looked like me in data science or analytics. I think that the black community is bit risk averse, and for good reason—particularly first generation college students from working families like mine. While growing up, people like me were often told, explicitly or implicitly, to get a a business degree, to work for the government or to become a doctor or a lawyer. Professions with a focus on engineering, data analysis, statistics, or visualization? Not so much. So much math!

People of color in the public school system were not exposed to math and science at the same level as students in private or parochial schools. There were specialized high schools or honors programs, but there was still a gap. In addition, career paths weren't clearly mapped for people like us. As a first-generation college student, I didn't have my parents or family to lean on to navigate college. They had government jobs because that was the best bet for good pay and fair treatment. There was no corporate uncle for me to get advice on how to play "the game."

Also keep in mind that most engineering programs were five years. This was longer and more expensive than regular four-year programs, not to mention the cost of textbooks. Some data science roles want you to have a graduate degree today. Think about all of those barriers to access within a system that was already keeping you 10 steps behind.

When you try to encourage people of color to enter a technical field, these are all mental barriers that you encounter. Of course, it also happens to women; gender is another factor.

Barriers are, therefore, intersectional:

> It's a result of how society has been in the past and all the way to the present. Being an engineer, an architect... all those are specialized fields. People tend to see data work in a similar way. Unless you get rigorous training, they think that you can't be a data professional or analyst. And because you aren't a professional, you don't feel that you have the authority or the right to leverage data. I think that this doesn't hold true.
>
> One of the reasons why I left my corporate job was to focus on teaching data science literacy. True, a degree in a data-related field, such as statistics, data science, computer science, or engineering can be a great benefit, but you don't need to be a data scientist formally to think like one. That's an artificial mental barrier that many people still have, and it's disproportionally prevalent in marginalized communities. I want to fight against that.
>
> No matter what career you choose nowadays, data is going to be part of it. Data is empowering and it can play a transformative role in equity and justice. I want to democratize it. For that I've been inspired by many people and organizations, including CodeHouse (https://www.thecodehouse.org/), which aims at strengthening the pipeline for students of color entering the tech field while dismantling barriers to access.

Allen has collaborated with multiple organizations, such as the Tableau Foundation and its Racial Equity Data Hub, on these matters. A personal loss made him transform a passion into a profession:

> My dad's passing caused me to do inventory. I wanted to move back to New York to take care of my mom. Verizon was offering out severance packages and I volunteered. I spent some time reflecting on what I really wanted to do with my life. I thought about writing, but soon realized that being a full-time writer wasn't a realistic prospect. I've been writing a lot about data science and visualization on the side, but my main focus in the past few years has been organizing workshops and classes. I enjoy teaching, which is another form of ambassadorship, I guess.

Along with Sarah Nell-Rodriquez, an expert in data literacy, Allen founded Be Data Lit! in 2021. Their company's statement says, "Our mission is to empower data literacy advocates so they will lower the barrier to data skills for everyone." Besides being the co-founder, Allen is the company's chief community officer:

> When I first came back to New York, I started organizing programs for the community where I grew up. I've done training for people who have a high school education or some college. It's important to me that people feel like they can be a part of the data world. They might not be able to wrangle the data or analyze it like a seasoned professional can, but they can certainly leverage it to make decisions.

The writings that Allen mentioned earlier have appeared in multiple publications, such as *Nightingale*, the magazine of the Data Visualization Society. He's written about inequality in data science, ethics, and also about key figures in the history of statistics and visualization:

> It's important to be aware of history. Take William Playfair, a data visualization pioneer—he wasn't a "data person," he was a polymath who happened to use data. Florence Nightingale. She wasn't a "data person" either. She was a nurse who leveraged data and graphics as analytical, rhetorical, and persuasive tools. I'd like people to stop seeing data as something esoteric and see it instead as an everyday thing. The reason is that data on its own is useless. You need context. A medical doctor who happens to also use data can provide valuable context about her field. Same for lawyers, journalists, engineers—any other profession, for that matter.

Data and visualization as rhetorical tools that people with any background can—and should—use... Allen's words reminded me of *Statistics as Principled Argument* (1995) by psychologist, political scientist, and Yale University professor Robert P. Abelson. It's a wonderful little gem of a book brimming with wit and humor. Here's a quote:

> From long observation of student struggles with statistics, I conclude that the difficulties lie not so much with computational mechanics as with an overall perspective on what they are doing [...] They ask questions such as, "Am I allowed to analyze my data with this method?" In the querulous manner of a patient or parishioner anxious to avoid sickness or sin, and they seem to want a prescriptive answer, such as, "Run an analysis of variance according to the directions of the computer package, get lots of sleep, and call me in the morning."

I think that I'll bring up that last line next time anyone asks me whether they're "allowed" to visualize their data with a pie chart, but I digress. Abelson next wrote:

> [The presentation of inferences from statistical analysis involves rhetoric [...] Statistical analysis also has a narrative role. Meaningful research tells a story with some point to it, and statistics can sharpen the story. Students are often not mindful of this. Ask a student the question, "If your study were reported in the newspaper, what would the headline be?" And you are likely to receive in response a rare exhibition of incoherent mumblings, as though such a question had never been even remotely contemplated.

Rhetoric and persuasion were central interests to the 19th century pioneers whom Allen mentioned earlier, William Playfair and Florence Nightingale, but also to others such as W.E.B. Du Bois and Ida B. Wells. Allen has written extensively about both.

Du Bois is known for being a brilliant polymath: sociologist, historian, writer, professor, and civil rights activist. He's less known for being a pioneer in the use of data visualization both for analysis and communication. Allen heard about it through RJ Andrews, publisher of the book series Information Graphics Visionaries, intended to unearth the work of many unsung geniuses in the history of the field.

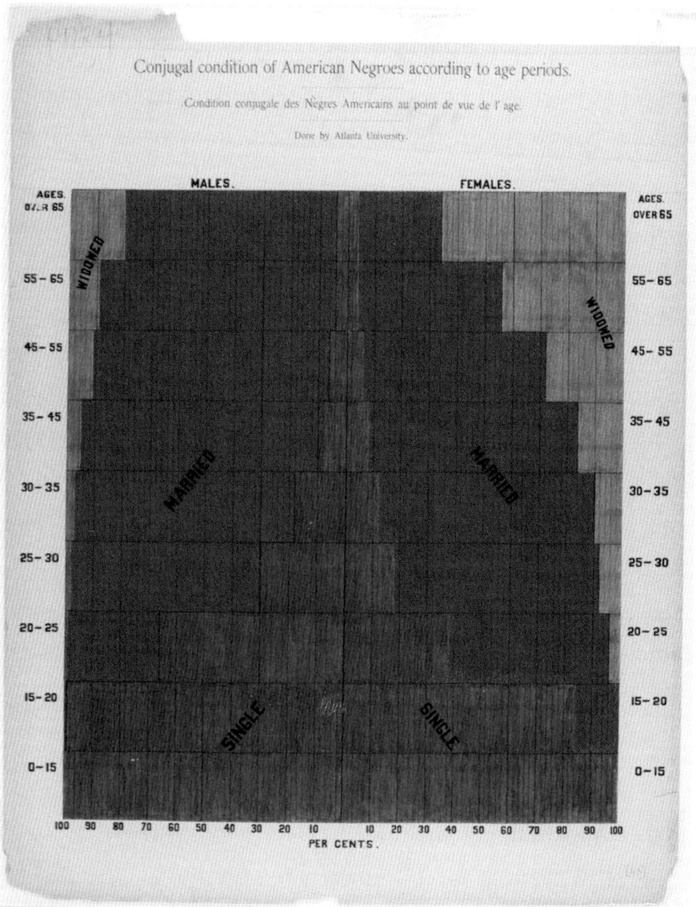

Figure 9.2: One of the charts from W.E.B. Du Bois's "American Negro Exhibit" and one of the photographs from the Exposition des Nègres d'Amerique

The Library of Congress / Public Domain

In 1900, Du Bois and a team of his collaborators, students, and alumni from Atlanta University, designed nearly sixty data visualizations (**Figure 9.2**) for the Exposition Universelle in Paris. Their graphics were part of an exhibit intended to demonstrate the great progress made by African Americans in the United States in spite of the many obstacles that they faced.

The exhibit included many other objects: photographs of anonymous people, portraits of relevant African American intellectual and political leaders, and copies of hundreds of publications by African American authors. As a whole, the exhibit wove a story of dignity, pride, and resilience at a time when scientific racism was dominant, and when former slaves and their descendants were told that they were "the architects of their fate because of racial inferiority, the wretched of the earth because God and nature planned it that way," in the words of Northwestern University professor Aldon Morris. Allen added:

> Du Bois's graphics are fascinating. He knew who his audience was. A key goal of the exhibit was to debunk social Darwinism. At the time there was this widespread theory that the black race was going to become extinct because of its allegedly inherent inferiority. Left on their own during Reconstruction, a few decades after slavery had formally ended, African Americans would disappear.
>
> Du Bois's graphics, and also the rest of the exhibit—the photographs of happy and successful people, the books that African Americans had authored—adopted an adversarial, confrontational stance. The visualizations seem to say, implicitly: Here we are, look at us and at our accomplishments. Despite discrimination and segregation, despite Jim Crow laws, despite all these obstacles and travails, *we're still here*. Not only that, we are also *flourishing*.

According to Whitney Battle-Baptiste and Britt Rusert, editors of *W.E.B. Du Bois's Data Portraits* (2018), Du Bois favored a sparse style, and "the protomodernist aesthetics of turn-of-the-century data visualization to gain the attention of an international audience." However, it's debatable that his visualizations alone would have been effective if not paired with the other elements of the exhibit, particularly the photographs of typical African Americans engaging in everyday activities:

> It wasn't just the data, but also the faces, that told a story of resilience. When you are trying to persuade an audience, you want to balance emotions. Du Bois used data and presented facts, he showed growth—and persistence, as growth hadn't come easy to African Americans. But to be moved, one has to see their faces. That's why the photographs and portraits were so relevant.

Allen has honored the work of Du Bois and other pioneers in multiple ways. In 2021, he launched the #DuBoisChallenge (**Figure 9.1** at the beginning of this chapter) in collaboration with visualization designers and data analysts Sekou Tyler and Anthony Starks:

> The #DuBoisChallenge was a Twitter campaign to celebrate Du Bois's graphics. Over several weeks, we challenged participants to recreate the visualizations from the famous exhibit. Designers then could tweet out their work and share their thoughts. It was an opportunity to use social media to bring attention to the accomplishment of Du Bois and his team.

Du Bois is also at the core of an honors class that Allen teaches at the City University of New York (CUNY), titled "Exploring W.E.B. Du Bois' Sociological Approach."

> I based the class on Du Bois's 1899 *The Philadelphia Negro*. The book is an in-depth sociological study of African Americans living in the Seventh Ward, in the center of the city. Du Bois' methodology was pioneering, combining quantitative analysis with more qualitative elements. He did surveys and thousands and thousands of interviews, which provided some needed context to the statistics. Du Bois used plenty of data, but he also focused on the stories of the people behind the numbers.
>
> I proposed my students to get some inspiration from Du Bois, choosing a neighborhood in New York City (Harlem, Chinatown, Jackson Heights...), investigating a problem that ails it (gentrification, opioid abuse, housing, or the unequal impacts of COVID) and then designing stories to explain it (**Figure 9.3**). I teach students how to handle census data, for instance, but I also want them to discover that data is a vehicle, a foundation, a piece in a much larger puzzle in which the contextual and even the anecdotal have a key role to play.

Before my conversation with Allen, I knew little about Du Bois's *The Philadelphia Negro* beyond the fact that it was a groundbreaking study. It can be found online legally in HTML and PDF formats, so I spent a few hours perusing it. It amazed me how carefully Du Bois annotated his graphs and tables, and how well he integrated text and visuals (**Figure 9.4**). Being the old bear I am, I sometimes long for the time before screens and e-books, when the layout of a book could be fully controlled.

Allen told me that he sees teaching as an opportunity for personal growth:

> I've learned so much myself by teaching classes or workshops like this and studying the parallel history of sociology, data analysis, visualization—and the city where I was born. There's a lot of stuff about the 1870–1900 period that isn't covered as it should be in basic education, such as the role that New York City had in slavery, being central to the cotton trade. Or the fact that African American residents were forced to move uptown from what is today the financial district to escape racism and become homeowners.
>
> I once did a workshop about Seneca Village, a dominantly African American neighborhood that was painted as a shantytown by the media, particularly *The New York Times*, [and eventually destroyed] simply because there was a desire to emulate Paris and create a large park in the city. Therefore people had to be displaced. That's of course Central Park.

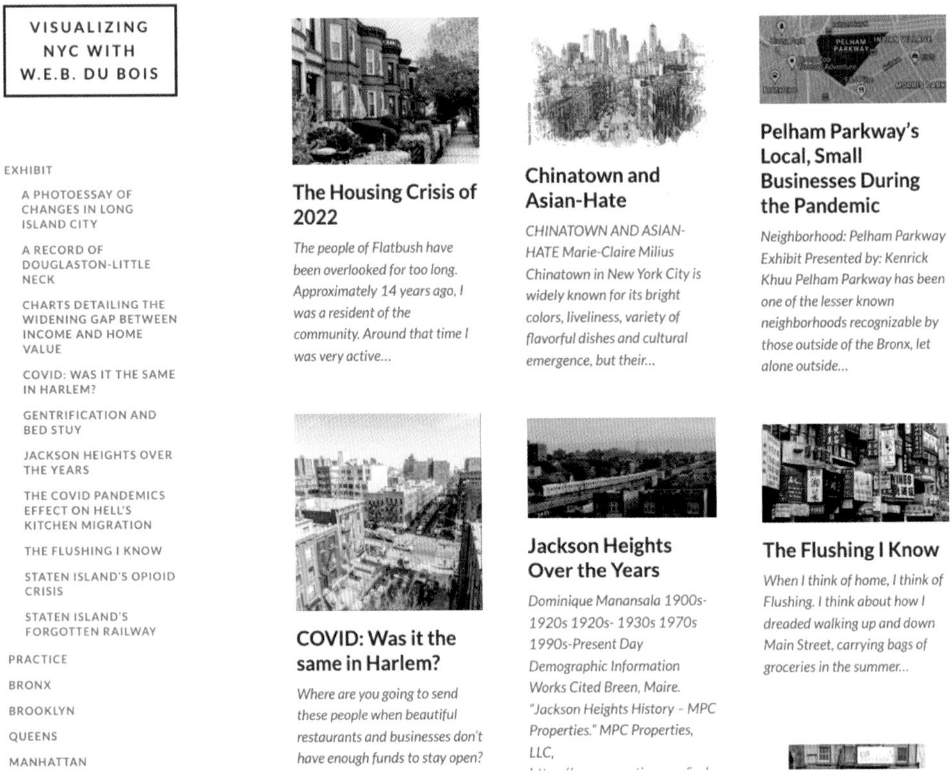

Figure 9.3: Visualizing NYC with W.E.B. Du Bois, class website

Visualizing NYC with W.E.B. Du Bois / https://eportfolios.macaulay.cuny.edu/visualizingnyc/ / last accessed Febuary 16, 2023

Recently, Allen has been focusing on another pioneer in the use of data for communication and social change, the civil rights activist and investigative reporter Ida B. Wells.

Wells is a fundamental figure in the fight against lynching, which become widespread in the 1890s and the early 1900s. She authored several pamphlets to denounce it using logic and numbers. Her most famous pamphlet is *The Red Record*, from 1895. Within its roughly 100 pages there are 14 that are just data she collected from news stories published in the *Chicago Tribune*. These pages are a long list of the 159 people lynched between 1892 and 1895. Allen said:

> I think that Wells's work against lynching could be labelled as "data humanism." She didn't want just to quantify these murders, their locations, dates, or circumstances. She wanted readers to envision each of those data points as an individual, so in her writings, besides the name and last name of every person, Wells also added vivid details about how they had been murdered.
>
> News publications at the time justified lynching by saying that there were a lot of black males who were raping white women. I don't know how Wells was able to figure out why each person was lynched, but when you look at those accounts, rape wasn't the reason.

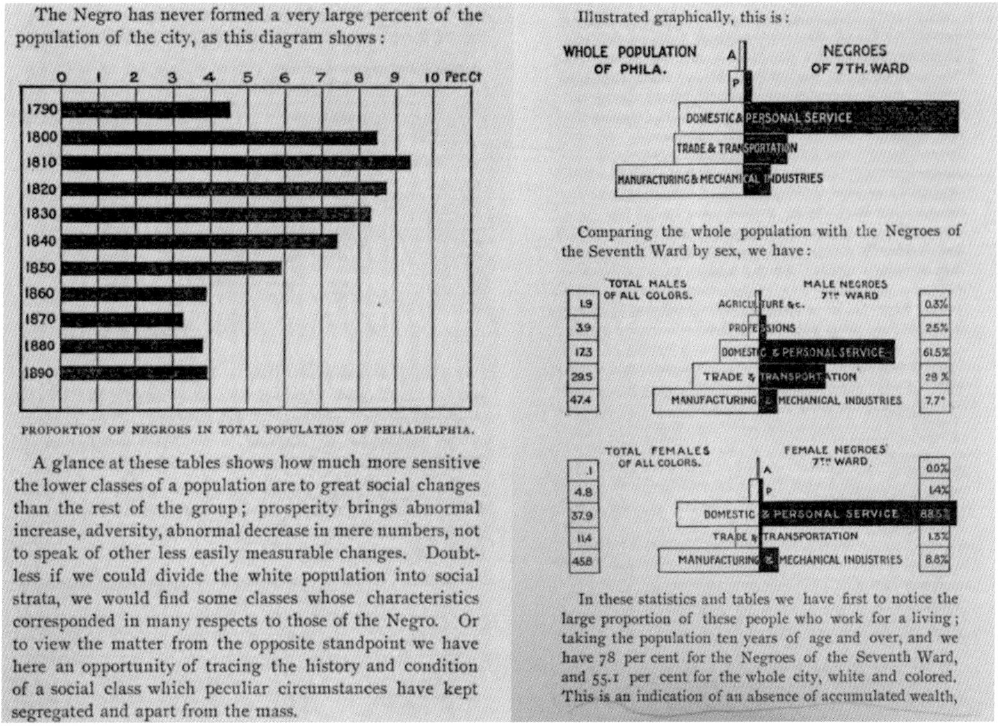
The Negro has never formed a very large percent of the population of the city, as this diagram shows:

PROPORTION OF NEGROES IN TOTAL POPULATION OF PHILADELPHIA.

A glance at these tables shows how much more sensitive the lower classes of a population are to great social changes than the rest of the group; prosperity brings abnormal increase, adversity, abnormal decrease in mere numbers, not to speak of other less easily measurable changes. Doubtless if we could divide the white population into social strata, we would find some classes whose characteristics corresponded in many respects to those of the Negro. Or to view the matter from the opposite standpoint we have here an opportunity of tracing the history and condition of a social class which peculiar circumstances have kept segregated and apart from the mass.

Illustrated graphically, this is:

Comparing the whole population with the Negroes of the Seventh Ward by sex, we have:

In these statistics and tables we have first to notice the large proportion of these people who work for a living; taking the population ten years of age and over, and we have 78 per cent for the Negroes of the Seventh Ward, and 55.1 per cent for the whole city, white and colored. This is an indication of an absence of accumulated wealth,

Figure 9.4: Two pages from W.E.B. Du Bois's *The Philadelphia Negro*

Paula J. Giddings's book *Ida: A Sword Among Lions* (2008) offers many examples of apologists alleging that lynchings were a response to rape. Giddings chronicles how Wells was able to show, through data (**Figure 9.5**) and argumentation, that this was untrue: "The South is shielding itself behind the plausible screen of defending the honor of its women."

Giddings says that one of the core themes in Wells's writings is that lynchings weren't isolated phenomena consisting of mobs bursting with fury and hatred in response to supposed crimes. Rather, lynching was a key piece of a structure of control in the white American South, and a reaction to fast societal change that included the liberation and progress of African Americans. In her writings and talks Wells demonstrated that white mobs would use any excuse, no matter how trivial, to lynch a person. Through her reporting, Wells discovered that many accusations of "rape" were made only after a liaison between a black man and a white woman had been made public.

Lynching was also a sign that the dark past of the South was very much alive, crawling under a thin veneer of modernity. Giddings wrote:

> Whites knew, beneath the humming mills, signs of material progress, and insistence about their superiority of Anglo-Saxon civilization, the New South wasn't new at all; it was the Old South,

1896

Murder	24	Arson	2
Attempted murder	4	Assault	3
Rape	31	Unknown cause	1
Incendiarism	2	Slapping a child	1
No cause	2	Shooting at officer	1
Alleged rape	2	Alleged murder	2
Cattle stealing	1	Threats	1
Miscegenation	2	Passing counterfeit money	1
Attempted rape	4	Theft	1
Murderous assault	1		

1897

Murder	55	Writing insulting letter	1
Attempted rape	8	Cattle thief	1
Mistaken identity	1	Felony	1
Arson	3	Train wrecking	1
Murderous assault	2	Rape	22
Running quarantine	1	Race prejudice	1
Burglary	1	Alleged arson	1
Bad reputation	1	Robbery	6
Unknown offense	3	Assault	2
Killing white cap	1	Disobeying Fed. regulations	1
Attempted murder	1	Theft	2
Insulting white woman	1	Elopement	1
Suspected arson	1	Concealing murderer	1
Giving evidence	2		
Refusing to give evidence	1		

1898

Murder	42	Theft	6
Rape	14	Miscegenation	1
Attempted rape	7	Unknown offense	2
Complicity in rape	1	Violation of contract	1
Highway robbery	1	Insults	2
Burglary	1	Race prejudice	3
Mistaken identity	1	Resisting arrest	1
Arson	1	Suspected murder	13
Murderous assault	1	Assaults upon whites	4

1899

Murder	24	Arson	8
Robbery	6	Unknown offense	4
Inflammatory language	1	Resisting arrest	1
Desperado	1	Mistaken identity	1
Complicity in murder	3	Aiding escape of murderer	3
Rape	11		
Attempted rape	8		

1900

Murder	30	No offense	1
Rape	16	Arson	2
Attempted assault	12	Suspicion of arson	1
Race prejudice	9	Aiding escape of murderer	1
Plot to kill whites	2	Unpopularity	1
Suspected robbery	1	Making threats	1
Giving testimony	1	Informer	1
Attacking white men	3	Robbery	2
Attempted murder	4	Burglary	4
Threats to kill	1	Assault	2
Suspected murder	2		
Unknown offense	2		

Year	Race prejudice	Murder	Rape	Total lynchings
1896	31	24	31	86
1897	46	55	22	123
1898	39	47	16	102
1899	56	23	11	90
1900	57	30	16	103
Total	229	179	96	504

Figure 9.5: Tables from Ida D. Wells's article "Lynching and the Excuse For It" (1901). They quantify excuses for lynchings. Notice that causes related to "Race prejudice," and not alleged murder or rape, were the most prevalent, as Wells had been arguing since her first writings about lynching in the early 1890s.

> replete with its past promiscuities of thought, action, greed, and hatred.

Allen told me that his mom had passed away a few months before we talked, and that he'd like to dedicate future work on Wells's data to her. "My mom had what I'd call a quiet strength," Allen said.

Wells's strength wasn't that quiet, though. She was a strong-willed, assertive woman with a fiery writing style, and I suspect that the "among lions" in the subtitle of Giddings's book doesn't refer just to white supremacists, but also to some civil right advocates Wells worked with.

According to Giddings, Wells could come across as abrasive, individualistic, and unwilling to compromise when she was part of an organization—but this was also true of some of her male collaborators, such as Du Bois himself. As is still the case to this day, what was seen as virtue in men was perceived as unacceptable demeanor in a woman. Allen's thoughts align with Giddings's:

> Wells was ignored late in her life by former collaborators, like the leaders of the National Association for the Advancement of Colored People (NAACP), even if she had been part of its foundation. This is unfair. She had collected so much data mostly on her own, without a team like the one Du Bois had. She used this data to slowly change people's minds and influence policy (**Figure 9.6**). She wrote articles, pamphlets, did speaking tours, was a leader in the women enfranchisement movement...Despite all her accomplishments, she didn't get much credit at her time, or even later.

Ida B. Wells passed away in March of 1931. In the last pages of her biography, Giddings says:

> Most of the obituaries about her were far from comprehensive; none captured the essence of her work and

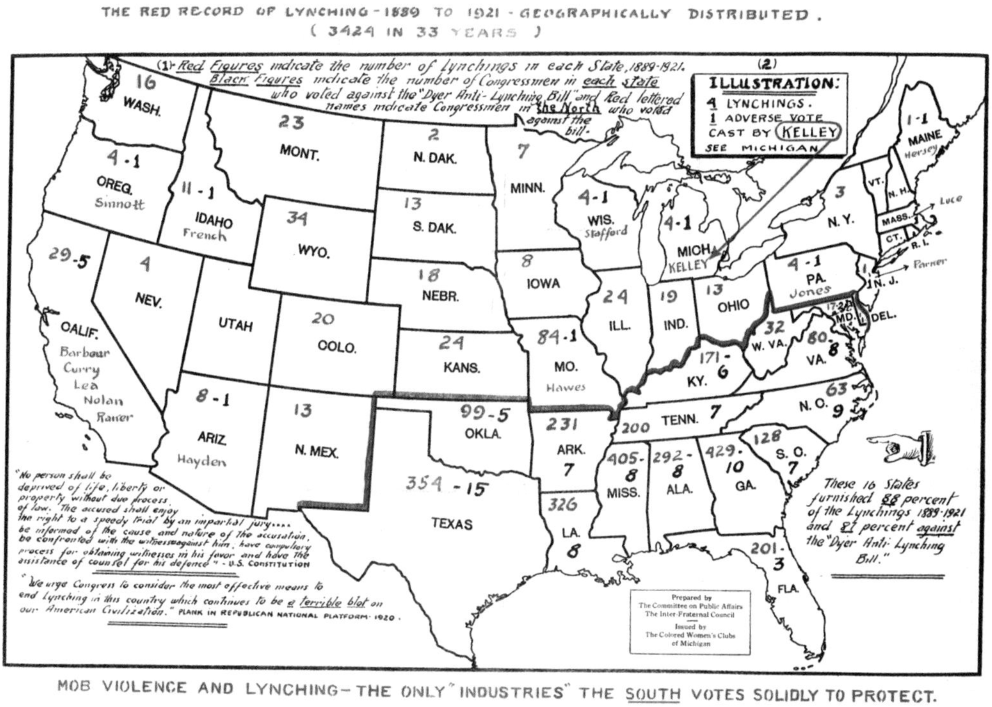

Figure 9.6: "Red Record of Lynching Map," based on Ida B. Wells's data. It was issued by the Colored Women's Clubs of Michigan to Congress in 1922 to support an anti-lynching bill introduced by Representative Leonidas Dyer of Missouri that had already passed in the House. The map displays lynchings per state and representatives who had voted against the bill in the House. Names in red identify Northern congressmen who opposed the Dyer bill by their names. The bill failed in the Senate. No federal anti-lynching bill passed both houses of Congress until March 2022.

A source I've found says that this map was designed by Wells herself, but I haven't been able to confirm it. Allen Hillery asked Wells' granddaughter, Michelle Duster, who replied, "I don't know for sure, but it would not be surprising." U.S. National Archives and Records Administration (NARA) / https://catalog.archives.gov/id/149268727 / last accessed Feb 17, 2022

> life, and others took the opportunity to marginalize her contributions [...] W.E.B. Du Bois called her "the pioneer of the anti-lynching crusade," who "began the awakening of the conscience of the nation." But churlish to the last, he added that the crusade had been easily forgotten because "it was afterward taken up on a much larger scale by the NAACP and carried to greater success."

I wonder how many champions for our craft like Wells have been lost to history because of their culture, race, or gender. I'd surmise that it's too many. This impoverishes us all. As visualization matures, it is my hope that some of us will keep building bridges to the past—unearthing rare or unknown historical gems and giving them the visibility they deserve—and bridges to the future—nurturing more diverse and equal communities where those destined to succeed my aging generation of designers will burgeon.

Figure 10.1: "The Mental Mindgames of Measuring Milk"
Medium / https://medium.com/nightingale/the-mental-mindgames-of-measuring-milk-3401113788d6 / last accessed June 19, 2023.

Chapter 10
with Amanda Makulec

The Good Fighter

Design [...] does not matter because it is pleasing to the eye, even though we applaud its beauty and its purpose and its presence in our lives. Design matters because of the why, not the what; the sentiment, not the acquisition. Design matters because people matter.

—Jessica Helfand

In March of 2020, **Amanda Makulec**, a bridge-builder like Allen Hillery (Chapter 9) an educator, and executive director of the Data Visualization Society, released the results of a home experiment. As someone with reasonable experience feeding babies, I found it endearing. Amanda was curious about the true capacity of a variety of baby feeding bottles, pump bottles, and breastmilk storage bags (**Figure 10.1.**)

While feeding her first baby, Amanda had perceived that volume measurements of bottles and bags vary widely, particularly when volumes are small; the same 100 milliliters of milk in one bottle may magically become nearly 120 in a bag. Amanda tested and confirmed her hunch with a non-representative sample of 25 bottles and bags, the latter having the highest variance by far. She explained that she had a good reason to be curious: "1.5 oz is very different from 2 oz when you're feeding a tiny human."

Two years later, on May 11, 2022, Amanda wrote a much sadder article about her family, this time for *The New York Times*. The title summarizes its content: "I Lost My Baby. Then Antivaxxers Made My Pain Go Viral." Amanda's second son, who was just three months old, had died unexpectedly in September of 2022. Amanda had shared the terrible news on Twitter, hoping to dodge well-intended questions from colleagues about how things were as a parent of two. The responses that she received were overwhelmingly supportive and empathetic; she has many followers and admirers, including me.

However, there were also people who weaponized her tragedy to push a partisan agenda. Within a day of her tweet, a stranger reposted a screenshot of it next to an older tweet where Amanda had shared that she had been vaccinated against COVID-19 while pregnant. That stranger wrote "Safe...and effective," implying that there was a causal connection between the vaccine and her son's death—needless to say, there wasn't. Amanda described her feelings in her article:

> The juxtaposition of the two images felt like a violation of the space my husband and I needed to grieve. Mixed into the emails with condolences were subject lines like, "Did you know you're on Reddit?" The misappropriation of our loss made me angry. The realization that people may still see bits of my story and have it influence their health choices hurt, both as a mother and as a public health professional [...] That's why seeing our loss misrepresented so boldly and spread so widely to further someone else's agenda has been so heartbreaking.

Amanda and her family received tremendous abuse. Anonymous ghouls writing in online forums and social media called her a "dumb mother" and a "murderer."

Reading those words in her article made me feel sorrow, horror, and then rage. One of my children is part of a minority that is subject to conspiracy theories and harassment in states led by religious fanatics, such as Florida, where we still live today (April of 2023). When I wrote for some news publications about what's happening to families like mine, I started receiving social media reactions and emails telling me "you're a terrible father," "you and your child are going to hell," and much worse. My responses to those messages were ten times more vicious.

Amanda is a much more measured person than I am. In her article she showed grace toward those who had hurt her, and even a scintilla of hope that vile people have the potential of becoming better human beings. Moreover, and despite her family's ordeal, to this day she's kept faith in data and evidence-based narratives to steer people's minds in the right direction.

But only if we designers are careful. Amanda also told me that she believes that the COVID-19 pandemic has changed the way that we should think about data and visualization:

> We should be cautious about what we post on social media or say in our daily lives. Let's say that you are a person who is knowledgeable about data in your circle of friends or in your family. They may listen to you over public sources. Therefore, we have a responsibility to think about how the information we share shapes the perceptions and behaviors of people around us.

I have a background in public health, research, and evaluation. In this field we pay a lot of attention to how data is collected, and to its quality and limitations. Lives are at stake when we use that data to inform budgets, policymaking, and program design which impact who has access to health services. Communicating data is also part of our mission, so I've thought a lot about how the pandemic made regular people more likely to look into public data often, but also to be wary about its shortcomings.

That sometimes leads to excessive skepticism on the part of public health practitioners, but there's a reason for it. Think about what happened at the beginning of the pandemic. The data we had was very imperfect, very incomplete, but COVID-19 figures were reported anyway, usually without proper context or caveats. This was a problem. In epidemiology we think a lot about dependencies between measures of cases, testing, and surveillance. If we face a rapidly spreading disease and see numbers vary widely, we recognize that those figures may not represent the true number of cases. You might simply be screening for the disease more effectively. This wasn't well explained, at least at the beginning. And those nuances need to be explained.

Since the beginning of the COVID-19 pandemic, Amanda has written several articles about data ethics. In "Ten Considerations Before You Create Another Chart About COVID-19" (2020), she said that before publishing any visualization, we should "consider if what you've created serves an actual information need in the public domain. Does it add value to the public and uncover new information? If not, perhaps this is one viz that should be for your own use only." Amanda told me:

Early on in the pandemic there were other mistakes that set the scene for people later becoming distrustful of public information. Should we wear masks or not, for instance? In early 2020 there were many limitations in the supply of masks and, as the virus hadn't spread widely yet, healthcare workers needed those masks the most. The public was told not to buy them. This recommendation flipped a few months later, when masks were more widely accessible.

The reasons for the initial recommendation and for the change weren't properly explained, I believe. At least part of the public heard, "Masks don't work!" when in reality the message was much more subtle and nuanced, much less simplistic: Masks do work (when worn properly); however, when facing scarcity, we needed those masks first for healthcare workers who treat people showing up in emergency rooms. Hospital personnel were at a much higher risk of being exposed to the virus than the general public.

Public messaging about COVID-19 was also too focused just on cases and deaths, and that led to misinterpretations. If the public is exposed to charts and dashboards showing that, say, cases are increasing but deaths are dropping, it creates a certain story in people's minds around what measures they should care about. But death isn't the only possible consequence of having COVID-19. We know now there are many potential long-term effects—this is what we would usually quantify with measures of morbidity (different than mortality), like disability or quality-adjusted life years, but those are much more complex measures to estimate or explain.

Finally, we need to consider that the United States is an individualistic society, That shapes the way that governmental organizations operate and make recommendations. Those individualist values also shape health law in many ways, limiting the authority of public health authorities to mandate interventions. During the pandemic I remember the Centers for Disease Control and Prevention basically telling people, "Look at your county each morning on this map and decide if you should wear a mask today." This is terrible advice. Being transparent about the data and making it public is important, of course, but so is distilling that data and giving people specific and plain-language recommendations based on it.

I mentioned to Amanda the research project about extreme weather and hurricane risk messaging that I'm part of (see Chapter 2). Like her, I believe that maps, charts, graphs, and tables are all necessary, but rarely sufficient to inform the public. I asked about the source for her intuitions about the interplay between data, visualization, and textual messaging:

The public health program I attended at Boston University exposed me to visualization early on, but not in a very deep way. For example, we had a dashboard design class, but it was focused on how to build them, but not on user-centered design practices or methodologies. We spent barely any time trying to understand audiences, how to grab their attention, or how to make graphics more understandable.

We also learned a very prescriptive approach to visualization design: Every type of chart has a role, and there's usually only one right way to design it. Bar graphs are for categorical data, line graphs are for trends, and so on.

After graduating I was part of an analysis and communications team on a project supporting content for the USAID website and annual reports to Congress about topics like maternal and child health or HIV-AIDS. From there, I moved into a joint evaluation and communications role on a larger maternal and child health project: those early years of my career, I spent learning how to transform lots of data into brief and readable documents.

During that period, I learned a lot from actual graphic designers. This sparked my interest in visualization, which was further ignited by the Stata 2012 conference in San Diego, which was my first exposure to Tableau and other tools that would allow someone like me to go beyond, say, Excel. When I came back I did several internal training sessions and eventually built a team to develop visualizations.

I learned a lot by doing—a bit of trial and error—but also started studying visualization seriously. Learning about the grammar of graphics [there's a book by Leland Wilkinson with the

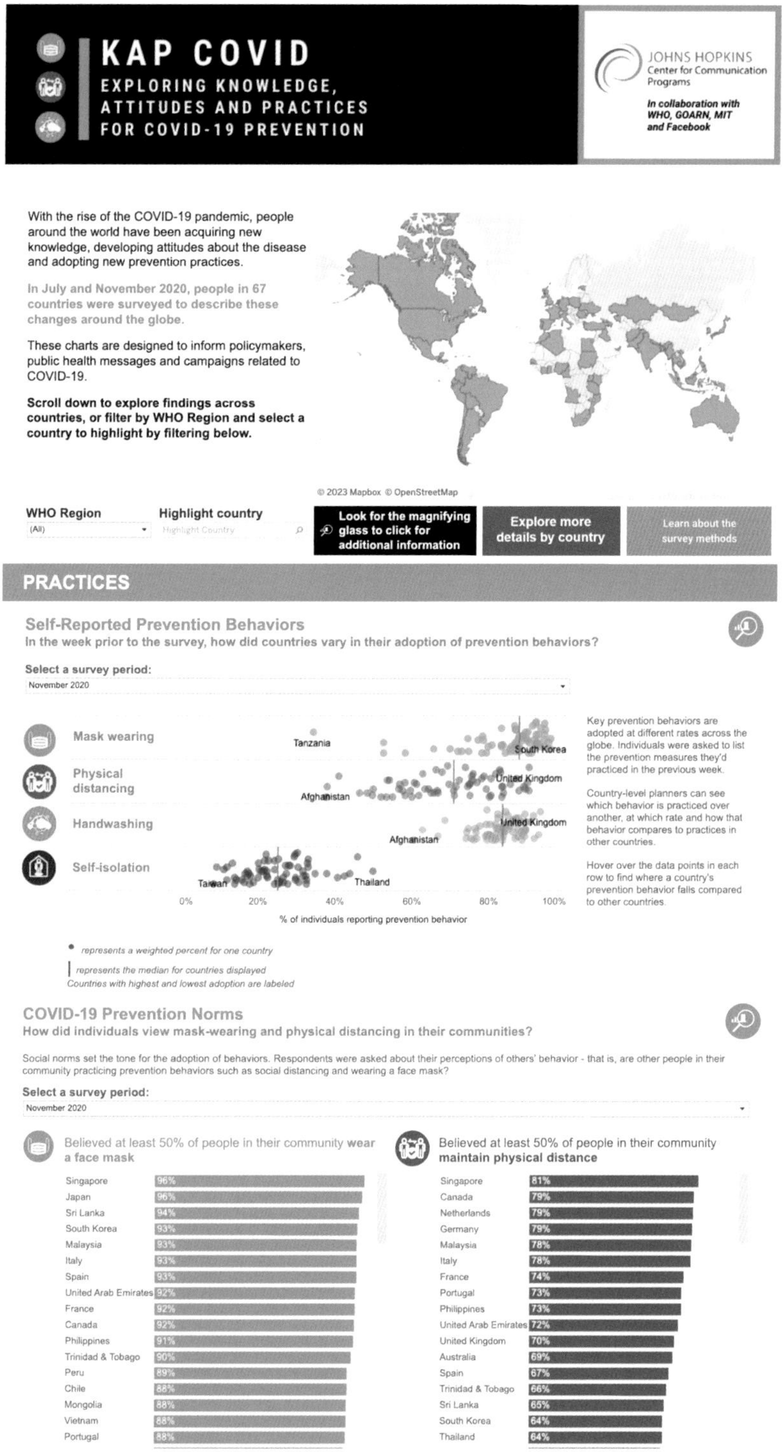

Figure 10.2: Some graphics from "KAP COVID: Exploring Knowledge, Attitudes and Practices for COVID-19 Prevention"
Johns Hopkins / https://ccp.jhu.edu/kap-covid/kap-covid-global-view-2/ / last accessed June 19, 2023.

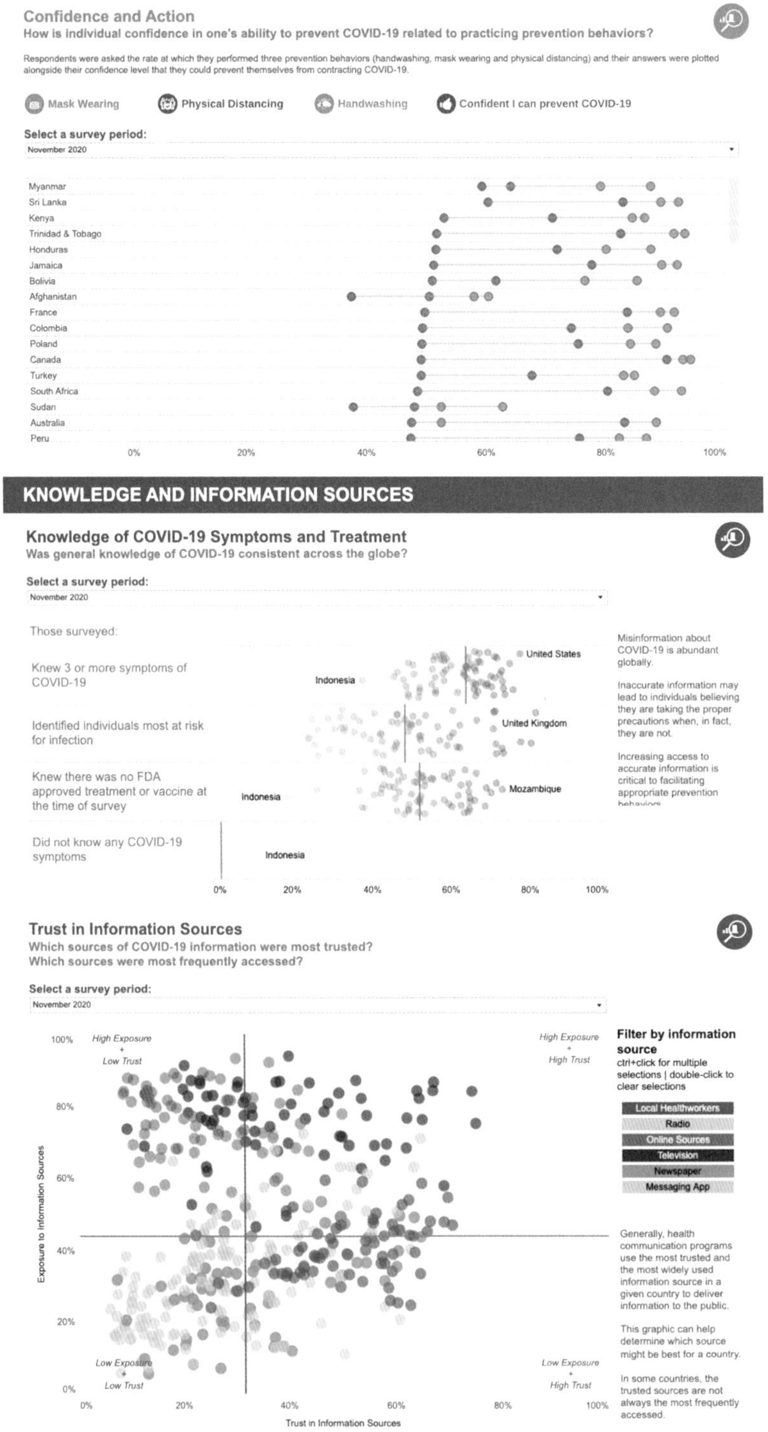

Figure 10.3: Screenshots from "KAP COVID: Exploring Knowledge, Attitudes and Practices for COVID-19 Prevention"
Johns Hopkins / https://ccp.jhu.edu/kap-covid/kap-covid-global-view-2/ / last accessed June 19, 2023.

same title] was eye-opening. Thinking about visualization in terms of taxonomies of charts—bar graphs, line graphs, pie charts, and so on—is useful, but also a bit limiting. Thinking instead in terms of symbols, encodings, and layers was freeing.

When I asked Amanda for examples of her visualizations, she chose two dashboards about worldwide attitudes toward preventive measures against COVID-19 that she designed with a team. They were the first releases of a series collectively known as "the KAP COVID dashboards." ("KAP" stands for Knowledge, Attitudes, and Practices, **Figure 10.2**.) They were later updated as a suite of visualizations about COVID behaviors.

These initial dashboards were the product of a collaboration between Johns Hopkins University Center for Communication Programs, the World Health Organization Global Outbreak Alert and Response Network (GOARN), MIT, and Facebook for Social Good, with support from Excella, where Amanda worked at the time. The data came from the COVID-19 Trends and Impact Survey (CTIS), conducted through Facebook between April of 2020 and June of 2022 by Carnegie Mellon University and other universities.

To give you an idea of the scope of this survey, around 40,000 people participated in it daily *just in the United States*. They were asked about their use of preventive measures—masks, distancing, handwashing—how frequent and effective they thought those measures were in their communities, and which sources of information they trusted the most (last graph in **Figure 10.3**.) Amanda told me:

Before I was involved in this project, the survey had been going on for a while; there had been six rounds of data collection already, but not much had been done to communicate the resulting data. However, there was a lot of demand for it from health communication professionals and policymakers worldwide. The data needed to be accessible—it filled in gaps around *why* people were adopting prevention behaviors or not, and what was happening in multiple low and middle income countries where case reporting was sparse.

An initial question we talked through with the team was whether we could put all the data into a single dashboard and tell people, "Here's all the data, go explore it and do whatever you want with it!"

We quickly realized that this wouldn't work. We had so much data that we decided to split up into four dashboards with different levels of granularity. For instance, one focuses on a global snapshot of the individual knowledge, attitude, and practices to prevent COVID-19 across countries, another on more detailed analysis of behaviors across demographic groups, and yet another on vaccine acceptance (**Figure 10.4**).

These were the ones used the most by health communication teams worldwide, in various webinars hosted with WHO, and in many news releases. Creating several dashboards rather than

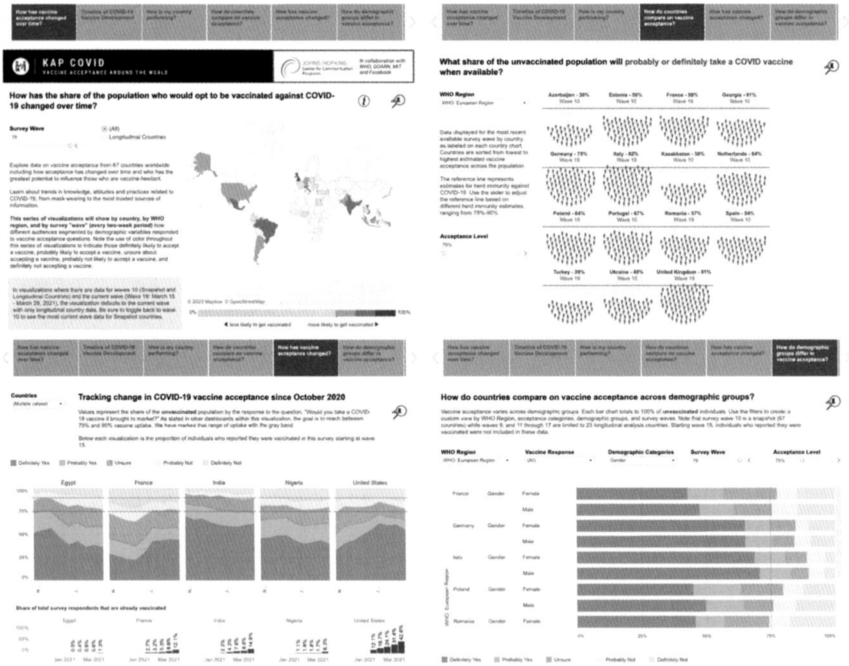

Figure 10.4: Graphics from "KAP COVID: Vaccine Acceptance Around the World"
Johns Hopkins / https://ccp.jhu.edu/kap-covid/vaccine-acceptance/ / last accessed June 19, 2023.

just one made it easier to provide an adequate level of granularity to answer different questions; in all these dashboards readers can get an overview and then explore detailed data about each topic and country.

As Amanda has thought and written so much about the limitations of data in public health, I asked her about the survey:

The survey was done through Facebook so, obviously, the sample was limited to people who visited that platform. That's certainly a limitation. On the other hand, it allowed the research team to collect much more data much more rapidly and at multiple points in time than would have been possible from more typical surveys conducted in every country.

Another limitation is that country sample sizes vary a lot. For some countries we had data that was more limited, but for others we had plenty, so a reader can drill into demographic groups and filter the data by education, gender, or age. It's possible to see interesting patterns thanks to this. For example, it seems that younger people tend to trust the government less than or are less influenced by the government than older people—important to consider around who is sharing information in the midst of a pandemic on sensitive topics, live prevention measures (that may be inconvenient to adopt), or vaccine adoption.

Designing a visualization based in such a large data set was challenging:

> When making a project like this you need to define your expected audience. Building a dashboard of complex survey data with the goal that everyone in the world can make sense of it is a fool's errand. Therefore, we decided that our audience would be policymakers and health communications professionals.
>
> Our idea was that you could go ahead and say, "If I'm a health comms person at the department of health in, say, Tanzania and I can see that we have really low adoption of mask-wearing based on what the survey data looks like, I both can see that as something that I need to potentially address and also be able to see which countries are more successful in adopting some of these behaviors."
>
> This step, which preceded the design, helped decide which questions from the survey to include on the dashboards and which ones to leave out, as well, and it influenced many design decisions. For instance, we knew that our audience would want to pull screenshots to include in PowerPoint slide decks, so we structured the dashboards in a way that makes this task easier.
>
> Notice also that the vaccine acceptance dashboard, which was the last to be developed, is less exploratory and much more prescriptive; each page on the paginated layout poses a question ("What share of the unvaccinated population will probably or definitely take a COVID vaccine when available?") and then it shows the data that can help a reader answer it. This was another deliberate design choice. We wanted to give readers the questions that we thought were more relevant for decision makers and the relevant data.

While Amanda explained the KAP dashboards, I was navigating them on my computer. I pointed out that there is an abundance of text everywhere: introductions, sidebars, long tooltips, and so on (**Figure 10.5**):

> We paid plenty of attention to the annotation layer. We tried to add human-readable text in many places for different reasons, one being that some of the graphics, such as the jittered strip plots or the scatter plots, are less common. We guessed that part of our audience would not be accustomed to them. The text helps readers not only understand the charts, but also see the points that they are designed to make.
>
> We also did two rounds of thorough testing and review with stakeholders from all partners involved in the dashboards, and we obtained feedback from readers who were using the dashboards worldwide, where they were leveraged by staff in local country offices and at the global level. Not only that, we organized multiple demos to teach people how to use the dashboards. All towards the goal that as many people as possible could use these visualizations, and that they could do it successfully and efficiently.

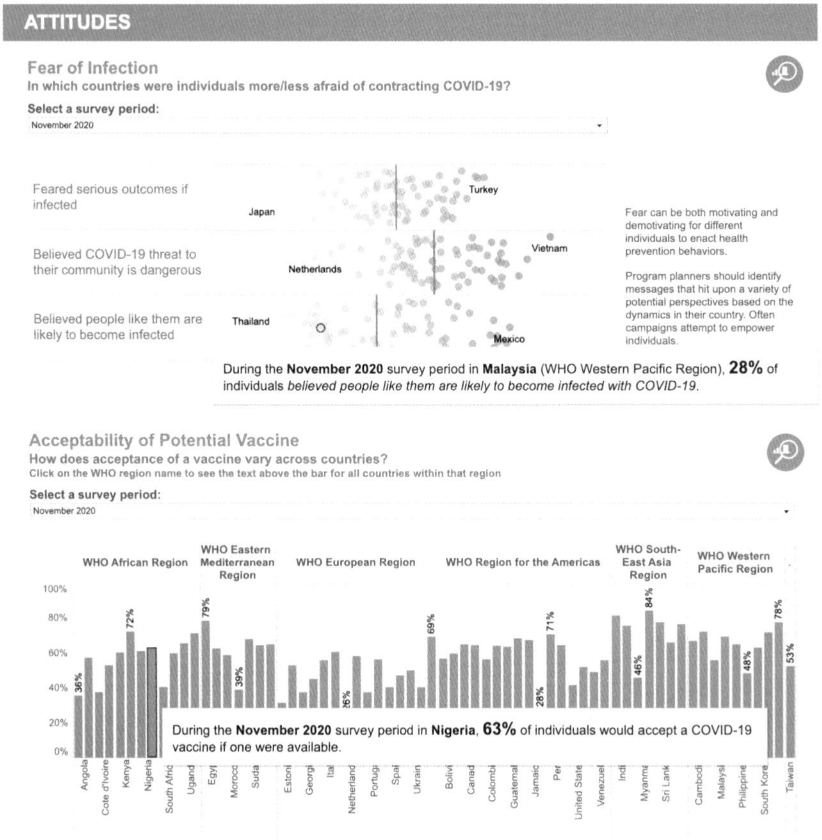

Figure 10.5: Examples of annotations from "KAP COVID: Exploring Knowledge, Attitudes and Practices for COVID-19 Prevention"

As a consulting team working with the researchers, we wanted to ensure they could also modify the dashboards, which were built with Tableau. I'm just not a big fan of being the kind of consultant or vendor that you have to come back to whenever you have any tiny change request. If I can empower you with the ability to go ahead and make those changes yourself, I should do that.

"Empowerment," I wrote in my notebook. I had suddenly realized that empowerment is a key motivation for some of the designers I spoke with for this section of the book, whom I'm calling "ambassadors." They aren't just interested in gathering, analyzing, presenting, or making sense of data for you, but also, whenever it's feasible, *with* you.

To do that, these designers create tools and tutorials, organize workshops, or write about the intricacies of data and graphics (**Figure 10.6** appeared in an article by Amanda) to bring as many people as possible up to speed. They sometimes warn us about the dangers posed by the widespread misuse of data, like Amanda does but, at the same time, they also wish to demystify it, to make it more approachable, less imposing—and much friendlier.

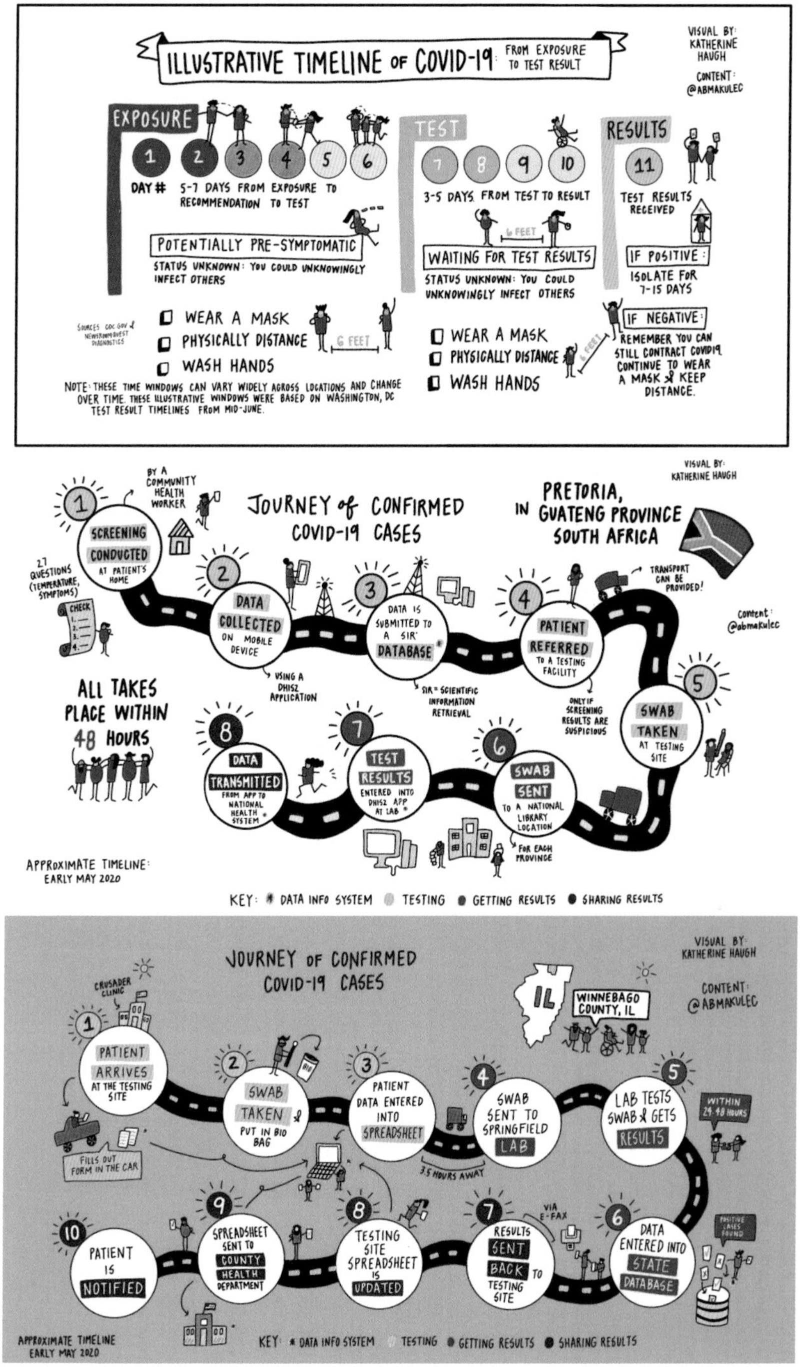

Figure 10.6: Illustrations by Katherine Haugh for "How Is COVID-19 Case Data Collected?" https://medium.com/nightingale/how-is-covid-19-case-data-collected-9afd50630c08

Figure 11.1: "An Illustrated Guide to Data Literacy: Base Rate Fallacy"
Alli Torban / Data Literacy / https://dataliteracy.com/an-illustrated-guide-to-data-literacy-base-rate-fallacy/ / last accessed under April 19, 2023

Chapter 11
with Alli Torban

Making Data Friendly

One is educated not merely because of what one knows, but as much or more for the manner in which one learns.
—Timothy Fuller

A couple of years ago, my mother phoned me to share her alarm at the large number of vaccinated people being hospitalized for COVID-19 in Spain, where she lives. That number was increasing, so she wondered whether vaccines and boosters were working as they were supposed to.

Alli Torban's data literacy comics brought back memories of that conversation. One of them in particular, about base rate fallacies (**Figure 11.1**,) would have come in handy. Vaccination rates in Spain have been high since COVID vaccines became available. However, even if you're vaccinated there's a chance that you'll get the disease and develop complications. When the number of people who get vaccinated increases and eventually becomes a substantial majority, more of them will end up in the emergency room; this might fool us into thinking that there's something strange going on.

Alli works for Data Literacy, a company founded by Ben Jones, who has written several books about data science and visualization. Like Allen Hillery (Chapter 9) or Amanda Makulec (Chapter 10) Alli is an information designer whose main aim is to make elementary scientific and statistical reasoning more accessible:

That's related to my own shortcomings. I come from a math family. My mom was a math teacher and I have a bachelor's degree in math, but understanding numerical things doesn't come quickly to me. I don't have a natural inclination for numbers, so it's always helped me to look at visuals and to design them.

I've been doing comics about these topics for a while, even before I began working at Data Literacy. I guess that what I'm trying to do with them is to not talk over people's heads. Rather, I want to bring more people into the circle of understanding data. I also want to make this circle wider and more accessible and inclusive. I want people, regardless of what their background is, to feel that thinking about data isn't something esoteric or beyond their reach.

I told Alli that her comics remind me of Ben Orlin, a math educator and author of a popular weblog and book titled *Math with Bad Drawings*. Ben's book is very quotable: "It is a funny paradox of design: utility breeds beauty. There is elegance in efficiency, a visual pleasure in things that just barely work." Alli agrees with that line of thought:

I became interested in information design, illustration, and data visualization gradually beginning in the late 2010s. Even before that I began designing seriously and making a living out of it. I also had a blog and a podcast. Back in 2018 I interviewed visualization designer Sonja Kuijpers [Chapter 5] and I got inspired by the way she uses glyphs and arranges them into landscapes. I wanted to do something along those lines. I got data from the Data Visualization Society about women in our field, and I visualized it (**Figure 11.2**).

I published this graphic online, and it quickly became really popular. However, if I had designed it today, I'd have done it differently. It's cute and amusing and it looks nice, but it makes it hard to see any sort of pattern in the data. Nowadays I strive for readers to be able to take something useful away from my graphics without having to dig too hard to get it. I'd love to maintain the friendliness of this graphic, though. Based on the reactions it got, I tend to think that it achieved what I intended, which was to connect the reader to the topic at an emotional level.

Alli's visual style is warm and friendly, and so are her voice and writings. In the past five years she's published numerous tutorials and judicious opinion articles in which she showcases examples of visualizations that are playful and approachable. For instance, when teaching readers how to design a bee swarm plot with a free visualization tool called RAWGraphs, and how to style the results in Microsoft's PowerPoint, she used a data set about—what else?—bees (**Figure 11.3**.) A bit obvious? Perhaps, but this is the kind of fun example that I'd use myself if I had to introduce young students to data science.

I've been following Alli for a while, first as a listener of her podcast and later as a fan of her design. Her path to becoming a visualization professional was different to those of other people in this book. It was conscious and deliberate—and also challenging:

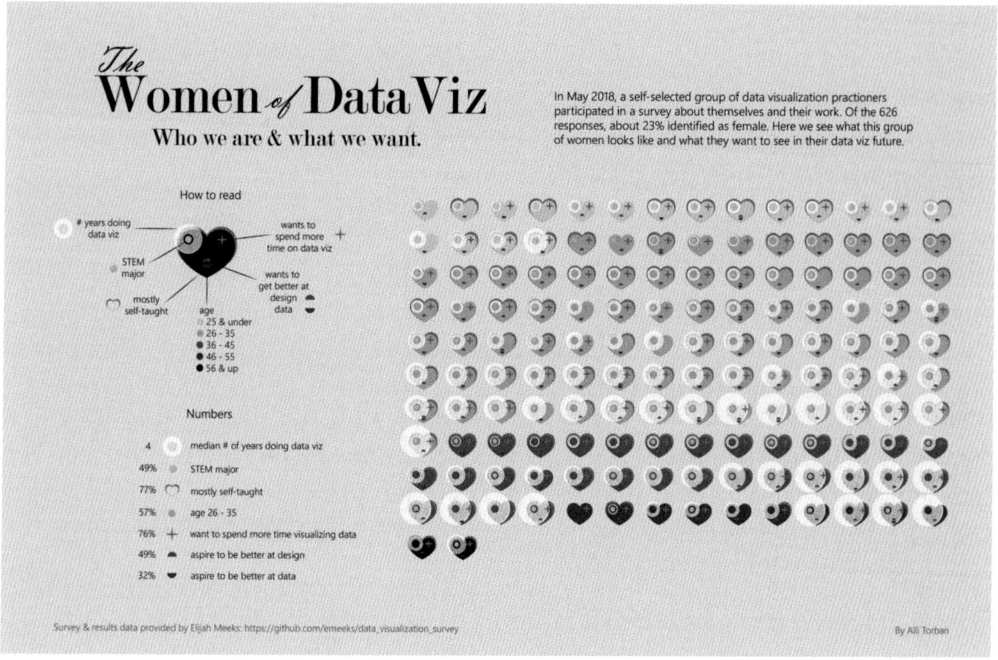

Figure 11.2: "The Women of Data Viz: Who we are & what we want"
https://dataviztoday.com/shownotes/28

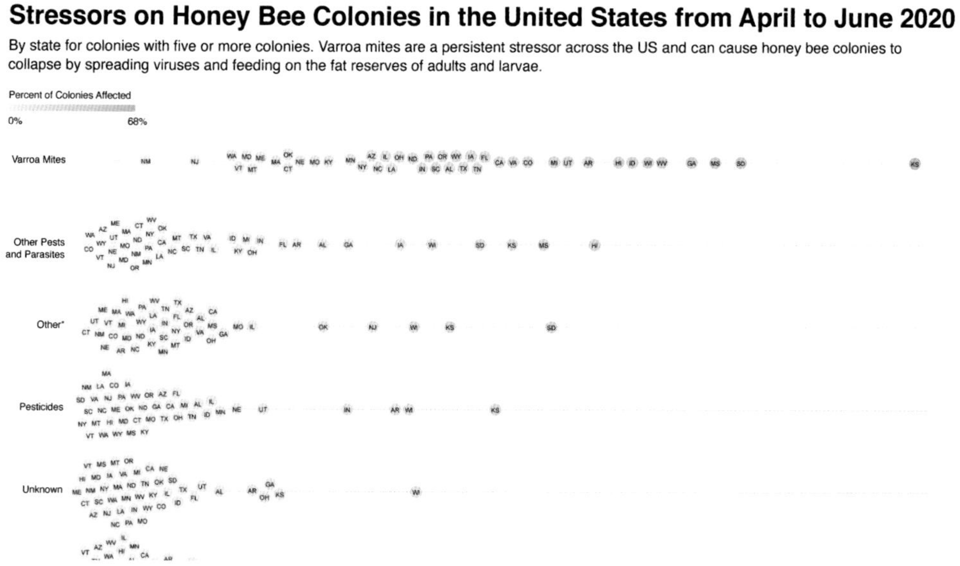

Figure 11.3: "Stressors on Honey Bee Colonies in the United States from April to June 2020"
https://dataliteracy.com/how-to-make-a-beeswarm-plot-in-rawgraphs/

Around 2008 I started working as a business systems analyst. My job involved a lot of software testing for government clients in the Washington, DC, area. I was receiving plenty of offers for jobs such as actuarial analyst, but my heart was elsewhere. I was already intrigued by visualization. I also needed a job that gave me some flexibility and allowed me to stay at home. My two kids were born in 2013 and late 2015, and I was their main caregiver.

Around this time I was listening to many podcasts. You know, when you're holding babies, doing chores, washing bottles, and all that, you try to keep your mind busy. One of my favorite podcasts was Moritz Stefaner's and Enrico Bertini's *Data Stories*. I think that I discovered it by happenstance, just by searching for data podcasts to listen to. Moritz and Enrico—their personalities are so infectious. They just make visualization sound so much fun! I realized, okay, this could be a career for me.

At the same time, I didn't want to do any formal courses. I couldn't spend money and I had two babies to take care of, so I looked for resources online and began teaching myself visualization and tools such as Mapbox, Tableau, and others.

I was perplexed. I take care of two teenagers, and being able to concentrate on any long-term endeavor—as a matter of fact, even writing this very book—is hard enough. I can't imagine how I'd get anything done if my kids were *babies*:

Well, I taught myself visualization mostly when the babies were napping during the day, or at night. It's really lonely being home all day with babies, so I thought that it was better to have something both enjoyable and productive to do.

And then the COVID-19 pandemic began. I was feeling anxiety at night. I couldn't sleep well and I was consuming too much news on TV and social media. I needed to get my mind and hands busy as a distraction, so I began designing dataviz-inspired wallpapers with a drawing app on my phone. One hundred wallpapers later, my illustration skills were at a point that I could start using them in my information design work. I was able to expand my dataviz skills to include infographics and illustration.

In fact, Alli became so much better at illustration that in the past few years she's authored several covers for visualization books, such as Jen Christiansen's *Building Science Graphics* (2023) or Neil Richards's *Questions in Dataviz* (2023).

I think that among my most recent projects, book cover illustrations are the ones I enjoy working on the most. They involve talking to authors and trying to capture some sort of essence of who they are and what they say in the book, and then reflect that essence through abstract drawings that resemble actual data visualizations. It's a lot like what I was doing with my dataviz wallpapers!

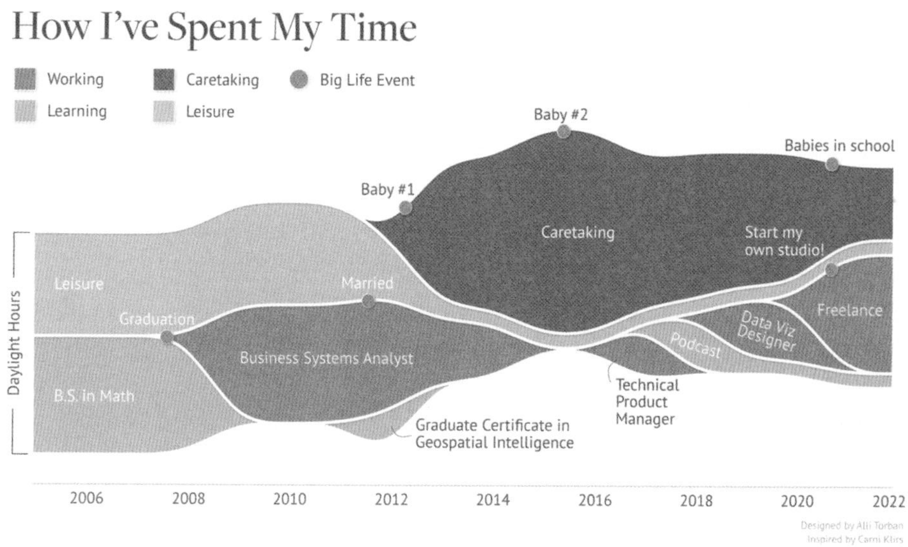

Figure 11.4: "How I've Spent My Time"
https://www.allitorban.com/iib/

Even Alli's most straightforward data visualizations have a certain artistic quality to them. In 2022 she visualized how her daily activities have varied due to shifts in her personal and professional life (**Figure 11.4**). Notice the subtle use of texture in the background, making the visualization look like it's painted on a canvas.

This chart shows many other things I've done in the past five or six years. For instance, I did some freelance data journalism on the side, but it paid very little. I love illustration and visualization, but I also need to get paid for it! For a while I had a wonderful job at the American Enterprise Institute (AEI), a conservative-leaning think tank.

I learned a lot as part of AEI's design team, and it was a golden opportunity for me because they agreed to hire someone who had little experience in visualization. At AEI I was able to interact with scholars who needed to show their data to the public, or to create interactive visualizations based on their numbers for the organization's website. And I was the only one in the team who knew how to do that. That gave me a lot of creative freedom.

Alli has continued collaborating with scholars to this day. One of her most recent projects is a series of illustrations for a paper by Eli Holder and Cindy Xiong titled "Dispersion vs Disparity: Hiding Variability Can Encourage Stereotyping When Visualizing Social Outcomes" (2022). It discusses how visualizations can perpetuate harmful stereotypes about minorities.

Imagine that you compare the incomes or educational attainments of four groups of people. Perhaps because you've heard the common mantra "in visualization, always keep things simple!" you decide to calculate measures of central tendency—the median, the mode, or the mean are typical. Then you plot just those statistics.

According to the experiments that Holder and Xiong conducted, by doing this you might be reinforcing fallacies and biases. One is the fundamental attribution error, our tendency to attribute other people's behavior to just their personality without considering environmental factors. The other is deficit thinking, which consists of explaining group differences by relating them to characteristics—or supposed defects—of individuals in those groups.

For instance, if you see a bar graph showing that Group A has a higher average income than Group B, you may be tempted to think that most—or even all—people in A are richer than people in B (first illustration in **Figure 11.5**.) You may even conjecture that such disparity is a result of people in A being more hard-working and *better* than people in B, and not a consequence of external constraints, obstacles, or incentives. This is stereotyping.

To reduce stereotyping when visualizing social outcome disparities, Holder and Xiong propose displaying distributions instead of measures of central tendency. Charts such as strip plots or jitter plots (third illustration in **Figure 11.5**) show that there's a lot of overlap between people in different groups. In any set of distributions, in-group variability may be larger than inter-group variability.

This is a difficult concept to grasp, so it was an opportunity for Alli to experiment with visual metaphors:

> Before I was involved in this project, some people reviewed the paper and were a bit confused, so they brought me in to design these illustrations. While brainstorming them, the word that stuck out to me was "optics," as I remembered the optic diagrams we all see in school. Depending on the lens through which you perceive a reality, your mind's eye's interpretation of it may vary substantially. The charts that we design to depict reality are those lenses.

One of Alli's early sketches for this project (**Figure 11.6**) is, in fact, an optic diagram. At the time of our conversation, Alli was working on her first book, tentatively titled *Data Unboxed: 10 Friendly Lessons to Develop Your Creative Practice in Data Communication*. I read its first draft, where she explains:

> The word metaphor derives from the Greek word *metapherein*, which means "to transfer." We use metaphors to suggest a point of similarity between two things. That's the power of metaphor.

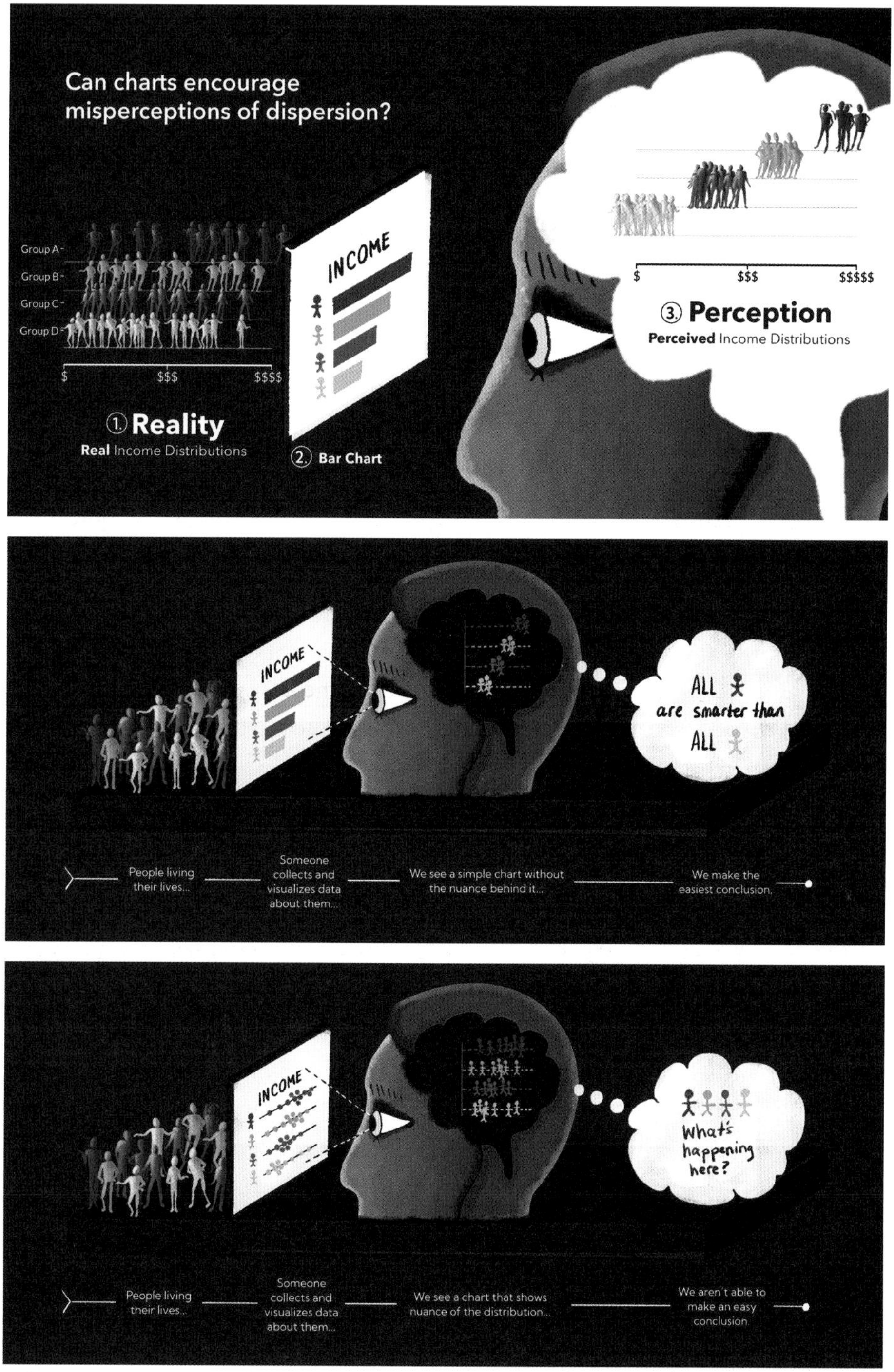

Figure 11.5: Illustrations for "Unfair Comparisons: How Visualizing Social Inequality Can Make It Worse" https://nightingaledvs.com/unfair-comparisons-how-visualizing-social-inequality-can-make-it-worse/

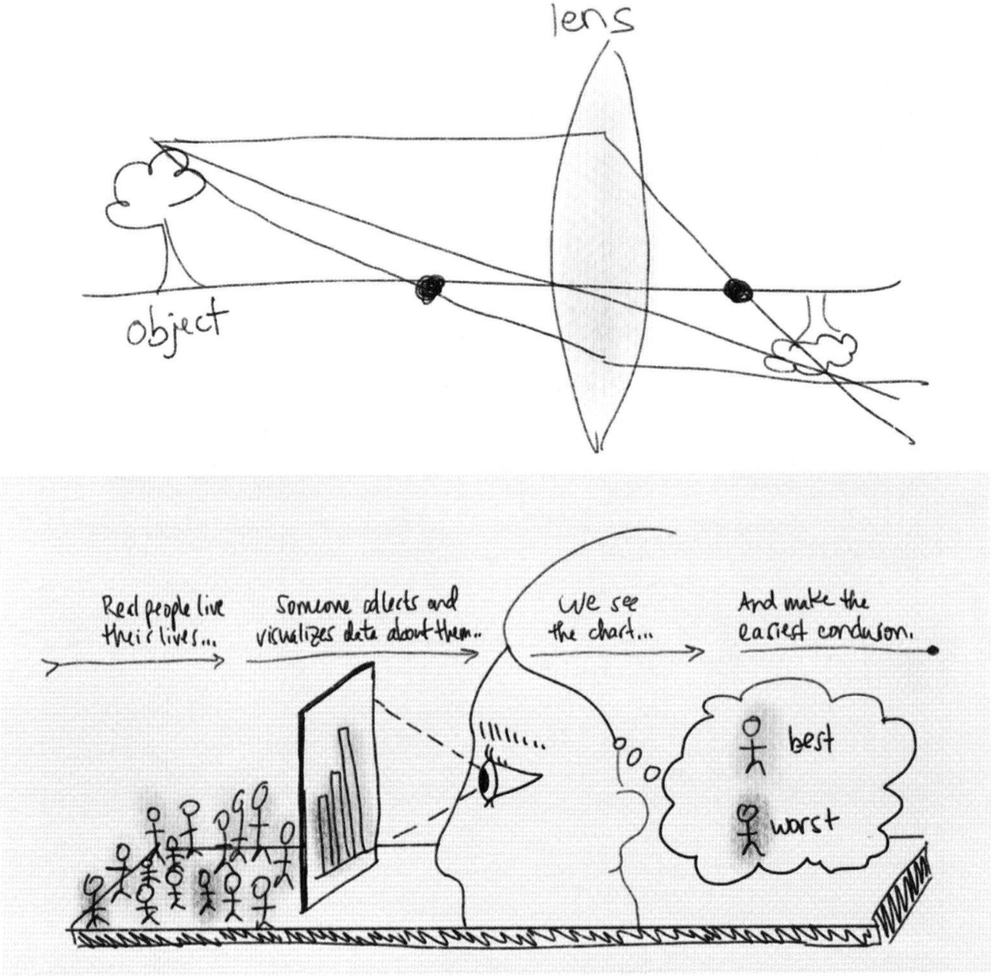

Figure 11.6: Sketches for "Unfair Comparisons: How Visualizing Social Inequality Can Make It Worse"

> So, what's a *visual* metaphor? It's when we use visual cues to convey the metaphor. When a designer uses a visual metaphor, they can seamlessly transfer information and trigger extra emotions in our minds, just like how we use metaphors when we write and speak.

Years ago, designer Mike Monteiro gave a talk to my students at the University of Miami. He told them, "We need to fear the consequences of our work more than we love the cleverness of our ideas." Mike's book *Ruined by Design* (2019) expands on this line of ethical reasoning. Mike wrote:

> You are responsible for what you put into the world. And you are responsible for the effects those things have upon the world [...] As long as you are a designer, you have a responsibility to make

> the world better for the rest of humanity. If you are a designer, you are a human being first. It is your job to stop those that would denigrate humanity for their own selfish benefit.

Think about Holder and Xiong's research and of Alli's illustrations next time you hear anyone suggest that "data speaks for itself" or that visualization designers should worry only about the correctness of their decisions and not about the consequences of those decisions; in the case of visualizations, how they might warp perceptions. Having evidence that certain choices can lead to spreading or solidifying harmful stereotypes gives us a good reason to act in a different way. Holder and Xiong wrote in their paper:

> Rather than chase false simplicity, our designs should lean into the messy truth.

In other words, visualizations intended to communicate or to reveal patterns in data should be as clear as possible; however, to make something clear we shouldn't remove crucial contextual detail just because we feel that it makes our graphic needlessly complicated or aesthetically cluttered. Instead, clarity depends on striking a balance between showing too little and showing too much.

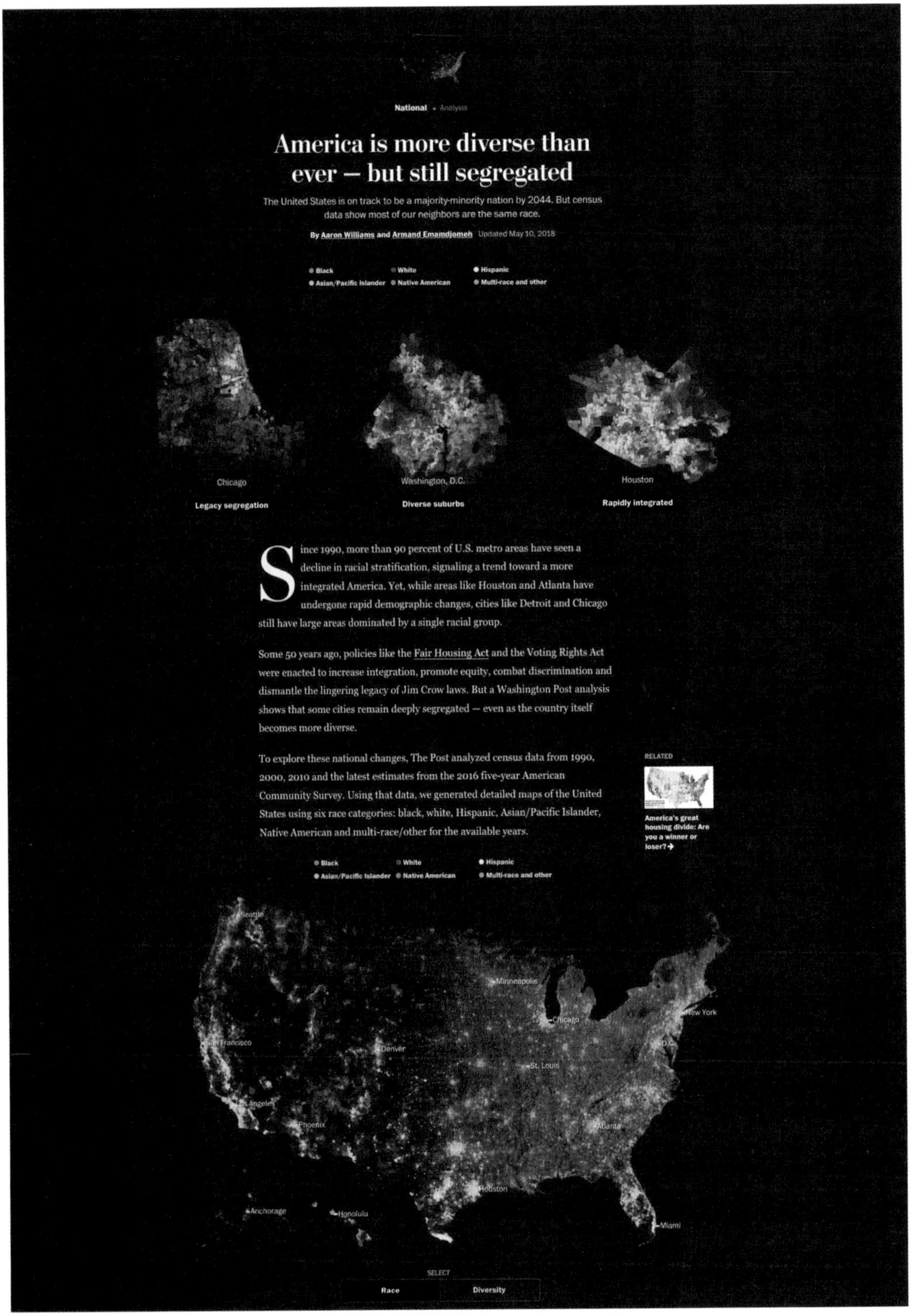
National • Analysis

America is more diverse than ever — but still segregated

The United States is on track to be a majority-minority nation by 2044. But census data show most of our neighbors are the same race.

By Aaron Williams and Armand Emamdjomeh Updated May 10, 2018

Since 1990, more than 90 percent of U.S. metro areas have seen a decline in racial stratification, signaling a trend toward a more integrated America. Yet, while areas like Houston and Atlanta have undergone rapid demographic changes, cities like Detroit and Chicago still have large areas dominated by a single racial group.

Some 50 years ago, policies like the Fair Housing Act and the Voting Rights Act were enacted to increase integration, promote equity, combat discrimination and dismantle the lingering legacy of Jim Crow laws. But a Washington Post analysis shows that some cities remain deeply segregated — even as the country itself becomes more diverse.

To explore these national changes, The Post analyzed census data from 1990, 2000, 2010 and the latest estimates from the 2016 five-year American Community Survey. Using that data, we generated detailed maps of the United States using six race categories: black, white, Hispanic, Asian/Pacific Islander, Native American and multi-race/other for the available years.

RELATED

America's great housing divide: Are you a winner or loser?

Figure 12.1: Opening images from "America is more diverse than ever – but still segregated" by Aaron Williams and Armand Emamdjomeh / washingtonpost.com / https://www.washingtonpost.com/graphics/2018/national/segregation-us-cities/ / last accessed under April 19, 2023"

Chapter 12
with Aaron Williams

A Reporter among Engineers

> *You don't work for the people who sign your checks.*
> *You work for the people who use the products of your labor.*
>
> *—Mike Monteiro*

"What does a journalist do at Netflix?" I once asked **Aaron Williams**. Before his current job, Aaron was a graphics reporter at *The Washington Post*. There he produced some of the most compelling data-driven journalism I've seen in decades (**Figures 12.1** and **12.2**.)

He laughed:

> Well, when Netflix reached out to me I was as confused as you are. I was like, what the hell? But, I learned that what I do today isn't that different to what I used to do at the *Post*.

Netflix hired Aaron in 2020. His current title is "data visualization engineer" although, contrary to what I thought before we spoke, his role isn't just designing dashboards or other visual tools to explore and analyze data:

> Like any other technology company, Netflix generates a large amount of data that is, on its own, incomprehensible. Think about what we data journalists are really adept at. We take a bunch of information and try to produce a narrative out of it so an audience can understand it. That skill is incredibly useful outside of the news media.

Figure 12.2: Screenshots from "America is more diverse than ever – but still segregated"

> There are folks out there who will say that I work in tech now, but I think that I still work for a media company that just happens to have a smart tech staff and a lot of infrastructure.
>
> In a lot of ways I feel that I am still effectively a data journalist, but now my readership isn't anybody out there who pays a *Washington Post* subscription, but people within Netflix who can benefit from understanding the data the company generates.

When Aaron left journalism—perhaps temporarily; he admits that he misses the daily grind of the newsroom—the website Open News interviewed him about his love for the craft, and the differences between his former job and his current one at Netflix. Aaron said:

> I spent large parts of my career convincing editors I was a journalist, full stop, and that the data and design aspects of my skill set aided in that endeavor. Early in my career, I was able to rise up the industry rather quickly and was offered far more competitive salaries than I would've gained had I just tried to compete as a beat reporter because of my software skills. Writing code felt like a cheat code to journalism job security. But that specialization over time yields friction. Data journalism is often treated as a singular beat, when in reality it's another type of reporting that can be utilized across newsrooms and for any topic.

These frustrations with journalism were somehow compensated by the freedom to pursue topics of personal interest, such as racial segregation, which he tackled in his famous "America is more diverse than ever – but still segregated" (2018.) It's a sobering piece consisting of a narrative that weaves maps of racial stratification and an interactive feature where readers can look for their own cities and zoom to their neighborhoods or blocks:

> This started as a passion project that I worked on during my spare time. It emerged from my personal experiences. I'm a Black American from the San Francisco Bay area, so I have an interest in the interactions between racial and ethnic segregation, gentrification, and diversity variation.
>
> That's why the project lets readers toggle between two different types of maps. The first type are dot density maps of races and ethnicities. These look beautiful, but they show you just where people live; a dot density map is just putting one dot per person in some kind of space, and you end up with population maps.
>
> If you want to say anything meaningful about the data, you need some way of measuring relationships. The second set of maps addresses this. They show a statistical index of racial and ethnic uniformity or diversity called the multigroup entropy index (**Figure 12.3**) for every census tract. Green areas are more evenly distributed in terms of race and ethnic groups, so they are more integrated than segregated.

I told Aaron that I thought that the style choices he made in this story—colors, type, the way he structured the narrative—were key to its popularity. He replied:

> Data visualization often gets talked of as a science, and it is in a lot of ways. However, when I talk about the segregation project with people, they ask me about its aesthetics. Why I used the dark background and those bright colors that pop out. Those are purely aesthetic choices.
>
> This story had been in the back of my mind for a long time but I felt that I had neither the technical ability nor the knowledge of aesthetics or visual design to execute it. As I slowly matured at the *Post*'s graphics desk as a journalist, a programmer, and a designer, things changed. When the segregation project was published I tweeted out that it was the most ambitious and complicated math reporting project I had ever created, and that still holds.

Figure 12.3: Diversity map of Miami from "America is more diverse than ever – but still segregated"

There was pride in Aaron's voice when he said that, so I probed him about his curiosity for new techniques and technologies:

> I'm self-taught on everything, and I've always felt the need to be on the cutting edge. Not just by showing the rest of the newsroom how powerful data journalism or data visualization can be, how they can enrich our stories, but also purely from a technical standpoint. How do we work with data as it scales higher and higher, for instance? The tools and techniques I used in the segregation project or in our investigation series about the opioid epidemic, titled "The Opioid Crisis," aren't revolutionary by any stretch, but they weren't that common in journalism back in 2018 or 2019.

"The Opioid Crisis" is a series of stories that was a Pulitzer Prize finalist for public service journalism in 2020. The first piece we discussed was "The Fentanyl Failure" (2018). It chronicles the Obama administration's missteps in dealing with the widespread use of that synthetic opioid between 2013 and 2017. Fentanyl was at the time the leading cause of overdose deaths in the United States:

> This story in particular was a good example to show the newsroom what data journalism can do. Our whole coverage of the opioids crisis is based on the biggest data sets the *Post* had ever worked with up to that year. Compared to the data sets I work with today at Netflix, some of these data sets were small, something like 170 gigabytes, but in a newsroom this was a big accomplishment.
>
> Sometimes data journalism is treated as some sort of secondary genre, like an offshoot of "real" journalism. However, at least from my perspective, there is no way you can actually do the work of a journalist without using at least some data. It's a prerequisite in order for you to tell a story accurately.

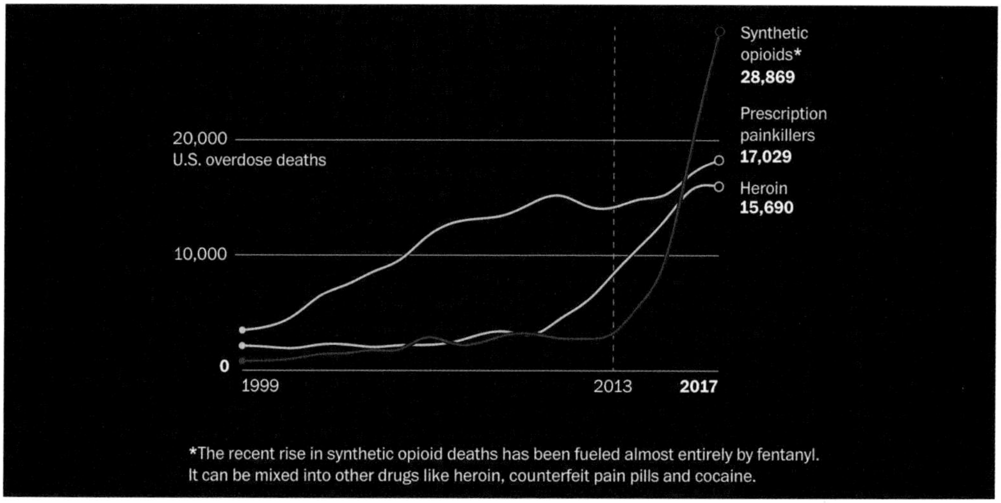

Figure 12.4: First chart from "The Fentanyl Failure"
by Scott Higham, Sari Horwitz, and Katie Zezima, with graphics by Aaron Williams
https://www.washingtonpost.com/graphics/2019/national/fentanyl-epidemic-obama-administration/

Back in 2019 my former graduate student Alyssa Fowers (Chapter 16), today a graphics reporter at the *Washington Post*, interviewed Aaron about the Fentanyl story. Alyssa and I were planning to write this book together, but her hiring by the *Post* got in the way. She allowed me to reproduce the part of her conversation with Aaron where they talked about the structure of "The Fentanyl Failure," and how it seamlessly combines photos, text, graphs, and a series of dot cloud charts:

> We wanted everything to feel like it belonged. Often when you see news stories that have graphics or any kind of visuals, they can feel like they were slapped into the story. It shouldn't be like, oh I'm reading text, now I'm looking at a graphic, now I'm looking at a photo, now I'm looking at text again. Your brain shouldn't have to do these kinds of cognitive switches. It should come to you very naturally. I was really trying to keep the cognitive burden as low as possible. You shouldn't have to think too hard.

> We thought a lot about the placement of the graphics. It's chronological, the story starts in 2013 and works its way to 2016. The line chart that opens the story [**Figure 12.4**] is straightforward, very Tuftean in style, very simple. I didn't use hard edges on any of the lines. I used a curved line to make it feel a little more organic.

> I could have opted for a bunch of other ways to visualize this, but these go-to forms are often the best. This chart is also a good example of the *Post*'s style of graphics, a mixture of annotation and visual elements, dropping most grid lines or tick marks, and letting the graphic blend with adjacent spaces.

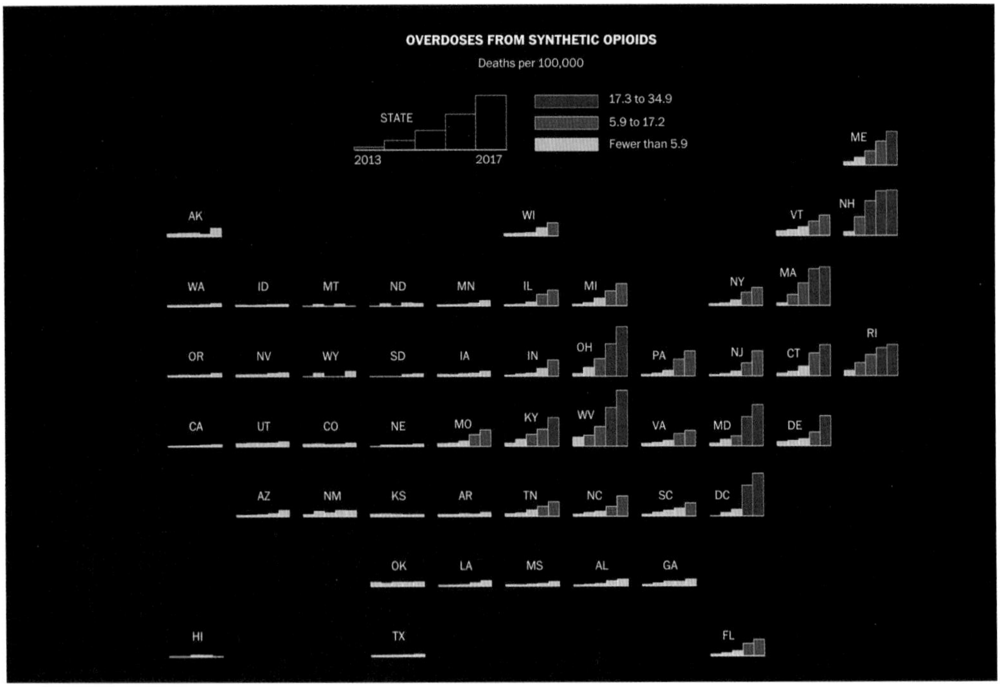

Figure 12.5: Cartogram from "The Fentanyl Failure"

Alyssa told Aaron that the colors in "The Fentanyl Failure" are striking. She usually thinks about colors such as purple and pink as friendly, but in this story they are anything but, especially in a cartogram that appears later in the article (**Figure 12.5**):

> I didn't want the visuals to cheapen the story or the victims or the impact of this drug. I almost always use counterintuitive colors, not because I like to be difficult, but because I want the data, not the color palette, to evoke a reaction. In a story about murder or violence, I avoid using red or any other color to evoke emotion at all cost. I'm not trying to manipulate anyone. I want you to look at the data and then have a human response.
>
> Regarding the way that the data is presented, I'd always wanted to do a small multiples cartogram. In many cases, if you can just see what you need to see with a very simple bar chart, I prefer to go with that form. Those forms exist for a reason! They're really effective at communicating information, so I try not to get too esoteric with my charts. But in this case, geography was an important component of the story because the epidemic begins in New England and makes its way to the Midwest.
>
> The hardest part of this wasn't the cartogram, it was the legend. As someone who has stared at this chart, I think it's intuitive, but I had to assume that a reader might have no idea what the hell they're looking at. The legend we put on the top of the graphic was the tenth legend designed for this, because there is so much packed in such a small space. Even if you don't sit here and study

Figure 12.6: Dot chart from "The Fentanyl Failure"

the legend, though, I think we were able to convey the big picture. If the reader can do a quick drive by and see the overdose hot spots, then I did my job as a designer.

Aaron then talked about a series of dot clouds in the middle of the narrative (**Figure 12.6**):

Data informs these graphics—the number of dots corresponds to the number of people who died that year. As you scroll through the article, this intense blob of dots gets larger and larger, and showcases the sheer size of this epidemic. But I didn't want readers to infer meaning that wasn't there, so I didn't group the dots in any way. In the beginning there wasn't a lot of tracking of fentanyl deaths, it wasn't even being tested for by morticians. So it's fitting that the visualization is kind of amorphous and foggy to represent that limitation of the data.

We didn't want to add too much annotation to these graphics, because then you would instinctively try to find patterns, when there are none. We were simply trying to illustrate the sheer amount of people dying year over year. Restraint was an important principle that stuck through the entire project.

The *Post*'s "The Opioid Crisis" contains some pieces that aren't linear, but exploratory, such as an interactive database of every single one of the more than 100 billion pain pills sold in the United States between 2006 and 2014 (**Figure 12.7**.) In hindsight, Aaron sees projects like these as critical for his current role at Netflix:

Sometimes we data journalists think this way: Do you want to see all this data we collected? Here is a giant interactive database! However, you soon realize that most readers aren't data analysts or researchers. Even analysts don't want to hunt and peck and seek and find data.

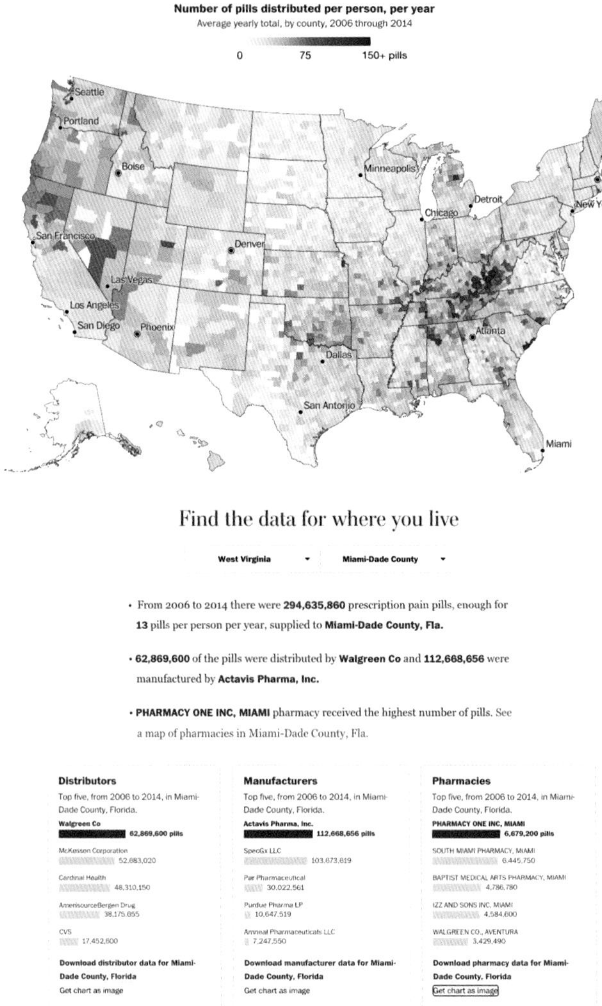

Figure 12.7: "Drilling into the DEA's pain pill database"
https://www.washingtonpost.com/graphics/2019/investigations/dea-pain-pill-database/

If every executive in the company needed to slice and dice through tons of different charts and dashboards, that would take a lot of their valuable time when they need to make a decision. They don't want to do the analysis themselves. They want the narrative. And even if you're designing an interactive dashboard, you can still lose the viewer if the information isn't presented in a way that makes sense.

This is why we're seeing several cases of data journalists and data visualization designers being hired at places like Netflix. We have a very unique skill set. I'm not talking just about tools. People who become journalists usually choose this career because they are curious and they care. You get to cover a lot of different topics and that forces you to learn how to get very smart about them very quickly.

This is something that I miss about working in a news organization. I also miss the impact that good journalism can have on the world. I don't miss the industry, though; there are glass ceilings for professionals like us. Once you reach a certain point, you can't climb up further. I also don't miss the politicking.

I often tell my University of Miami students that there's a difference between working *in journalism* and working *as a journalist*. You can of course do both, but the former is a job and the latter is a way to be in the world and to look into it. Aaron doesn't work in journalism anymore, but he keeps being a journalist at heart.

My information design and visualization classes at the University of Miami are part of our Journalism and Media Management program. However, nine out of ten of my students are never going to work in journalism or in any related field. They come from data science, computer science, statistics, climatology, biology, or our medical campus.

I see this as a sign of an increasing awareness among specialists of the need to communicate information truthfully and accurately, but also clearly, elegantly, and concisely—without losing much depth. Ideally, that's what journalism should be about.

Figure 13.1: "History of Philosophy," early 2014 version
Deniz Cem Önduygu / https://www.denizcemonduygu.com/portfolio/the-history-of-philosophy/ / last accessed under April 19, 2023

Chapter 13
with Deniz Cem Önduygu

The Therapy of Visualization

Let nobody put off doing philosophy when he is young, nor slacken off in philosophy because of old age. For nobody is either too young or too old to secure the health of the soul.

—Epicurus

On October 8, 2018, philosopher Daniel Dennett tweeted to his more than three hundred thousand followers: "Here's a surprisingly useful thinking tool for anybody interested in the history of Western philosophy: a sort of garden of forking paths of argument." That thinking tool was an interactive arc diagram by information designer **Deniz Cem Önduygu** (**Figure 13.1**.) If you aren't into philosophy, maybe Dennett's name might sound unfamiliar, but I can tell you that at the time I thought that his praise was a big deal. Dennett is one of the foremost philosophers of science and of mind, author of books such as *Consciousness Explained* (1991) and *Darwin's Dangerous Idea* (1995.) His tweet prompted me to look into Deniz's visualizations and to ask him for a conversation, which began with some details about his childhood:

> My mother was a neurologist and my grandfather was an engineer, so I grew up around lots of medical illustrations and mechanical drawings. My home was a nurturing environment that allowed me to explore many areas of knowledge. Also, since I was very young I was interested in drawing both figurative art and abstract diagrams. I ended up studying industrial design and did an MA on visual communication design, but I've always kept an eye on other areas, such as

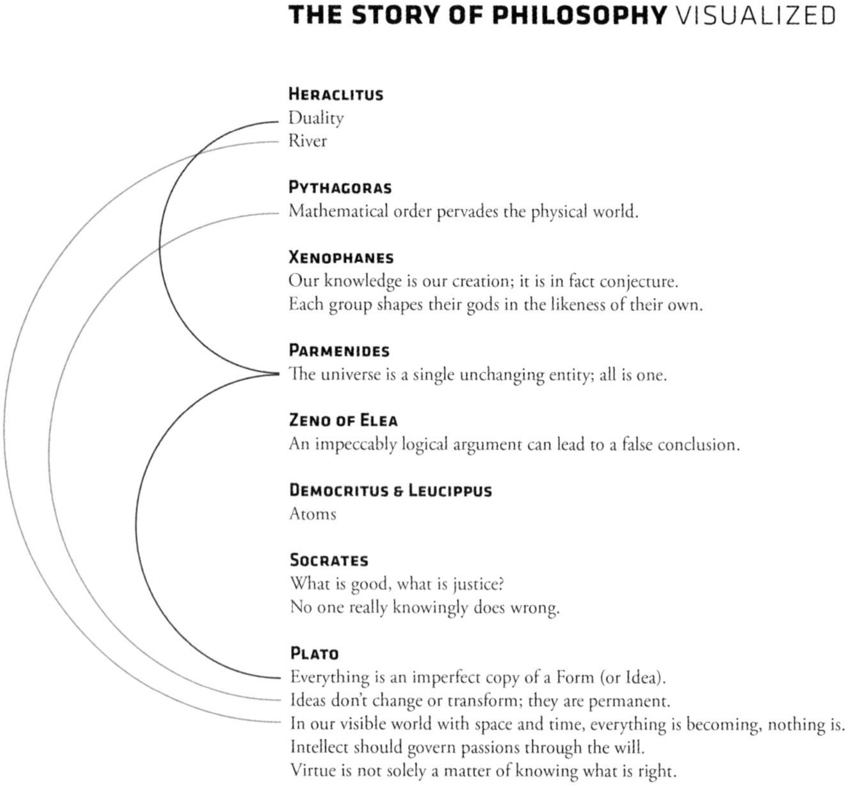

Figure 13.2: One of the first sketches for "History of Philosophy"

the natural sciences, the visual arts, neuroscience—and philosophy. In 2010 I even started doing a PhD in biology, but the life of a PhD student wasn't for me, partly because I have a hard time being told what to read! I enjoy the freedom to dig deeply into any subject that I find fascinating. That's one of the reasons I love doing information design.

Around 2004 I read Bryan Magee's *Story of Philosophy* (2001). I found myself taking tons of notes, probably too many for a visual thinker like me. The history of philosophy consists of people building on other people's ideas, agreeing or disagreeing with them, expanding on them or trying to refute them. To understand how thinkers interacted with one another, I used color-coding and tables in Word documents. One night in 2012, I had the idea of listing sentences and connecting them with lines and I created some crude diagrams.

Those early sketches (**Figure 13.2**) remained in my computer for two years before I produced the first version of the project in 2014 in collaboration with my friend Eser Aygün who is a computer scientist. Then we started developing an interactive version in collaboration with Hüseyin Kuşçu. The visualization is generated algorithmically from a spreadsheet, so I have been

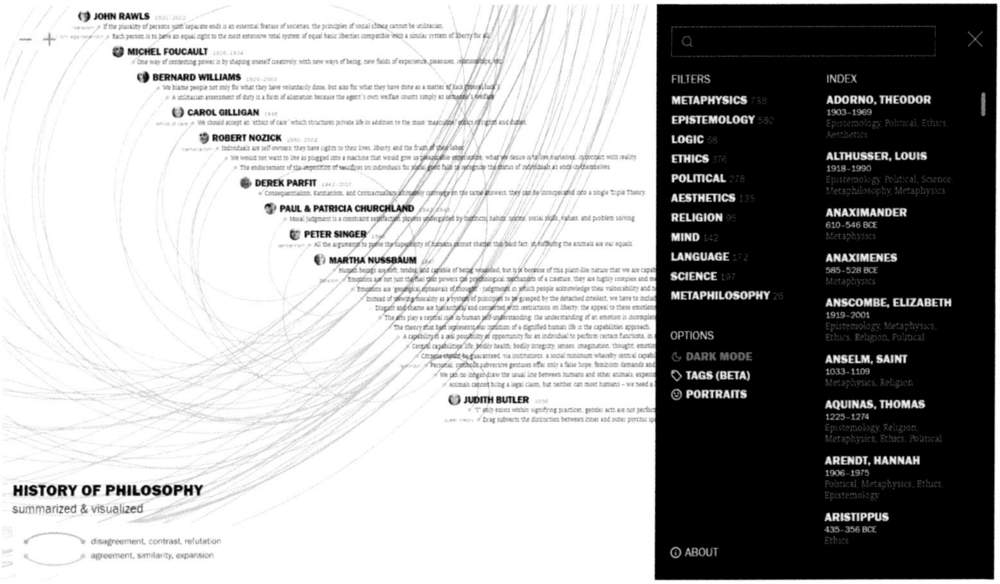

Figure 13.3: A screenshot from "History of Philosophy" centered on philosopher Martha Nussbaum

> updating it with new information for the past decade. Whenever I read a new philosophy book or article, I incorporate new thinkers, sentences, and connections. It started with 377 sentences and now it has 1,626. As years go by I've also improved the interface and added new features.
>
> I strive to be true to what each author said but, ultimately, this is a diagram that I designed as a mnemonic aid for myself, so there's some subjectivity to it especially in what I choose to include in the summaries. It's a reflection of my own interpretations of what I read, but I constantly get messages from readers telling me that they have benefited from it. I also know it's being used in schools around the world. I get a lot of satisfaction from that.

I've benefited from Deniz's "History of Philosophy" myself. I've explored it multiple times, looking for topics that intrigue me—epistemology, ethics, or the philosophy of mind—and for thinkers that I've enjoyed reading, such as William James, Bertrand Russell, Derek Parfit—or Martha Nussbaum (**Figure 13.3.**)

Throughout a long and fruitful career, Nussbaum has touched upon too many topics to be captured in a visualization. Deniz's graphic correctly displays, for instance, her many agreements with Aristotelians and her disagreements with Platonists or Stoics on matters of human emotions. However, connections to other thinkers whom I know she's written about, such as the Hellenistic philosophers, are missing.

I don't see these gaps as a shortcoming, however. When I was a high school student my father encouraged me to draw mnemonic diagrams for myself. I ended up being able to

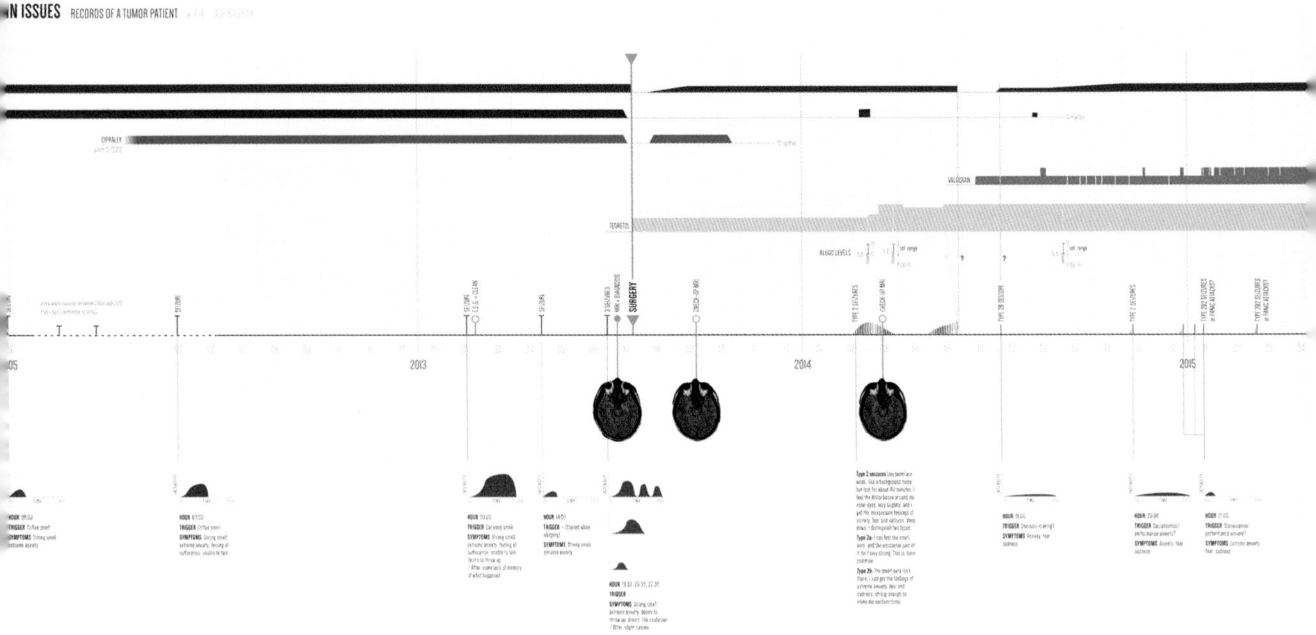

Figure 13.4: "Brain Issues"
Deniz Cem Önduygu / https://www.denizcemonduygu.com/portfolio/brain-issues/ / last accessed under April 19, 2023

summarize long books in just two or three pages of dense and intricate network charts and I know that they don't need to be thorough and comprehensive to be useful for their authors.

A typical misconception about mnemonic diagrams is that they are mere records, external ways to store what we learn and want to remember. That's inaccurate. Mnemonic diagrams interact with preexisting knowledge. They may prompt remembrance thanks not only to what they show, but also to what they omit.

The lack of connections in Deniz's graphic between Martha Nussbaum and the ancient Hellenistic philosophers—Epicureans, Skeptics, Stoics—summoned in my mind memories of her encyclopedic *The Therapy of Desire* (2018). That book explains that Hellenistic thinkers conceived of philosophy as a medicine for the soul: "They practiced philosophy not as a detached intellectual technique dedicated to the display of cleverness but as an immersed and worldly art of grappling with human misery."

These thinkers saw philosophy as the practice of weeding out false beliefs so true ones can flourish and lead to happiness.The sheer process of acquiring knowledge about ourselves and our very nature as sentient creatures, they claimed, mitigates anxiety and al-

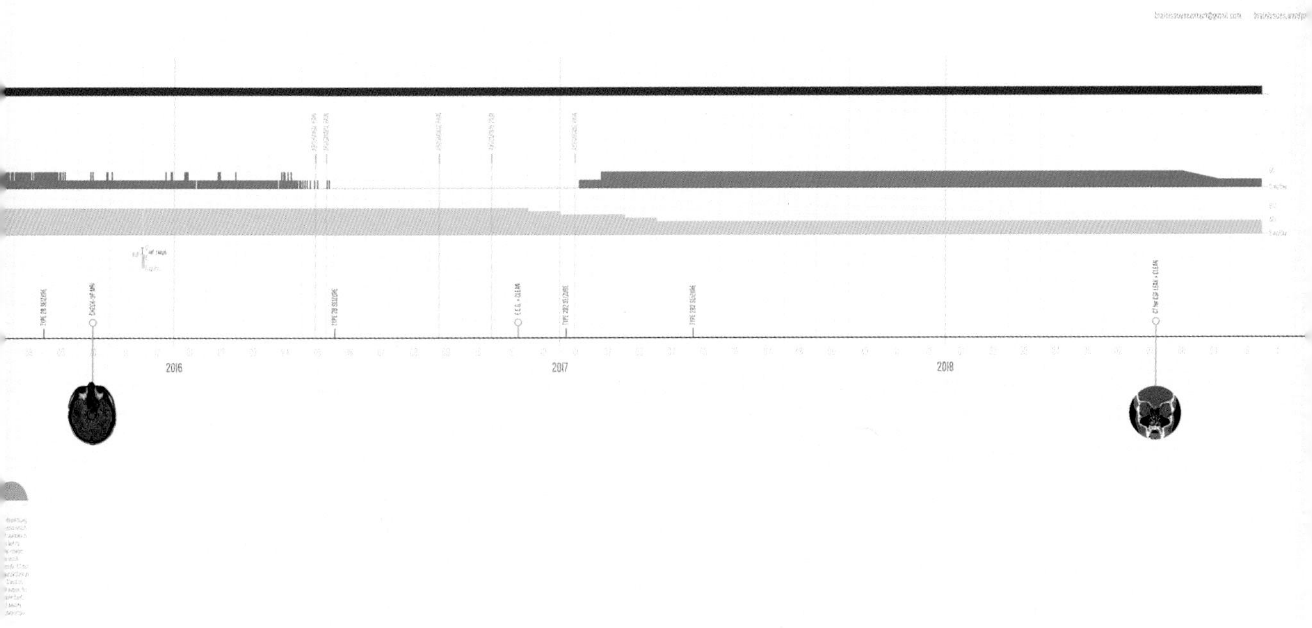

leviates suffering. Deniz mentioned a similar restorative aim when we discussed some other visualizations, such as his "Brain Issues" (**Figure 13.4**):

> In 2013 I had surgery to extract a brain tumor. I had probably had it for a long time, but it didn't cause symptoms. Eventually, though, its growth led to my experiencing seizures.
>
> Before and after a surgery like this you have to take medications every day, go to regular check-ups and make many decisions about your health. You also need to control other variables such as the amount of sleep you get, how you feel physically and mentally, and so on—and you're encouraged to monitor them. I'm a visual thinker, so is there a better way to do that than a visualization? There have been many cases where these visualizations led to important insights about my health which were instrumental in making decisions.
>
> Friends and family have told me that this project and also my "Vital Signs" (**Figure 13.5**), where I record many other variables about my life besides health-related ones, are expressions of my desire for control. It's true. Temperamentally, I'm a bit of a control freak. For years I've been trying to slowly lower that impulse and to reduce my level of alertness. Besides leading to actionable insights, seeing data about myself from a distance, making it something external to me, probably helps manage anxieties.

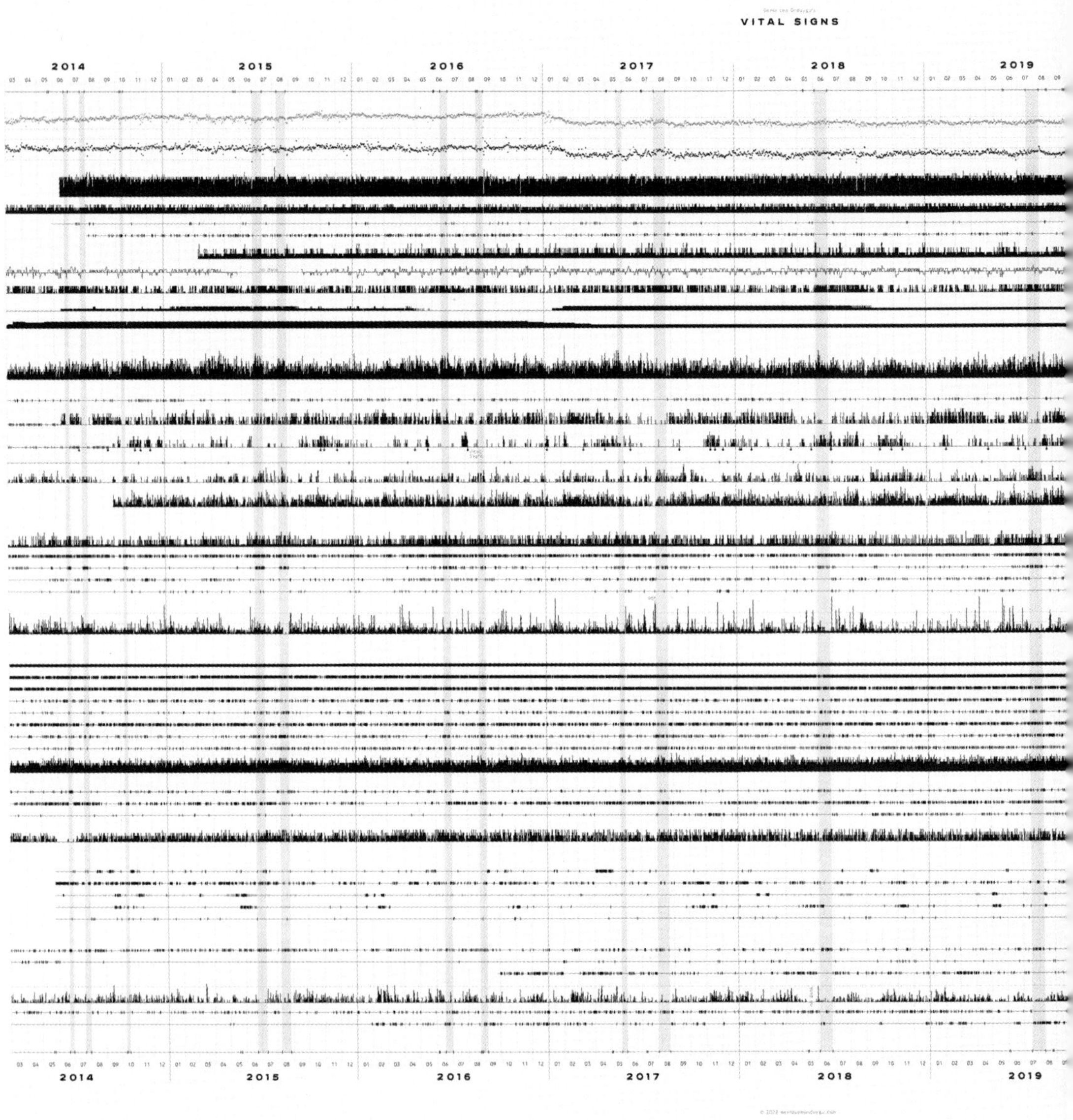

Figure 13.5: "Vital Signs"
Deniz Cem Önduygu / https://www.denizcemonduygu.com/portfolio/vital-signs/ / last accessed under April 19, 2023

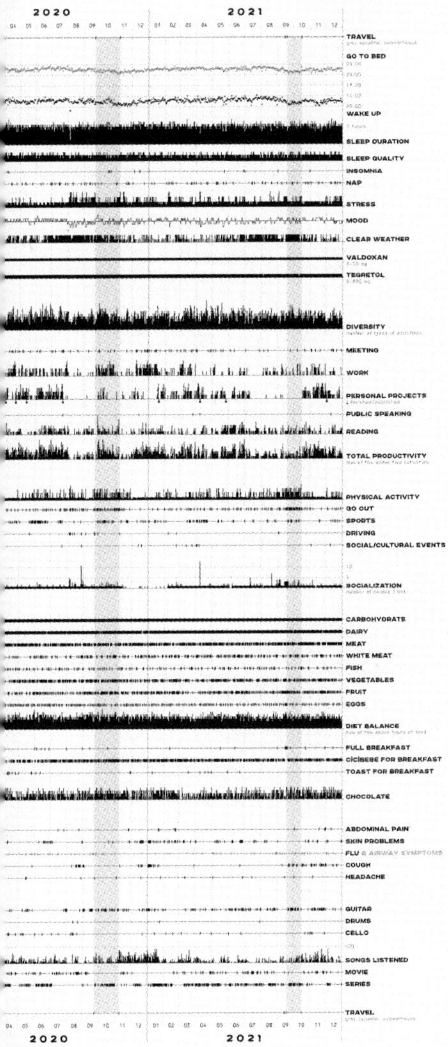

Deniz's self-tracking projects are reminiscent of Nicholas Felton, a designer who between 2005 and 2015 published personal annual reports quantifying and visualizing many aspects of his life. Deniz discovered his work years after he began tracking his own personal data, but Felton's software tools came in handy:

> I use Felton's app Reporter twice a day to log my daily data, when I wake up and when I go to sleep. In the evening I fill out a questionnaire that I devised for myself in that app. It takes me about five minutes, and I've been doing it for nearly a decade. I visualize the data and publish the updated version every year.

We then switched to the style of his graphics. Deniz deliberately employed a sterile style in "Brain Issues," and even more so in "Vital Signs":

> These graphics look "boring" to most people, I know! I'm using that word in an ironic sense. I guess they might be boring if you expect visualizations to always be colorful eye-candies. I wished to defy that expectation. When the data or the concept is strong, visual simplicity can make it stronger.
>
> I also like the tension between how I see life—full of rich experiences, sights, smells, tastes—and how it's depicted in "Vital Signs," as a large collection of black-and-white, very simple charts. Obviously there is an insufficiency, a desperation in representing our experience of life with bar charts, and I like the humor in this. But, however desperate and funny it is, this project is a tool that can reveal patterns I wasn't aware of.
>
> I know that you and I share this love for simple and functional designs with rich data. I believe that in visualization we need to have a good reason for every choice we make and every feature we add. I formulate

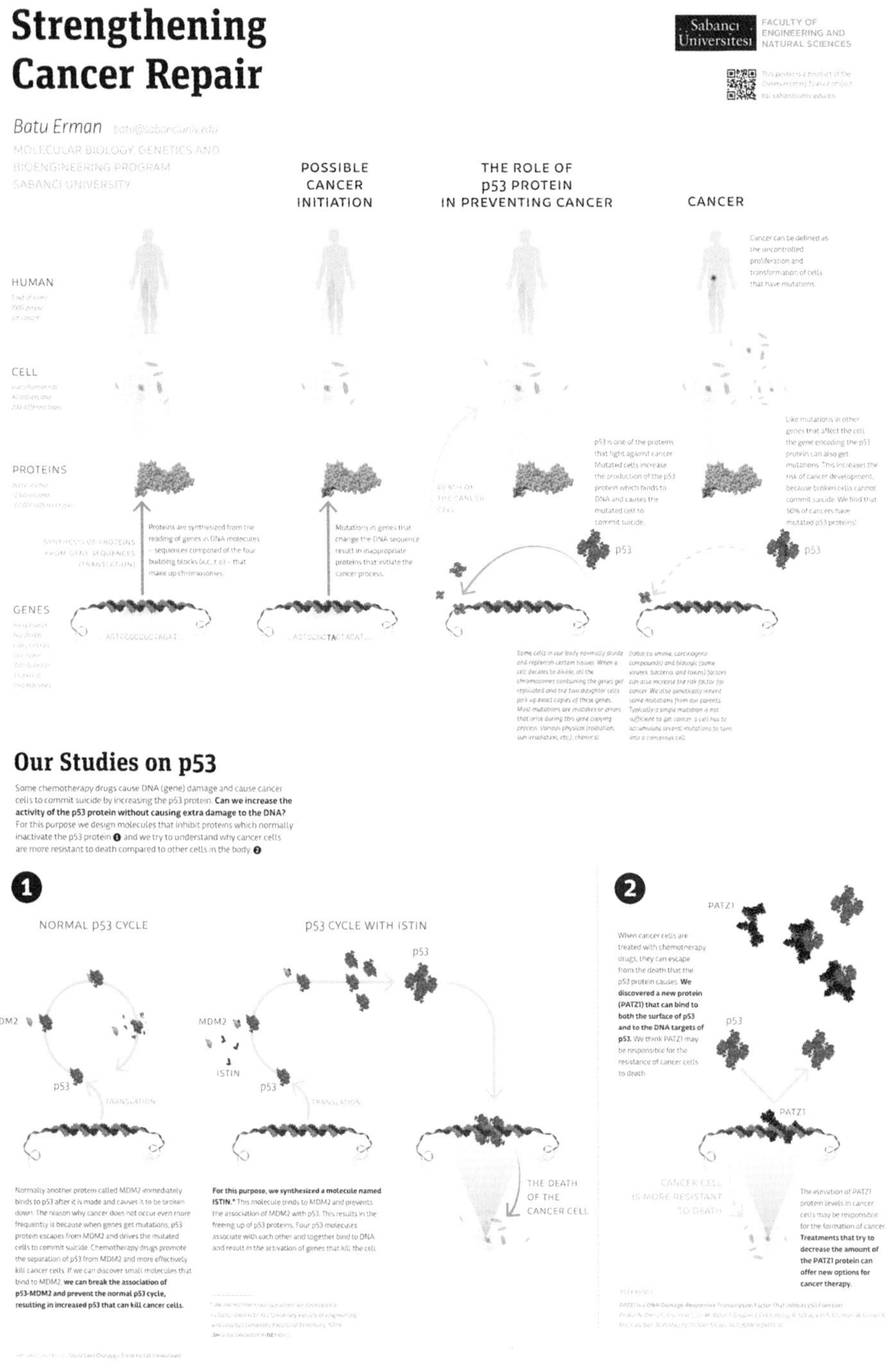

Figure 13.6: "Communicating Science"
https://www.denizcemonduygu.com/portfolio/communicating-science/

my methodology in two questions: "What can I add (in terms of data, concepts, media)?" and "What can I remove (in terms of visual elements)?"

Since I come from a design background, I have a solid sense of the standard distinctions between art and design, decoration and function, etc. I've always felt close to modernism and minimalism ever since I had my first college courses on art and design history. I respect designers having different theories, styles, or priorities, but I see what I do as visual engineering for analytical thinking. I'm less interested in appeal, impact, or memorability in my personal work, so the evidence that decoration can increase these things doesn't convince me to use it.

Deniz is both a designer and an educator. He's taught his minimalistic style to researchers and science students in a series of events organized by Sabancı University, near Istanbul:

Sabancı University is where I did my masters degree. Years ago they invited me to organize a few workshops to help scientists communicate their research outside of their fields. I don't "teach" in these workshops. What I do instead is to demonstrate how a collaboration between researchers, their students, and designers can work if the purpose is to translate the science to general audiences.

Scientists in attendance and I first brainstorm every component of a scientific poster that we intend to create. We discuss its information architecture, the elements that it should contain, and we write the copy for it. After discussions and plenty of sketching, I take care of the execution of the poster itself. I draw any illustrations, graphs, or diagrams we agree on.

The posters that Deniz and his collaborators have created are spare and elegant (**Figure 13.6**). Thanks to these workshops, Deniz says, many scientists have realized that information design isn't just about assembling pretty visuals:

Some scientists were a bit skeptical at the beginning. Perhaps because of their lack of experience and exposure to information design, they thought that it's just decoration, and not worth their time. Moreover, some of them didn't even feel the need to communicate with the public, they don't see the value of that side of science, and wish to focus just on their research. That's a respectable position.

That said, many of the participants realized that the brainstorming portion of the workshop was useful. During our discussions they didn't just think about how to present their work to their peers, to future grad students, or to non-specialists, but often they also encountered questions about their work that they hadn't thought about before.

Of course, they were happy to end up with well-designed posters and graphics to use at conferences and in their publications or presentations. However, I have never been able to persuade

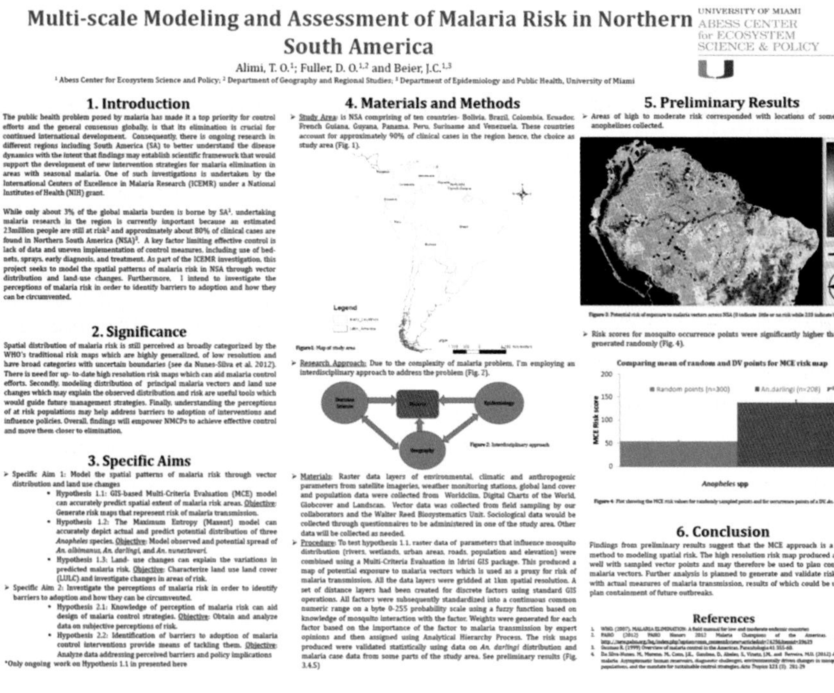

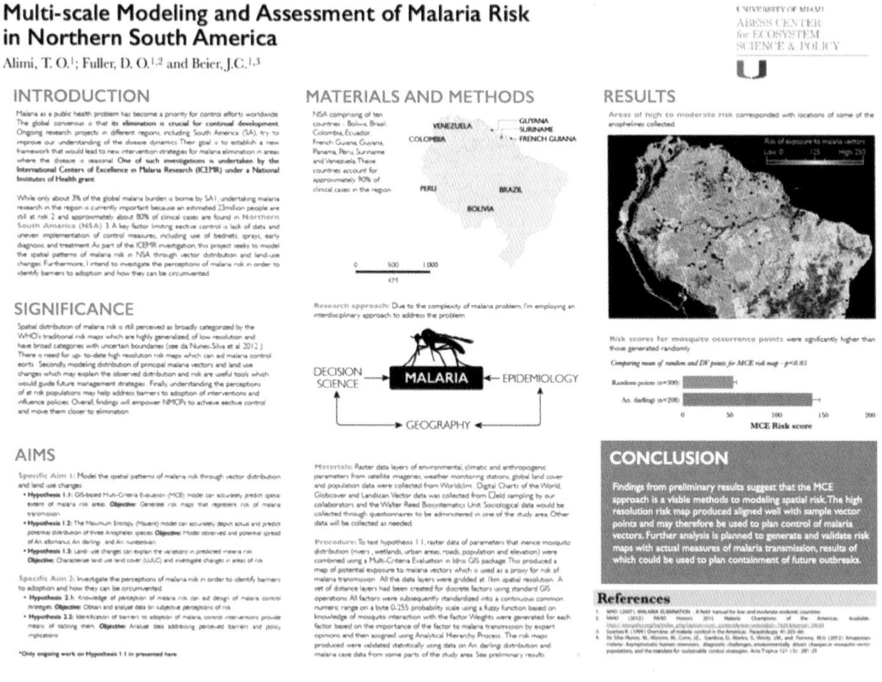

Figure 13.7: A poster by University of Miami students and a quick makeover to exemplify some elementary design tricks

100% of attendees of the value of information design—but I guess that convincing a smaller percentage is still good progress.

Changing a handful of hearts and minds at a time is indeed progress. For years I've wished that more historians, librarians, philosophers, or literature scholars would pay attention to their colleagues in the digital humanities or at least—like Daniel Dennett did when he saw Deniz's "History of Visualization"—that they'd acknowledge that graphics can be tools for reasoning. It's the same with scientists.

Something that Deniz told me at the end of our conversation made me smile: "I always wonder why scientists love putting everything inside boxes." **Figure 13.7** shows a poster designed by graduate students and faculty from the University of Miami's Abess Center for Ecosystem Science & Policy who attended one of my workshops. Below it there's a quick-and-dirty makeover that I created to exemplify some design fundamentals, such as hierarchy, stylistic unity and variety, the importance of negative space, and so on. I also encouraged workshop participants to use fewer background boxes, and only when they are needed to emphasize a piece of information or a section.

Moreover, I asked them to strive to override software defaults. "You don't want your graphics to look like they come from a mindless computer tool," I said, "as you wouldn't want your writing to sound like it was spouted by a word generator." As a reader, I like to notice that there are actual human beings behind the writings and designs I engage with, making sensible choices to improve my experience.

Did I persuade everyone at that workshop? I guess not. However, a few weeks later some of the graduate students in attendance sent me a few new charts and posters. There were far fewer boxes in their designs, and their style was much more pleasant and polished. My brief ambassadorship to their realm had succeeded.

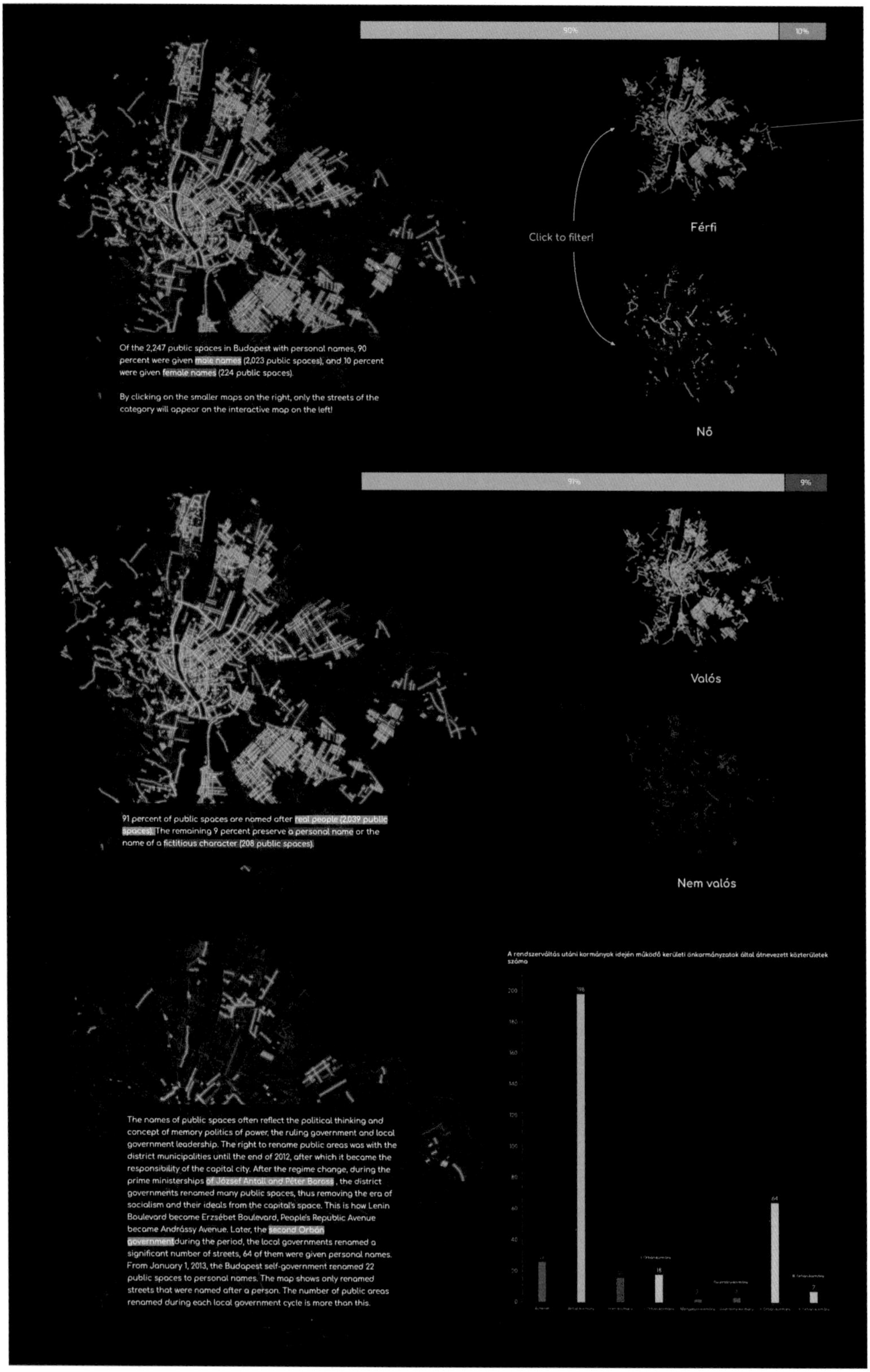

Figure 14.1: Screenshots from "Names and Spaces: Street Names of Budapest" by Attila Bátorfy and Krisztián Szabó / http://adatvizualizacio.bparchiv.hu/budapestiutcanevek/ / last accessed under April 19, 2023

Chapter 14
with Attila Bátorfy

The Public Intellectual

Liberty is a tunnel that must be dug by hand.

—Paul B. Preciado

"I notice that many streets in Budapest were renamed during the second prime ministership of Viktor Orbán," I told data journalist, visualization designer and professor **Attila Bátorfy**. We were talking about his "Names and Spaces: Street Names of Budapest" (**Figure 14.1**). In it, a bar graph quantifies streets that were renamed after the fall of communism. Orbán's three terms—out of four; he was reelected in 2022—are colored orange. I asked Attila, "who were those streets renamed after?" He replied: "Some named after fascists, antisemites—it was a big scandal."

Countries where authoritarian ideologies are growing deep roots fascinate me. Hungary is among them. Since 2010, Viktor Orbán, his political allies, and the cronies and oligarchs he's cultivated have transformed the country into a postmodern kleptocractic autocracy or, as they prefer to call it, an "illiberal Christian democracy."

In a 2016 paper, political scientist András Bozóki listed the key strategies of this type of regime. First, gaining hegemonic power by manipulating the electoral system and taking over key institutions, such as education or the judiciary. Second, developing a nationalism based on race and ethnicity. Third, denigrating and excluding certain groups—cosmopolitan intellectuals, immigrants, gays, transgender people, and so on. Fourth,—the most relevant for this chapter—colonizing culture and their symbols. Bozóki calls this "symbolic politics." Renaming streets and other public spaces is part of this fourth strategy, as it helps shape perceptions of history and national identity.

Attila's project shows that the highest number of street name changes, nearly 200, happened during the transition from communism to parliamentary democracy under Prime Ministers József Antall and Péter Boross (1990–1994.) The second highest occurred with Orbán, this time to glorify a mythical past inhabited by ancient Magyar heroes, and to whitewash dark episodes of Hungarian history, such as its alignment with Nazi Germany during World War II. Attila told me:

> I've seen similar visualizations about other countries, but I believe that "Names and Spaces" highlights the peculiarities of Hungary. For instance, the disproportionate amount of streets named after men, more than 90 percent, the politics behind name changes, such as the first democratic governments dropping the names of socialist personalities, or Orbán's prioritization of figures cherished by the far right. I designed this project for myself, it wasn't commissioned by anybody. However, one of my main sources for it was the Budapest City Archives, and they ended up publishing it.

Attila is an accidental investigative data journalist in a country whose government systematically smears critical news publications:

> To be frank, 15 years ago, fresh out of college, I didn't think about becoming a journalist. I have degrees in art history and in media studies, and my original goal was to become a media scholar. However, I was educated in the most liberal and most socially aware media studies department in the entire Hungarian educational system. It pushes you to become a public intellectual. It also teaches you that the responsibility of any public intellectual is to go after the government and the powerful, holding them accountable, forcing them to be transparent. When I had the opportunity to get a job in the news industry, I realized that, at least ideally, journalism shares those values.

That job was at *Kreatív*, a weekly magazine about creativity, media, and advertising:

> It was in 2008. The job paid relatively well. In 2010, around the time of the second Orbán government, I started to investigate corruption in the media, and the many newly created companies that were getting public money to design advertising and promotional campaigns for the state. Many hadn't done this type of work before. "Who was behind them?," I asked myself. It turns out that many were created by oligarchs close to Orbán's party, Fidesz.
>
> The tipping point for me was that I obtained a very large data set from a market research company that I needed to process somehow. That forced me to learn data analysis tools. In 2015 *Kreatív*

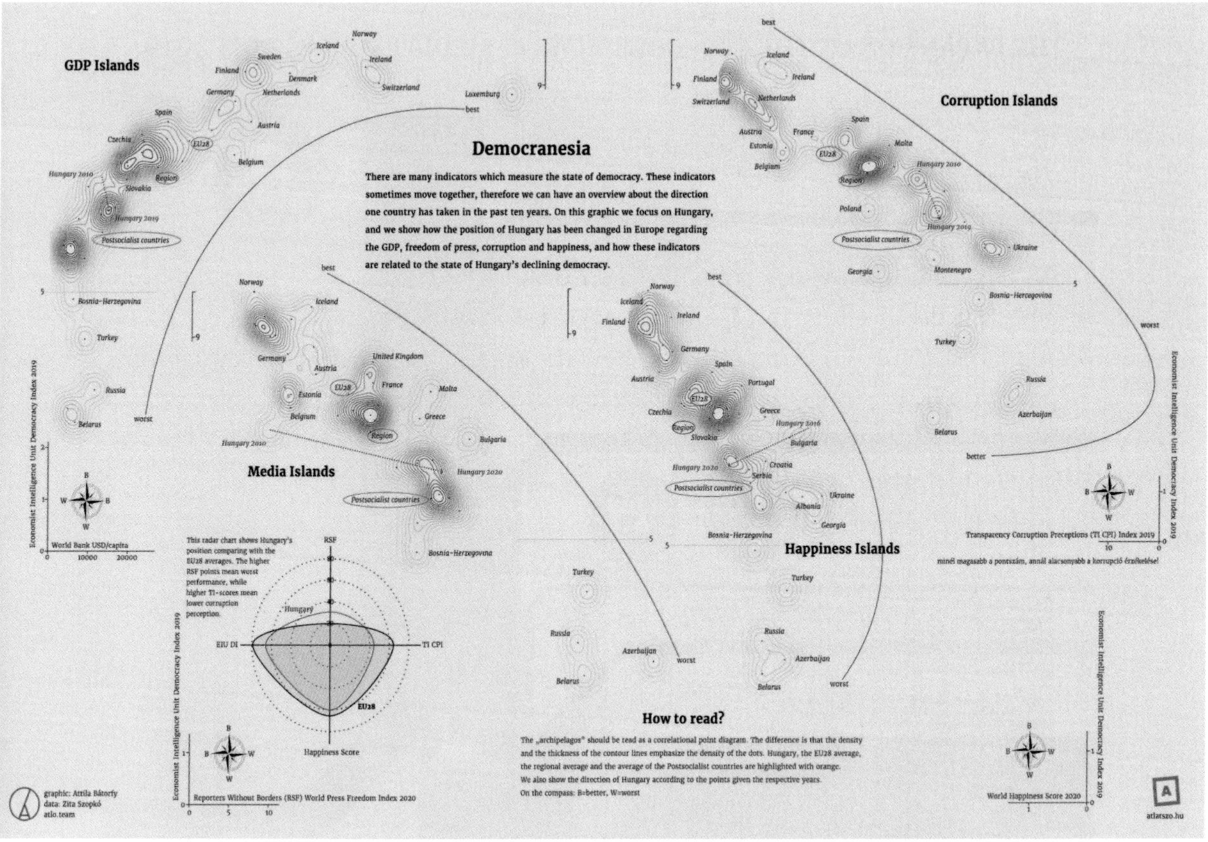

Figure 14.2: "Democranesia" by Attila Bátorfy and Ziza Szopkó
https://attilabatorfy.com/wp-content/uploads/2022/08/demokranesia.jpg

> published the result of my work, a long report about corruption in publicly funded advertising. Its print version was almost 100 pages with very basic and crude graphics, and it exploded on the Hungarian internet. I became a public figure, appearing regularly on television and radio, both local and international, to comment on Hungarian media and advertisement.
>
> From that point on, my colleagues called me a data journalist. This was new not just for me, but in the Hungarian media landscape. The minority of Hungarian news publications that aren't controlled by the government can do excellent journalism, and they publish some data and infographics. However, they don't do it at the same level of ambition as, say, the *Washington Post* or *The New York Times* which, by the way, I started copying at the time. For a while, I was the only person doing this kind of work, *the* data journalist in Hungary.

Attila has done extensive work on the connections between political corruption and democratic decline in Hungary. "Democranesia" (**Figure 14.2**) consists of a series of contour plots comparing indicators of well-being or happiness with levels of press freedom, perception of corruption, or democratic quality. The design of this project is very unique, so I asked Attila about it:

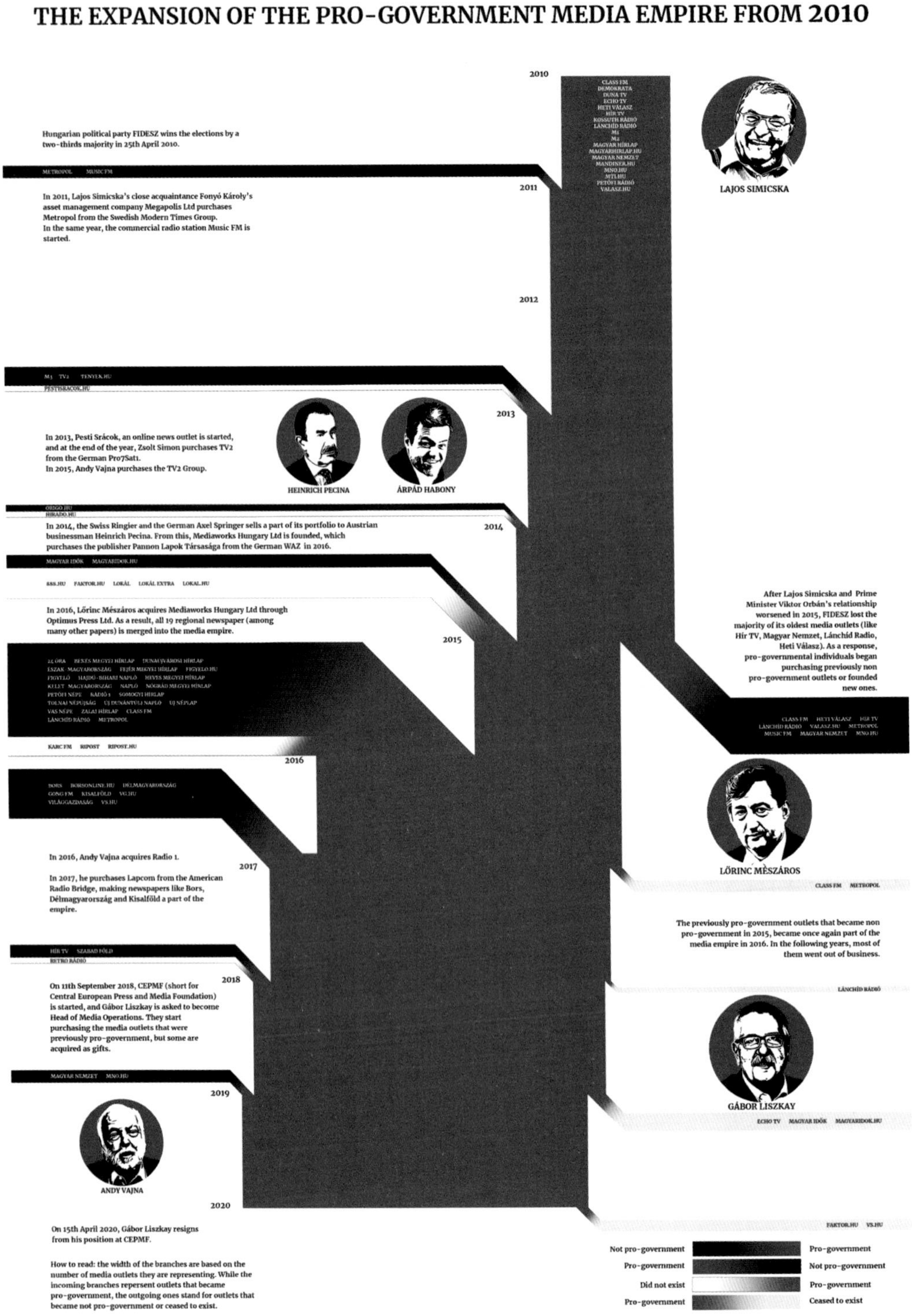

Figure 14.3: "The Past Ten Years of Hungarian Media" by Krisztián Szabó and Attila Bátorfy
https://atlo.team/media2020/

"Democranesia" is a more creative project that I also designed for myself, but that was picked up by the weekly magazine *Magyar Hang*. These charts are, in essence, scatterplots comparing two variables each, one on the horizontal axis and another on the vertical one. The density contours give the graphics almost a topographical feel, making them look like a map of an archipelago, especially over the blue background.

You may notice that Hungary appears twice in every plot. That corresponds to two points in time, for instance 2010 and 2020. I connected the two points with a line and an arrow to emphasize that most Hungarian scores have worsened.

Much of Attila's visualization work is a result of his collaboration with *Átlátszó* (which means *transparent*), a nonprofit investigative media publication launched in 2011 that acts as a watchdog. *Átlátszó* is funded through subscriptions, crowd-sourced contributions, and donations from entities such the International Press Institute (IPI), and Hungarian-American billionaire George Soros's Open Society Foundations. Soros is a *bête noire* of the far right worldwide. To certain people, he embodies a supposed vast Jewish mind-control conspiracy to spread liberal and globalist propaganda.

In November of 2018, *Átlátszó* and Attila launched ATLO (atlo.team) a publication dedicated to data journalism and visualization. Attila built a small team of designers and developers that, up to this day, has produced more than 60 stories. One of them, "The Past Ten Years of Hungarian Media" (**Figure 14.3**) is related to Attila's past work chronicling the takeover of the Hungarian media market by allies of Viktor Orbán's.

This project depicts the vanishing of real journalism in Hungary since 2010, and a phenomenon that experts call "media capture." Instead of trying to close down critical news publications, modern autocratic governments act in more insidious ways. For example, oligarchs allied with a ruling party fund hostile takeovers of independent media and, at least at first, they try to maintain a simulacrum of ideological diversity. Most publications controlled by the Hungarian government—directly or indirectly, through public advertising money—are still nominally independent, but they all avoid criticizing it.

The data sets that Attila has collected about the Hungarian media market have been used in academic research, some that he has co-authored himself. However, and despite the quality of its work, funding a project like ATLO in a small country like Hungary is hard:

Back in 2019 ATLO was about to close down, but the coronavirus hit Hungary and I told my editor-in-chief, Tamás Bodoky, that I wanted to do a monitoring site. Thinking that the pandemic would be over in a couple months, he was skeptical, so he told me to do it in my free time. This website quickly became a big success.

> That success was in part due to the fact that the government was disclosing only very basic data. We had to consult with dozens of other sources, such as hospitals and public health experts. My job became to manage more than one hundred emails a day and process all the data we got. We became the main source of information about the pandemic in the country, and even the Hungarian statistical office asked us for our data. We were making our data public anyway, as the main purpose of the project was to hold the government accountable.

My friend Luís G. Prado has lived in Budapest since 2016, and he's written two books of essays about Hungary, *Crepúsculo en Budapest* (*Twilight in Budapest*, 2021) and *Vida en un clima iliberal* (*Life in an Illiberal Climate* 2022). The second chronicles Orbán's disastrous management of COVID.

Orbán used the pandemic to expand his executive powers and blame immigrants for the spread of the virus. Meanwhile, Hungary had some of the highest rates of contagions and deaths in the world between late 2020 and mid-2022. Moreover the Hungarian government became obsessed with controlling the flow of data about the pandemic. About this, Attila told me:

> And it's not just COVID data. Getting any type of public data in Hungary has become increasingly difficult. The government and academia generate data using public funds, but then refuse to make it public. They either refuse to collaborate with you or they make you pay for it. This is absurd. If you use, say, money from the European Union to run a study, you should make public not only the results, but also the underlying data, shouldn't you?
>
> Another problem is how reliable the data is. In fact, I think twice about using data provided by the Hungarian Central Statistical Office because I don't trust it anymore; even data as elementary as unemployment or poverty rates have become dubious. I have some evidence that counting methodologies are fudged when there's a need to make the government look better.

Attila's most recent long-form story for ATLO is "And the Earth Shakes" (**Figure 14.4**, next spread) published in the aftermath of the large February 6, 2023, earthquakes that killed nearly 60,000 people in southern Turkey and northern Syria. Attila told me that he considers this project the realization of his ideals when he founded ATLO five years ago:

> This project has the ambition, quality, and visual sophistication that I wanted to reach years ago, but that I couldn't achieve at the time because of my lack of experience. It has everything that I always imagined that ATLO stories should have: a tight connection to newsworthy events, and also detailed context.

I've already mentioned that Attila is a professor and a scholar; that's his current job. He teaches information graphics and journalism at Eötvös Loránd University (ELTE) in Budapest. His main research focuses on the history of information graphics and data visualization in Hungary.

When I was becoming a data journalist and educating myself into the history of visualization I collected what I think is the largest data visualization library in Hungary. I read authors such as Michael Friendly or Sandra Rendgen, who have written wonderful articles and books about the history of the field.

That said, it annoyed me that most examples I saw were Western, and that typical histories of visualization talked about it as mostly a Western phenomenon, as something that gained prominence only in, say, Great Britain or France. I wanted to know what had happened in Hungary.

What I discovered by poring through archives is fascinating. In a famous paper, "The Golden Age of Statistical Graphics," Michael Friendly says that there was a massive growth in the use of data visualization in the second half of the 19th century. That's the "Golden Age" he mentions in the title. Many types of charts that we use to this day were invented at the time.

In that paper, Friendly also argues that the first half of the 20th century was the "Dark Ages" of graphics because there was a shift in the way that statisticians and other scientists thought about their work. They moved away from visualizations and focused instead on precise quantification and statistical modeling. Graphics started to be seen as mere pictures that didn't have the same accuracy as figures on a table.

What I have discovered through my research is that the 19th century graphics revolution missed Hungary. Instead, our treasure trove comes after, during the time of Friendly's Dark Ages. The first Hungarian data graphic that I've found is from the late 18th century, but it's only near the end of the 19th century that we see an explosion in the production and publication of visualizations in Hungary. The pinnacle was the decades between 1920 and the end of World War II, where you could see pretty sophisticated and dense charts even in newspapers.

Attila explained the reasons for these historical patterns in a 2023 interview with *Nightingale*, the magazine of the Data Visualization Society. As Hungary was part of the Hapsburg Empire, up to the end of the 19th century it lacked a dedicated statistical office that collected data about the country in a systematic manner.

Also, at the time Hungarian statisticians were disdainful about charts (they were more permissive about maps.) They considered graphics inferior and simplistic ways of analyzing or communicating statistics compared to text or tables. According to them, visuals were unworthy of educated minds and only appropriate for the illiterate masses.

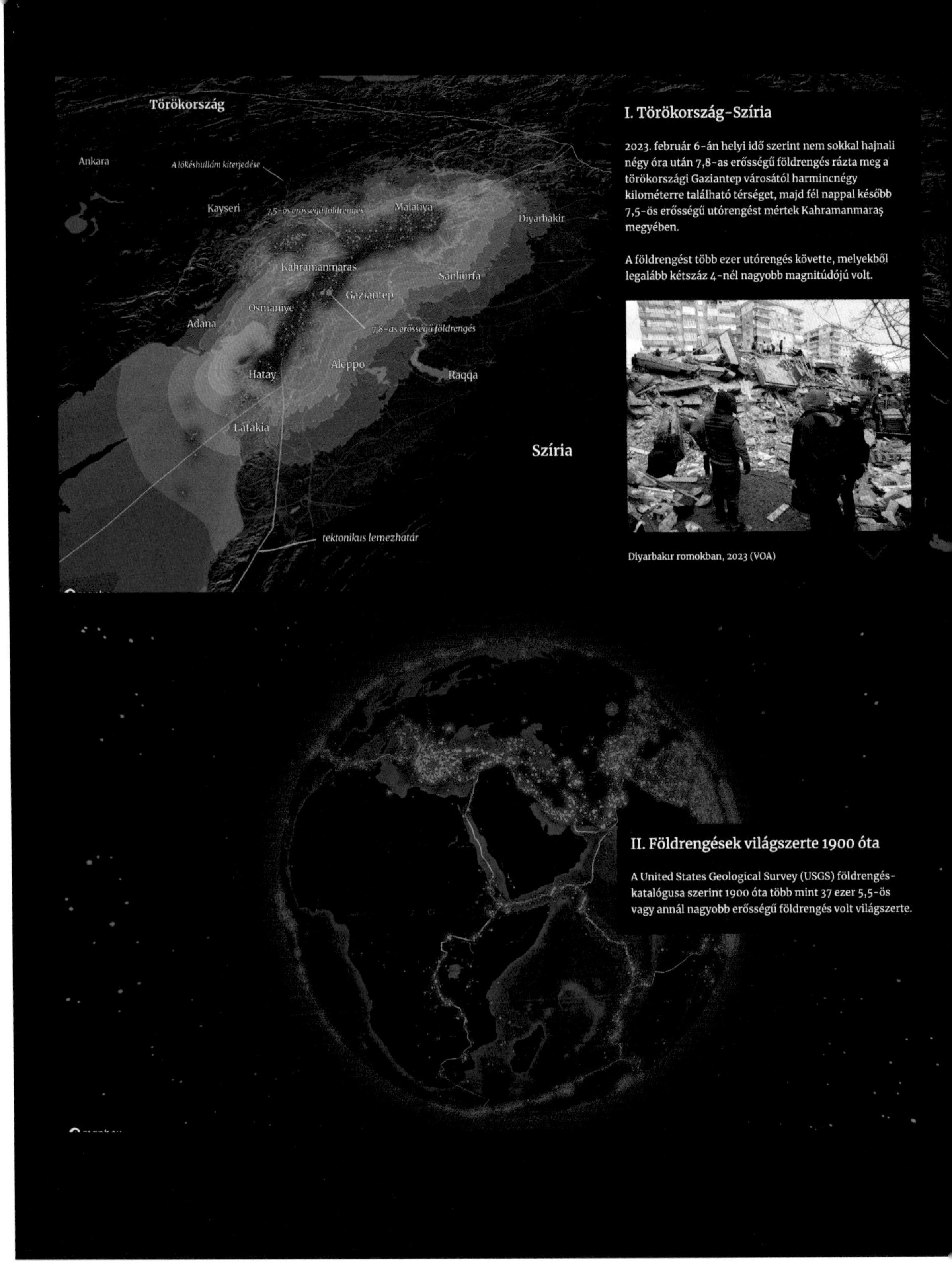

Figure 14.4: Screenshots from "And the Earth Shakes – Earthquakes from 1900 to Nowadays" by ATLATSZO / Attila Bátorfy and Krisztián Szabó / https://atlo.team/wp-content/uploads/2023/02/foldrengesatlasz.html / last accessed under April 19, 2023

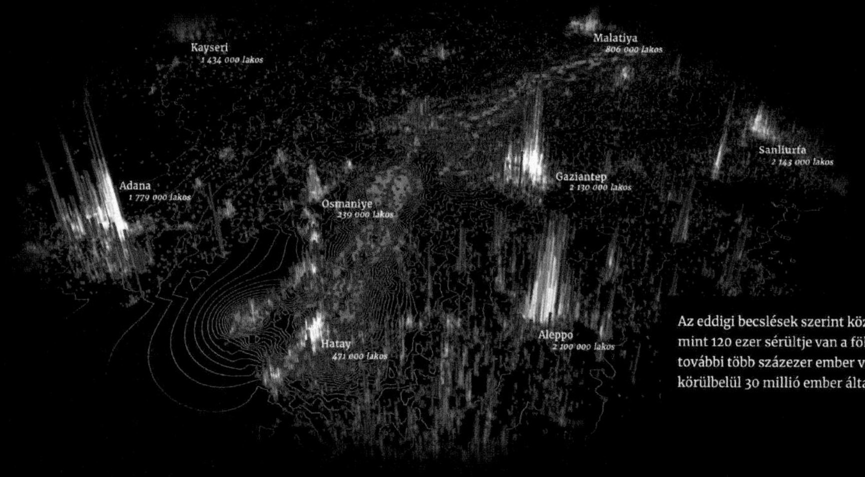

Az eddigi becslések szerint közel 50 ezer halottja és több mint 120 ezer sérültje van a földrengéseknek. Ezen felül további több százezer ember veszítette el az otthonát a körülbelül 30 millió ember által lakott térségben.

A földrengésben érintett terület népsűrűsége

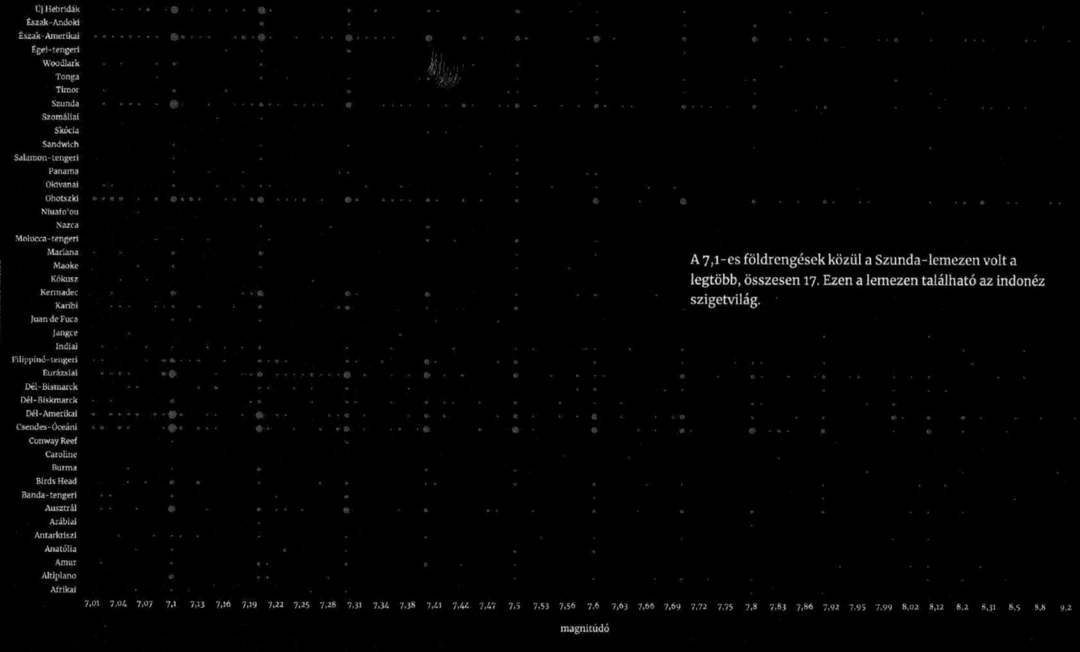

A 7,1-es földrengések közül a Szunda-lemezen volt a legtöbb, összesen 17. Ezen a lemezen található az indonéz szigetvilág.

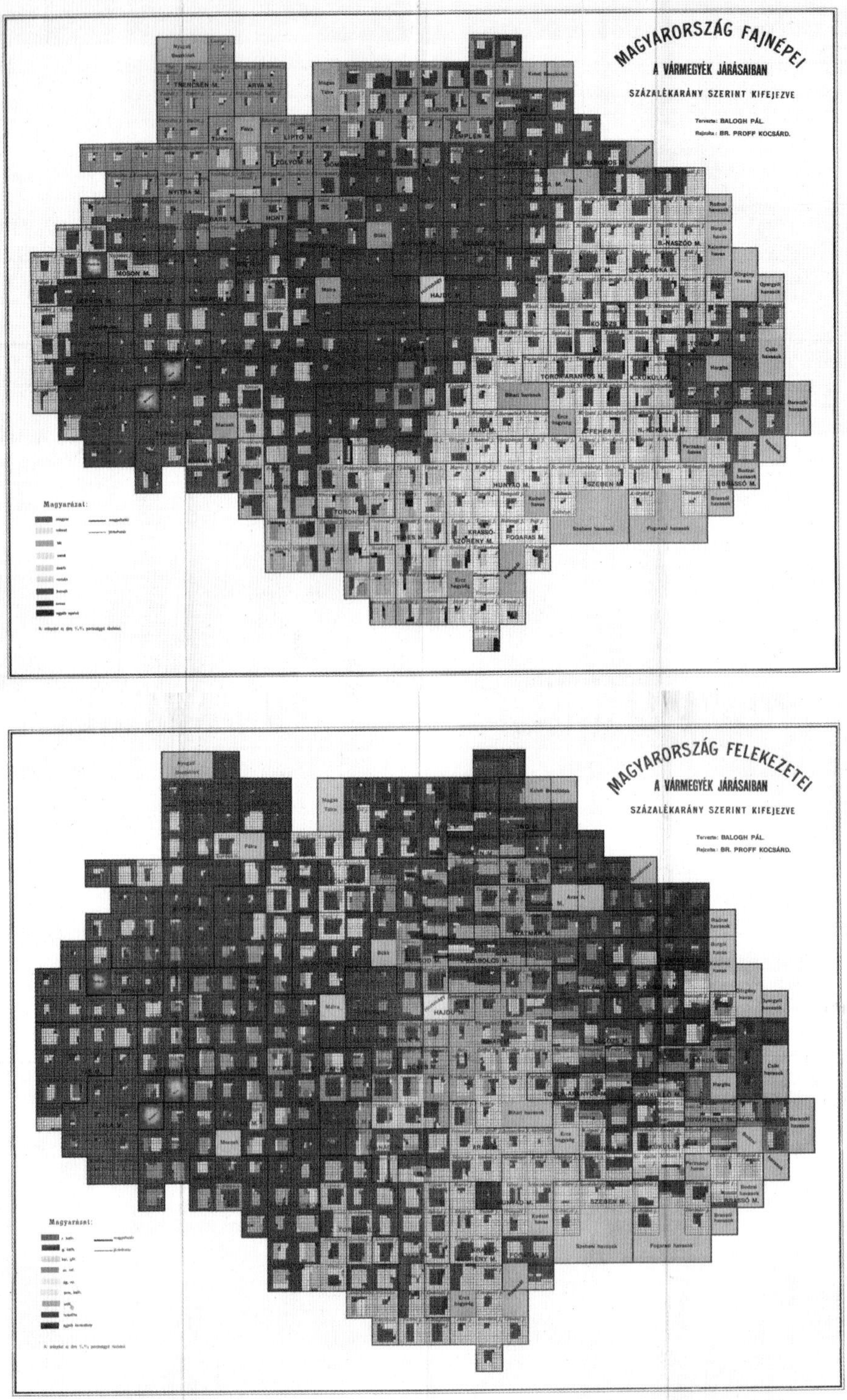

Figure 14.5: Ethnic and religious maps of Hungary by Pál Balogh and Kocsárd Proff, 1902
https://nightingaledvs.com/exploring-hungarian-data-graphics-with-attila-batorfy/

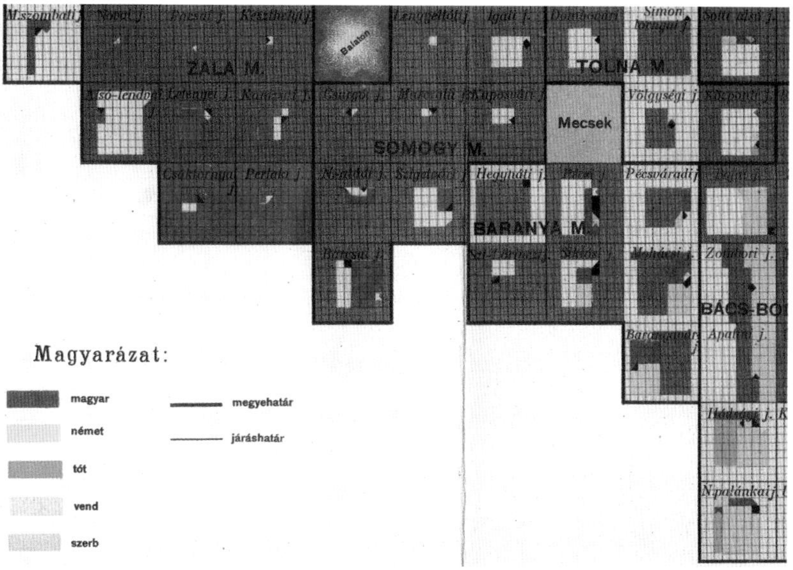

Figure 14.6: Detail from the ethnic and religious maps of Hungary by Pál Balogh and Kocsárd Proff

Attila showed me several graphics from his "treasure trove," an extensive collection of 19th and early 20th century graphics. Some of them, like a couple of tile maps of ethnic and religious groups in Hungary, look very modern and unique (**Figure 14.5**).

> These were designed by journalist Pál Balogh and painter Kocsárd Proff in 1902. Balogh, who was responsible for the concept, understood that the thematic maps that were used at the time, such as choropleth maps, can distort our perception of the numbers because some countries, regions, or provinces are larger than others. That's why he made the size of all 413 districts in Hungary the same.
>
> Notice that these are also waffle charts. Each district is divided into a 10-by-10 grid (**Figure 14.6**). Each little square represents 1 percent of its population. The colors are the ethnicities on one map—red is Hungarian, yellow is German, and so on—and religious affiliations on the other—red is Catholics, yellow is Evangelicals, and so on.
>
> I think that these might be the first equal area tile maps ever published. Or, at least, two of the first ones, as so much research remains to be done in other countries.

Attila doesn't think that Hungary is an isolated case. To him, our understanding of the history of data visualization is grossly incomplete and, because of that, skewed. He's familiar with statistical atlases from other countries in Eastern Europe such as Finland, the Baltic countries, Romania, or Poland, and says that there's an urgent need for scholarship to analyze them and situate them in their historical context. Many treasure troves might be waiting for intrepid explorers to find.

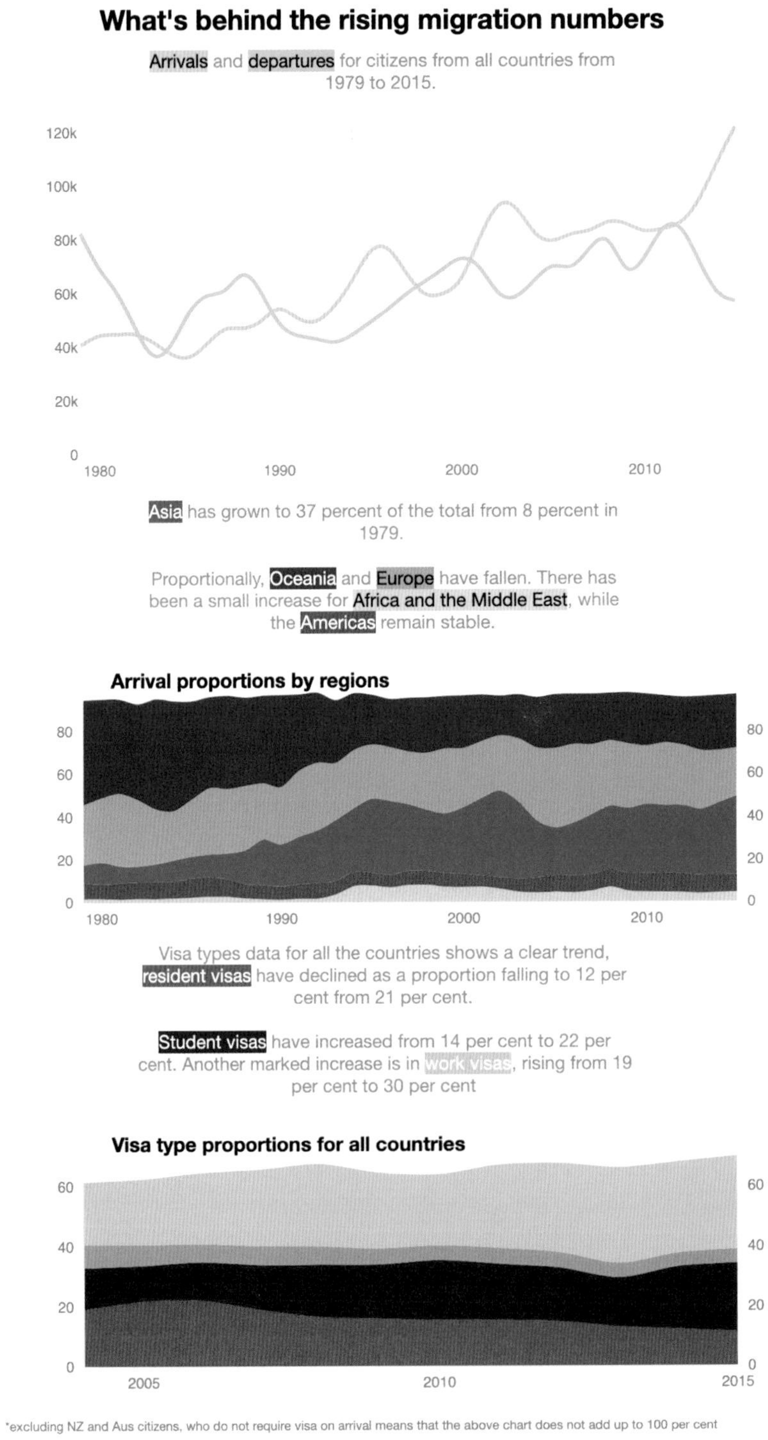

Figure 15.1: Graphs from "What's behind the rising migration numbers" by Harkanwal Singh and Lincoln Tan
https://insights.nzherald.co.nz/article/rising-migration-numbers-nz/

Chapter 15
with Harkanwal Singh

The Discerning Outsider

The sunset, like survival, exists only on the verge of its own disappearing.
To be gorgeous, you must first be seen, but to be seen allows you to be hunted.

—Ocean Vuong

The poet Ocean Vuong once said about immigrants that we feel the estrangement of "being forever arriving, never truly having arrived," and that our experiences are filled with wonder, but also with a sense of loneliness. In my conversation with **Harkanwal Singh**, he shared his story of moving from India to New Zealand and becoming the first data journalist in the country, and his thoughts about how his identity as an outsider shaped many of his stories, such as "What's behind the rising migration numbers" (**Figure 15.1**). Harkanwal's experiences in New Zealand reminded me of Vuong's words. He told me:

> I studied mechanical engineering, but I wasn't good at it, so I came to New Zealand in 2009 to study journalism. In my last year [as a student], I made a WordPress website for the journalism school. Thanks to it, in 2012 I got a web editor job at *The Waikato Times*, a regional newspaper in Hamilton. This was a big deal because it isn't common for an immigrant to get a job in New Zealand media.
>
> At that time, *New York Times* designers like Shan Carter and Mike Bostock were making incredible interactive visualizations. I found them fascinating. As I often finished my daily work in a few hours, I was able to devote my spare time to learning how to handle data with tools such as Fusion Tables. I began designing graphics to be published on the newspaper's website.

A turning point for me was a small project that got a lot of attention. The city of Hamilton was getting its main road rebuilt, and I had obtained photographs of it before and after the construction. I built a simple before-and-after interactive. My editors were puzzled because that story became the most viewed on the website that week.

The Waikato Times is owned by a media conglomerate called Fairfax [renamed Stuff in 2018,] located in Wellington. Their main news website, which is the largest in the country, hosts the websites of all their regional newspapers. After acquiring some data and graphics experience locally, I decided to fly to Wellington to convince the management to create a job for me at the main website. It was the first data journalism position in New Zealand. I spent just eight months there, though, as I was hired by Fairfax's main competitor, *The New Zealand Herald* (in Auckland).

Harkanwal was the first data journalist in New Zealand, but not the first news graphics designer:

The *Herald* had and still has a really good graphics desk. However, I wasn't part of it; I worked mostly by myself at least for the first year of the four that I was at the newspaper.

When I was hired, I was determined to prove that data journalism was a thing, that it's useful, and that it can illuminate stories that we don't understand well. I was also determined not to be pushed into a niche.You know, an immigrant journalist who writes almost exclusively about Indian communities in New Zealand.

I also wanted to push against certain stereotypes. For instance, more than once I've met people who think that I must be good at math simply because I'm Indian. (I do like math, and I've never given up on it.)

Since early in my career, I observed that New Zealand media too often popularizes stereotypes like this, and even casts a negative light on immigration and foreign students. This affected me. One day I should write a lengthy piece about the role that identity plays in how we choose what data stories to tell, and how we tell them. People sometimes wrongly think about data as if it were neutral. Even I, at least at the beginning, believed that my being an immigrant had little to do with my work. Well, it did.

I brought up "What's behind the rising migration numbers," which Harkanwal designed and co-wrote with reporter Lincoln Tan:

Some stories can be encapsulated in just a few charts, but migration patterns in New Zealand cannot. Ben Goldacre [a British medical doctor and journalist] has a book about data reasoning titled *I Think You'll Find It's a Bit More Complicated Than That* [2015]. I think that this title captures how I approached this story in 2016.

Many Kiwis [New Zealanders] believe that immigration is a simple phenomenon. Some right-wing politicians such as Winston Peters [more about him later] constantly push this narrative that the country has open borders, that there's a flood of Asian people—Filipinos, Indians, Chinese—coming in, that they take jobs from Kiwis, and so on. This narrative is echoed ad nauseam in the media. If they instead looked into the numbers, they'd notice that the story is, as Ben Goldacre wrote, "a bit more complicated than that." There are many nuances.

Immigration and visa data is published every month by Statistics New Zealand. There's data going back to 1979, and I decided to create a step-by-step explainer based on it.

It's true that arrivals to New Zealand from Asian countries have increased in the past decade or so, but not that impressively. In fact, as a percentage of all visitors or immigrants that require a visa, the numbers from Asian countries aren't that different from what they were in the early 2000s. Moreover, arrivals from Europe are still a significant proportion, and the percentage of people traveling from Oceania [mainly Australia] Europe, or the Americas has remained stable or declined a bit.

The central reveal of the story, though, is that if you break down the data by visa type, you realize that a large portion of visas granted to Asian people are student visas, not work or resident visas, and that each Asian country is different. Take the Philippines (**Figure 15.2**.) New Zealand gets plenty of people from the Philippines to work as nurses and in low-paying jobs. However, student visas [among Filipinos] have also been on the rise.

This pattern is even more prominent if we look at India or China. Indians usually travel to New Zealand to attend school or college, and some transition to work visas or residency later on, like I did. You can see that in the data. Student visas for Indians have increased drastically since the 2010s, while work, resident, and visitor visas have remained low and stable (**Figure 15.3**).

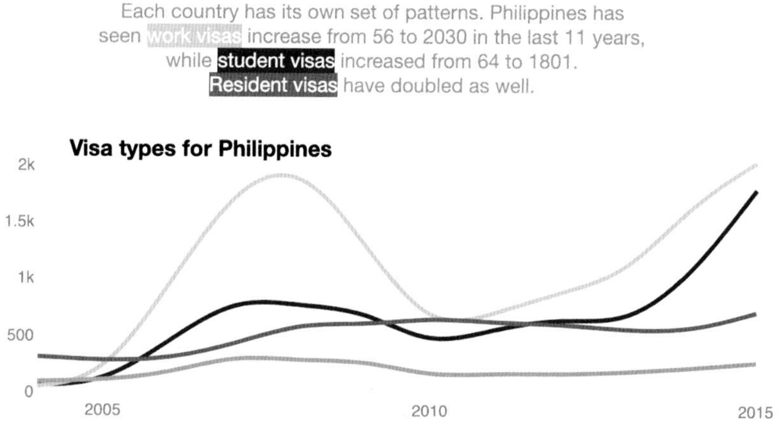

Figure 15.2: Visa types for the Philippines from "What's behind the rising migration numbers"

Reproduced with permission of NZME, the owner of *The New Zealand Herald*

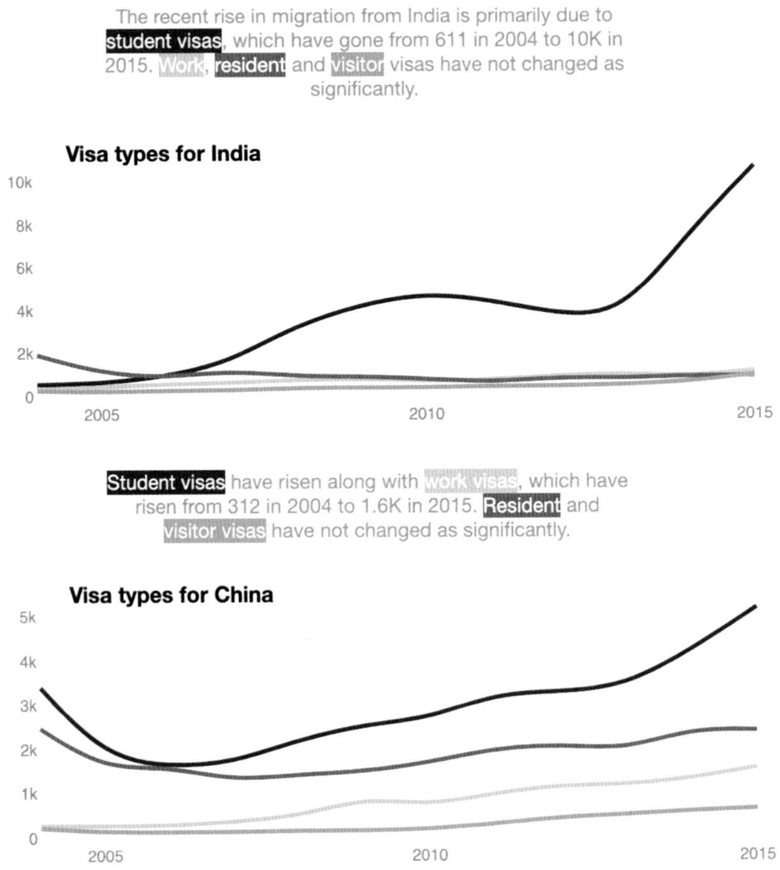

Figure 15.3: Visa types for India and China from "What's behind the rising migration numbers"

Reproduced with permission of NZME, the owner of *The New Zealand Herald*

> China is yet a different case. Many Chinese people also move to New Zealand to study, but other types of visas, such as visitor visas—tourist visas—are also noticeable.
>
> Think about this: Students bring in money, *lots* of money. In fact, New Zealand universities have historically run and grown on international students. If you don't want migration from Asian countries, you can simply stop accepting international students, and the pipeline that goes from student visas to work visas will stop. That is the complicated narrative that wasn't being discussed at the time. Covid has changed it, as universities suffered without international students.

I was confused. I told Harkanwal that I didn't think that this is a complex story. It doesn't require advanced knowledge of, say, statistics or demography, just some inquisitiveness, some data slicing and dicing, and a few deep conversations with experts to put the numbers in context. Why hadn't a story like this been published before?

> I guess that it is because not many people are that interested in this level of nuance. Who knows, some people might even enjoy the outrage caused by yet another story focusing just on the overall increase of immigrants from Asian countries since 1979.
>
> My perspective is different. As an immigrant myself, and as someone who has met and talked with many other immigrants, each of them with their own story, I know that the aggregated data and one chart or two aren't enough. There's a person behind every one of those tens of thousands of numbers, a person trying to make their life, or the lives of their family members, better.

"What's behind the rising immigration numbers" was followed in April of 2017 by "Rising work visas drive migration." The government of New Zealand, under the pressure of local xenophobic voices, and influenced by worldwide trends—Brexit in the UK and the 2016 election of Donald Trump in the United States—tried to curb immigration from Asian countries by tightening the requirements to obtain skilled work visas.

However, according to the story, the top source countries for New Zealand work visas in 2017 and even earlier—the countries that would likely be more affected by the proposed regulations—weren't Asian countries, but the UK, Germany, Australia, South Africa, and the United States. Revealing this fact didn't sit well with some politicians, Harkanwal told me:

> At the time I was studying statistics part-time (I have yet to finish all papers for the diploma) at the University of Aukland. A couple of days after this story launched I was sitting at my computer at home preparing for an exam. I had Twitter open and I suddenly saw my name in a press release by Winston Peters [the leader of the nationalist-populist party New Zealand First]. Imagine my shock.
>
> Peters acussed Lincoln [Tan] and me of lying, of writing propaganda and "fake news." He went after us because both of us are Asian immigrants; he said that explicitly in his press release.
>
> I was somewhat disappointed by the response in the newsroom. It panicked. I was repeatedly asked, "What do you make of these accusations? Does this critique have merit?" One of the main opinion writers in the newspaper, someone I had never spoken with and who is sympathetic of anti-immigration policies, called me up to ask about the story and the analysis.
>
> My response to all that was that Peters was lying. Points that he made in the press release had already been addressed in our story. Even considering that, I wrote a rebuttal the very same day his press release came out. Moreover, three statistics professors from the University of Auckland, James Curran, Thomas Lumley, and Chris Triggs, published a post in the statistics department's blog saying that, of course any data can be subject to interpretation, but they also endorsed our conclusions. This type of external validation is great, but not having the same internal backing in your own workplace takes a toll.

"And that's why you left journalism," I said. Harkanwal said,

> And that's why I left journalism little by little, yes, at least for a while and at least for now. It's challenging to be an immigrant and also one of the first people working in a novel field, data journalism, in a country that didn't have a tradition of it. You need to constantly prove your own value, constantly think harder than others, constantly be in the public eye—and you need to do all that while facing difficult situations like the one we've just talked about. It became exhausting. I got tired of struggling.
>
> After leaving the *Herald* I did a bit of everything, consulting, freelancing, and so on. I also wrote five papers in statistics and computer science. I got into advanced statistical modeling, Bayesian statistics, and statistical theory.
>
> I eventually switched to data engineering and data visualization development, as I needed some job security and a steady income. I've worked for Westpac NZ, the New Zealand division of an Australian bank, and today I'm at Woolworths, a retail company.
>
> In between those two jobs I collaborated with a small independent news organization in New Zealand, *The Spinoff*, not so much as a data reporter, but more on helping them plan their data strategy, and providing training on data journalism. That was a good experience. *The Spinoff* is a pretty diverse news organization.
>
> If I were to go back to journalism full time one day, I'd like to return to India and do it there. After all these years in New Zealand, I still feel like an outsider, and that the journalistic stories that I want to tell somehow don't belong here.

"But perhaps they do," I said. Some of the most perceptive reflections about Spain, my home country, were written by outsiders—George Orwell, Albert Camus, Hugh Thomas, Giles Tremlett, and so many others—people who were able to look into Spanish culture and society with fresh eyes unburdened by history, conventions, or prejudices.

Perhaps the same is true of New Zealand, its colonial past, its latent distrust for non-Western immigrants, or its historical inequalities that largely affect Māori and Pasifika communities. (Pasifika refers to immigrants belonging to indigenous populations from other parts of Oceania, such as Samoa or Fiji.) Harkanwal continued:

> I love boring data sets, those numbers which a newsroom would never pick up. I think that the fact that I'm an immigrant has made me sensitive to data sets that local people aren't that likely to look at closely. For example, of all the work that I produced at the *Herald*, I feel most proud of a series of stories about education inequality in New Zealand.
>
> Since 1995 and up to this year [2023], New Zealand has had a peculiar way to group schools into socioeconomic deciles. The Ministry of Education used census data to assign each school to one decile. This system was based on variables such as household income, or the jobs that

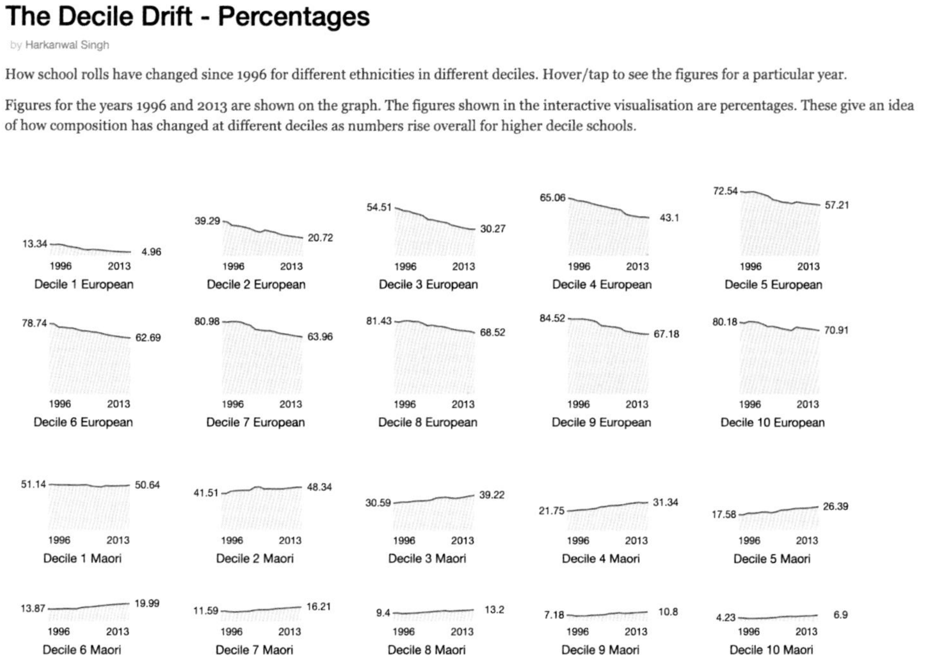

Figure 15.4: Graphs from "The Decile Drift"
https://insights.nzherald.co.nz/article/decile-drift/
Reproduced with permission of NZME, the owner of *The New Zealand Herald*

parents had, and was used to distribute funding to schools. Schools in lower deciles, those with a larger proportion of students coming from poorer households, would get more support from the government.

One day I'll write a history of deciles and how they have shaped New Zealand society. Even though they have been removed, they've had an outsized impact on NZ society and housing.

Harkanwal's story mentions several consequences of the decile system. Schools in the higher deciles tend to have more students of European descent, while indigenous students represent a higher proportion in schools in low-decile schools (**Figure 15.4**). Even if deciles are not a measure of school performance, New Zealanders tend to interpret them that way, and try to avoid their local school if it's in the lower levels.

Moreover, indigenous students and those in low-decile secondary schools are more likely to take a higher proportion of vocational, skill-based courses, rather than courses that are approved and qualifying for university entrance. Another story in Harkanwal's series of investigations about New Zealand's educational system, "What's beneath rising NCEA pass rates?," explains this disparity (**Figure 15.5**). NCEA (National Certificate of Educational Achievement) has three levels, which students can complete in their last few years of their secondary education.

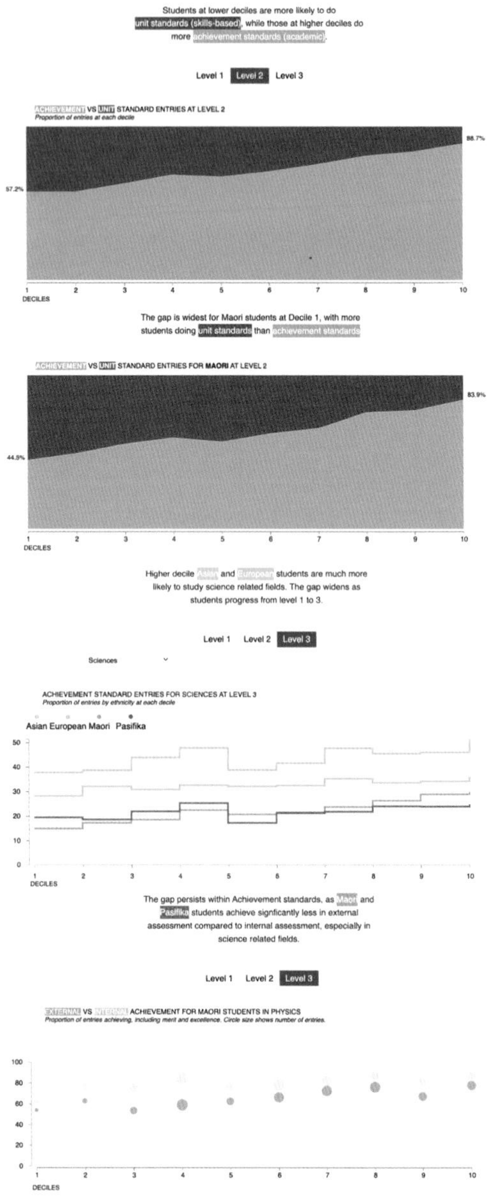

Figure 15.5: Graphs from "What's beneath rising NCEA pass rates?"
by Kirsty Johnston and Harkanwal Singh
https://insights.nzherald.co.nz/article/whats-beneath-rising-ncea-pass-rates/
Reproduced with permission of NZME, the owner of *The New Zealand Herald*

Harkanwal's graphics reveal that students at lower deciles are more likely to do "unit standards" (components of courses that are skill-based) while students at the higher deciles finish their secondary education with a much larger proportion of "achievement standards" (part of academic courses). Also, students of Asian or European descent are more likely to enroll in science courses than Māori or Pasifika students *across all deciles*:

There are inequalities in New Zealand's education, and also a few mysteries. Another project I designed was about a certain gap in educational assessment and achievement (**Figure 15.6**). This was the first time that this data set was visualized; I got it through an Official Information Act request, and later several academics reached out to me because they wanted to use it for their research.

Assessments in New Zealand, measures of what students have learned according to certain criteria, can be "internal" or "external." Internal assessments are done by teachers and in the classroom. External assessments are usually standardized exams.

[In these graphics, the red and purple bubbles correspond to "achievement standards," the academic ones. These can be assessed externally or internally. Yellow bubbles are assessments for "unit standards," the skill-based ones.]

Look at schools that are in the higher socioeconomic deciles [second column in Figure 15.6]. Notice that there's a gap between the achievement rate in achievement standards

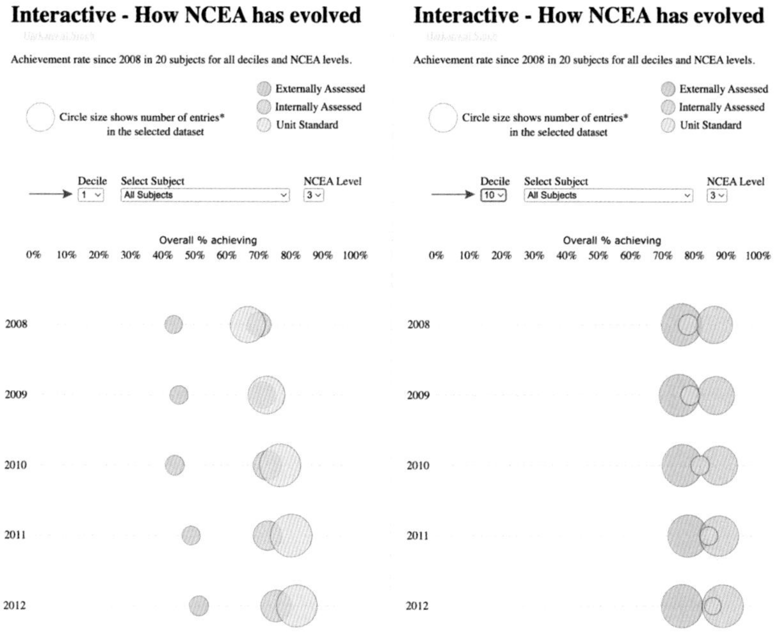

Figure 15.6: "How NCEA has evolved?"
http://media.nzherald.co.nz/webcontent/infographics/358/datavis5.html
Reproduced with permission of NZME, the owner of *The New Zealand Herald*

> when students were assessed externally or internally. The latter is slightly higher. Now look at schools at the lowest deciles [first column on Figure 15.6]. The gap is much larger. A classic example of this would be math (calculus) in the final year of high school. Huge gap.
>
> Now, something very important: The data shows that there's a gap, but doesn't explain *why that gap exists*. It's too easy to make up explanations for these numbers. An editor suggested to me that the lower-decile schools are likely cheating, but we don't know that. Perhaps students from lower-income backgrounds feel more pressure when assessed externally, who knows? A researcher called this gap "the NCEA puzzle at the core of New Zealand's education," and he asked the Ministry of Education about it. No one has an explanation for it yet.

While Harkanwal spoke animatedly about the minutiae of the data, I thought that his case is similar to Aaron Williams's (Chapter 12); I wouldn't be surprised if his temperament, characterized by an impulse to scrutinize complex phenomena and to explain them to others, leads him back to a newsroom one day—or, at a minimum, to regular collaborations with news publications.

Once a reporter, always a reporter.

Second Coda

The designers featured in this third section of the book, each in their own way, have a knack for disseminating awareness of data science, information design, or visualization. They are bridge-builders and ambassadors who journey beyond the boundaries of our domains not as evangelizers or colonizers, but as gentle emissaries carrying a message such as, "Would you let me talk to you about something I've learned? I find it fascinating; perhaps you'll find it fascinating, too."

There's something exemplary in that impulse. In fact, I'd argue that I've found something worth imitating in everyone I interviewed for *The Art of Insight*—either their work, their passion and commitment, their ethical stance, their mockery of reactionaries and despots, their willingness to demonstrate and teach, or a combination of all of those.

The Spanish philosopher Javier Gomá Lanzón has written eloquently about the role that imitation of exemplary people plays in human progress. In his *Imitación y Experiencia* (*Imitation and Experience*, 2019) he said:

> In our postnihilistic times, when authoritarism and coercion have forever lost their cohesive power, only the persuasive force of the virtuous example, as a source of civic customs, is able to promote the emancipation of the citizen. [I write] for those who are still able to be moved by everything that is grand, noble, and beautiful in this world.

Lanzón added that "all of us are examples surrounded by examples, entangled in a mesh of mutual influences." There's an ethics implicit in his thinking: If we humans learn largely by imitating others, a decent heuristic for a good life is to strive to act in ways that other human beings will find admirable and worth imitating of their own volition. Lanzón's philosophy of imitation of exemplarity is, therefore, anti-authoritarian and forbearing:

> [This is a] benevolent ideal of what it means to be human, one that is demanding with oneself and indulgent towards others, and that doesn't choke individuality with the rope of moralism, but leaves space to error, to detours and withdrawals, to the failed experiments, revisions, corrections that are part of anyone's natural learning process.

A common reaction when facing human beings whom we find exemplary—inspiring visualization designers are among them—is an urgent and rousing "*I want to be like them.*" That's a beautiful feeling for sure, but it also poses risks.

The first is what designer Manuel Lima has called in his book *The New Designer* (2023) the cult of heroes and geniuses. It's too easy to worship certain individuals while ignoring the circumstances, environments, or communities from where they emerged. Lima suggested, and I agree, that we're all the result of historical and cultural networks of being. It's fine to admire people, but we ought to be appreciative of their surroundings, as well.

There's a second danger that Lima warned against, the paralyzing obsession with perfection and excellence. How common it is to admire other designers while feeling stuck because we think that the quality of our work will never be comparable to theirs? It's pretty common; I've been in such a quagmire.

However, why should we agonize over whether our work is—or will one day be—as good as the work of those we admire? All that matters is that we perceive that our work today is somehow a bit better than it was yesterday.

Striving for "excellence"—whatever that means to each of us, as I've never found a coherent definition of it—isn't a bad idea, but expecting that we can *reach* excellence is. Excellence isn't a static Platonic ideal, but a path with no destination. Therefore, let's get our work done ethically and to the extent of our knowledge and skills today, and let's enjoy and celebrate the products of our efforts.

My friend Simon Rogers once wrote for *The Guardian* newspaper that "Data journalism is the new punk" (2012), meaning that the abundance of data in digital form, and the ubiquity of tools to manage, analyze, and visualize it, were lowering barriers of entry.

Simon quoted the British fanzine *Sideburns* (1977), which explained how to make punk music: "This is a chord… this is another… this is a third. NOW FORM A BAND." Central to the ethos of classic punk is the subversive and liberating notion that "anyone can do it."

I tell my visualization students something similar at the beginning of every semester: Here's some data, here are a few easy-to-use software tools, and here are some common types of graphics. Now let's practice, discuss, and learn how to use all these things responsibly because the fact that *anybody can do it* doesn't imply that everybody will do it *equally well*. In his essay, Simon wrote:

> The theory goes that the punk bands we remember best are the ones that were good—but there needed to be a whole lot of kids experimenting and sounding awful before they got there.

In Chapter 11 I mentioned Mike Monteiro's thoughts on design ethics. Mike has also written about the importance of belonging to communities of mutual support. In his online essay "On my second birthday we landed on the moon" (2017), he reflected on what it was like to grow up in the Philadelphia of the 1970s as the child of recently arrived Portuguese immigrants.

Mike suffered racism and xenophobia, and learned that he himself was racist against Jews, Puerto Ricans, and African Americans. "In our eagerness to show Americans we belonged," Mike wrote, "we adopted their racism. (We also brought some of our own with us.)" He added that as a teenager he felt like an outcast.

Mike changed when he enrolled in art school, discovered punk rock, and found himself immersed in a delightfully anarchic, fluid, inclusive, and creative community:

> The world doesn't want to include me. But the world didn't want to include a lot of people. And for a brief moment in time we found each other. *We* met in abandoned halls, *we* met in the back of steak shops, *we* met in shitty bars, *we* met in basements. But *we* met. And we supported each other.
>
> It didn't matter that we couldn't play instruments very well. (I never even attempted.) We played them anyway and if you played them faster, no one realized you messed up. It didn't matter that no one would publish our writing. *We* made our own zines. It didn't matter that no one made clothes we liked. *We* put our own together with safety pins. *We* didn't need you to let us into your community. We made our own. And our community was made up of all kinds of people. All backgrounds. All sexual orientations—with revolving doors to choose a new one whenever you liked. In these basements, in these halls, in these art school classrooms, I met the most amazing fucked-up people and they loved you for who you were. Here in these halls of kindness I met

> people who I'd previously avoided, been afraid of, mocked, reviled, and flat-out hated and they were calling me brother. And I loved them back.

"These halls of kindness," what a great title for a book, should life be long enough to write it one day.

Information design, data journalism, data visualization, the worlds that I've inhabited all my life, would benefit from building many halls of kindness, venues, forums, anarchic spaces where old-timers and newcomers mingle in conversation and shared joy for their crafts and trades. Those worlds, those fields and disciplines, are too wide, wondrous, and unexplored to be monopolized by an oligarchy of professed experts, some of whom prefer to be *gatekeepers* rather than *gate openers*, bridge-builders, or ambassadors.

I shall return to these musings in the Epilogue, after I visit people whose experiences and careers are the most similar to mine. I've called them narrators.

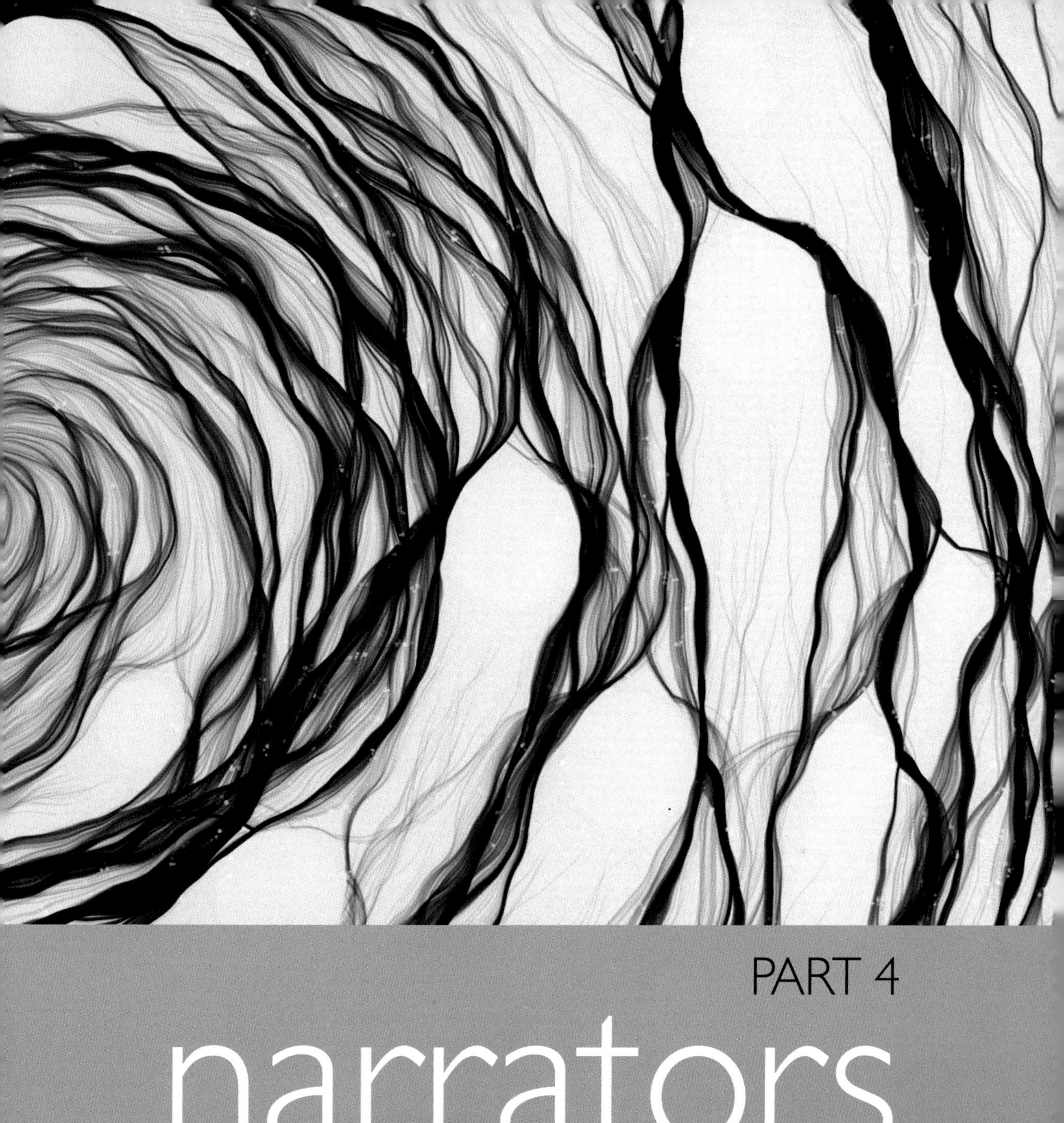

PART 4

narrators

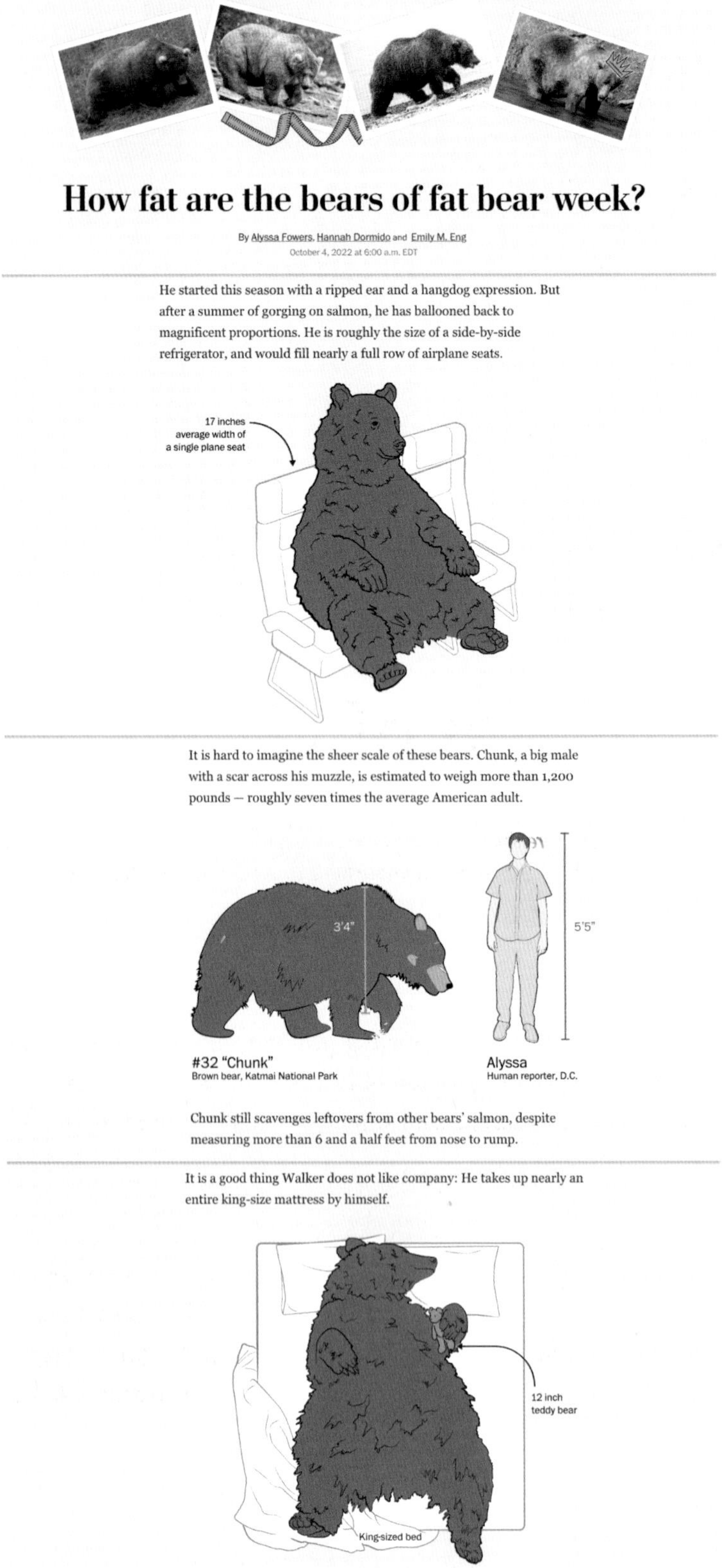

How fat are the bears of fat bear week?

By Alyssa Fowers, Hannah Dormido and Emily M. Eng
October 4, 2022 at 6:00 a.m. EDT

He started this season with a ripped ear and a hangdog expression. But after a summer of gorging on salmon, he has ballooned back to magnificent proportions. He is roughly the size of a side-by-side refrigerator, and would fill nearly a full row of airplane seats.

It is hard to imagine the sheer scale of these bears. Chunk, a big male with a scar across his muzzle, is estimated to weigh more than 1,200 pounds — roughly seven times the average American adult.

Chunk still scavenges leftovers from other bears' salmon, despite measuring more than 6 and a half feet from nose to rump.

It is a good thing Walker does not like company: He takes up nearly an entire king-size mattress by himself.

Figure 16.1: Illustrations from "How fat are the bears of fat bear week?" by National Park Service / https://www.washingtonpost.com/nation/2022/10/04/how-fat-are-bears-fat-bear-week/ / last accessed under April 19, 2023

Chapter 16
with Alyssa Fowers

A Journalism of Care

That which we ignore reveals more than what we give our attention to. It's in these things that we find cultural and colloquial hints of what is deemed important. Spots that we've left blank reveal our hidden social biases and indifferences.

—Mimi Ọnụọha

In February of 2023, **Alyssa Fowers**, a former graduate student of mine and a graphics reporter at *The Washington Post*, gave a talk to my University of Miami students. After presenting many of her graphics, she said something that I rushed to jot down:

> Nothing you love is a waste of time. Nothing you learn from is a waste of time. The only waste of time is caring more about how you look than about what you do.

I believe that this quote captures Alyssa's character. Her best work comes from both the heart and the mind, combines the personal and the empirical, and emerges from love and care. Her stories, regardless of whether they are grim and serious or funny and light-hearted, always derive from an interest in the *un*expected, the *un*counted, the *un*told, and the *un*shown:

> My main beat at the *Post* when I was hired was the economy, which has been depressing for a long time, and I also like to make visualizations that try to humanize mass tragedy. But I also love other things, sometimes weird ones. For instance, fat bears (**Figure 16.1**.)

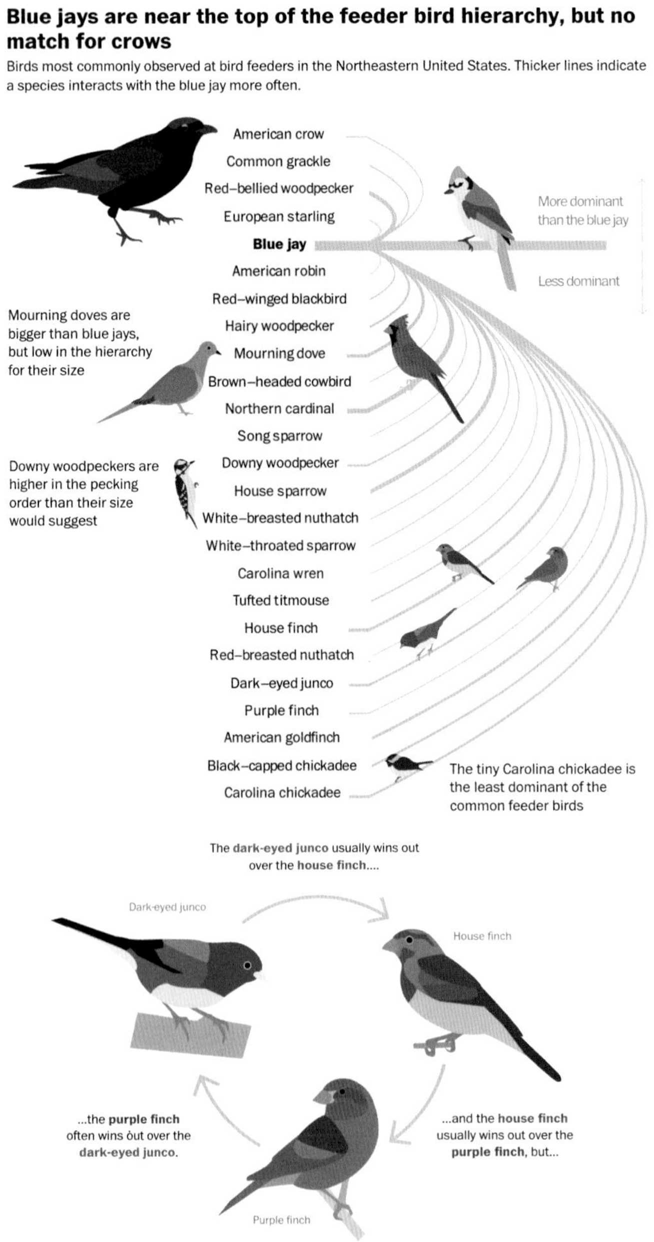

Figure 16.2: Illustrations from "Which birds are the biggest jerks at the feeder?" by Andrew Van Dam and Alyssa Fowers
https://www.washingtonpost.com/business/2021/11/28/bird-feeder-pecking-order/

Years ago my wife, Zoe, and I started watching live streams of Alaska's Katmai National Park. We were mesmerized by the brown bears fishing in the Brooks River. When you watch them repeatedly, you start identifying individuals and becoming attached to them. Every October, Explore, a multimedia documentary organization, organizes Fat Bear Week, a competition in which thousands of bear fans can vote for their favorite Katmai bears.

Through livestreams and photographs you can see the bears, but it's hard to get a sense of how big they truly are after months of eating fish and accumulating fat in preparation for the winter. That's why I and my collaborators, Hannah Dormido and Emily M. Eng, decided to draw vector illustrations comparing the bears to everyday objects and people; I myself appear in the graphics.

Alyssa is devoting time to projects like this after years of making graphics about unemployment, evictions, mental health care, or the COVID pandemic:

After so many tough years I thought, why don't I delight our readers a little? I did another project about which bird species bully each other the most at bird feeders (**Figure 16.2**.)

There's a funny origin story behind this one. My colleague Andrew Van Dam had bookmarked a research paper that defined a hierarchy of power among bird species. When interacting with each other at feeders, some birds are much more dominant than others, and the biggest bully is the American crow. Andrew would verify the data analysis that the paper authors conducted and write the story, and I'd take care of the illustrations and graphics.

My conversation with Andrew happened two days before Thanksgiving, which is a slow news period. Our editors were not in the newsroom, so we thought, hey, we can do this really fast and no one can stop us!

I laughed out loud, remembering my own misdeeds when I worked in newsrooms, and replied: "Been there, done that!"

About once or twice a year I get to do something that delights me and that I hope delights readers. The rest of the time, my graphics are about more serious matters, like the end of pandemic-related federal unemployment aid in 2021 (**Figure 16.3**.)

According to this story, Monday, September 6, 2021, was the date of "one of the largest and most abrupt ends to government aid in U.S. history." Seven and a half million jobless people saw all unemployment benefits disappear, and 2.7 million more lost a $300-a-week boost to their benefits. Just a month earlier, 1.6 million workers had lost their benefits and 1.1 million had seen their benefits reduced.

The main graphic in the story is an alluvial diagram, a type of chart intended to show a total quantity branching out into its components, or vice versa. It's an unusual graphic form, but one that I believe fits the story adequately:

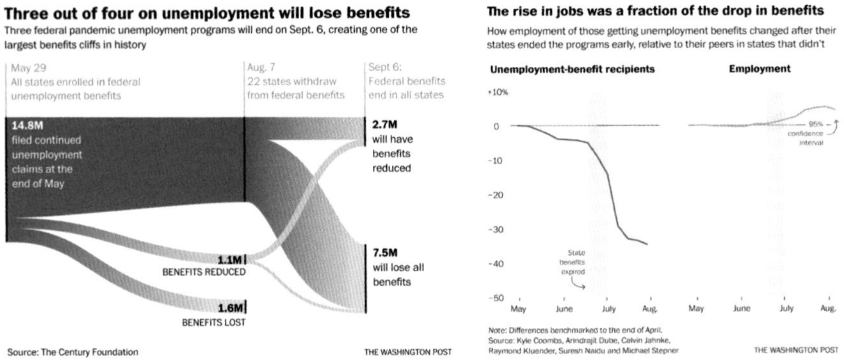

Figure 16.3: Charts from "Millions in U.S. lose jobless benefits as federal aid expires, thrusting families and economy onto uncertain path" by Yeganeh Torbati, Andrew Van Dam, and Alyssa Fowers https://www.washingtonpost.com/business/2021/09/05/unemployment-benefits-economy/

I guess that I could have used more traditional charts, such as stacked bar graphs. However, this story belongs to our in-depth coverage of pandemic-related federal aid programs, and many stories in it indirectly conveyed the idea of a system that was piecemeal and sort of broken. Metaphorically, the alluvial diagram communicates that; it looks discontinuous and complicated to navigate.

Some pandemic-related aid programs, such as the emergency rental assistance program, were hard and time-consuming to get. It was funded by the federal government, but administered through state or local community organizations, each with their own procedures.

Alyssa has a soft spot for graphics that depict flow. We next talked about a stream graph showing the factors that contributed to inflation in 2021 and 2022 (**Figure 16.4**):

It's a wibbly wobbly chart, isn't it? The total width corresponds to how much different items contributed to overall inflation growth each month. On the left I put necessities (housing, energy, groceries) and on the right, items that aren't that essential, such as dining out or cars.

Those patterns are related to the origins of the graphic. I was frustrated by the way that a lot of people were talking about inflation. In 2021 there were so many scary headlines focusing just on aggregate price growth, and not so much on its components. And when there was a story about a particular thing becoming 3 times as expensive, 10 times as expensive—they were usually items that don't have a substantial impact on the everyday experience of most people.

Prices for leisure and vacation increased in 2021 because people started going out again, there was a lot of demand and the supply hadn't recalibrated yet. Then you got into used cars. Then, things changed: the war in Ukraine led to a big bulge of energy price inflation. Housing and groceries also suffered big increases, and this is much scarier to me than what happened in 2021, as it does affect everyday lives.

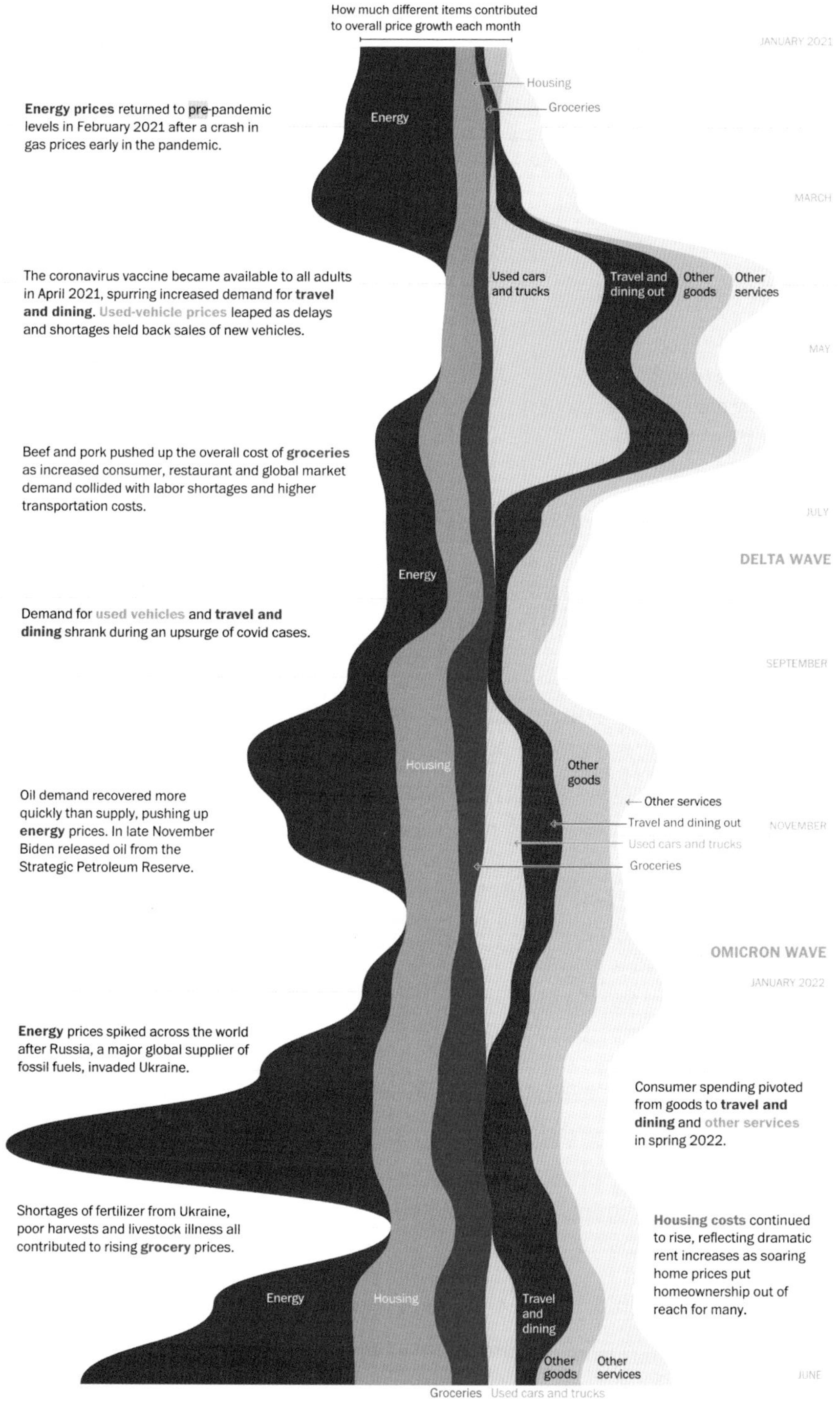

Figure 16.4: "What is causing inflation: The factors driving prices high each month"
https://www.washingtonpost.com/business/2022/07/26/inflation-causes/

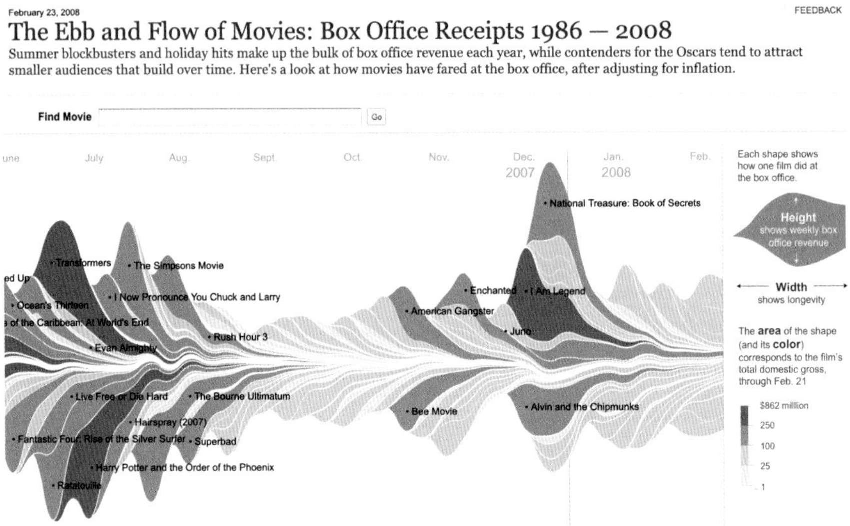

Figure 16.5: "The Ebb and Flow of Movies: Box Office Receipts 1986 — 2008" by Amanda Cox
https://www.nytimes.com/interactive/2008/02/23/movies/20080223_REVENUE_GRAPHIC.html

> Stream graphs are not common in newspapers, and I also made some unusual design choices on this one. If it was intended to be published as a stand-alone piece, perhaps I would have designed it differently, but it was part of a series of stories that contained more traditional graphics, such as bar graphs or line graphs. On this particular one I wanted to focus just on overall patterns of change, not on letting people see those changes in a lot of detail.

Stream graphs are indeed uncommon in journalism. The first one I saw, back in 2008, was designed by Amanda Cox and published by *The New York Times* (**Figure 16.5.**) It shows movie box office revenues since 1986. At the time, I unfairly criticized this graphic because it's hard to see the performance of every movie, as the graphic lacks any common baseline.

In hindsight, I think that Amanda's choice of graphic form was right and I was wrong. Her graphic was not only groundbreaking, in journalism at least, but it also emphasized what she thought was the most relevant aspect of the story: not the performance of every movie—a series of line graphs would be better for that—but the seasonality of total box office revenue and movie longevity.

Alyssa reminded me of a principle that I teach to this day: No single visualization can reveal all meaningful patterns in a data set. We have to choose which ones matter the most:

> An organizing principle of everything I do in visualization is making sure that you don't have to spend 30 minutes with something to understand it. I'd love to make graphics that reward spend-

> ing a lot of time reading them, but I know that I'm usually not going to get it. If something is very well covered elsewhere, I prefer to give readers insight into patterns that they haven't seen before, and I'll probably pick charts that might be a bit less precise, but more intuitive to understand.

Alyssa applied that personal design strategy to one of my favorite visualizations of hers, titled "Cut short" (**Figure 16.6**):

> Back in 2020, a friend of mine, who is a Wikipedia editor, was tweaking an article about a scholar who worked in the early 20th century. In the article there were tons of links to other articles about people whom this person had worked with or was influenced by. My friend spotted a pattern: the length of the articles varied a lot, some were very long, some very short. The reason was that many of these people had been killed by the Spanish flu.
>
> When he told me this story I envisioned this visceral pattern of lives being cut short. I imagined a visualization that honored one victim of COVID for each week of the pandemic. I'd write a sentence about every person, and the sentence would be cut off at a certain place. The result is a bar graph, with the bars being unfinished sentences that you can reveal by hovering over them.

Alyssa got the story idea approved around March of 2022, when the United States was approaching the one-million–COVID deaths landmark, which happened two months later:

> I worked with my colleague Leslie Shapiro, who greatly improved my original design ideas. Very few people in the newsroom believed that we could get this project done in such a short time.
>
> The challenge was manually curating the data. I used an obituary aggregator called Legacy.com to find people who died of COVID; all I did in three weeks was to read obituaries, and select a large sample of 400 that described what those people liked to do, what their plans in life were, things like that. I also tried to match the demographics of the sample to reality. I didn't do a perfect job but the visualization is as representative as possible. The sentences in the story aren't actual quotes. I wrote every single one of them based on those obituaries.
>
> I also tried to reach out to as many families as I could to make sure that they were OK with the story. I ended up talking to about a third. The only way I reached out to them was through places mentioned in the obituaries, such as funeral homes and churches. This was rough. There was a funeral home director who wanted to make sure that I wasn't a scammer. When he had enough proof that I was really a reporter, he started crying. So many people he knew had died or had been disabled by the Omicron wave...He also felt that nobody wanted to talk about the pandemic anymore, so his response was like, oh my God, somebody still cares.

"Somebody still cares." But we should always care, shouldn't we? Too often in my journalism career I've seen reporters who don't think much about the impact that their reporting might have on the people they cover. They treat them as subjects, numbers, *things* to be explored, analyzed, understood in a detached, statistical, sanitized manner.

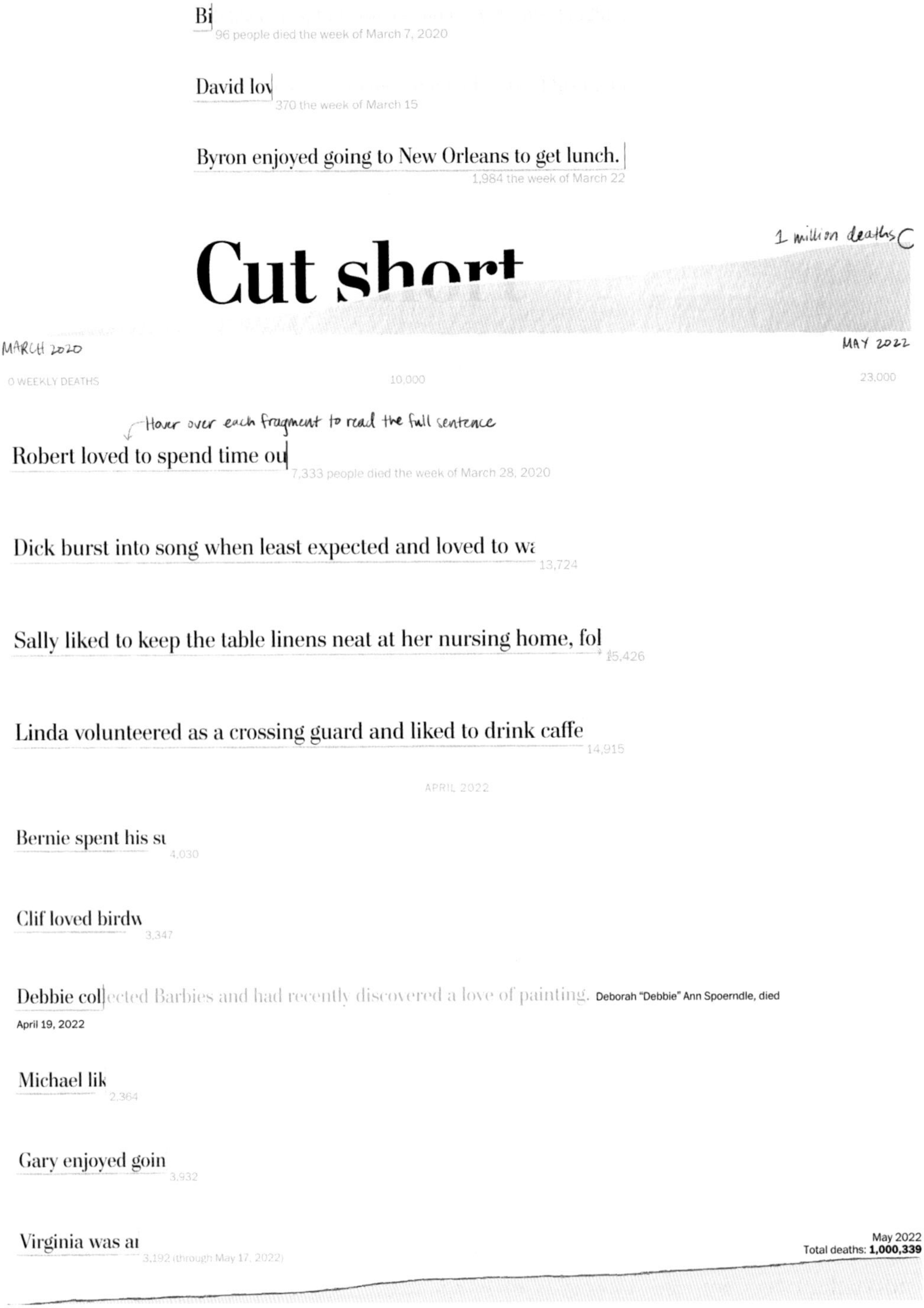

Figure 16.6: Screenshots from "Cut short" by Alyssa Fowers and Leslie Shapiro
https://www.washingtonpost.com/health/interactive/2022/1-million-covid-deaths-us/?

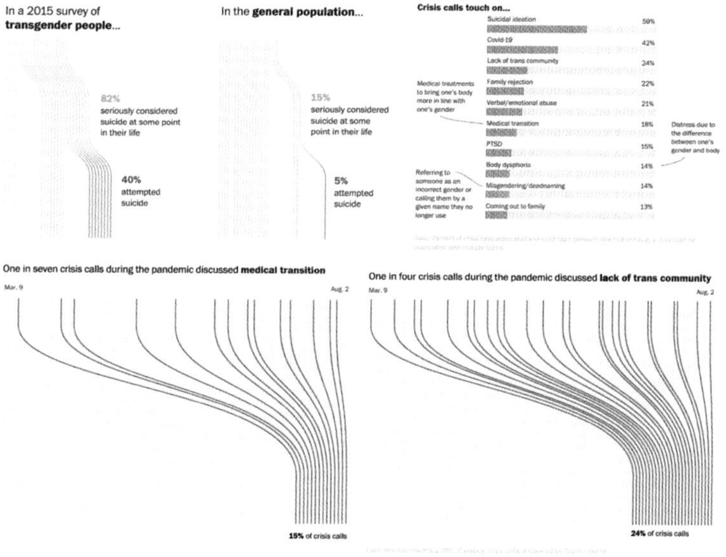

Figure 16.7: Charts from "Pandemic places pressure on transgender mental health" by Alyssa Fowers and William Wan
https://www.washingtonpost.com/health/2020/08/18/coronavirus-transgender/

Recently—I'm writing this in early 2023—we're witnessing this unconscionable behavior in the way that news media covers transgender people, particularly transgender youth, their access to gender-affirming care, and their increasing presence and visibility in society. Transgender rights are often framed as a "debate" or a "controversy," and not as what they truly are, human rights. This is insulting and demeaning.

It's also the opposite of Alyssa's approach. I think that she's representative of a generation of journalists who try to not only get their data right and to present it as accurately and fairly as possible, but who are also emotionally invested in their stories. Theirs is a journalism that transgresses decrepit notions of journalistic "balance" and, as a result, it becomes more humane.

A story that Alyssa contributed to, which describes how the COVID pandemic worsened the mental health of transgender people (**Figure 16.7**,) showcases elegant variations of Sankey diagrams and bar graphs, but what makes this piece compelling isn't these graphics or the numbers behind them. Instead, it's the writing and the visual style; they signal a profound empathy toward the people whose lives are being written about and visualized.

Essayist Rebecca Solnit once said that "empathy is first of all an act of imagination, a storyteller's art" because it consists of imagining ourselves in somebody else's place. Perhaps that should be a requirement to all who gather, analyze, visualize, or write about data on human beings.

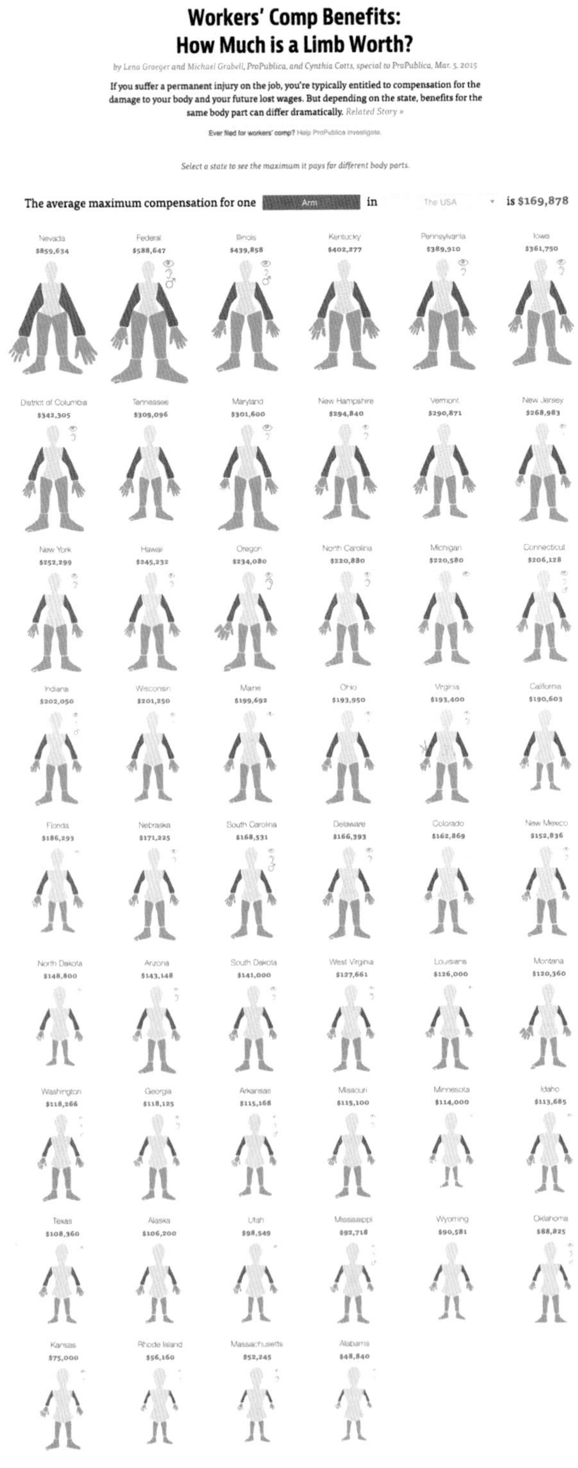

Figure 17.1: "Workers' Comp Benefits: How Much is a Limb Worth?" by Lena Groeger, Michael Grabell, and Cynthia Cotts
https://projects.propublica.org/graphics/workers-compensation-benefits-by-limb
Context: https://www.propublica.org/article/five-things-i-learned-making-a-chart-out-of-body-parts

Chapter 17
with Lena Groeger

No Treasure Hunts

Life can surprise us in giving us the work we are here to do.

—Dacher Keltner

In the fall of 2014 **Lena Groeger**, graphics director at ProPublica—in my opinion the gold standard when it comes to data and investigative journalism—emailed me to ask about a project she was working on. It was a visualization of the compensation that U.S. workers receive for damaged body parts. The amount depends on the state where the worker is. Lena wanted my opinion about using "a little person that represents each state, and size each body part according to difference from the national average."

I replied that I wouldn't do it. I told Lena that her illustrations looked so creepy that they sent "shivers down my spine." Instead I recommended traditional maps and graphs.

Lena is a wise journalist and designer, so she ignored me. The result was one of the most widely read and discussed graphics she's ever created (**Figure 17.1**). It was picked up by multiple news organizations—Gawker linked to it with the title "How Much Are Your Balls Worth?"—and fueled policy discussions in several states.

Consider this anecdote whenever you hear visualization "thought leaders"—I've always rejected that label; it *really* sends shivers down my spine—claiming to know what we're talking about. In my defense, though, in her first email Lena had attached some early prototypes that she acknowledges are spooky, if not utterly terrifying (**Figure 17.2**).

Lena and I began our conversation laughing about our exchange almost a decade ago, and quickly moved on to more serious matters:

This project exemplifies how I think about graphics. For instance, it reflects my love of small multiples. I think that it's a design strategy that is useful in many contexts.

Small multiples are trellis charts, arrays of graphics that share the same characteristics—for instance, axes or scales—organized as a grid to enable comparisons. Lena continued:

This project reveals another feature of my work and ProPublica's in general: trying to take advantage of the data that you have, and to do something unique with it, asking yourself "what is it that I can do with this data set that I can't do with other data sets?" Both in terms of how the data is displayed and of the overall design of the story. In a case like this we're talking about body parts, so we can use the body parts to encode the data. And there's a reason to choose something a little more visually compelling: by visualizing the data as little human figures, we attracted over a million readers into a project about, of all things, insurance.

Another reason for the success of this piece might be that readers can interact with it and get pretty deep into the numbers:

That is also a very ProPublica thing. ProPublica's style is related to its ethos of investigative reporting and being as transparent as possible, showing receipts, so to speak, and all the data we have. Our projects use a design strategy that my colleague Scott Klein calls "the far and the near." The "far" consists of presenting an overview of the data at a glance. The "near" is giving the reader the opportunity to drill down as deep as possible.

We've used this strategy multiple times. For instance, in a project titled "Reopening America" (**Figure 17.3**) the "far" is a map made of arrows that indicate whether positive COVID tests increased or decreased over the previous two weeks. That gives you the big picture. The "near" is

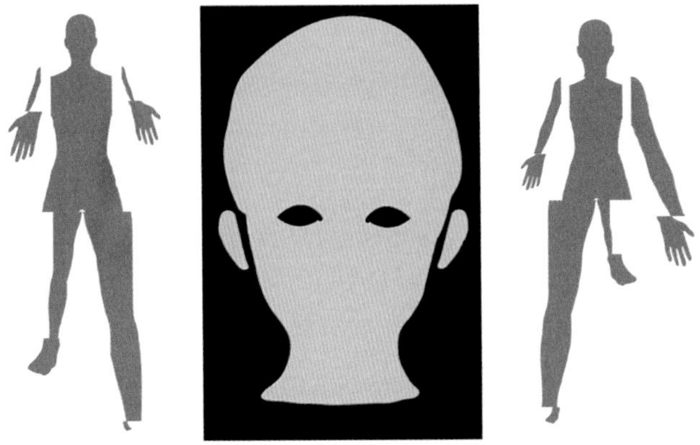

Figure 17.2: Early sketches for "Workers' Comp Benefits: How Much is a Limb Worth?" See more at https://www.propublica.org/article/five-things-i-learned-making-a-chart-out-of-body-parts

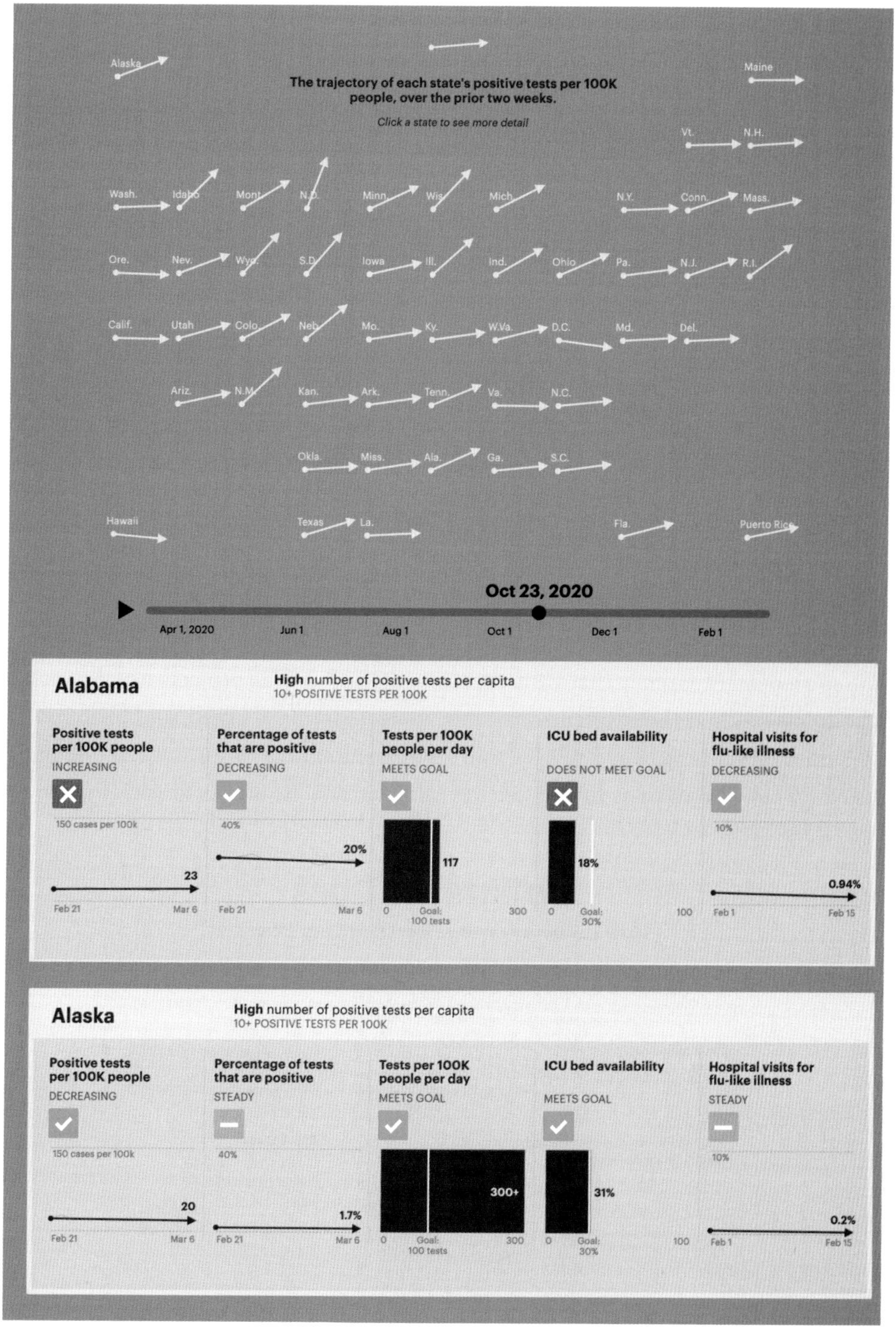

Figure 17.3: Charts from "Reopening America" by Lena V. Groeger and Ash Ngu
https://projects.propublica.org/reopening-america/

> that readers can click on those arrows and see a lot of detailed information. The "near" consists of trying to let readers find themselves somehow in the data, by seeing their own communities, in the numbers.

In a project titled "Dollars for Docs" (**Figure 17.4**), one of the most-read pieces that ProPublica has ever published, any reader can search for the names of their caregivers and see how much money they have received for "promotional talks, research and consulting." My primary care doctor was paid $15 for this in the latest year reported, 2018; not a hefty sum!

ProPublica calls interactive projects like "Dollars for Docs" "news applications" because their primary goal is to make large databases accessible and useful. As secondary goals, they can also reveal patterns in data or explain a topic. Unlike traditional news graphics that are published once and then abandoned for the next project, news apps are updated frequently with the hope that people use them again and again:

> News applications keep attracting readers well after they are published. We updated "Reopening America" daily with new COVID numbers for a year, and some of our health-related news apps, like "Dollars for Docs" or "Nursing Home Inspect," we've updated for over a decade.

In the spirit of transparency that Lena mentioned, ProPublica's projects usually include a methodology section that explains how they collected, transformed, and analyzed their data. Sometimes this section discloses sources of inspiration. For instance, the explanatory piece "What Coronavirus Job Losses Reveal About Racism in America" (**Figure 17.5**)

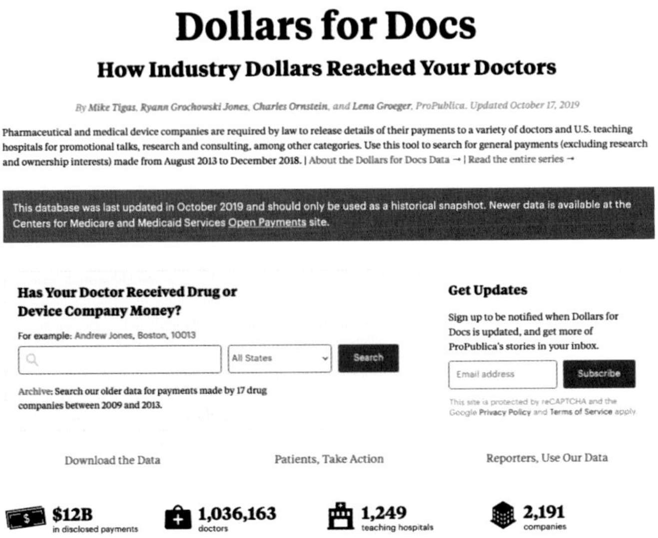

Figure 17.4: "Dollars for Docs"
https://projects.propublica.org/docdollars/

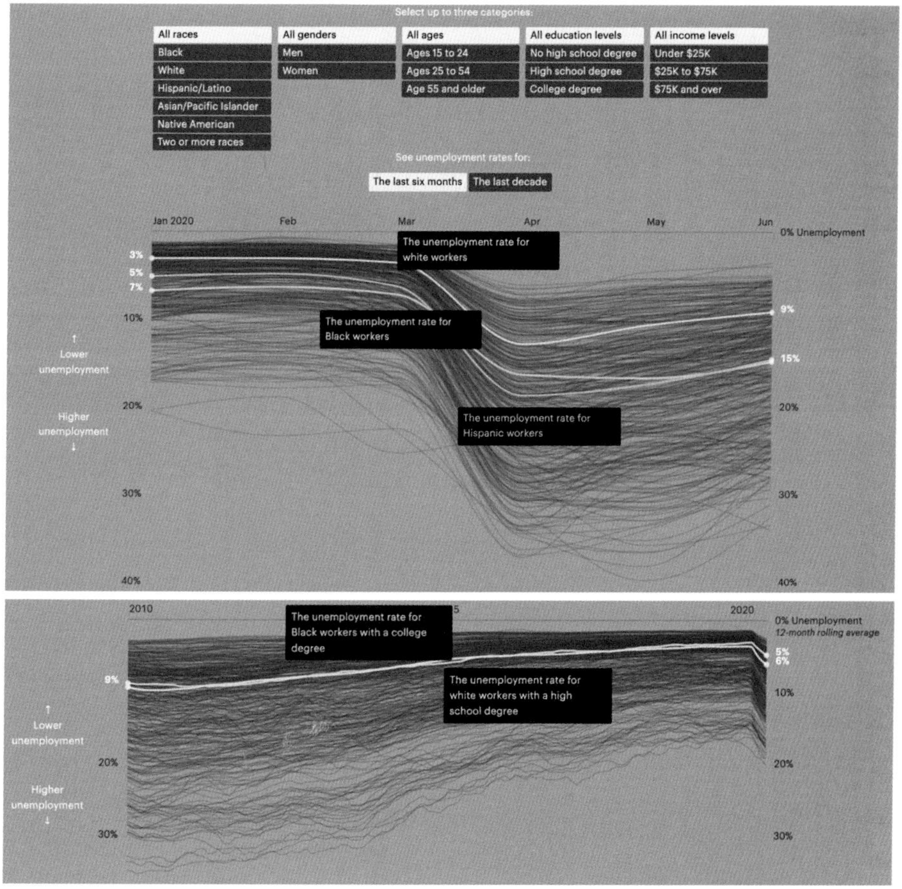

Figure 17.5: Charts from "What Coronavirus Job Losses Reveal About Racism in America"
https://projects.propublica.org/coronavirus-unemployment/

is influenced by a 2009 *New York Times* interactive visualization titled "The Jobless Rate for People Like You."

Giving other designers credit for the ideas we borrow from them is unusual, but it shouldn't be. I told Lena that I wish it would become common practice. I myself have learned a lot from emulating people I admire. Lena explained:

> I guess that I wanted to honor a certain spirit of generosity, recognizing what came before us. At ProPublica we want other organizations to "steal" our stories, to republish them. We want to get credit for that, of course, but also to give credit back.

From the original *New York Times* visualization Lena borrowed the idea of an upper menu that lets readers select races, genders, educational levels, and other variables, to see their corresponding unemployment rates in the past two decades. To that she added her own spin, a narrative. When readers scroll the piece, certain lines are highlighted, and explanatory text gradually appears over the graphics. There's a term to refer to this type of story, "scrollytelling":

> Maintaining the interactivity of the original visualization, but then adding the narrative element and the annotations is related to a pet peeve of mine. At ProPublica we use to say "No treasure hunts!" What we mean by that is that when interactive data visualizations started to become common in journalism, back in the 2010s, the "treasures" (the insights from the data) were often behind a click or a hover. Readers had to work hard to navigate graphics by opening menus, clicking on buttons, or using their cursors to reveal tooltips. This was self-defeating. If certain data points or patterns are important, they should be visible straight away.
>
> Some interaction is still necessary in pieces like this, but we can also help readers by highlighting the most relevant or interesting parts of the data.

The highlighted parts are indeed interesting. I knew about the racial unemployment gap in the United States, but I hadn't seen it visualized along with educational levels. It was striking to see that the unemployment of African Americans who have college degrees is similar to the unemployment rate of white people who have just high school degrees.

The COVID pandemic made unemployment increase for all groups in the first six months of 2020, but not at the same rate. Workers of color were more affected. This worsened a historical pattern, revealed by the graphic:

> If we zoom out to the past decade, we see that Black Americans have faced unemployment levels for years that would be considered an economic catastrophe if they were the national average.

Much of Lena's work at ProPublica combines interactive features with a linear narrative, but she's also designed stories of stark simplicity and depth, such as "Lost Cause" (**Figure 17.6**). It consists of a series of maps that highlight the counties that supported the losing candidate in every presidential election between 1828 and 2008. The maps are interspersed with text that provides historical context and explains the patterns in the visuals:

> In many stories we begin with a question or a conjecture and then we try to find data to analyze it. This is the opposite. This is a case similar to the workers, compensation visualization, an example of my finding a data set and thinking, "What can we do with it?" Years ago I discovered the work of Frédéric Salmon, a French geographer who has these massive historical election data sets of different countries. I started thinking about how to use it.
>
> The 2016 presidential election was approaching, and I wondered what would be the ProPublica way of covering it. We aren't a traditional news organization, so we don't follow campaigns, we don't do forecasts or predictions, and we don't publish results after the vote. We thought, well, everyone is going to be covering the winner on election day—why not make a story about the loser's perspective? We published it one day before the 2022 election.

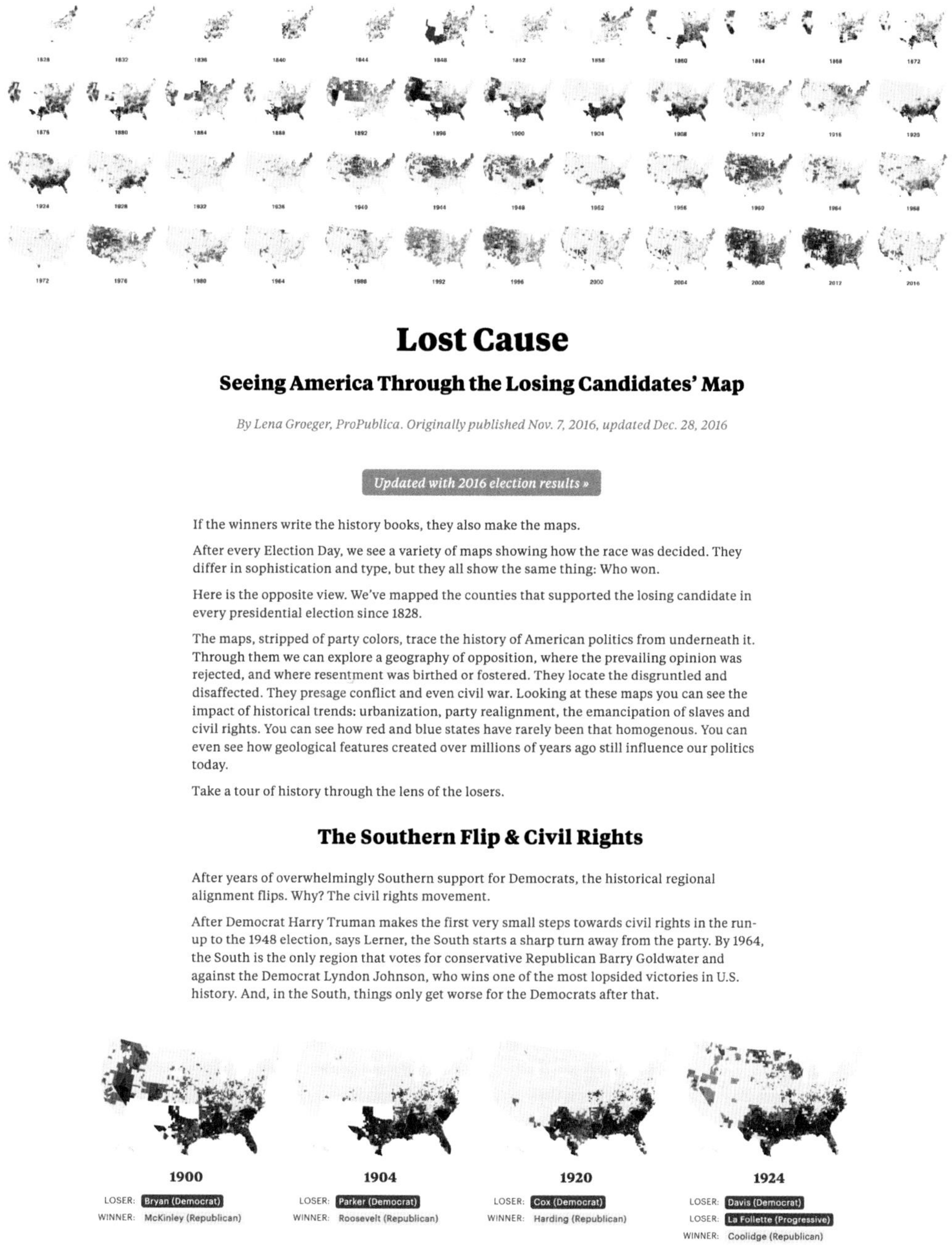

Lost Cause

Seeing America Through the Losing Candidates' Map

By Lena Groeger, ProPublica. Originally published Nov. 7, 2016, updated Dec. 28, 2016

Updated with 2016 election results »

If the winners write the history books, they also make the maps.

After every Election Day, we see a variety of maps showing how the race was decided. They differ in sophistication and type, but they all show the same thing: Who won.

Here is the opposite view. We've mapped the counties that supported the losing candidate in every presidential election since 1828.

The maps, stripped of party colors, trace the history of American politics from underneath it. Through them we can explore a geography of opposition, where the prevailing opinion was rejected, and where resentment was birthed or fostered. They locate the disgruntled and disaffected. They presage conflict and even civil war. Looking at these maps you can see the impact of historical trends: urbanization, party realignment, the emancipation of slaves and civil rights. You can see how red and blue states have rarely been that homogenous. You can even see how geological features created over millions of years ago still influence our politics today.

Take a tour of history through the lens of the losers.

The Southern Flip & Civil Rights

After years of overwhelmingly Southern support for Democrats, the historical regional alignment flips. Why? The civil rights movement.

After Democrat Harry Truman makes the first very small steps towards civil rights in the run-up to the 1948 election, says Lerner, the South starts a sharp turn away from the party. By 1964, the South is the only region that votes for conservative Republican Barry Goldwater and against the Democrat Lyndon Johnson, who wins one of the most lopsided victories in U.S. history. And, in the South, things only get worse for the Democrats after that.

Figure 17.6: Maps from "Lost Cause: Seeing America Through the Losing Candidates' Map"
https://projects.propublica.org/graphics/lost-cause

My work is often easy in comparison to my colleagues' at ProPublica. Many of them are tough investigative reporters who constantly have to deal with people who don't want to talk to them because they are involved in misdeeds or are hiding something. It's the opposite for me. I talk to experts who are eager to share some obscure research or data set! While working on "Lost Cause" I showed these maps to political geographers, historians, social scientists, and asked, "What do you see here? What patterns do you notice? What is this map telling us?" The story is structured around a series of the most interesting tidbits that these researchers gave me.

Projects like this are the closest to my idea of what journalism was when I was in college: a job that would give me the chance to talk to a bunch of experts, condense what they say, and then package it as a coherent narrative.

I wondered where Lena's interest in "obscure research" came from. It might be a natural follow-up to her peculiar and winding educational path with excursions into the medical sciences, neuroscience, the philosophy of mind, morality and, ultimately, journalism and design:

I've always liked design. I fell in love with typography in middle school and made it a hobby. I never imagined that design could be a real job, and I had this weird idea that it was just about illustration and making things look pretty.

In college I studied philosophy, biology, and even planned to go to med school, but I also took classes on poster and magazine design that helped me understand that design could have a practical purpose. I even took a job at Brown University's health education department putting together public health posters about consent and sexual health. After that I spent a year in Europe deciding what I wanted to do with my life and taking odd jobs. In fact, my first writing job was maintaining a weblog at University of Oxford's Uehiro Centre for Practical Ethics.

When I came back to the United States I did a master's degree in science communication at New York University. I discovered data journalism and visualization thanks to it, and I ended up at ProPublica, where I first did some writing and eventually moved to the News Apps team.

After years in ProPublica's News Apps team, led by Scott Klein, Lena was recently named the head of a newly created graphics team. As a former graphics director at several news publications myself, in Spain and Brazil, I was intrigued about the differences between those two departments:

When ProPublica was launched, back in 2010, it didn't have an art department or a graphics department. People who designed visualizations were in the News Apps team, where they were also in charge of information graphics, databases, etc.

We worked like any other reporters or editors. We pitched story ideas, investigated them, and then created our own projects. We could spend many months working on a single story, but we didn't make many smaller-scale graphics for stories by other reporters in the newsroom, the type of daily graphics you see in traditional news publications. We did work with other people in the newsroom regularly, but there wasn't a formal process to do so.

At some point ProPublica decided that we needed a team devoted to collaborations with reporters and editors, and less centered on designing our own pitched stories. This led to a newsroom reorganization in which news applications and graphics are both part of a broader Visuals team that also includes photo, illustration, and video teams.

My new job, then, consists of reading story memos and pitches early on, and assessing them for their graphics potential. I can propose ideas for graphics to supplement those stories—or sometimes I can simply mention that no chart is needed! If a simple good sentence or a table are enough to tell a story, why design a visualization?

While Lena was talking I thought back to my first days in journalism, back in the late 1990's. At the time, graphics departments in news organizations were treated as service desks. We didn't do any reporting or editing. Rather, we were artists who waited for people from other desks to bring requests for graphics to fit into the stories that they were writing. I mean "to fit" in a literal sense, as I'm talking about print newspapers. We were given a specific space on a page, which was rarely negotiable, and we had to make our graphics squeeze in it.

I was part of a generation of news graphics journalists who pushed for an overhaul of this antiquated hierarchical and unidirectional workflow. Why couldn't we, graphics journalists, be autonomous, do reporting, and write our own stories, besides designing the graphics for them?

However, this model can also be taken to the extreme, to a point where a news graphics desk becomes too isolated from the rest of the newsroom. The proactively collaborative and horizontal workflow that Lena described for her new graphics desk at ProPublica sounds ideal. It's an attempt to find a middle point between total dependency and total autonomy.

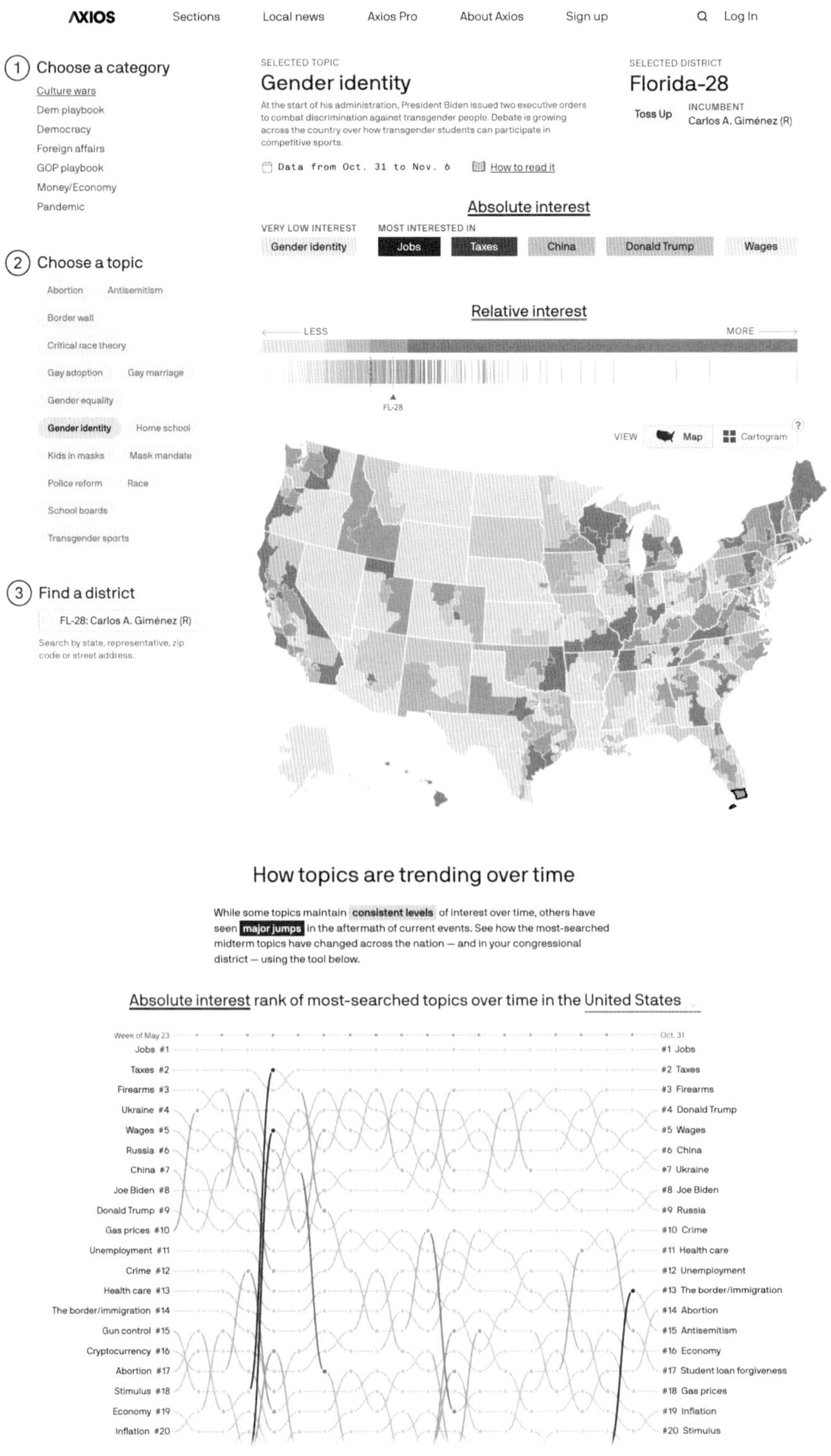

Figure 18.1: Screenshots from "Midterm elections 2022: The issues that matter to Americans" by Jacque Schrag and Will Chase Axios / https://www.axios.com/midterms-elections-2022-issues-americans-care / last accessed June 19,2023.

Chapter 18
with Danielle Alberti, Jacque Schrag, and Will Chase

Smart Brevity

Our job is to find stories in *the data, rather than finding data* for *the story.*

—Erin Davis

In most countries where I've lived or worked, traditional news organizations, particularly newspapers, have been declining for decades. To get a sense of the scale of the crisis, consider this: According to the Pew Research Center, daily print newspaper circulation in the United States in 1990 was more than 60 million; thirty years later it was less than 25 million. Newspaper revenue has suffered a similarly steep downward slope.

Nonetheless, data and visual journalism still thrives nowadays at a handful of national newspapers—*The New York Times* or *The Washington Post* come to mind—and at smaller, more nimble organizations that have been able to specialize and offer something unique. ProPublica (Chapter 17) chose the path of in-depth, long-form investigative reporting. Axios, the focus of the current chapter, took a different road. Its founders, journalists Mike Allen, Roy Schwartz, and Jim VandeHei call it "Smart Brevity."

I've been an advisor for some Axios projects in collaboration with Google Trends and its data editor, Simon Rogers, so I've witnessed Smart Brevity at work. One of the projects I advised on is "Midterm elections 2022: The issues that matter to Americans" (**Figure 18.1**), which visualizes Google search data about topics of political interest. Axios's Smart Brevity

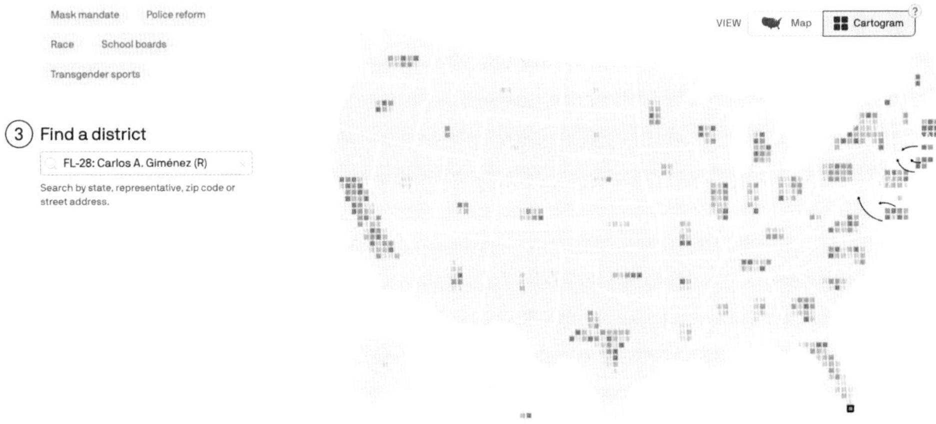

Figure 18.2: Cartogram from "Midterm elections 2022: The issues that matter to Americans"

doesn't consist of mere reduction or simplification—"Midterm elections 2022" contains plenty of maps and charts—but of using plain language and presenting just a sufficient amount of information to make a story clear—no more, but also *no less*; another motto at Axios is "short, not shallow."

Danielle Alberti, Axios's data visualization editor, told me that achieving the right balance in every story demands ruthless editing:

> We journalists and designers tend to be too attached to every single bit of the data that we gather and report on. Something that my team really excels at is trying to narrow the data down, and to keep and highlight just the relevant parts, the main takeaways. Very often in the newsroom we tell each other, "That's not Axios!" meaning that a story that we are discussing may be too long and complex or too short and superficial.

Jacque Schrag and **Will Chase** designed our midterm elections project. Jacque reminded me of the moment when I got excited about it, during one of our early meetings:

> Sometimes the most obvious or traditional graphic form isn't the right choice even if your main goal is to make a visualization that is as clear as possible. Remember that our first drafts for this story, based on typical maps and charts, were a bit unexciting? And remember how the mood in the meeting changed when I presented our ideas for slightly more unusual graphics?

I remember it vividly.

In the first drafts of this story, the main visual was a congressional district-level choropleth map. A well-known challenge with choropleth maps is that the area of geographic units—countries, states, counties, districts, and so on—can vary a lot, and it doesn't correspond to the population that inhabits them. Sparsely populated states such as North Dakota or South Dakota have a single electoral district, which looks gigantic in comparison to, say, the 28 districts that Florida is divided into.

This gives a designer with pragmatic sympathies like me a justifiable reason to let readers see the data in a complementary way, for instance through an equal area cartogram where all districts have exactly the same size (**Figure 18.2**).

However, it was Jacque and Will's second idea that intrigued me the most. Its first version is shown in **Figure 18.3**. In this barcode plot, every row corresponds to a search topic, and every dash is a congressional district. The position of the dashes on the horizontal axis is the search interest for that particular topic. "Search interest" is a normalized variable that goes from 0 (no interest) to 100 (maximum interest) in relation to all Google searches in the same places and time.

Most designers I know are inexplicably attached to certain graphic forms. I have a soft spot for graphs where each symbol corresponds to an individual data point, such as scatter plots or strip plots (a barcode plot is a variant of the strip plot that uses dashes instead of dots). I find them visually pleasant, and I believe that they gently prompt scrutiny.

A polished and interactive version of this plot became a key element in the story. Notice that topics related to financial well-being—wages, taxes, or jobs—were the most

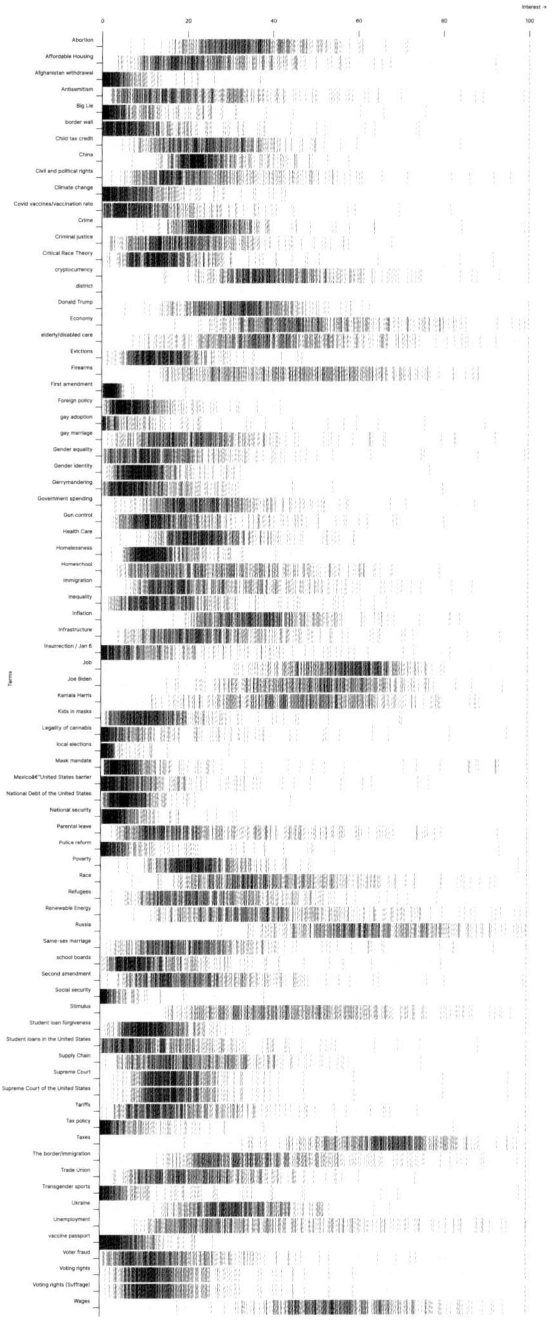

Figure 18.3: First barcode plot sketch

searched for in most districts. There are also subtle patterns of concentration and dispersion: some topics are of very low interest in some districts but of maximum interest in others.

Since I was online graphics director at the Spanish newspaper *El Mundo* from 2000 to 2005, I've been interested in the structure and evolution of news graphics desks whose work I admire. As Axios is among them, I asked Danielle about it:

> Our graphics team was created by Lázaro Gamio [currently a graphics editor at *The New York Times*]. He created all the graphics styles and made a lot of hires. He also oversaw our first chart-building tool for internal use in the newsroom, built by Gerald Rich (now at AP) and Harry Stevens (*Washington Post*)—all that while he was in charge of data viz and illustrations.
>
> Axios has grown a lot since it was founded in 2016 and launched in 2017. We have a presence in more than 30 cities in the United States, and we're producing many graphics on a day-to-day basis. My graphics team (12 people) is divided into three parts: Sara Wise's daily requests team, which collaborates with reporters on graphics produced on a deadline; the storytelling team, led by Will; and the engineering team, led by Jacque.
>
> There aren't rigid boundaries between these teams; most of us aren't just on one team or the other all the time, but become part of either on a project-by-project basis.

The main task of Jacque's engineering team is to maintain, expand, and improve Axios's newsroom tools to automate data and data visualization design. Jacque explained:

> As the Axios newsroom has continued to grow, so has the need to scale our processes, tools, and templates. The chart-making tool is key. It allows anyone in the newsroom to produce simple visualizations such as bar graphs, line graphs, or heat maps, write a headline, and then send them to us so we can edit them before publishing. This allows the graphics team to spend more resources and time on more ambitious and custom projects. Developing templates also contributes to this goal.

Jacque has a background in web development and she's worked for think tanks in Washington DC. Switching to Axios and adapting to its Smart Brevity mentality was a challenge because of her previous experience, she told me:

> I have an undergraduate degree in history and a master's in international peace and conflict resolution, but I've also done website design and development since I was a kid. I've worked for organizations such as the National Democratic Institute, Interaction, Mennonite Central Committee, and the Center for Strategic International Studies (CSIS), which is where I was before joining Axios.

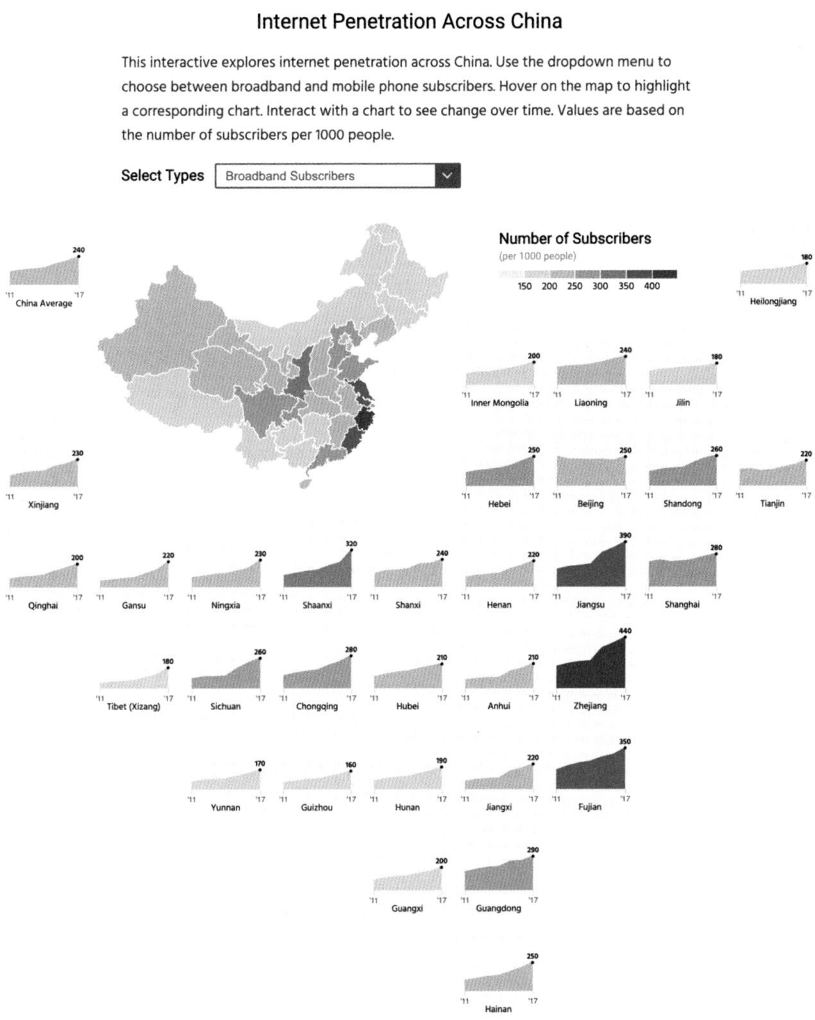

Figure 18.4: "Internet Penetration Across China" by Jacque Schrag Center for Strategic and International Studies. / https://chinapower.csis.org/web-connectedness/ / last accessed June 19,2023.

I made hundreds of data visualizations at CSIS. My job there was my first kind of foray into how you deal with big numbers and make them understandable to any audience. The skills that I learned there turned out to be useful later at Axios, but my current job is very different. At CSIS I designed many rich and complex interactive visualizations with menus, buttons, and tooltips [**Figure 18.4**, "Internet Penetration Across China," is an example.] At Axios we're more limited.

Part of the limitation is the Smart Brevity thinking, of course, but it's also due to trying to adapt our visualizations to the medium that we work in, and to the needs of our audience. Many of Axios's readers get our content via email newsletter, and you can't have a whole lot of fancy interaction in a newsletter! In my previous job my bread-and-butter was interactive data visualization. Moving to Axios was a big learning experience. At the same time, I believe that my visualization skills have become better because of the need to be concise and to have a clear point in the charts and maps I design nowadays.

We still publish plenty of interactive graphics at Axios, but we think very carefully about their design to make sure that they are understandable regardlesss of whether readers interact with them. In other words, never put relevant information behind a tooltip!

I asked Danielle, Jacque, and Will whether there was anything that revealed to them that a career in data journalism and visualization might be an exciting prospect. Danielle mentioned statistician Nathan Yau's website, Flowing Data, and his first book, *Visualize This!* (2011); both Jacque and Will said that *Data Sketches*, the project and book by Shirley Wu (see the Introduction) and Nadieh Bremer (Chapter 4), opened their eyes. Jacque said:

In 2017 I traveled to Boston to attend the Open Viz conference. I remember that trip for two reasons. One, my then-boyfriend came with me and we got engaged that weekend. Second, Nadieh and Shirley were presenters that year, and they talked about *Data Sketches*. It was their first talk about the project. I just sat there in complete awe and said to myself, "Holy sh*t, you can do amazing, creating things with visualization." I left the conference telling myself, "I want to be them!"

Will was similarly enthusiastic:

I studied microbiology in college. That background in science has been very helpful to this day. After all, what is science but building data stories, at least in a sense? I was also interested in programming and designed many visualizations for my research and classes. And one day I stumbled upon *Data Sketches* and it was like a spark in my brain, "Oh my God, I want to do this! This is the thing!"

Fast forward a few years and I got to meet Shirley Wu at a conference about D3.js. She was amazing, we chatted all night and I decided, "OK, I can do this. This is a career that I want to pursue." Coincidentally, at that conference I met some people from Fidelity investments, and that led to my first full-time job as a visualization designer. It was part of their internal business intelligence team, which builds all the dashboards and data reports. That was the largest amount of data I've ever dealt with.

Every generation of visualization designers has its heroes. My generation of visual journalists grew up under the radically opposing influences of Nigel Holmes—who favors simple, direct, and often illustrated and gently humorous graphics—and Edward Tufte's stern writing and design style. What does it feel like to have people like Nadieh Bremer and Shirley Wu as your heroes instead? I asked Jacque, who replied:

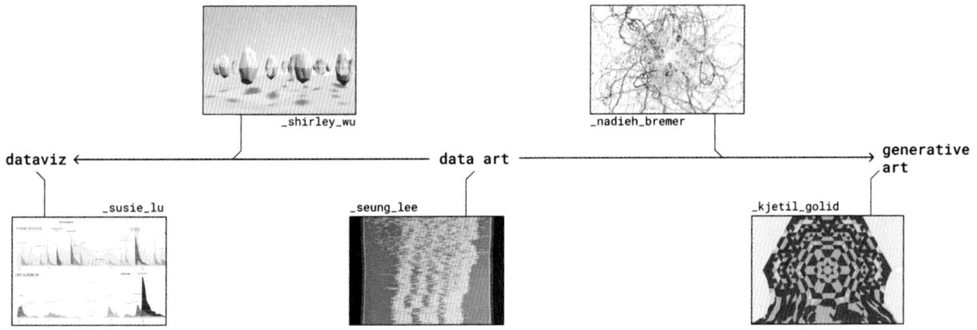

Figure 18.5: "The generative art <--> dataviz spectrum"
https://buttondown.email/willchase/archive/the-generative-art-dataviz-spectrum/

It pushes you to be creative and to innovate, but to also think about when it is appropriate or not to do so. You can't be artistic all the time, or even most of the time. I encountered *Data Sketches* when I still was at CSIS and, even if I had plenty of freedom to make choices about design, I had to consider who my audience was: analysts, researchers, and policymakers. Those are people who won't spend a lot of time staring in awe at an incredible chart, no matter how beautiful it is.

This creates some tension between what you would like to do and what you *actually* need to do. I'd love to use more of those so-called *xenographics*, [a term coined by designer Maarten Lambrechts, who has a website with the same name], strange, unusual, creative, artistic graphic forms. However, I also understand that this isn't the best approach if the goal is to inform a reader quickly and efficiently. Part of my personal growth as a designer has been coming to appreciate when someone designs a very readable, very functional chart, but also makes it look novel and fresh. That's what I try to do at Axios.

Will added:

The *Data Sketches* approach to visualization I think is aspirational, in a way, for many designers, including myself, someone who in the past had to design business graphics.

Related to this, in 2020 I wrote a newsletter based on a talk I gave about creative coding. I titled it 'The generative art <--> dataviz spectrum" because I see a continuum (**Figure 18.5**) between the type of visualization that we make at Axios, which strives to be easy to read and understand, data art, and generative art. I see no clear boundaries between them; they are connected to one another.

Sometimes you need your graphic to be clear and efficient, and in other times you need to aim for a higher emotional resonance and memorability, perhaps because you're trying to create

> social change; in that case sacrificing some efficiency to come up with a more unique visualization is acceptable.

Will echoed Jacque's point about Axios not being the right place for unfettered artistic experimentation—"We do experiment, but we also try to put the reader first; we never do experimentation for experimentation's sake"—but he added that his storytelling team has plenty of creative freedom:

> We have a lot of room to pitch our own stories, following our interests and passions. The newsroom encourages that, and there's barely any editorial quashing of ideas or direction. Our approach to story choices is bottom-up, rather than top-down. If you have an idea for a story, usually the reaction is, "We'll probably find a place for it."
>
> My team is different to the daily requests team within the graphics desk in the sense that we are not that restricted on subject matter or even space. This has led to some self-doubt. Axios is all about Smart Brevity, isn't it? But we have done plenty of long-form stories and deep visualizations.
>
> We've come to believe that graphics-driven stories help circumvent one of the main challenges with long-form journalism, which is that too often it ends up being these very large walls of text, these large essays that turn many readers off. In our graphics-driven stories there's usually not much text. I think that inherent to the medium of visualization is Smart Brevity, we reduce the word count and try to distill core messages.

The visualization stories that Will's team produces are long, but they don't *feel* long to me because they are tightly designed to be a service to readers; they don't try to show off. I asked Will to pick a project created by his team to exemplify their aims and processes:

> The first long project I created for Axios was our coronavirus variant tracker (**Figure 18.6**). It was published in April of 2021, when the many variants of COVID—six at the time—were starting to become a big deal. There were many stories in the news about each of them, but no centralized place that offered information about all variants at the same time.
>
> It was a confusing time. You could search on the Internet for one variant and you'd find dozens of news stories about it, and all of them would have slightly different information. How much more virulent is it? Can you still get this new variant if you are already infected with other variants? And many other questions.
>
> We asked ourselves, what if we take all that information, we verify it, and we package it in a way that can be digested easily, using iconography and illustrations? We ended up distilling the information about each variant down to five key points, the essential information that any reader needs to know. Following that opening section we added some maps and graphs to provide

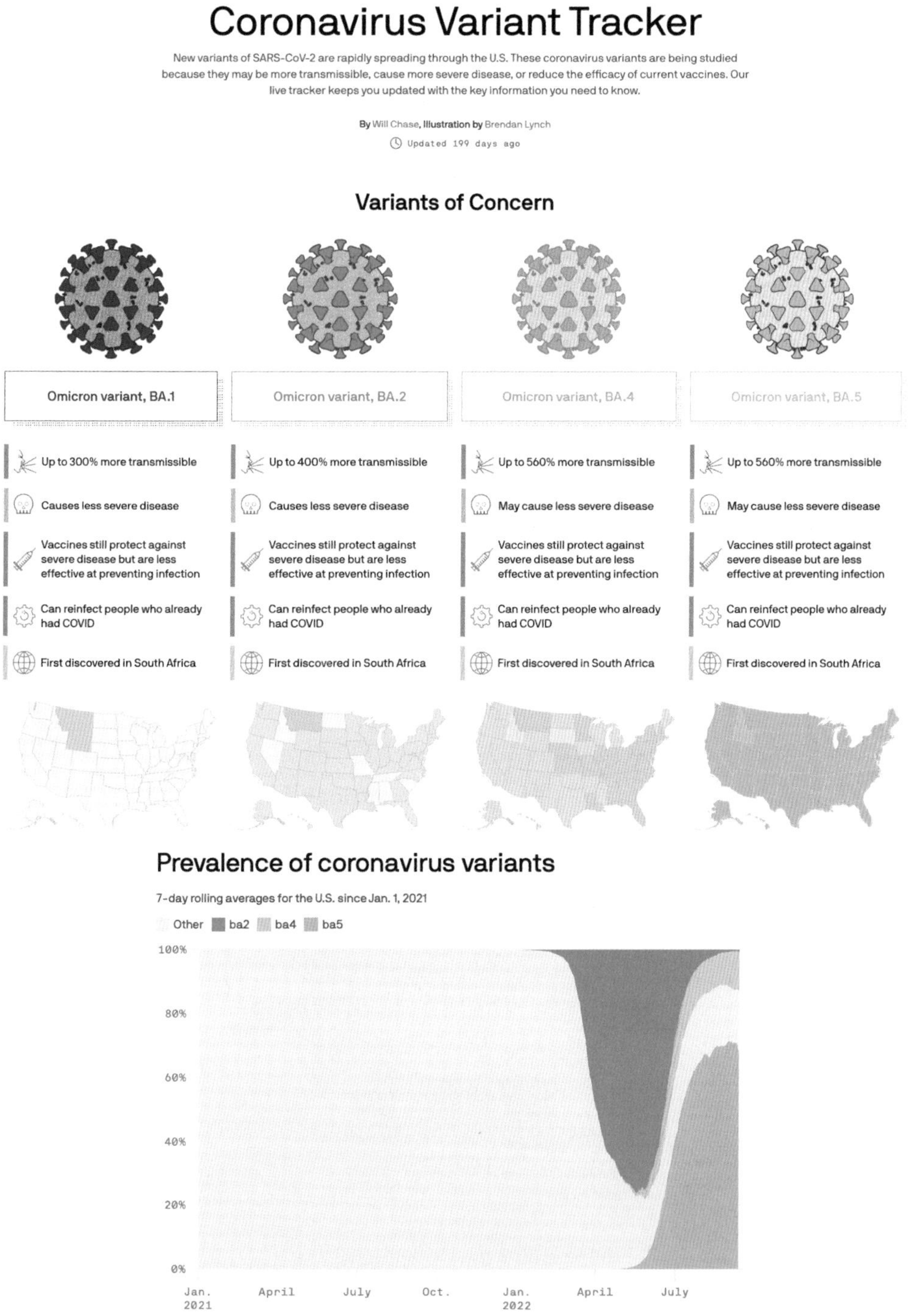

Figure 18.6: Graphics from "Coronavirus Variant Tracker" by Will Chase, illustrations by Brendan Lynch https://www.axios.com/variants-tracker

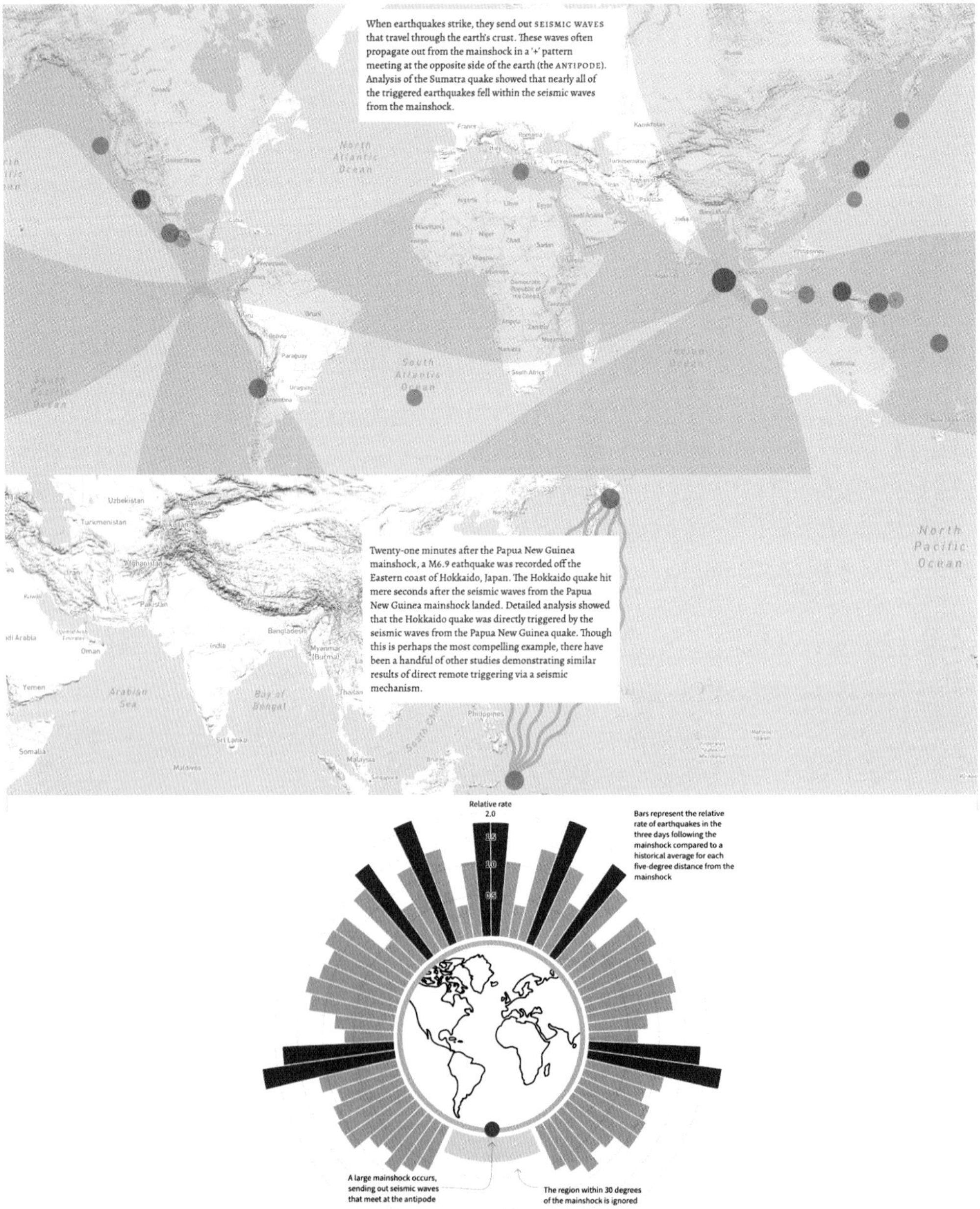

Figure 18.7: Graphics from "Can one earthquake trigger another on the other side of the world?" by Will Chase
https://will-r-chase.github.io/eq_bw/

context. We've also updated the project until early 2023; the last update has information on fourteen COVID variants. Considering the overwhelmingly positive response we received from readers, it seems that they appreciated the thoroughness but also the brevity of the project.

The coronavirus tracker was the first long-form story that Will published in Axios, but not the first he's made. In the summer of 2019, Will self-published "Can one earthquake trigger another on the other side of the world?" (**Figure 18.7**).

I designed this story for a competition run by Mapbox and the Data Visualization Society. The challenge was to make graphics about natural disaster risks. I began researching which natural disasters could trigger others, and ended up with earthquakes.

I this story Will wrote that anyone who lives in a place exposed to natural disasters knows that they "can cause others in their immediate vicinity, for instance, hurricanes are often accompanied by flooding, and earthquakes are followed by aftershocks." But earthquakes triggering other earthquakes in distant parts of the world? I confess that I hadn't heard of that, so I read Will's piece in its entirety. It's fascinating. I learned that when an earthquake occurs, it generates seismic waves that propagate through the Earth's crust often in a pattern that resembles a cross. If these waves meet again on the antipode—the opposite side of the planet—they can unleash earthquakes there.

Visualizations don't just inform us of things that we should know; they can also lead us to discover things that we never thought we'd like to know.

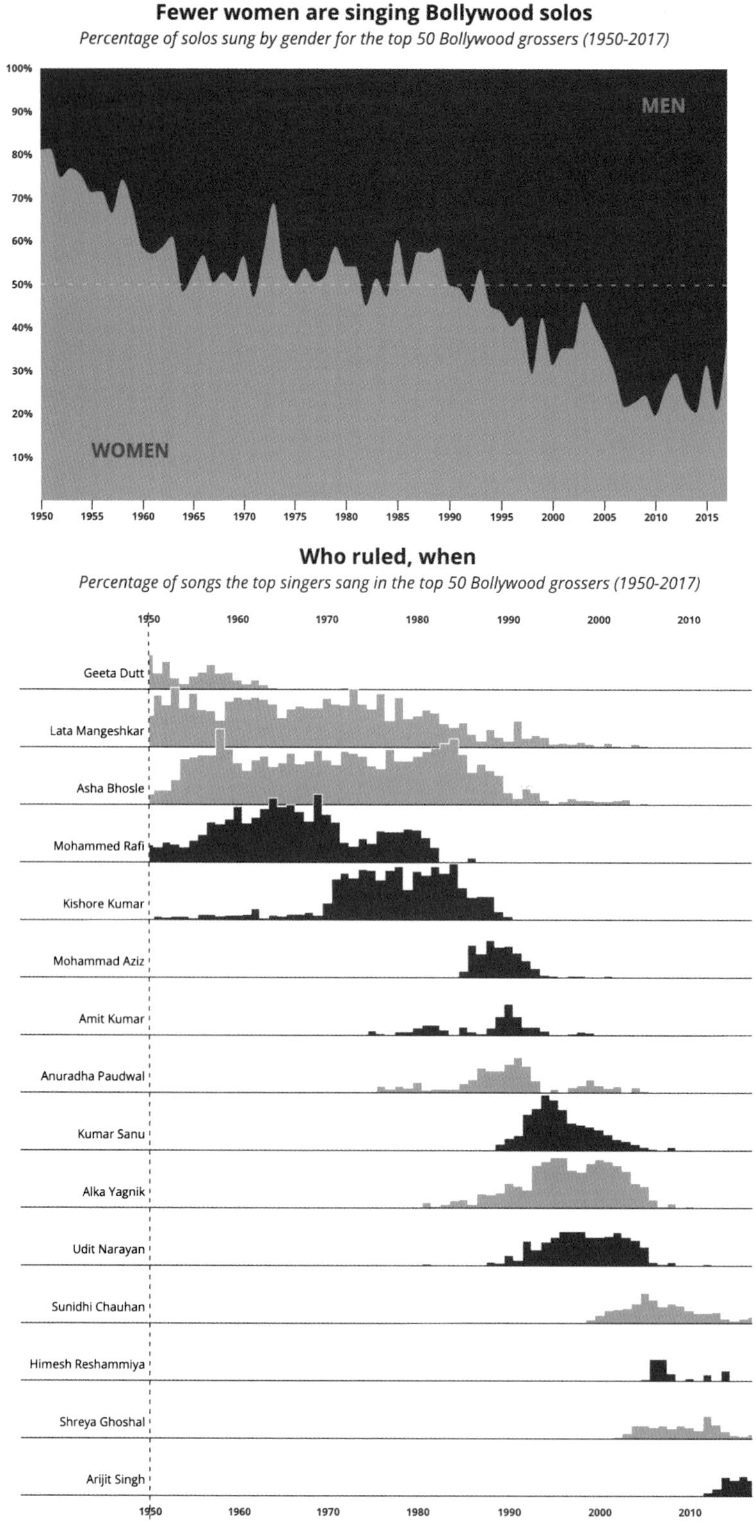

Figure 19.1: "Women are fading out from Bollywood music: An analysis of over 24,000 songs" https://www.hindustantimes.com/interactives/bollywood-songs-gender/

Chapter 19
with Gurman Bhatia

Visceral Visualizations

The mind that harbours philosophy should, by its soundness, make the body sound also. It should make its tranquillity and joy shine forth; it should mould the outward bearing to its shape, and arm it therefore with a gracious pride, with an active and sprightly bearing, with a happy and gracious countenance. The most manifest sign of wisdom is a constant cheerfulness.

—Michel de Montaigne

Michel de Montaigne may have been right when he said that wisdom—a deep serenity of the soul—is conducive to cheerfulness, I thought while talking to data journalist **Gurman Bhatia**. However, the eminent French essayist forgot to add that cheerfulness is contagious (wisdom, on the other hand, might not be).

In my conversation with Gurman I got carried away by her cheerfulness and enthusiasm about her work. It made me long for a time when, as a young visual journalist myself, I could speak for hours about any story I was working on. We began with "Women are fading out from Bollywood music" (**Figure 19.1**), published by the *Hindustan Times*:

> Like all good projects, this one is the result of happenstance. In 2017, I was listening to an interview with a few female Bollywood singers conducted by a film critic. One of those artists said something in passing about how playback singing in Bollywood movies has changed significantly in the past few decades. From albums sung entirely by women, the soundtracks of today were much more male dominated. It was just a few anecdotes, but something clicked in my brain, and I began wondering whether those anecdotes were supported by trends and patterns in the data.

The data that Gurman collected corroborated that the number of songs sung only by women in Bollywood movies has decreased a lot:

> The data itself was a challenge. There was no beautiful and neatly organized database I could go to. I first spoke to a friend of mine who is a Bollywood reporter, and she gave me a few suggestions for sources. I quickly realized that looking into every single Indian movie in the past six or seven decades would be impossible, so I decided to explore the top 50 grossing movies every year from 1950 to 2017. [The story was published in March of 2018.]
>
> I wrote the list of movies and wrote a script that scraped several websites and matched movie titles with the more than 20,000 playback songs they contained. Then I faced a challenge: tagging all singers as male or female. That's very hard to do. You can't do it with names because lots of Indian singers have ambiguous names. You can also not say, I'm going to play the song and analyze the tone of voice, because lots of female singers have deep voices.
>
> This last part of the data collection process was very manual. I had first obtained a list of singers from a list of songs, and then tagged every singer manually. I sometimes looked for information about the playback singers, and even ran a few names by my mother, who has a degree in music and a very good memory. It took me months to slowly collect and verify the database.

Gurman's story opens up with a time-series area graph that reveals that, back in 1950, more than 80% of solos were sung by women. In 2017, that percentage was around 40%. Why such a large drop?

> The style of filmmaking in Bollywood has changed. In the past there were many family-centric movies, and almost no song would play in the background of a scene. If there was a song, somebody was lip-synching it on camera. Often this could be an entire family with lots of female characters. You'd have the main character's mother, sister, or love interest, and all of them would get a song.
>
> Modern Bollywood movies are different. They are sometimes shot outside of India, and they tell stories of strong, independent, career-driven characters. That calls for a different style of filmmaking and music. Nowadays there's barely any lip-synching in Bollywood movies. Instead, songs play in the background. A woman can be, for instance, walking around the city in a scene, and there can be a song playing that is sung by a man.
>
> Another pattern that my story reveals is that the variety of singers in Bollywood movies has increased. In the past the majority of songs in the 50 highest grossing Indian movies were sung by just a handful of artists, such as Lata Mangeshkar, Asha Bhosle (women), Mohammed Rafi, or Kishore Kumar (men). In the present no artist sings more than 10% or 15% of the songs in all top-grossing movies. Therefore, it's not that today there are fewer women singing

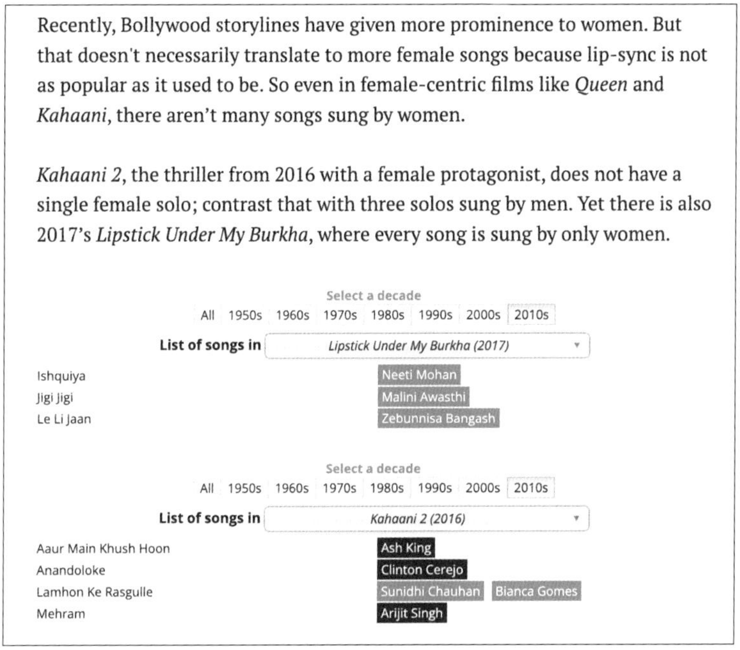

Recently, Bollywood storylines have given more prominence to women. But that doesn't necessarily translate to more female songs because lip-sync is not as popular as it used to be. So even in female-centric films like *Queen* and *Kahaani*, there aren't many songs sung by women.

Kahaani 2, the thriller from 2016 with a female protagonist, does not have a single female solo; contrast that with three solos sung by men. Yet there is also 2017's *Lipstick Under My Burkha*, where every song is sung by only women.

Figure 19.2: Searchable movie song database from
"Women are fading out from Bollywood music: An analysis of over 24,000 songs"

songs in movies; there are still many women singers, but they sing fewer songs. This includes female-centric movies (**Figure 19.2**). Moreover, even when women sing in duets they get only, say, a fifth of the lines of the song.

Gurman used her Bollywood music piece to talk about some of her professional ideals:

I think about the type of journalism I do as a way to make readers more mindful or data literate or, like in the case of the Bollywood story, to talk about topics that have already been covered, but that could benefit from being explained in new ways, from a different angle.

I'm also interested in making work that sticks with readers. Graphics have that power. Take the story that my *Hindustan Times* colleague Aparna Alluri and I made around the 70th anniversary of the Partition of India, which happened in August of 1947. It focuses on how Delhi changed in just a decade around that time. Everybody in India learns about Partition, but it is different to see its consequences through maps (**Figure 19.3**). It's a more direct, more visceral experience.

"The decade that changed Delhi" consists of a series of paired before-and-after maps that appeared in the print paper—in large format—and also online. The 1942 maps show Delhi as little more than a few scattered neighborhoods. By 1956, nearly a decade after the Partition between India and Pakistan, the city was a metropolis. The story explains it this way:

Figure 19.3: "The decade that changed Delhi" by Aparna Alluri and Gurman Bhatia
https://www.hindustantimes.com/static/partition/delhi/

> In the wake of India's hellish Partition, thousands of Muslims fled, while Hindu and Sikh refugees poured in. Delhi took in nearly half a million refugees from Pakistan in those heady but brutal months before and after August 1947. Large parts of today's Delhi grew out of the refugee camps that sprung up along its limits 69 years ago.

Gurman's roots are in India, but since she was in her early twenties she's moved wherever she felt she could learn something new:

> I studied journalism first in Delhi, where I was born, and after in New York, at Columbia University. There I didn't just improve my storytelling skills with audio, photo, or video, but I also learned about graphics and data journalism in a class called "Interactive Design and Storytelling." I was blown away. I've always loved math, I had done a little bit of programming in high school, and it all came back to me quickly.
>
> While I walked home after the first class I called my parents and told them, "This is why I came here!" I felt like I was in Disneyland. Do you know that kind of excitement? I'm in the Disneyland of news nerds!

After Columbia University, Gurman moved to the Poynter Institute and the *Palm Beach Post*, both in Florida, and then to the *Milwaukee Journal Sentinel* in Wisconsin:

I had zero qualms about moving around the United States. I told myself that I'd go wherever I needed to, I wanted to see it all and do all kinds of journalism. I didn't say no to anything. I covered anything and everything.

I've kept my enthusiasm for journalism and my journalistic curiosity up to this day even if, now that I'm a freelancer [since 2021] I prefer to call myself an information designer or data storyteller. I felt that journalism skills could be used in other areas, such as education or science communication, so I started moving in that direction.

That would come later, though, so let's go back to Wisconsin. I had to apply for a work visa, but it remained pending for a long time. It didn't make sense to wait for it in the U.S., where I couldn't work, and I was very homesick at that time. So I packed my bags and came back to Delhi, where I've been able to work for news publications such as the *Hindustan Times* and Reuters Asia. I've enjoyed it so much that when my visa application finally got rejected, I woke up my parents in the middle of the night and danced while yelling "Yeah, my visa got rejected!"

This momentous event led to some of Gurman's best work, not only for the *Hindustan Times*, but also for non-governmental organizations such as Greenpeace, and for Reuters, where she's covered the COVID pandemic ("It was emotionally taxing," she told me), several Indian elections, and the challenges of access to water and environmental pollution in her country of origin.

Earlier in our conversation, Gurman had described her maps of the India Partition as *visceral*. She used the same term to refer to the story that we talked about next, 2018's "A window into Delhi's deadly pollution" (Reuters).

According to this project, pollution has become so bad in the city that in 2017 the authorities declared a public health crisis, shut down schools for a week, and told residents to remain indoors. The World Health Organization says that India has 14 of the 15 most polluted cities in the world, and Delhi isn't even the worst among them:

The months of October and November are the pollution season in north India. Pollution isn't really news in my country It's a story that is told every year, and everybody knows about it. You can see it, smell it, feel it, and read it in the news constantly. How do you tell a story like this in a new way?

For quite a long time Simon Scarr [deputy head of graphics at Reuters] had this idea of placing a camera on the rooftop of Reuters bureau in Delhi and getting a large sequence of photographs of its pollution. He took inspiration from similar projects that were made in Beijing and other places, and in 2018 he was able to get some approvals to make the project happen.

Two photographers in the Delhi bureau, Adnan Abidi, Altaf Hussain, got a person to create a makeshift room for the camera to protect it against wind and rain. After it was set up, it would

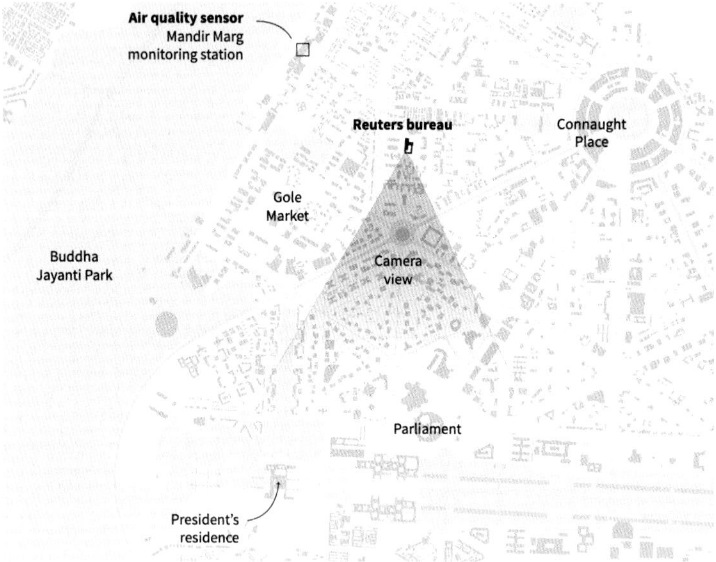

Figure 19.4: Map from "A window into Delhi's deadly pollution"
by Simon Scarr, Han Huang, and Gurman Bhatia
https://www.reuters.com/graphics/INDIA-POLLUTION/01008173281/index.html

take a picture every hour for nearly a month. We got hundreds of photographs that revealed how smog ebbs and flows during each day depending on variables such as temperature or traffic.

We positioned the camera to point at the President's residence and India's Parliament (**Figure 19.4**.) We also got data about air pollution from the Central Pollution Control Board, which is part of India's Ministry of Environment (**Figure 19.5**.) The concentration of dangerous fine particles in the area where Reuters' offices are, close to the Mandir Marg monitoring station, can get very high but, on average, it isn't worse than the rest of the city: 191.34 micrograms of particles per cubic meter. This is typical in Delhi, but it's really bad for your lungs and your health in general!

Therefore, on one hand, we had these numbers. On the other hand, we had the many photographs that our camera had taken (**Figure 19.6**.) Our goal was to merge all of these into a cohesive narrative, and also give readers a comprehensive understanding of the problem. Sure, everybody knows that fine particle concentrations of, say, 200, 500, or even more than 1,000

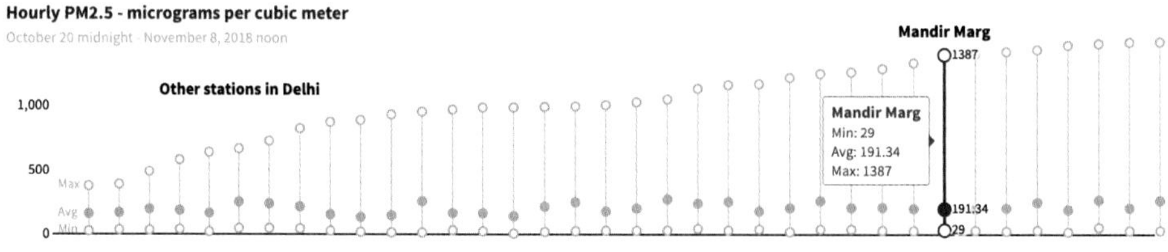

Figure 19.5: Data from "A window into Delhi's deadly pollution"
by Simon Scarr, Han Huang, and Gurman Bhatia
https://www.reuters.com/graphics/INDIA-POLLUTION/01008173281/index.html

Figure 19.6: Photos from "A window into Delhi's deadly pollution"

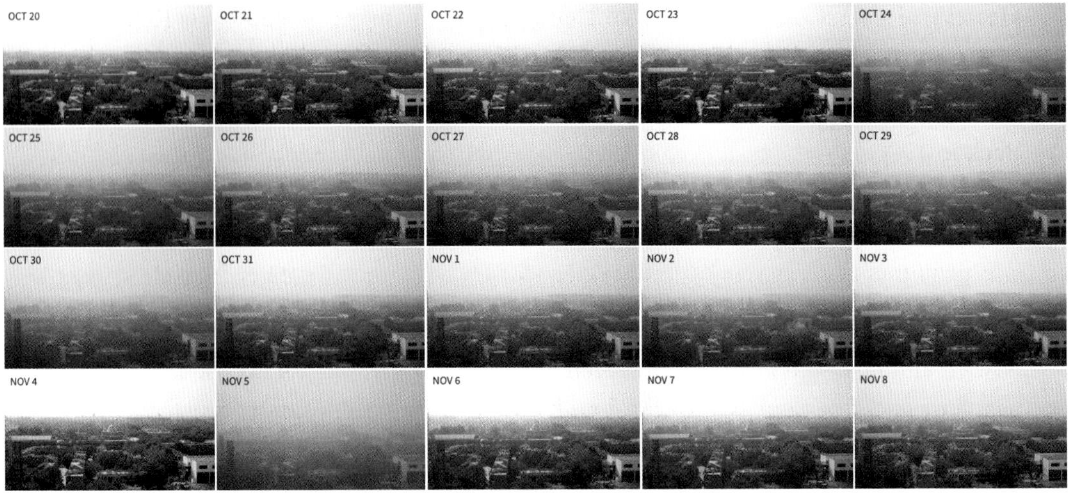

Figure 19.7: Photos from "A window into Delhi's deadly pollution"

> micrograms per cubic meter is bad, but what does "bad" really look like? Just hearing about the numbers tells you little.
>
> Moreover, anybody who lives in Delhi or has visited the city has witnessed pollution at different times of the day, and noticed that there are times when you can't even see what's 20 meters ahead of you. But you never notice what pollution looks like throughout an entire day, or throughout several days [**Figure 19.7**] all at once. When you do, it hits you in the face, "Oh God, it's *that* bad!" We got that kind of reaction from readers.

In 2016 Nicholas Felton, whose self-quantification projects I mentioned in Chapter 13, coined the term *photoviz* in a series of talks and a book with the same title. Gurman referred to it when discussing her Delhi pollution project. Felton has said:

> In a world overwhelmed with both data and photography, there is an increased need for both aggregating photos and for making data stories more evocative [...] Like data, photography reduces the world's complexity into a form that is suitable for manipulation and data visualization. By combining the goals of data visualization with the beauty and fidelity of photography, photoviz is able to represent the world in illuminating ways.

Gurman told me that photo visualizations are not only illuminating, but also far more visceral and vivid than traditional visualizations. I think that she has a point. A priori, I'm not the target audience for a story about Delhi's smog. If this story consisted of just maps, charts, and perhaps some testimonials from inhabitants of the city, it's unlikely that I'd spend time reading it.

However, I did read "A window into Delhi's deadly pollution" when I saw Reuters promoting it in social media. The juxtaposition of photographs, and their sequencing on an interactive timeline made me stop, pay attention, and think.

Back in 1980, in their book *Human Inference: Strategies and Shortcomings of Social Judgment*, social psychologists Richard E. Nisbett and Lee Ross suggested that information presented in a vivid manner—"emotionally interesting, concrete, imagery-provoking, and proximate in a sensory, temporal, or spatial way"—has a greater impact on people than neutral or abstract messages.

Nisbett and Ross's book and the research on health communication that it inspired in the past four decades is one of the reasons why cigarette boxes often showcase fear-arousing photographs of decayed teeth, rotten lungs, or cancer patients.

Evidence for the efficacy of these messages in persuading people to take better care of their health is mixed. However, they seem to have *some* effect; at a minimum, they make people seek scientific information and think twice about exposing themselves to risks. Perhaps the same is true of vivid design in journalism? Maybe news stories that employ photographs as visualizations mobilize public support and put pressure on authorities to improve air quality much more than your typical 1,000-word piece with some standard visualizations.

If you're a researcher, there's something that might be worth studying.

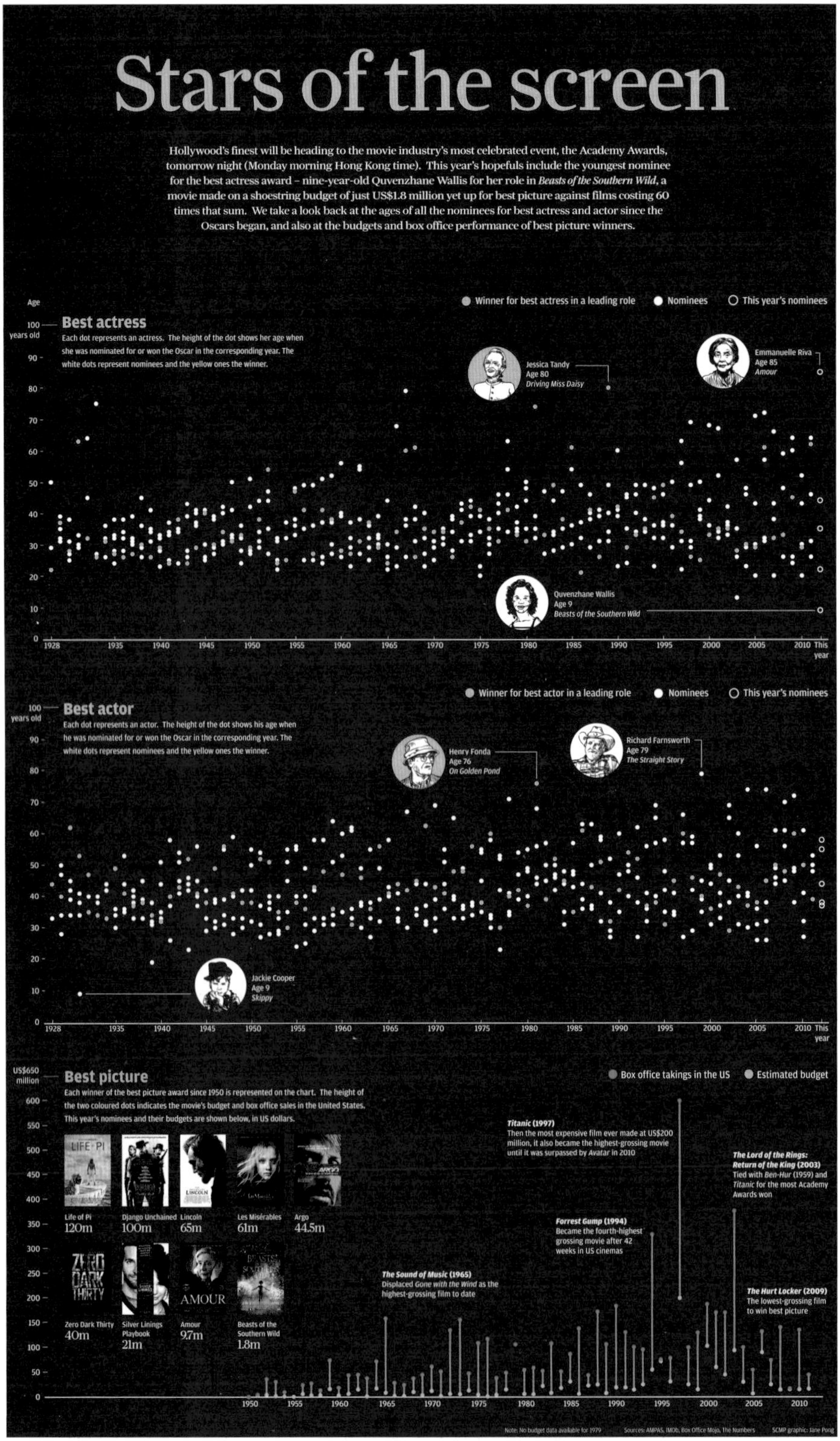

Figure 20.1: "Stars of the screen" by Jane Pong / *South China Morning Post* https://multimedia.scmp.com/culture/article/SCMP-printed-graphics-memory/lonelyGraphics/201302A283.html / last accessed June 19, 2023.

Chapter 20
with Jane Pong

The Determined Learner

Authentic living isn't judged by whether you are successful or not. Authenticity flowers in making intentions and in following through with actions. Authenticity is a process of boldly embracing our freedom, resolutely striding into life, and creating our essence and the world around us. When we set off on a quest to live authentically, we affirm freedom for ourselves and others. We create a world worth living in.

—Skye C. Cleary

Back in 2012, **Jane Pong** designed the graphic that led to her first job in visualization—**Figure 20.1** is a polished version of it, published a year later. Her career began, of all places, at a Starbucks in Hong Kong:

> I had recently quit my job for reasons that we can talk about later. At the Starbucks where I was sitting, there was a copy of the *South China Morning Post* [one of Hong Kong's main newspapers]. I picked it up and began casually leafing through it. And there it was, a data visualization! It was a very clear moment in my mind where it was like, "Wait a minute, this is exactly what I want to do, and there are other people already doing it here in Hong Kong."
>
> There was a tiny byline in the corner of this graphic, Simon Scarr. I searched for Simon on Twitter, found his profile, and wrote to him: "I saw your graphic in the paper today. I love it, and this is exactly what I want to do. Do you have any internships available?"

We met Simon Scarr, former graphics director at the *South China Morning Post* (SCMP) and today the deputy head of graphics at Reuters, in Chapter 19. Simon has a well-deserved reputation in the news graphics industry for finding and nurturing talent. Curious about Jane's determination, he invited her to the SCMP newsroom, but with a warning: He'd treat her visit as a job interview. Jane explained:

> I was supposed to visit after the Oscars weekend. I found this story in the SCMP about how wide the age range of nominees for Best Actor or Best Actress was. The oldest nominee was in her 80s and the youngest was around 9. I thought, "Well, this is a prime example of when to use a visualization in a story."
>
> Over the weekend I created a spreadsheet with every Oscar nominee in history. At the time I didn't have many data skills, so I didn't know how to find or scrape that type of data. I Googled every nominee to find out their date of birth, put together the spreadsheet manually, and designed a visualization based on it.
>
> When I met Simon and Stephen Case, former art director, at the SCMP, I told them, "I saw this story in the newspaper. I think that this is a graphic that could have fit in it. I know that it's very rough but I wanted to show you that I'm serious about this. What do you think?" Stephen called me the following day and asked, "Would you like to come work with us? You begin next week."

Before this meeting, Jane had already designed some data visualizations:

> I grew up in Australia. I have a bachelor's of science and a bachelor's of art because I've always been curious about a variety of things. I studied chemistry, linguistics, psychology, and art history. Funnily, after I graduated I found myself working at a research center doing things that I hadn't studied for, marketing and economics. I learned tools such as MATLAB or Stata, I did a lot of statistical modeling, and I was seriously exposed to data visualization, which fascinated me. I thought that it was the perfect way to encapsulate the results of the studies I was conducting. I fell into a rabbit hole and spent a lot of time online reading about visualization.
>
> In 2011, Information is Beautiful [an organization led by David McCandless, see Chapter 2] had this challenge to visualize the economic crisis. They gave you a few data sets and asked you to design visualizations with them. I told myself, "This sounds fun, let's try it." But I knew nearly nothing, so I asked a few designer friends for advice.
>
> I designed a series of connected scatter plots in Adobe Illustrator [**Figure 20.2**] and got third place in the competition. That was a tremendous confidence boost. I realized that visualization was what I wanted to do as a career, and that I needed to learn more about it. So I quit my job; that's what led me to that fateful day at Starbucks where I stumbled upon the SCMP.

I discovered Jane's work thanks to these charts, which work like frames in an animation: Read them from left to right to see the covariation of two variables in several countries, bond yield (X-axis) and unemployment rates (Y-axis.) It impressed me that an absolute

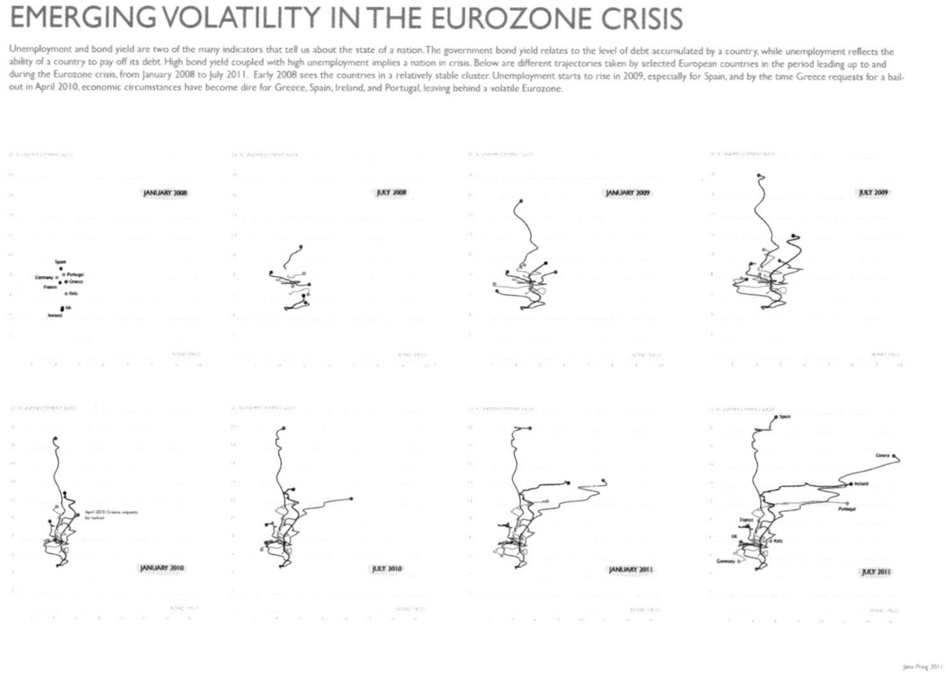

Figure 20.2: "Emerging volatility in the Eurozone crisis"

beginner was using such an unusual graphic form, and that she already had a mature, sophisticated sense for design. I asked Jane about it:

> I honestly didn't know much about design or journalism when the SCMP hired me, but I was willing to do anything, any type of task, and to learn from anyone and everyone, reporters or designers in the art department. It's good that I did that because, not long after I became part of the newsroom, Simon came to me to say, "You know, there was something that I didn't tell you during our meeting. There's a reason why we got you in so quickly. I'm leaving in two weeks." He was moving to Singapore to work for Reuters. This was a shock because that meant that there would be no one left at the SCMP to make data visualizations—other than me.
>
> My first reaction was, "But I'm here because of you! What am I supposed to do now?" But then I immediately switched to, "Well, OK, would you mind teaching me everything you know in the time you have left?" I asked to see every data visualization that the SCMP had published. I also sat behind Simon, looking over his shoulder, and asking questions, "Wait, what was that shortcut again? What did you do there? How did you design that?" I must have been the most annoying person on Earth.

I doubt that Jane was annoying to Simon. In fact, I have a hunch that he was delighted. A common trait among news graphics designers is that we can't stop talking to anyone who shows an interest in our relatively obscure trade. I told Jane about my own graphics internship, back in 1997. It was at *La Voz de Galicia*, a regional newspaper in northwest Spain. My colleagues at the graphics desk weren't simply welcoming; they were eager and happy to spend endless hours teaching me not only design or software tools, but also how to navigate the tricky waters of newsroom politics.

I learned something else that Jane said she experienced, as well: Being alone forces you to learn fast and to boost your self-reliance. My internship was during the summer, so many of my colleagues were on vacation—sometimes *all of them at once*. I was left in charge of the graphics desk on some slow news days, usually Sundays. Imagine the overwhelming feeling of being an intern and also responsible for graphics that you knew would be seen by tens of thousands of readers the following day. Jane nodded:

> It was very challenging, but also one of the best times in my professional life. I was part of the art department and, even if I was the only one who could make data visualizations, I had the support of other members of the team. For instance, Adolfo Arranz, who didn't know much about data, but is an incredible illustrator.
>
> I had a lot of freedom to pitch ideas to editors. Sometimes my ideas required drawings, so Adolfo and I collaborated on many projects. During my time at the SCMP, the graphics desk expanded, hiring other designers, such as Alberto Lucas [both Adolfo and Alberto are from Spain.]
>
> SCMP gave us this freedom without considering whether our ideas were part of the news cycle. We were all encouraged to pursue topics that could be of local interest to SCMP readers and for which we had data in Hong Kong.

I think that this is a key reason for the consistent high quality of the SCMP's news graphics. In my previous books I showcased projects by several of its designers, including Adolfo and Jane herself; for instance, her "Rain patterns" (**Figure 20.3**) published in 2013 at the start of the monsoon season:

> I got data from the Hong Kong Observatory going back a century. I used Processing [a programming language for visual design and creative coding] to generate the base plots; D3.js [a Javascript library for interactive data visualization] was not even a thing back then. After that, I tweaked the graphics manually and added the annotations for key historical events.
>
> Something that I learned from Simon Scarr and that has stuck with me to this day is the use of visual metaphors. He is very good at employing metaphors in his work to give readers an intuitive sense of what the data is about even before they read the graphic. I've tried to emulate him many

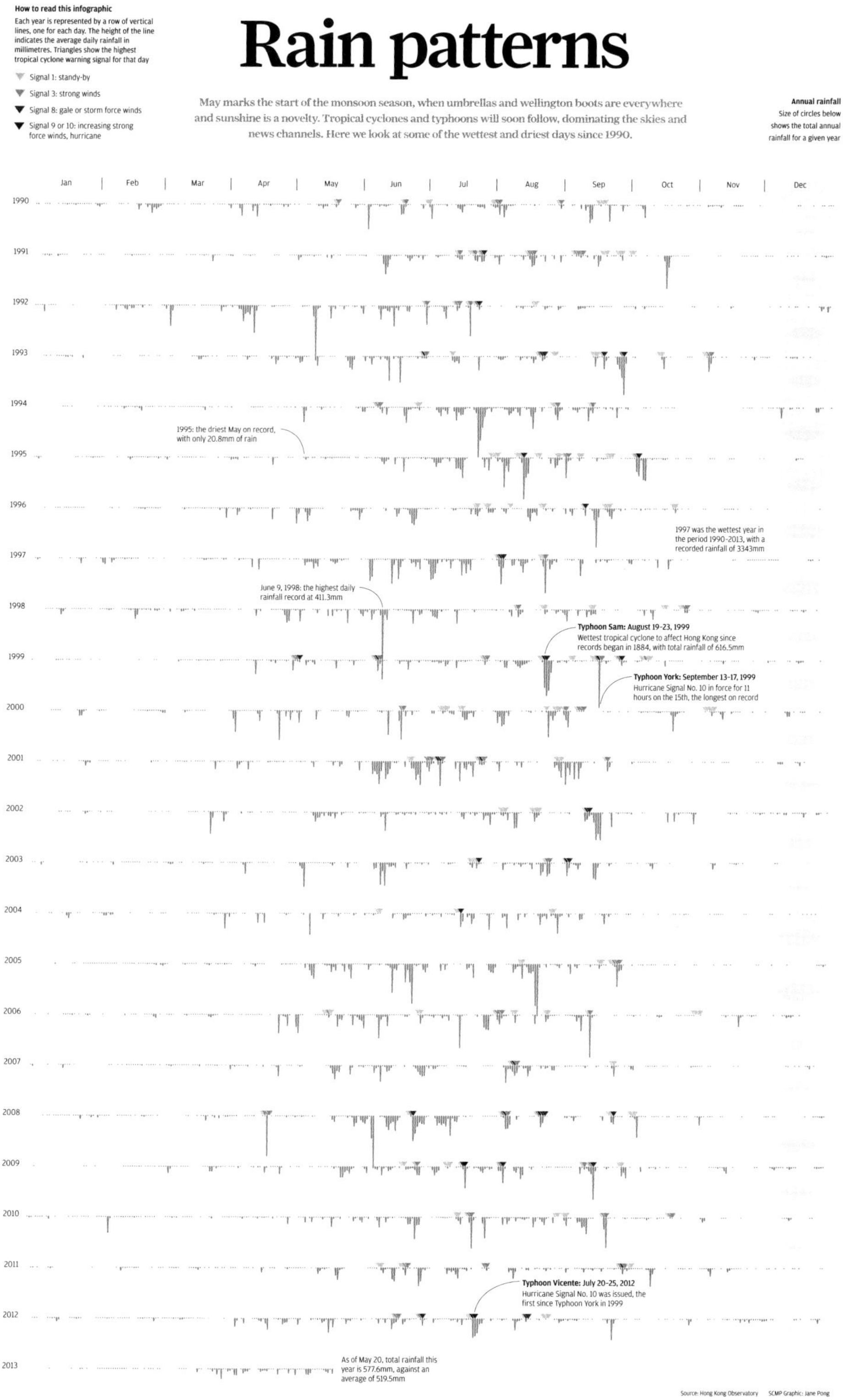

Figure 20.3: "Rain patterns" by Jane Pong / *South China Morning Post*
https://multimedia.scmp.com/rainfall/

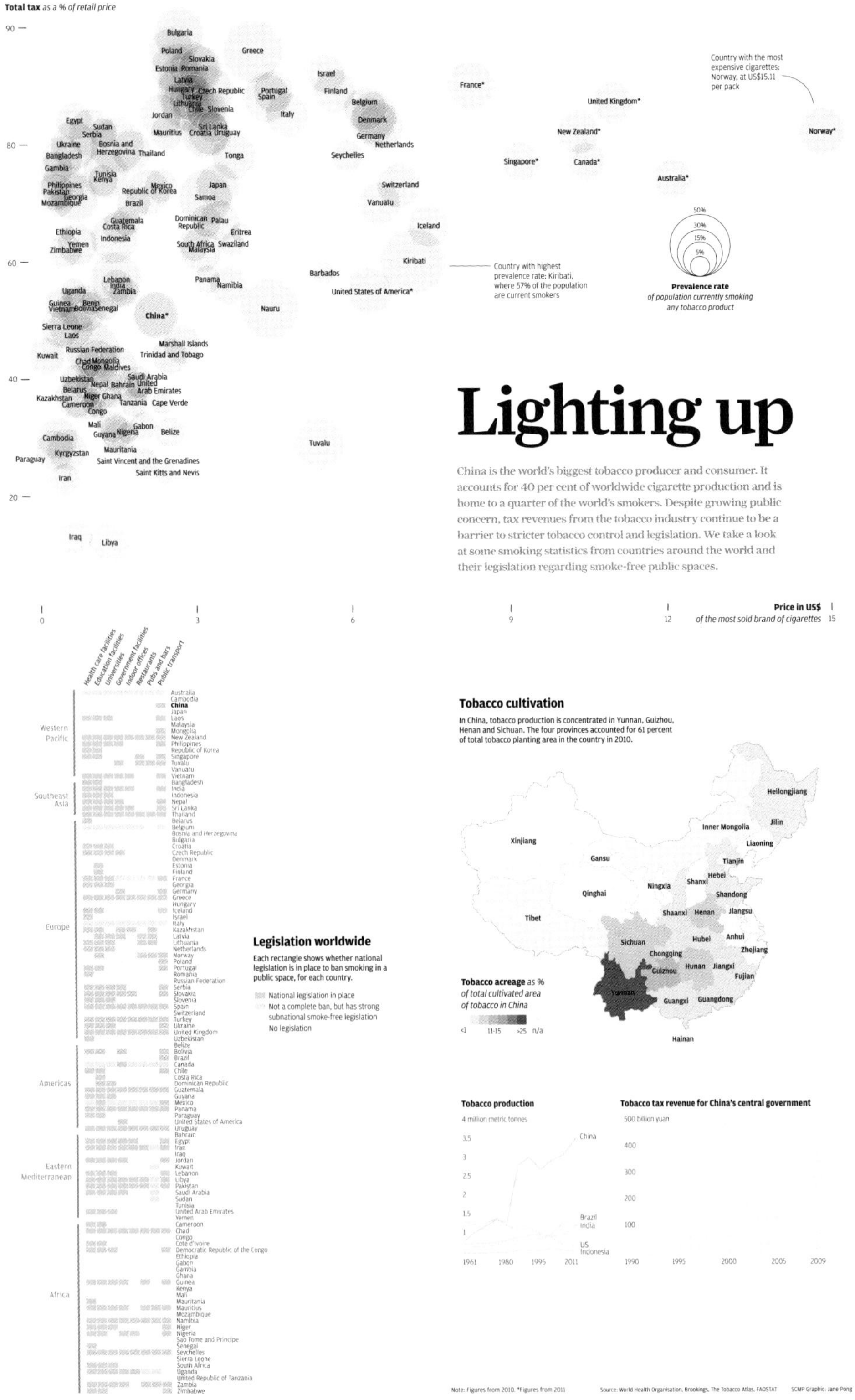

Figure 20.4: "Lighting up" by Jane Pong / *South China Morning Post*
https://www.scmp.com/infographics/article/1350765/lighting-biggest-tobacco-producer-and-consumer-china

> times, not only in the rain patterns graphic, which looks like a windowsill, but also, for instance, in "Lighting up," about tobacco production and consumption in China (**Figure 20.4**). The heat map at the bottom looks like a cigarette and the scatter plot on top looks like smoke coming out of it.
>
> It's funny, I've never thought of myself as someone who could be creative. I've always associated creativity with artists. My family, friends, and teachers would say that I am a perfectionist, very conscientious and practical.
>
> One of the reasons I fell in love with data visualization when I discovered it was that, for the first time in my life, I could be creative in a very *me* way. I felt that I could make beautiful things while being true to data and to stories. I don't think that I could ever design anything that isn't practical in some way, something that is merely aesthetic. It's just not in my DNA.

However, Jane said something that reminded me of several of the designers that I showcased in the second part of this book, those most interested in creativity and novelty, such as Nadieh Bremer (Chapter 4) and Sonja Kuijpers (Chapter 5); Jane even mentioned feeling flow while handcrafting visualizations:

> Efficiency is rarely my main goal when I am working on a graphic. I like doing things that take time. I'm an efficient person, but when it comes to designing visualizations, I really like spending a lot of time with the data and the design itself. I mean actually looking at the data line by line, and cleaning spreadsheets. I feel that it gives me more of an intuitive and intimate sense of what the numbers mean. I also spend a lot of time doing my graphics by hand; it's like putting together a puzzle piece by piece. I get into a state of flow.

Since she left the SCMP, Jane has worked for the *Financial Times* and, today, she is a graphics editor at Bloomberg. She's continued designing graphics that are intricate and elegant, such as the heatmap matrix in "How remittances flow around the world" (**Figure 20.5**). And she emphasized that she still lives in Hong Kong:

> I've always wanted to stay in Asia. Simon Scarr got me a dream job at the SCMP when I had barely any experience. He also gave me the opportunity to learn while in the newsroom. That changed my life. I'd like to do the same for others here. I also feel a connection to this continent and want to tell Asian stories more often.
>
> Graphics teams in Asia, particularly at news organizations, are small and scrappy, if they exist at all. There are some independent organizations, such as Kontinentalist.com, that produce excellent work, but visualization has always been a bit behind here.
>
> Also, visualization as a field is too American and European-centric. I want this to change, but there are many obstacles to overcome. One is that data is hard to come by in most Asian countries. Freedom of information acts are rare. For a while I was involved in the open data

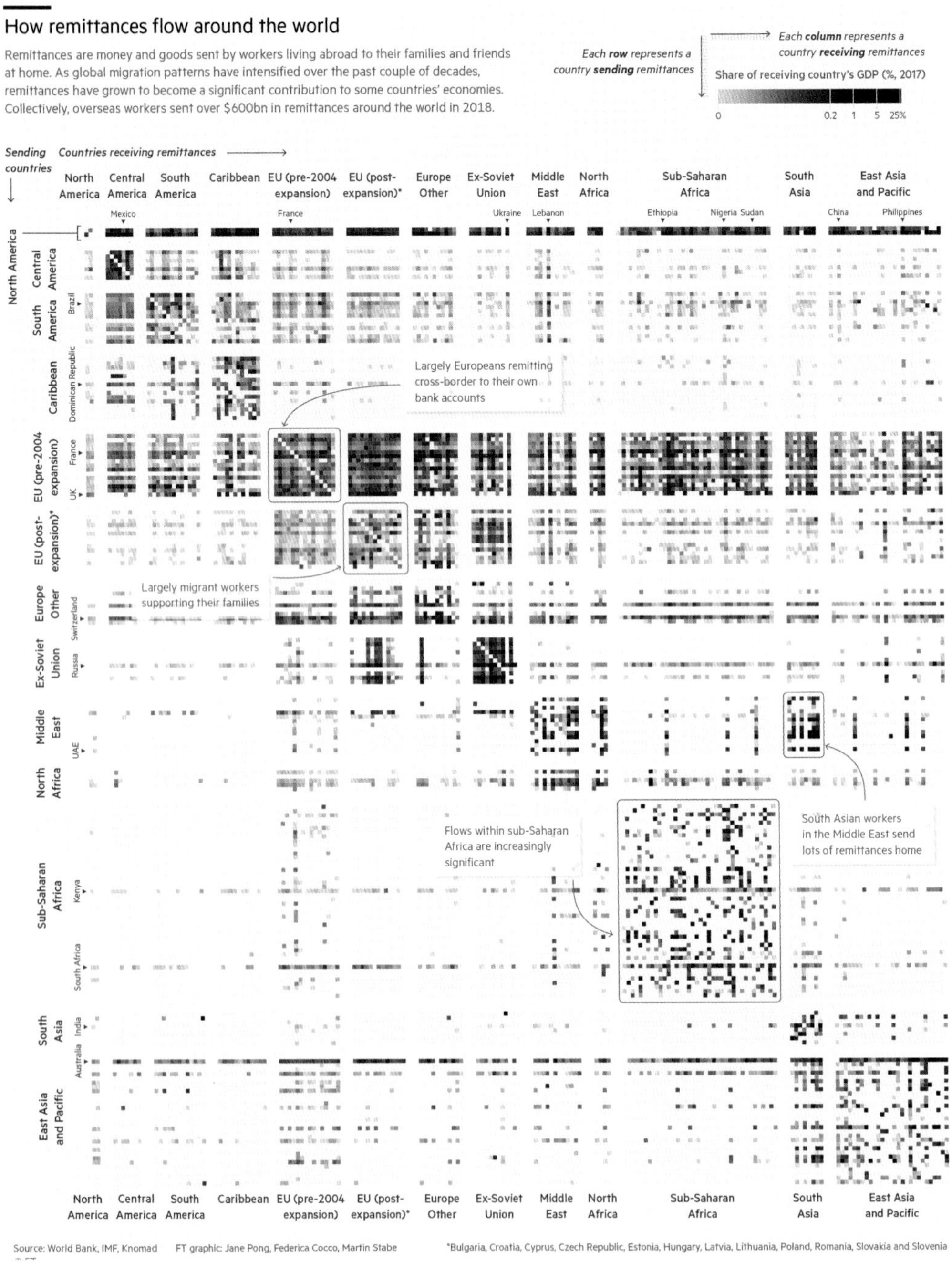

Figure 20.5: "How remittances flow around the world" by Jane Pong, Federica Cocco, and Martin Stabe for the *Financial Times*
https://ig.ft.com/remittances-capital-flow-emerging-markets/

movement in Hong Kong, and even participated in talks with government officials, but that didn't really go anywhere. Moreover, data literacy in this region is low.

Some publications, the SCMP among them, try to face these challenges by using illustrations when not so much data is available. A pictorial illustration can be useful as an explanation even if it's not based on a comprehensive and detailed database. Making the case for hiring an artist to work in a data visualization team can be hard, but I think that it makes sense.

It does. In fact, I'd say that any news graphics desk that has at least one jack-of-all-trades who can design both data visualizations and pictorial explanations can consider itself lucky. Allow me to introduce you to one of them next.

Figure 21.1: "Capivara Weather"
Simon Ducroquet / https://cargocollective.com/ducroquet/CAPIVARA-WEATHER / last accessed June 19, 2023

Chapter 21
with Simon Ducroquet

The Jack-of-All-Trades

Stories are compasses and architecture; we navigate by them, we build our sanctuaries and our prisons out of them, and to be without a story is to be lost in the vastness of a world that spreads in all directions like arctic tundra or sea ice.

—Rebecca Solnit

I've never been a devoted video gamer but I was able to understand something that the Brazilian news designer **Simon Ducroquet** told me about *Doom*, the pioneering first-person shooter released in 1993:

> Remember that you could go beyond playing the game and design your own levels for it? Well, I did that. I truly was a nerdy guy when I was in school and in college—I still am!

I do remember *Doom*. I had a college friend who created scenarios for it. One was a reproduction of the magnificent cathedral of Santiago de Compostela, the city where I studied journalism. Those were the days.

Why did Simon and I talk about a video game for a visualization book, you might wonder? He was demonstrating a recent side project, which draws some inspiration from video games and was still in development. It's a phone application that recommends what to wear, depending on the weather. Instead of showing humans in the app, though, he Simon used cartoon capybaras—a rodent species that is common in part of Brazil. (**Figure 21.1**). He said, "I wanted to do something different, something more fun than a typical weather app."

Simon, today a graphics reporter at *The Washington Post,* is one of the most—if not *the* most—versatile designers I've ever met. He can make data visualizations; he can code; he can draw and paint; he can model and animate in 3D software; he's designed excellent pictorial explanation graphics for news publications; and he's experimented with virtual and augmented reality. Moreover, and contrary to the jack-of-all-trades stereotype, he can do all that rather well. Are people like him born or made, I wondered?

> Since a young age I've been absorbing influences from all kinds of visual media, news publications, art, comic books, video games, board games—you name it. I know that you're into tabletop games; my college friends and I used to play things like *War* [a Brazilian variation of the popular strategy game *Risk*] and *Settlers of Catan*. We never got into the more "serious" stuff, like the historical and simulational war games that you enjoy so much.

Indeed, I do like games that simulate historical events and conflicts, not only wars. I also think that visualization designers and tabletop game creators have a lot to learn from one another, a topic that I should write about one day. Simon continued:

> Beginning at 12 I began teaching myself software tools such as Photoshop. I would do photo collages or scan hand drawn illustrations and color them.
>
> And I was a news reader. I grew up in a small town in the state of Santa Catarina. We didn't have a local newspaper there, but there was one newsstand in town. Our father took us every week to buy comics and magazines, particularly about games, computers, technology, and science. This was around the late 1980s, and my favorite was *Superinteressante*; it had a lot of illustrations and infographics.
>
> I was inspired to design my own fanzines. There was always a curiosity in me on trying to understand how things I liked were built and then crafting them by myself. I guess that all this learning about computers, software, and journalism foreshadowed what came later.

I have fond memories of *Superinteressante* ("Super Interesting") too. It's a compelling and widely read popular science magazine published by Editora Abril. In the summer of 2008, I spent a couple of months there as a consultant (I was later hired by Abril's main competitor, Editora Globo). *Superinteressante* and other Abril magazines, such as *Mundo Estranho* ("Strange World") employed great designers like Alessandra Kalko or Luiz Iria, who pioneered the use of infographics in Brazilian media.

I met Simon in 2008. He was taking his first steps as a visualization designer at *Folha de São Paulo*, one of the main national newspapers. Simon produced excellent work for *Folha*, such as a timeline of the labyrinthine history of Brazilian political parties (**Figure 21.2**) published ahead of the 2010 presidential elections that resulted in a victory by Dilma Rousseff, from the Worker's Party (PT). This graphic greatly helped me figure

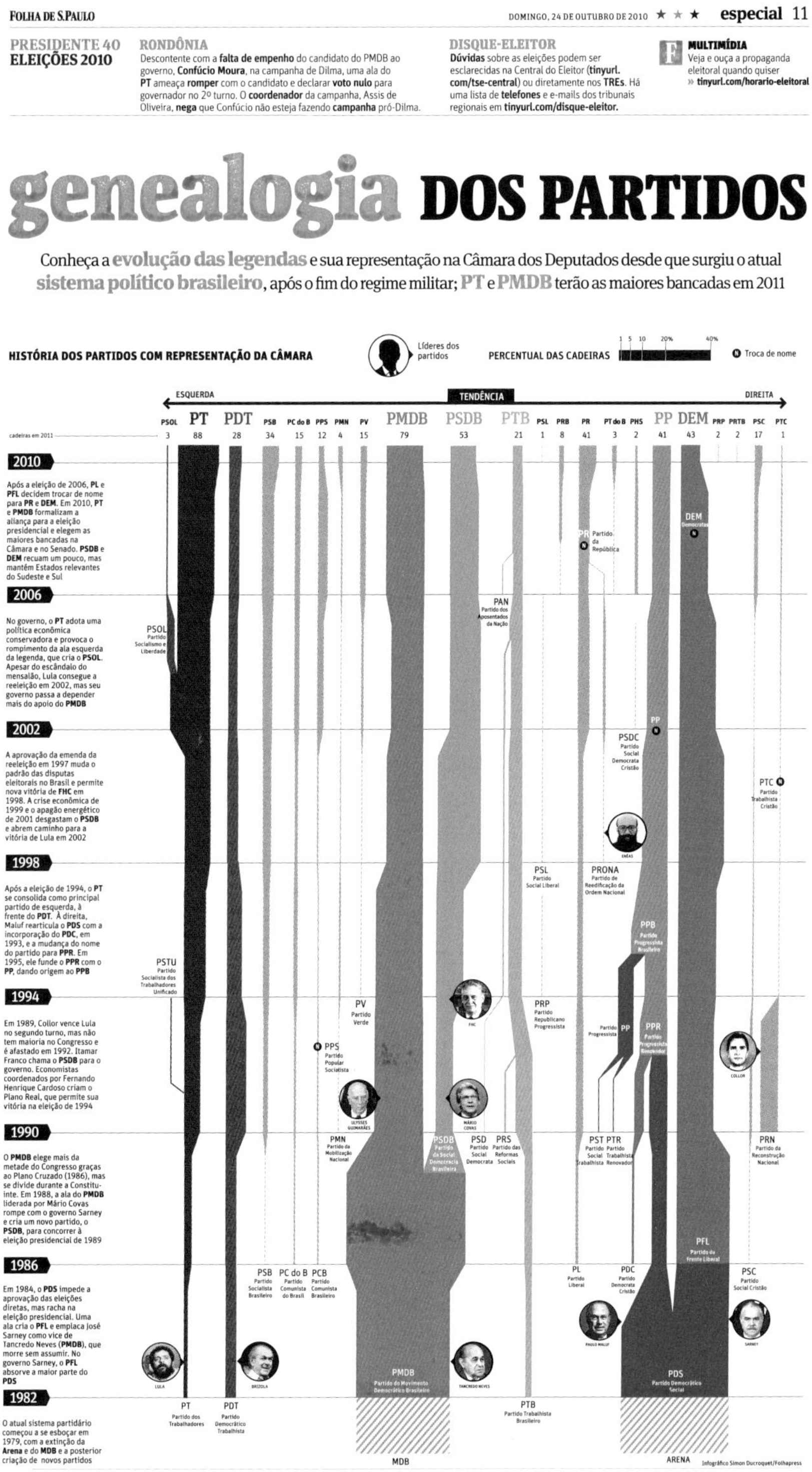
FOLHA DE S.PAULO — DOMINGO, 24 DE OUTUBRO DE 2010 ★ ★ ★ especial 11

PRESIDENTE 40
ELEIÇÕES 2010

RONDÔNIA
Descontente com a **falta de empenho** do candidato do PMDB ao governo, **Confúcio Moura**, na campanha de Dilma, uma ala do **PT** ameaça **romper** com o candidato e declarar **voto nulo** para governador no 2º turno. O **coordenador** da campanha, Assis de Oliveira, **nega** que Confúcio não esteja fazendo **campanha** pró-Dilma.

DISQUE-ELEITOR
Dúvidas sobre as eleições podem ser esclarecidas na Central do Eleitor (**tinyurl.com/tse-central**) ou diretamente nos **TREs**. Há uma lista de **telefones** e e-mails dos tribunais regionais em **tinyurl.com/disque-eleitor.**

MULTIMÍDIA
Veja e ouça a propaganda eleitoral quando quiser
» **tinyurl.com/horario-eleitoral**

genealogia DOS PARTIDOS

Conheça a evolução das legendas e sua representação na Câmara dos Deputados desde que surgiu o atual sistema político brasileiro, após o fim do regime militar; PT e PMDB terão as maiores bancadas em 2011

2010

Após a eleição de 2006, **PL** e **PFL** decidem trocar de nome para **PR** e **DEM**. Em 2010, **PT** e **PMDB** formalizam a aliança para a eleição presidencial e elegem as maiores bancadas na Câmara e no Senado. **PSDB** e **DEM** recuam um pouco, mas mantêm Estados relevantes do Sudeste e Sul

2006

No governo, o **PT** adota uma política econômica conservadora e provoca o rompimento da ala esquerda da legenda, que cria o **PSOL**. Apesar do escândalo do mensalão, Lula consegue a reeleição em 2002, mas seu governo passa a depender mais do apoio do **PMDB**

2002

A aprovação da emenda da reeleição em 1997 muda o padrão das disputas eleitorais no Brasil e permite nova vitória de **FHC** em 1998. A crise econômica de 1999 e o apagão energético de 2001 desgastam o **PSDB** e abrem caminho para a vitória de Lula em 2002

1998

Após a eleição de 1994, o **PT** se consolida como principal partido de esquerda, à frente do **PDT**. À direita, Maluf rearticula o **PDS** com a incorporação do **PDC**, em 1993, e a mudança do nome do partido para **PPR**. Em 1995, ele funde o **PPR** com o **PP**, dando origem ao **PPB**

1994

Em 1989, Collor vence Lula no segundo turno, mas não tem maioria no Congresso e é afastado em 1992. Itamar Franco chama o **PSDB** para o governo. Economistas coordenados por Fernando Henrique Cardoso criam o Plano Real, que permite sua vitória na eleição de 1994

1990

O **PMDB** elege mais da metade do Congresso graças ao Plano Cruzado (1986), mas se divide durante a Constituinte. Em 1988, a ala do **PMDB** liderada por Mário Covas rompe com o governo Sarney e cria um novo partido, o **PSDB**, para concorrer à eleição presidencial de 1989

1986

Em 1984, o **PDS** impede a aprovação das eleições diretas, mas racha na eleição presidencial. Uma ala cria o **PFL** e emplaca José Sarney como vice de Tancredo Neves (**PMDB**), que morre sem assumir. No governo Sarney, o **PFL** absorve a maior parte do **PDS**

1982

O atual sistema partidário começou a se esboçar em 1979, com a extinção da **Arena** e do **MDB** e a posterior criação de novos partidos

Figure 21.2: "Genealogy of Brazilian Parties"
https://cargocollective.com/ducroquet/GENEALOGIA-DOS-PARTIDOS

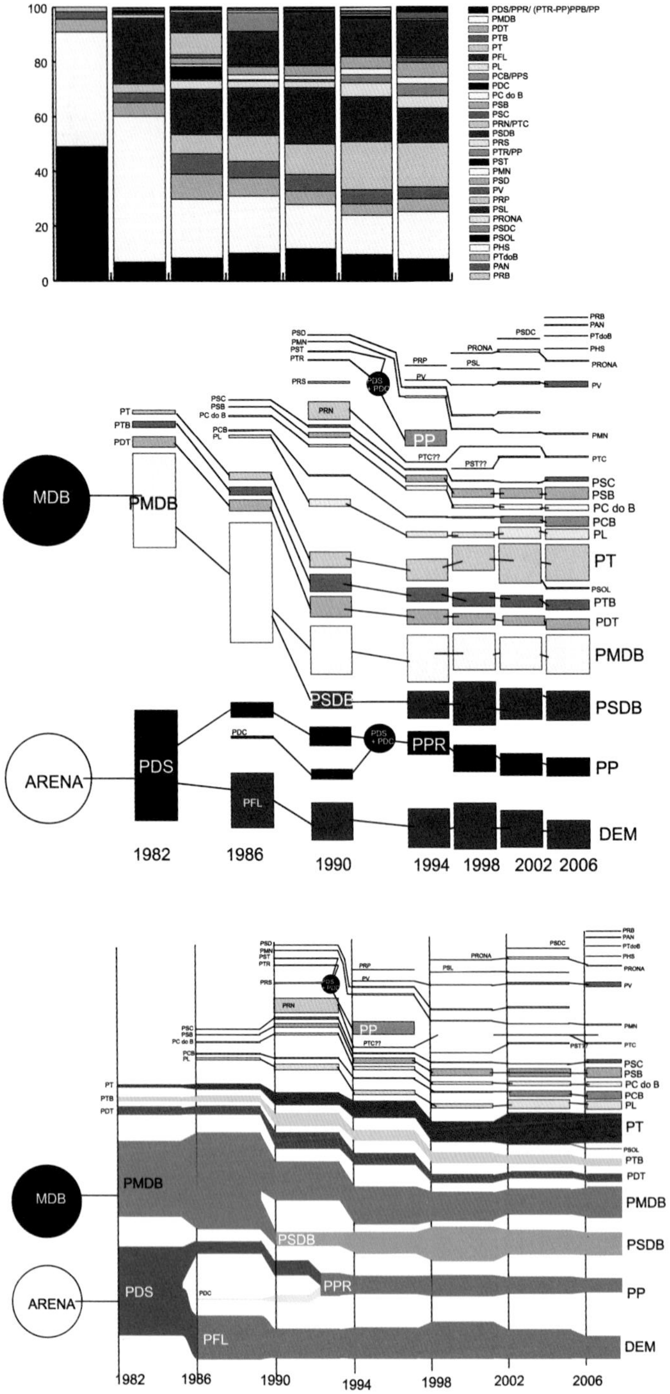

Figure 21.3: Early sketches for "Genealogy of Brazilian Parties" made in Adobe Illustrator

out a few books I had been reading that year about the complex modern history of Brazil. Simon explained:

> In Brazil parties often appear out of nowhere, they branch out from others, or they merge with one another. Their history is very convoluted—and that makes it perfect for a visualization.
>
> I didn't code at the time, so I made this full-page graphic in Adobe Illustrator. I began with a stacked bar graph representing the percentage of vote that each party received in every election, and then I moved the segments apart to build the final graphic (**Figure 21.3**).
>
> I got the graphic published in my second year at *Folha de São Paulo*, and the way that I made it was a bit unusual, in the sense that it went against the culture of the newspaper. It wasn't typical that a designer acted like a journalist, piching a story and doing all the research for it.

Finding a way to make things happen, even when lacking resources or skill, became a constant in Simon's career:

> Here's something that is typical in Brazil's news media: Structures are relatively informal and, even in the biggest newspapers and magazines, roles within a graphics department are vague. It's hard to specialize because you have to cover a wide range of topics and visual formats from one day to the other.
>
> This is different in the graphics desks of big newspapers in the United States, where you

can find developers, cartographers, statisticians, and so on. To survive in Brazil's news graphics one needed, and still needs, to be able to do a bit of everything, from writing to design. And you also need to always find ways and workarounds to get things done against the odds. I did well in that environment. It suits my personality, I guess.

Simon's news graphics aren't just nicely designed, but they are also thoroughly reported. I asked him about this, and we went back to his college years:

When I was in college I temporarily put my love for the arts and journalism aside, and focused on science. I enrolled in an engineering and biotechnology program. This was in the late 1990s and early 2000s, and genome studies was all the rage. It sounded like science fiction, you know, all those stories about Dolly, the cloned sheep, and the like. My father was a researcher in agronomy so I thought that I could pursue a similar career.

I grew a bit frustrated with the program, though. Sure, I had always enjoyed mathematics, science, and logic, but I also felt that I was not feeding my creative side, which I guess comes, at least in part, from my mother. She's a school teacher and also someone who engages in a large variety of crafting hobbies; she also has a great interest in animals and the environment, which I share.

So I left the engineering program and enrolled in two majors at the same time, graphic design and journalism. That worked out because one held classes in the morning, and the other in the evening. Even though I switched careers, I've maintained an ongoing interest in research, science and environmental issues.

From my brief foray into engineering I've kept an interest in understanding how complex things work. To do that, I sometimes try to learn how to build them, and then I feel a need to explain it to others. In journalism, those "others" are the readers. The highest satisfaction I can get from my designs is when anyone (including me) reacts to them by saying, "Wow, now I understand this thing!"

Simon's interest in science and his concerns about the environment show often in his work. Among his most popular projects—because it was groundbreaking when it was published—is a virtual reality animation that he created for *Fusion* in 2014. *Fusion* was a TV channel launched in 2013 by an alliance between ABC-Disney and *Univision*, the main Spanish-language TV network in the United States. It was intended to attract young English-speaking Hispanic and Latino audiences (unfortunately, it failed and closed less than a decade later). Simon, who had moved to Miami, where *Fusion* had its headquarters, was part of a team led by our common friend Mariana Santos tasked with researching and experimenting with novel digital storytelling formats:

Virtual reality was getting some serious traction in the mid-2010s. Cell phones had become powerful very quickly, and could be paired with other devices like the Google Cardboard [an app and a fold-out cardboard viewer] to track the motions of your head. We wanted to give these technologies a try, but we didn't want to create just a gimmick. Using technology for technology's sake isn't something that appealed to us. We wanted whatever we designed to have value, and to help us think about what applications these technologies might have.

For example, could we use this technology to give viewers a sense of scale about something? A blue whale, the largest animal on earth (**Figure 21.4**)? To do that in a traditional infographic you'd put an illustration or a photograph or a whale next to the silhouette of a person. That's fine, it works. But with virtual reality we thought that we could give viewers a completely different, much more natural, and much more accurate, perception of the size of this amazing animal. We could let the viewer stand next to it.

I've continued exploring 3D in journalism to this day. Recently I've been focusing on tools that allow real time 3D rendering in the browser, something similar to what video games do. Modern phones have amazing processing power for graphics; they are as capable as video game consoles from just a few years ago. Another thing that helps experiment with these technologies is that the software for building 3D experiences on the Internet, like Three.js [a Javascript library] is much more accessible than it used to be.

These days I'm playing with tools to capture objects and spaces in the real world and convert them into 3D models. I think that these tools will prove to be very useful in journalism, and they are getting better very rapidly. 3D used to be a very laborious process, but now we have promising AI solutions that may allow us to do it easily. I see endless possibilities; I'll never get bored.

Simon returned to Brazil in 2015 to work in a news startup, *Nexo Jornal*, an online-only newspaper dedicated mostly to explanatory journalism—its main aim is not to break news, but to put the daily news in context. Since its launch, *Nexo* has favored infographics, data visualizations, and video narrations. Simon was in charge of all these visuals:

When I joined *Nexo Jornal*, the newsroom was small, maybe 15 journalists. I oversaw everything and anything visual: photo, video, design, animations, infographics, data visualizations, and so on. I was able to put together a tiny team that included a designer and a video editor, plus a design intern. We also teamed up with a data scientist, who was very talented, but had never worked in a newsroom environment before.

Simon's team was tiny, but its output was impressive. Visual explanations such as "Pedaladas Fiscais" ("Fiscal Maneuvers," **Figure 21.5**) won multiple international design awards thanks to their simplicity and clarity.

The "pedalada fiscal" ("fiscal pedaling") is an accounting trick that the Brazilian government used to make itself look better to the public and to financial markets. There are three boxes in the bottom-left illustration in Figure 21.5. The first box is the taxes that

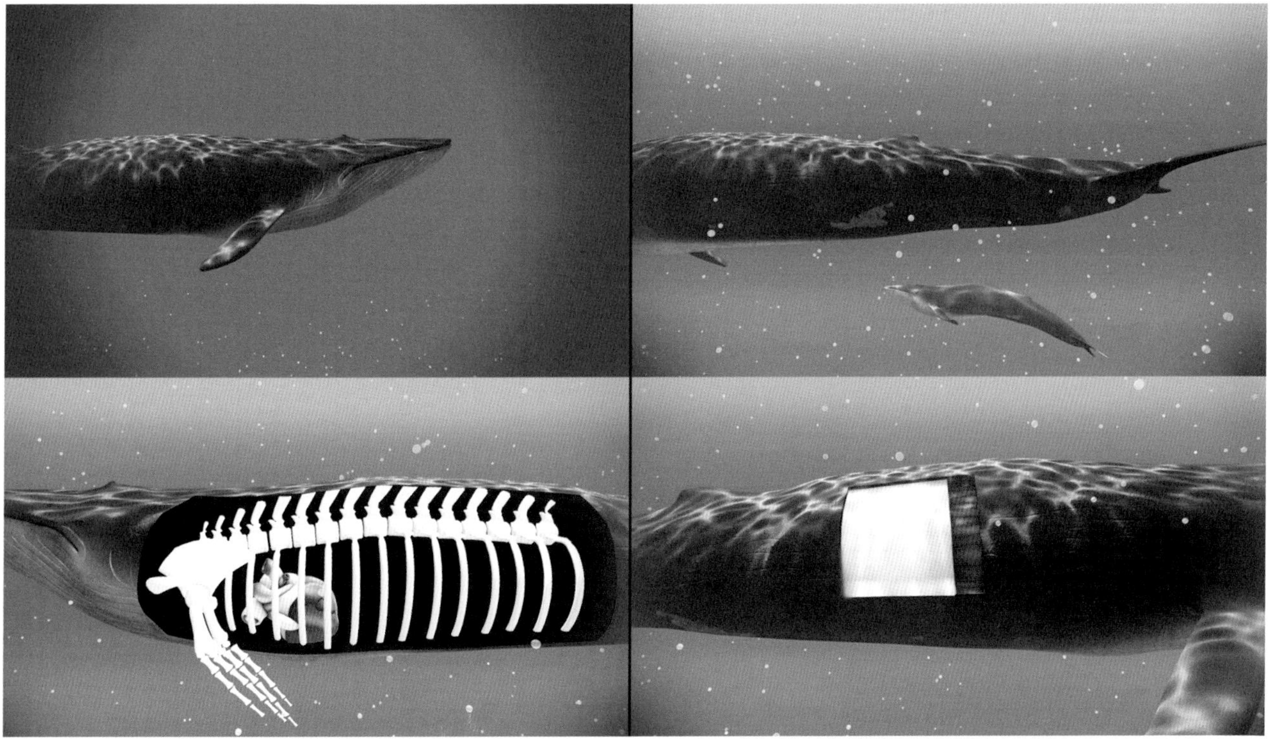

Figure 21.4: "Blue Whale VR," personal renders
Simon Ducroquet / "https://cargocollective.com/ducroquet/BLUE-WHALE-VR / last accessed June 19, 2023."

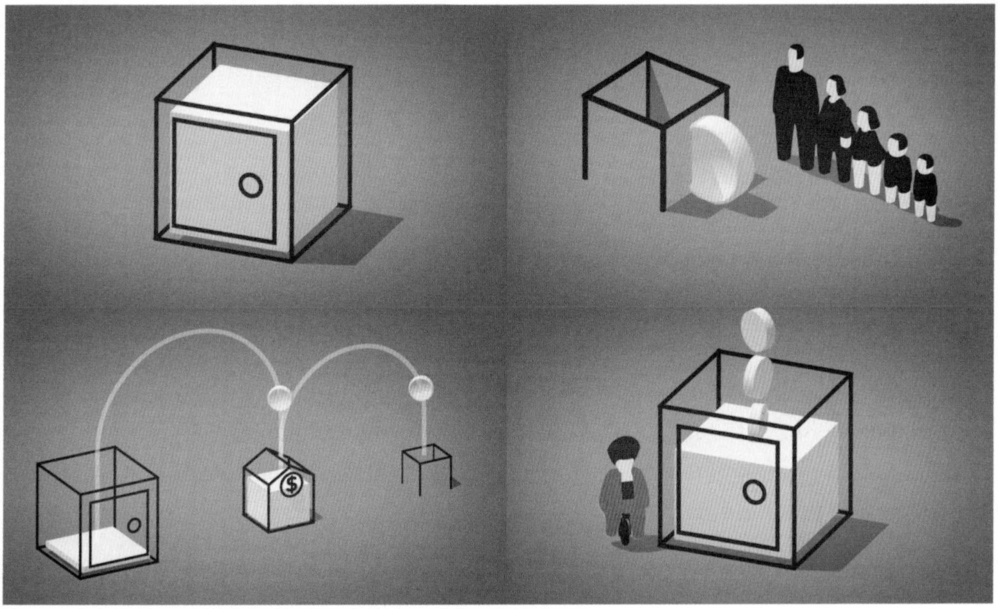

Figure 21.5: "Fiscal Maneuvers" by João Paulo Charleaux, Lilian Venturini, and Simon Ducroquet for *Nexo Jornal*
https://cargocollective.com/ducroquet/PEDALADAS-FISCAIS

the government collects. The third represents public expenditures, such as social services. The box in the middle is the banks (some state-owned) who work as intermediaries.

In theory, the Brazilian government should periodically send the banks a sufficient amount of money to cover public expenditures; however, in times of economic uncertainty, or to conceal budgetary flaws, the government could delay this process for a few days, leaving the banks to use their own resources. That way, and at least temporarily, the government created a misleading appearance of fiscal health. The "pedaladas" were a key argument in the 2016 controversial impeachment of then president Dilma Rousseff.

Referring to projects like this, Simon told me:

> Thinking retroactively, I think that there is a constant in my career, a desire to disassemble certain news events or phenomena—to understand their logic and their inner workings; and then a drive to reassemble the components of those events in ways that are compelling and clear to viewers. This reassembling is a crafting process that is unique to each story; it's very deliberate, very manual, and I sometimes fail at it. The process itself is useful for me to also understand the information I'm dealing with.

That constant is present in many of Simon's graphics, including those that are more data-driven. In 2018 Jair Bolsonaro, a right-wing populist, was elected president of Brazil. Bolsonaro had been very active in social media as a candidate, and he kept building a large following after the election. His posts were consistently aggressive, seemingly intended to fire up his conservative fanbase.

But how far to the right were Bolsonaro's followers, really? A series of visualizations published by *Folha de São Paulo* that Simon contributed to in 2019 (**Figure 21.6**) showed that Bolsonaro had a pretty conservative following indeed, but not as much as I had guessed. These graphics were based on an analysis of a thousand political figures and of a sample of nearly 2 million accounts that followed them. Each circle is a political influencer, and its horizontal position corresponds to the ideological leanings of their followers.

This said, the actual focus of the piece was a pattern of ideological sorting; profiles all over the political spectrum typically followed and interacted with those with whom they aligned ideologically (right-wing profiles were even more insulated than those on the political center or on the left). "The ideology of Twitter influencers" explains this first through a visualization of the data set in its entirety, followed by others that disassemble it to zoom into its specifics.

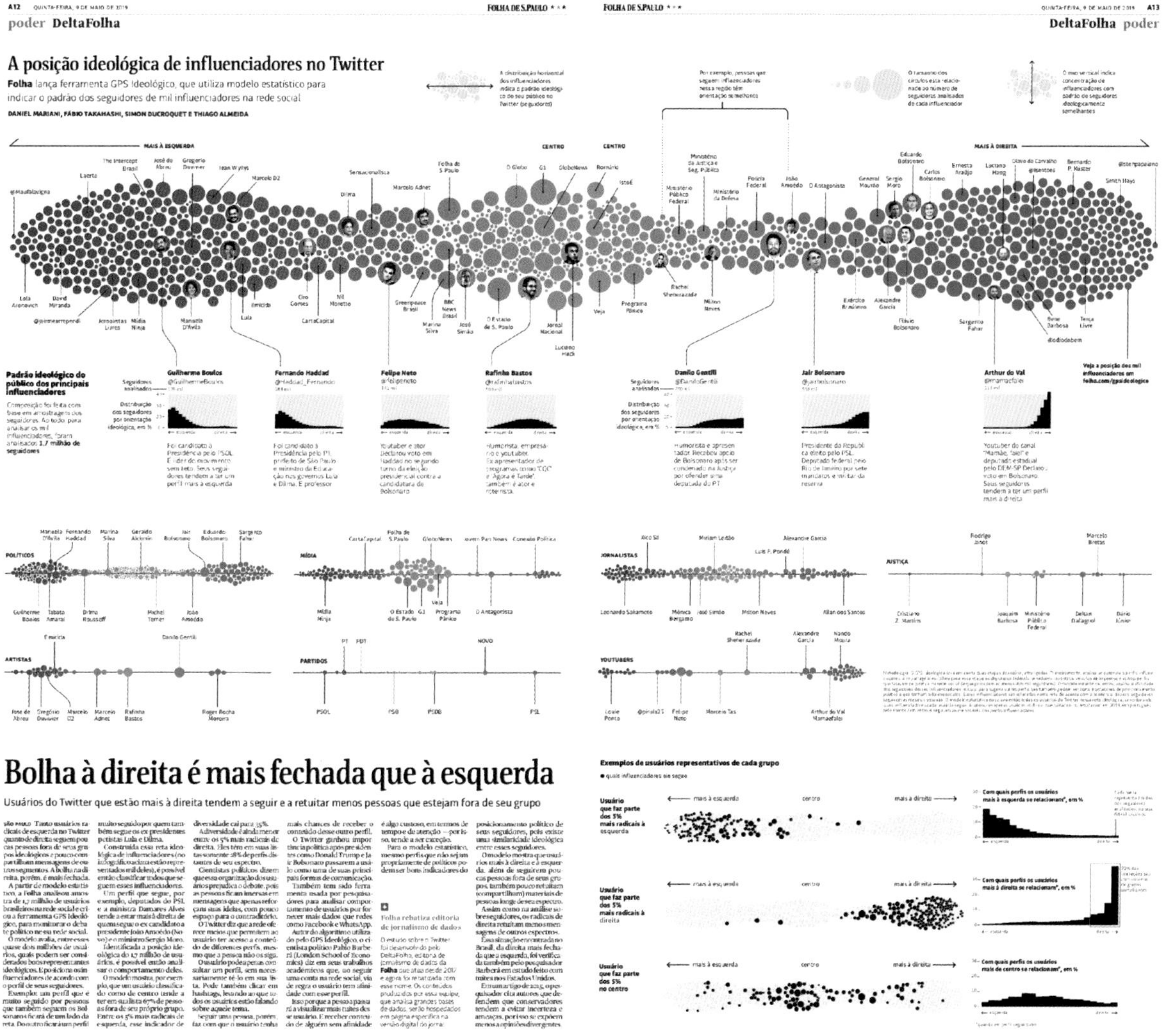

Figure 21.6: "The ideology of Twitter influencers" by Daniel Mariani, Fábio Takahashi, Simon Ducroquet, and Thiago Almeida
https://cargocollective.com/ducroquet/GPS-IDEOLOGICO

"How strange visualization can be," I wrote when I found this project in Simon's portfolio, and I struggled to make sense of and give order to some banal thoughts that crossed my mind: "I find these charts as beautiful as I find the story that they tell concerning, even terrifying. What a paradox."

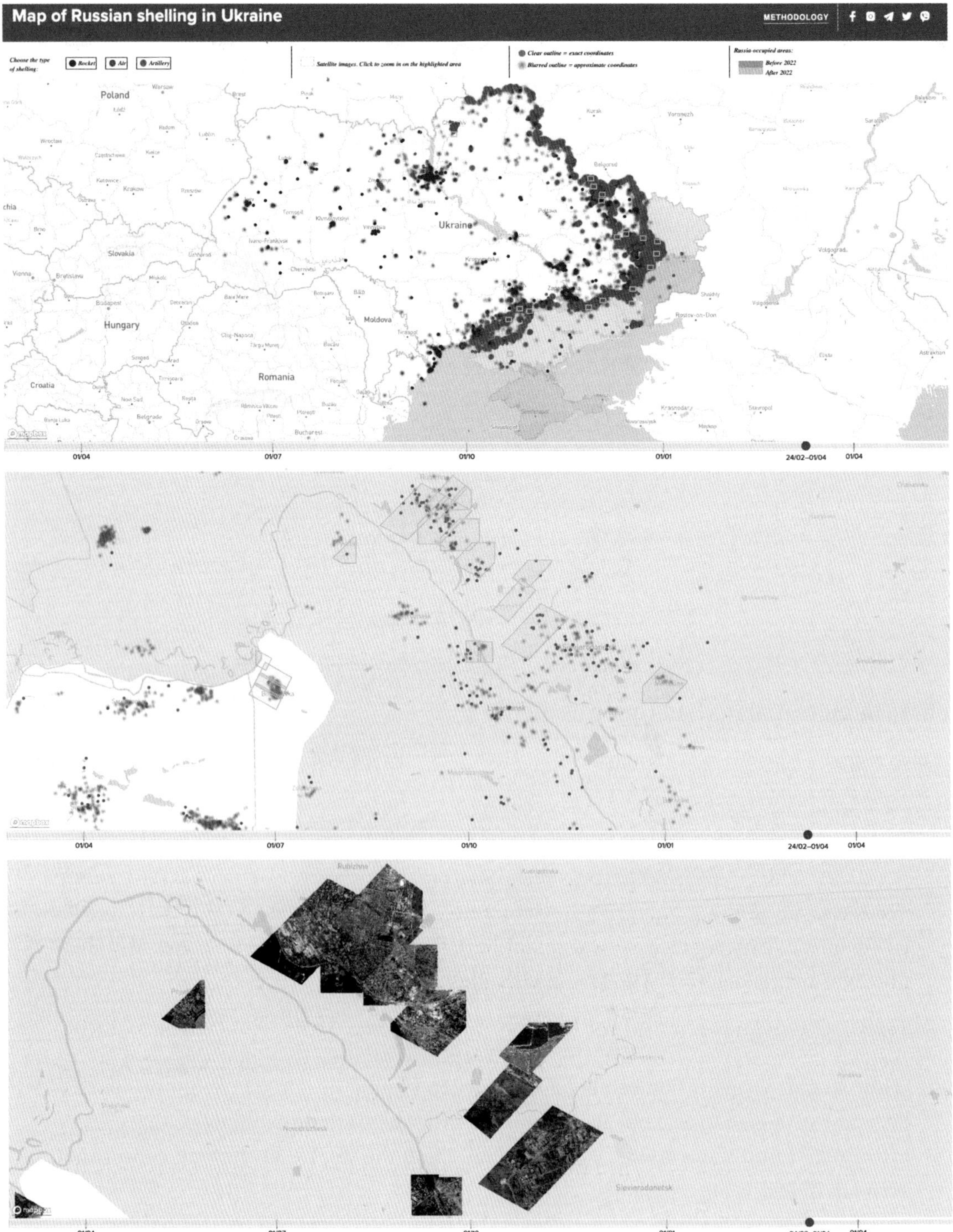

Figure 22.1: "Under attack. What and when Russia shelled in Ukraine" by Petro Bodnar, Yevhenia Drozdova, and Nadia Kelm
Simon Ducroquet / "https://texty.org.ua/projects/107577/under-attack-what-and-when-russia-shelled-ukraine/ / last accessed June 19, 2023."

Chapter 22
with Anatoliy Bondarenko

A Journalist at War

Just as others might take pleasure from a good horse, or a dog, or a bird,
I take even more pleasure from good friends.

—Socrates, quoted by Xenophon

"My friend is at war," I wrote in my notebook when **Anatoliy Bondarenko** told me in an email that he had joined the Ukrainian army as a captain. Since February 24, 2022, when Russia launched its invasion of Ukraine, not a week has passed that I have not thought about him, his family, or his team at the nonprofit investigative journalism publication he co-founded, Texty.org.ua. The war might have been decided by the time you read these lines, written in late May of 2023—in Ukraine's favor, I hope.

Texty isn't well known outside of Ukraine. That's a shame. The quality of their visualizations is comparable to publications with far more reporters and designers on staff. At the start of the invasion, Texty launched an impressively detailed tracker of Russian artillery and air strikes, and they've updated it to this day (**Figure 22.1**). Anatoliy told me that they used satellite data provided free of charge by Planet Labs, a U.S. imaging company:

> It's so great to talk to you, Alberto. It brings a sense of normalcy and memories of better times. Yes, about this piece. I'm really proud of my team; they made this graphic in my absence; I was already in the army when we launched it. Texty has been very active not just since the beginning of the current invasion, but since Russia's illegal annexation of Crimea. We've made many

projects about the ongoing conflict, for instance a tracker of pro-Russian propaganda and disinformation in Ukraine (**Figure 22.2**).

This interactive visualization monitors hundreds of local websites (bars pointing up) and Russian websites (bars pointing down) that spread propaganda. The height of bars is the prevalence of a topic—war-related stories, for example, which become more common the closer we move to the present—as a percentage of all the stories published by those websites.

Something that caught my attention when I first read this piece is that its "Methodology" section occupies more space than the visualizations themselves. Anatoliy told me:

It took us half a year just to research how to build and train machine learning models to identify stories that possibly included propaganda or disinformation, and then to experiment with those models and test them for accuracy. It felt like a research project.

In Ukraine there's a large information ecosystem devoted to spreading disinformation. Our initial training data was a relatively small sample of a couple of hundred stories from what in Ukraine we call "junk websites," pages created to disseminate clickbait or propaganda. To this day we've been adding more websites to this list of pages to track.

The second step was to build the infrastructure to maintain the project. We have a powerful server that visits all these websites constantly and, using Python scripts, scrapes their content, separates what we think is relevant (politics, the economy, international affairs) from content that we don't analyze (weather or sports, for instance) and transforms the results into data. We trained a machine learning model to do this using topic modeling, a method to identify clusters of similar words or terms.

However, the most time-consuming part was to develop a method to classify stories and to estimate the likelihood that they contain manipulative or false information. This required plenty of human judgment. We collaborated with nearly 10 journalists. They spent a lot of time first analyzing a random sample of a thousand stories one by one to identify propaganda, disinformation, or emotionally manipulative content. After that, they grouped stories into categories. This resulted in the hierarchy and sub-hierarchies that you can see in the project. We've also kept constantly refining the underlying model to increase its accuracy.

We went back in time. Anatoliy's professional trajectory began in the 1990s, around the time of the fall of the Soviet Union:

I'm from a province in central Ukraine. I studied physics at the Moscow Physical Engineering Institute, and when I finished I moved to Kyiv. This was the time of the end of the Soviet era and the transitional period when Ukraine gained its independence. Those were difficult times economically, and a career in science was out of the question. There wasn't much funding for

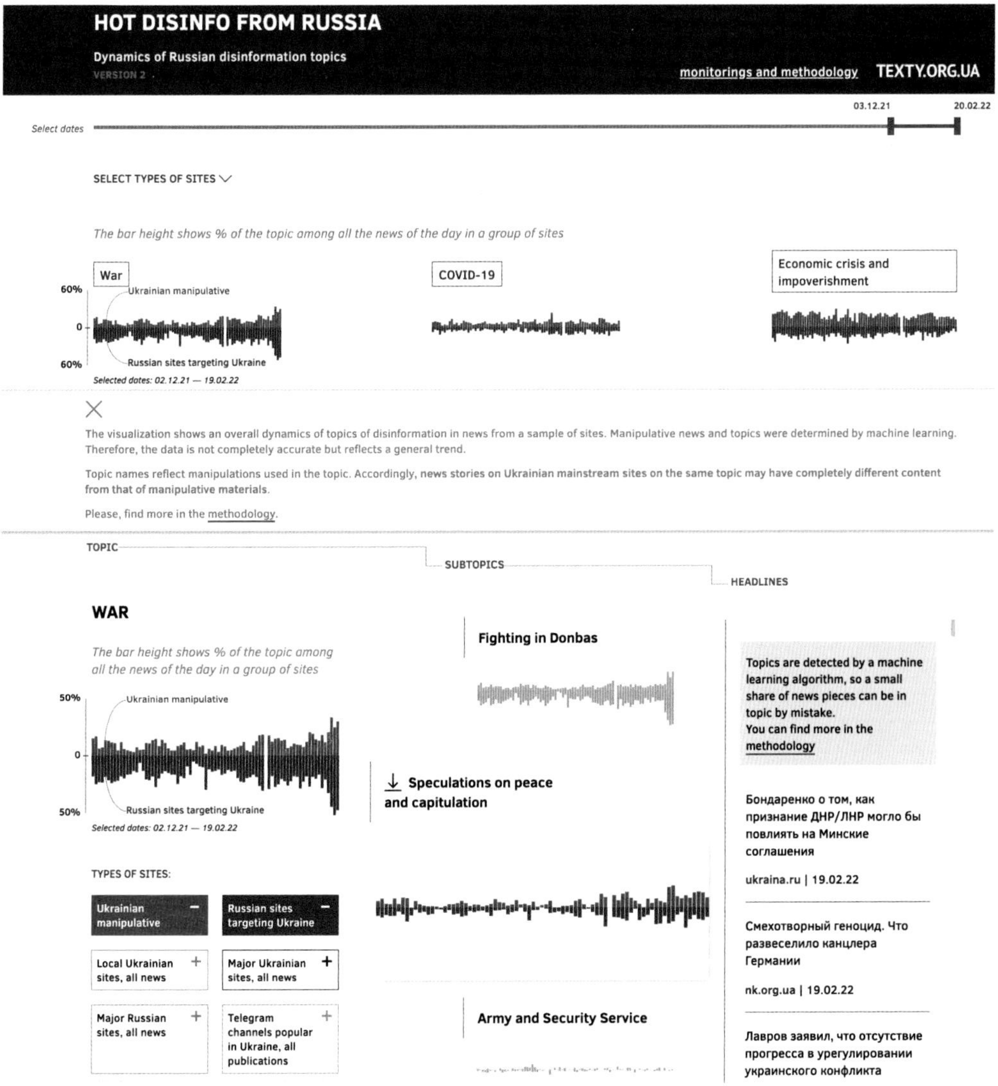

Figure 22.2: "Dynamics of Russian disinformation topics"
by Nadja Kelm and Nadia Romanenko
https://topic-radar.texty.org/

research, so the options for me were to either move to a different country or to get an industry job. I did the latter. I began doing a bit of everything, IT, website development, and I even worked for an investment company, trading stock in the Ukrainian market. Actually, this is where I designed my first visualization around 1998. I used C to visualize the performance of stocks all over the world. The graphic I created was useless, but very pretty.

The late 1990s and early 2000s were a time of hope, but also of increasing corruption, strife, and even violence. Paul D'Anieri, a professor of political science at the University of California, Riverside, has chronicled the recent history of Ukraine in his *Ukraine and Russia: From Civilized Divorce to Uncivil War* (2023). It contains a thorough explanation of the attempt by the second post-Soviet president of Ukraine, Leonid Kuchma, to eliminate independent news media in the late 1990s, consolidate power, and transform the country into an autocracy.

A pivotal moment of Kuchma's presidency, D'Anieri wrote—and Anatoliy confirmed—was the murder of journalist Georgiy Gongadze, who was very critical of the government, and had exposed many corruption scandals during Kuchma's two terms. Four policemen kidnapped and killed Gongadze in November of 2000. A few weeks after his mutilated body was found, tape recordings were released that implicated Kuchma in the case.

Anatoliy told me that Gongadze's murder changed everything not only for him, but for his country:

> It's a fundamental historical episode of modern Ukraine. It infuriated me, and millions of others. Civil society was already pretty active at the time, but the murder of Gongadze ignited it. It led first to the Ukraine without Kuchma protest movement in 2000, and that movement is the foundation of the protests that came after, the Orange Revolution of 2004, and the Maidan Revolution of 2014.
>
> All these protests in Ukraine are based on informal networks that emerged from Ukraine without Kuchma. I was involved in this movement. When the murder happened I began having a double life, one at my daily job and another as protest organizer. I was part of the eight-person team that launched Maidan.org.ua, the main website of the movement. The word "maidan" [related to Kyiv's Maidan Nezalezhnosti, Independence Square] has been used in Ukraine as a synonym for "place of protest" ever since.

Activism took Anatoliy to news media and, eventually to data journalism:

> What I saw around me in Ukraine—the corruption, the violence, the protests, the Russian meddling—made me think that I could not just sit and do nothing. I started to write, and that led to my first journalism job in 2008. It was in a magazine, *Ukrainskiy Tyzhden* (*Ukranian Week*). I was hired as its politics editor.
>
> My main job was to manage journalists and edit their pieces, but I also insisted on having pages dedicated to infographics. That was one of my side activities. The other was to think about how programming could make our work easier. For example, I wrote a program to compare state budgets (you can't imagine how messy Ukrainian state budget data is) and another to compare the programs of political parties. I quickly realized how powerful these data-driven techniques were to enrich traditional journalism.

Figure 22.3: "Here's how Ukraine was swept by populism. History of voting since 2006" by Yevheniia Drozdova, Nadja Kelm, and Anatoliy Bondarenko
https://texty.org.ua/d/2020/elections_history/en/

Anatoliy brought his enthusiasm for data and computational journalism to his next venture, Texty.

> *Ukrainskiy Tyzhden* laid me and most of the editorial team off at the end of 2009 due to a conflict with the owner. At the time I was increasingly worried about the diminishing landscape of independent media in Ukraine, so I founded Texty in 2010 with my partner Roman Kulchynsky. At the beginning it was a really scrappy operation. We used our personal savings to pay for it, but eventually we started getting funding from donors, non-governmental organizations, and we set up a crowd-sourcing system for individual readers to support our reporting.
>
> In the first couple of years Texty was a typical online news publication, consisting mainly of written stories, but around 2011 or 2012 I started pushing for more data and more visualizations. In the last decade we've produced hundreds of graphics-driven stories ranging from exposés of government corruption to overviews of parliamentary elections (**Figure 22.3**).

In these maps, each dash is a voting location. The color corresponds to the party that received more votes than others on each. Blue are mostly pro-Western and Ukrainian nationalist parties; red are communist or largely pro-Russian coalitions; and yellow are populist forces. The slope of dashes is the support that the dominant party or coalition received in comparison to the others: the steeper the slope, the bigger the support.

Notice the presence of pro-Russian parties in 2005 and 2012, particularly in Eastern and Southern Ukraine, and the tide turning in 2014, the election after the Maidan Revolution, which expelled president Viktor Yanukovych. The last map I chose displays the 2019 victory of former comedian Volodymyr Zelenskyy, who ran on a populist, anti-establishment platform. Zelenskyy led Ukraine during the Russian invasion that began in 2022 and became an international icon.

Texty has published many analyses of the intricacies of the Ukrainian political system. I asked Anatoliy to pick just one as an example, and he chose a sophisticated historical overview of voting patterns in parliament since the Maidan Revolution of 2014, which eventually led to the presidency of Petro Poroshenko, backed by a coalition of parties associated with the Orange Revolution of 2004. These parties, yellow, green, red, and pink in the charts (**Figure 22.4**) tend to be pro-Western and anti-Russian. Anatoliy told me:

> To design this story we first imagined a perfect deputy [in Ukraine, the parliament is called the Verkhovna Rada, and representatives are called People's Deputies of Ukraine]. What we mean by "perfect" is a deputy who would vote in favor of every single reformist, anti-corruption, pro-Ukranian, or pro-democracy bill since the independence of Ukraine. We gathered a sample of more than two thousand parliamentary bills, and we manually classified them as reformist or not. This is obviously based on our own subjective assessment, but we did our best to be fair.
>
> Take a look at the line graph in this piece. The voting record of our fictional and ideal deputy who votes for beneficial bills 100% of the time would be the upper horizontal grid line, the 1.0. Below that line you'll see Ukraine's political parties, each represented by a color. If a party's line moves up, that means that a higher proportion of its deputies were voting in favor of "good" bills. The opposite is true if the line goes down.
>
> The lowest lines correspond to the pro-Russian block of opposition parties, the post-Yanukovich coalition. But the most interesting lines to me are the ones representing the governing coalition. There are so many stories in those lines. There are periods when the parties are very close to each other, meaning that their deputies were voting very much alike. However, starting in 2015, they began diverging. The red line, for instance, is the Radical Party of Oleh Liashko, a small party that initially was part of the coalition, but exited it and then came back to it. The pink line is Yulia Tymoshenko's party, Batkivshchyna (Fatherland). Notice that it left the coalition, as well.
>
> This story also contains several radar charts. The central dot is our ideal deputy, and the other dots are real deputies. You can see them moving closer or farther away from the center, but also

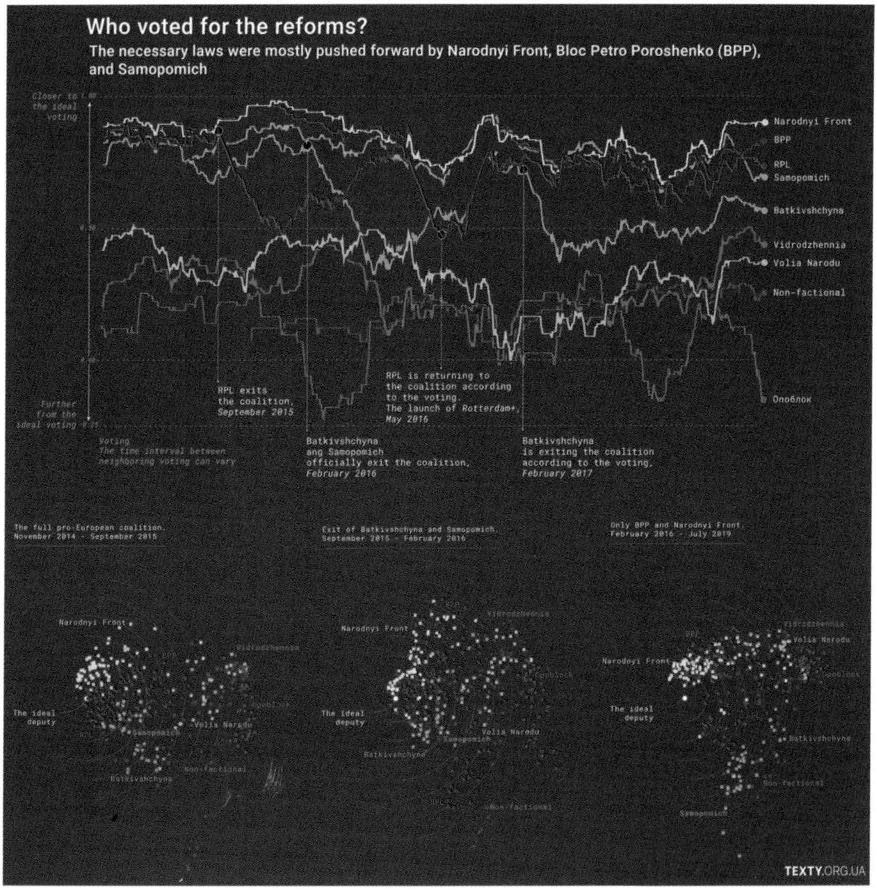

Figure 22.4: "Who voted for the reforms?" by Anatoliy Bondarenko, Nadja Kelm, and Yevheniia Drozdova
https://texty.org.ua/d/2019/verhovna-rada/

clustering or dispersing or moving upwards and downwards, indicating the level of support for the Poroshenko administration.

Anatoliy enjoys stories about topics that are apparently lighter, but that may reveal relevant societal patterns. In 2021 Texty published an analysis of the most commonly stolen products in one of Ukraine's biggest grocery store chain, ATB (**Figure 22.5**). The highest on the ranking, both in terms of total stolen value and in the number of court cases, are alcohol, candy, cosmetics, and caviar.

Anatoliy also mentioned a piece about vehicle registration plates (**Figure 22.6**). It consists of a series of plots displaying the frequency of digits and digit combinations (Ukrainian plates have four digits). The visualizations reveal that these combinations aren't always random. Some appear much more frequently than others.

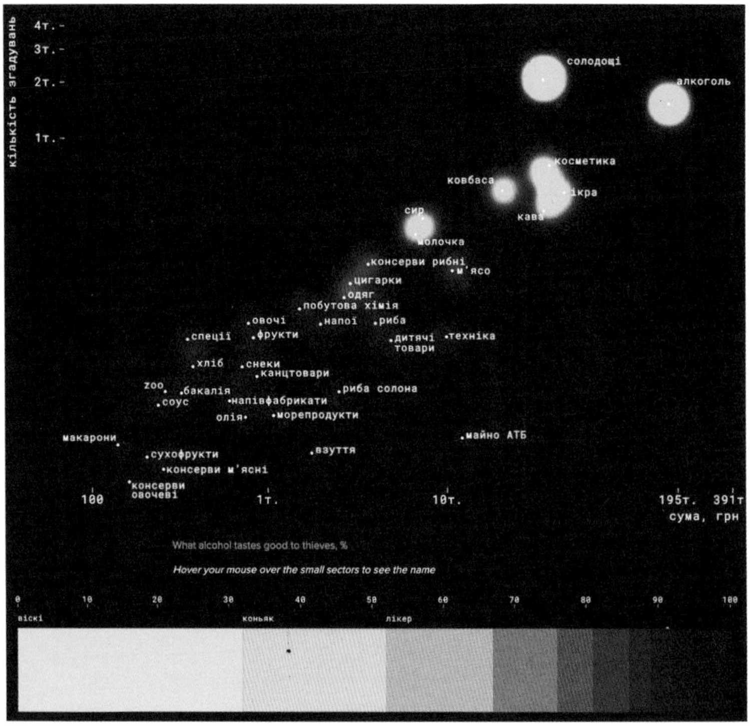

Figure 22.5: "Whiskey, chocolate, red caviar: What is most often stolen in ATB?" by Yevheniia Drozdova, and Nadja Kelm
https://texty.org.ua/d/2021/atb/

The reason is that in Ukraine there's a market for "prestige" plates. A wealthy person can pay extra money—sometimes hundreds or even thousands of dollars—to get a digit sequence that looks nicely symmetrical, or that is associated with popular culture products or celebrities:

It may sound silly, but having a nice-looking plate number is a symbol of social and economic status. I guess that you could compare it to wearing nice jewelry, gold chains, or big rings. If you have a nice car and you pair it with a cool plate number, you're showing not only that you have money, but also the possibility of making even more money. Wealthy car owners have all sorts of strange (or not so strange!) beliefs, such as thinking that they might get better treatment by the police if they are stopped for speeding or unlawful parking. This is a pattern that Ukraine inherited from the first post-Soviet years, when corruption was extreme.

You said that this type of project is more light-hearted, perhaps funny or more inconsequential than others. I disagree. This type of story reveals important facts about Ukrainian society.

"Well, my friend," I replied, "you titled the piece '0007, Like a Bond, James Bond'," so I'm not the only one who found it funny, am I? We both laughed, sharing a fleeting, pleasurable moment of normalcy and obliviousness to the uncertainties of our time.

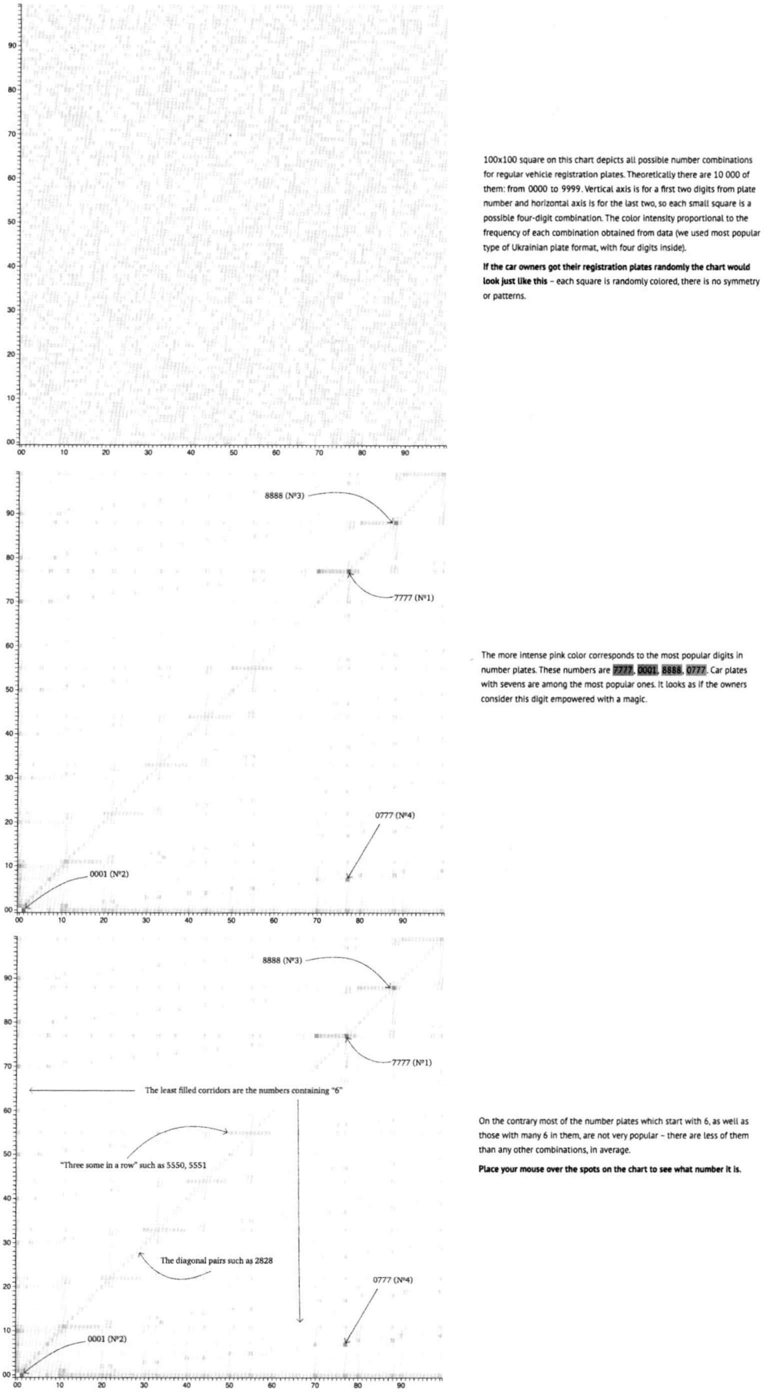

Figure 22.6: "0007, Like a Bond, James Bond: Who buys fancy number plates 3,000USD worth and what for?" by Yevheniia Drozdova, Nadja Kelm, and Anatoliy Bondarenko https://texty.org.ua/d/2019/numbers/en/

Epilogue: Teachers, Mentors, and Meaning

Our knowledge has made us cynical. Our cleverness, hard and unkind. We think too much and feel too little. More than machinery we need humanity. More than cleverness we need kindness and gentleness. Without these qualities, life will be violent and all will be lost.

— Charlie Chaplin

My wanderings are about to come to an end. In Chapter 2, I quoted a passage from David Le Breton's *Marcher la vie: Un art tranquille du bonheur* (2020), "Like Ulysses, sometimes we need to travel around the world and lose ourselves in a thousand follies before returning to Ithaca." Have I returned to the place from where I departed? I think I have, reinvigorated and, like Shirley Wu in the introduction, hopeful.

Pierre Hadot's *What is Ancient Philosophy?* (2004) is one of those books worth revisiting regularly. To Hadot, philosophy isn't just an academic discipline, but an inquiry into what a good life is and how to pursue it. He also wrote that philosophical theories and schools are influenced by the temperament (innate dispositions) and character (learned traits) of the people who construct them.

For example, we can better understand Plato's ideas by studying where and when he lived, his biography, and his personality. A tale popularized by one of his biographers, Diogenes Laertius, says that Plato wanted to burn all works by Democritus, a far more interesting rival, in my opinion. This is an uncorroborated anecdote, but I find it amusing nonetheless.

To understand a practice, then, it's helpful to learn about its practitioners. I believe that this applies to information design and data visualization, and perhaps to any field of human inquiry. The myriad ways in which we make visualizations, the ways that we think about the craft, the ways that we share it and teach it to others—all of them intertwine with who we were born to be, how our environment and experiences hew us, and how we decide to conduct ourselves at every step of our journeys.

Here's an early step of such a journey: When I was 12 years old, one of my least favorite classes was geography, not because of its content (what's not to like in a class that relies on maps so much?) but due to the teacher, a cruel, hollow soul who enjoyed belittling his students. He was that type of man who revels in power, knowing that it's unlikely that those whom he considers inferior will dare to punch back. Of people like him J.R.R Tolkien once wrote, "From splendour he fell through arrogance to contempt for all things save himself, a spirit wasteful and pitiless." But I digress.

One of the assignments for the class was to draw and color a map of Europe, labeling every ocean, sea, country, capital city, major river, and mountain range. I've enjoyed maps since I was little, so that evening I returned home brimming with excitement.

My dad and I purchased a big cardboard sheet, black pens, and colored pencils. Before he retired, dad was a medical doctor, but he's also a humanist, a poet, a novelist, and a pretty decent visual artist, so he offered his help. I haven't kept the map that I made under his guidance, but I remember that it was colorful, intricate, baroque even. When I was a kid I read an unhealthy amount of fantasy, horror, and science fiction, and I tried to emulate the lush maps I had seen in books. I've kept handcrafting maps with almost the same style to this day as a hobby. **Figure E.1**, which I drew in 2021, should give you a rough idea of what my class project looked like.

A few days later, we had the in-class review session. My geography teacher dismissed most maps, and singled out mine as a particularly dreadful example. He harshly laughed at several distinctive details—triple parallel lines and shading to emphasize coastlines, pictorial representations of mountains and rivers—that he said were decorative and, therefore, needless. He also compared my map with the ones in our textbook; these were stylistically spare and conventional and, to my younger eyes, also uninspiring, uninviting, *boring*.

I don't remember my teacher's exact words. However, beyond their crude prescriptivism —maps ought to be made in a specific way, *or not be made at all*—they reeked of sexism. My map, he suggested, looked soft, infantile, *feminine*. I guess that, deep in his withered mind, there was a vague idea that *real* boys and men ought to favor rugged and masculine minimalism.

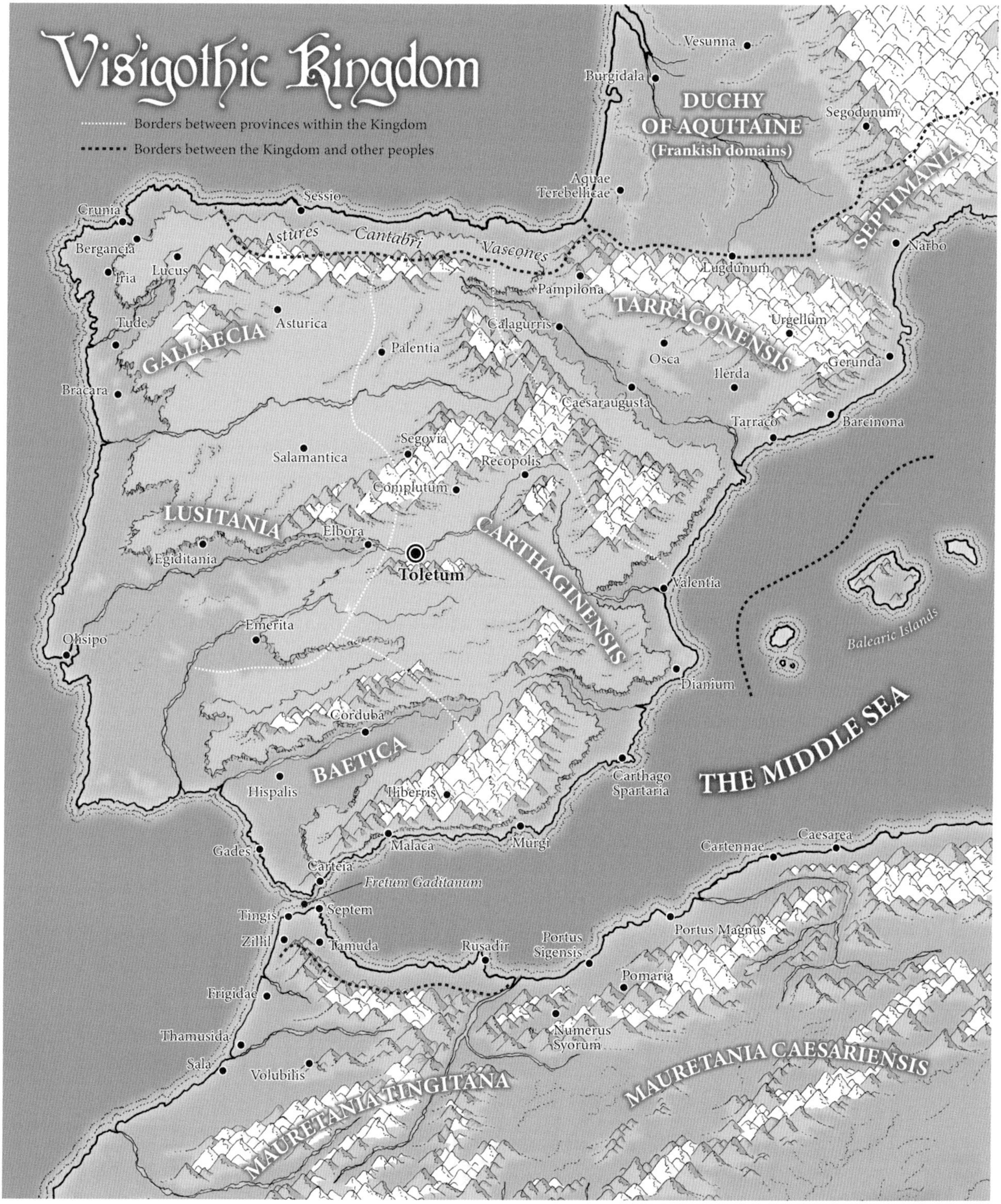

Figure E.1: A map of the Visigothic kingdom of Spain and its neighbors in the late 7th century. I used pencil, black pen, and Photoshop for coloring and shading.

I didn't reply to the teacher. I felt hurt for a few hours—and mightily motivated to keep drawing immediately after. “Screw that bastard,” I thought (in Spanish that'd be, *Que se joda ese cabrón*).

I've sometimes fantasized about crossing paths with this teacher one day, only to say, “Hi, you don't remember me, but here's what you said about a map I drew for your class when I was a kid. Let me now tell you about who I've become, where I am, and what I do for a living.” On a second thought, though, there's no point in that. That man, if he's still alive, is of advanced age, retired, and unable to hurt students anymore.

Many times in the past three decades I've reflected on this formative experience. Destructive feedback motivated me, but what would have happened if my temperament were different? What if I weren't as combative—in a quiet, stoic way when I was a kid— as I am? Perhaps I'd have given up illustration and mapping, activities that not only have brought me great pleasure, that also have led to a fruitful career in journalism, information design, and data visualization.

I also wondered, what if my geography teacher had acted like my math, history, or philosophy teachers? These were tough and rigorous, but none of them rushed to judgment (“Tell me, how did you get that idea, where does it come from?” was a typical question they asked), and they always offered a word of encouragement along with suggestions for improvement. Would I have felt even more motivated about mapping had my geography teacher been like them?

In the Second Coda, which closes Part 3 (Ambassadors) of this book, I wrote that emulating exemplary and admirable people is a decent heuristic for a good life. Here's a complementary one: It's advisable to model ourselves against the people whose ideas or behavior we find unsavory or harmful.

While working on the conversations for this book I realized that, consciously or not, I've slowly become the opposite type of person that my geography teacher was. Nowadays I even hesitate to call myself a *professor*, an *instructor*, or even a *teacher*. I'd rather be a mentor and a conversationalist—one among a community of many—who asks, listens, ponders, chats, and, pretty often, holds judgment, sometimes indefinitely. An instructor walks ahead of you; a mentor walks *with* you while you both either travel existing paths, or trace new ones that others may later traverse.

If my geography teacher had acted more as a mentor, he might have learned about a long tradition of fantasy and science fiction artists. His horizons would have been expanded. But people like him—or like *me* somewhere in the not-so-distant past—talk too much and listen too little. As a consequence, we tend to prescribe even before we understand what or why we're prescribing.*

Fixing English (2014) by linguist Anne Curzan chronicles the interactions between descriptivists and prescriptivists in the history of the English language. Descriptivists are those who observe and analyze how languages are used and how they evolve. Prescriptivists take a normative approach, trying to "fix" languages in the sense of either making them "better" in some way—standardized, more stylistically elegant, or more culturally inclusive—or of preserving them in their current form. I see *The Art of Insight* as a descriptivist book, albeit not a systematic one by any stretch.

Curzan is sympathetic to both descriptivists and prescriptivists and says that their interplay is essential to the history of any language. They are engaged in an endless dance between heterodoxy and orthodoxy, progress and preservation. She also warns about a few risks in both approaches. On the one hand, descriptivists may focus too narrowly on dominant forms of a language, privileging them and implicitly conveying the idea that minoritarian or emerging varieties of that language are somehow inferior, less sophisticated, not well formed.

In visualization, this is a danger that Lauren Klein and Catherine D'Ignazio wrote about in *Data Feminism* (2020). For instance, too many histories of visualization, data journalism, and adjacent domains are limited to just a handful of key figures in a few Western countries. That's why people such as Allen Hillery (Chapter 9), Attila Bátorfy (Chapter 14), and so many others who explore visualization in different cultures and places, past and present, are so relevant. I'm still appalled that I hadn't heard of Ida B. Wells's extraordinary investigative reporting before Allen prompted me to look into it. There's a book waiting to be written about Wells's data work.

What about prescriptivism? Citing linguist Deborah Cameron, who coined the term "verbal hygiene," Curzan wrote that "the desire to regulate, improve, and clean up the speech of others, is a natural part of all speech communities." Prescriptivists can't stop language evolution, but they can steer it in certain directions. They can do it through persuasion, example, and forbearing authoritativeness—think of the *The Elements of Style*, by William Strunk and E.B. White, which has been used as a writing manual since the

* Once again, I break my self-imposed rule of not using footnotes. When my friend, geographer Nick Cox, read part of these musings, he sent me a quote by historian Geoffrey Elton: "Sympathy for a variety of concerns and manners of approach does not preclude the existence of some severe discrimination in the judgment." Point taken, but severe self-examination must always precede any opinion.

1920s—or sometimes, like in the case of my geography teacher, through scorn, mockery, and cruelty. Too often, prescriptivism can turn into an exercise of illegitimate, arbitrary power.

Unfortunately, pious and unrequested gatekeeping is still too common in information design and visualization. Remember Ed Hawkins (Chapter 1) hearing from some designers that his "Warming Stripes" wasn't following established rules; or Sonja Kuijpers (Chapter 5) encountering people who told her that her work doesn't belong in visualization; and here's a passage that Federica Fragapane (Chapter 7) wrote on Instagram in December of 2022 about the responses that her unique and organic visualizations—some of which are part of New York's Museum of Modern Art (MoMA) Permanent Collection—sometimes receive:

> Projects of mine about women rights/women rights violations are more likely to attract technical—and sometimes unkind—remarks from men. That's an interesting pattern. What strikes me the most is how such comments completely ignore the topic to jump directly to technical considerations: data on rights violations take second place to the fact that "it should have been a bar chart." I'm convinced it's possible to do both: constructively criticize and be respectful. But I also think that this is part of a broader issue that finds its roots in a common practice: delegitimisation. Delegitimisation of a subject, delegitimisation of an approach, delegitimisation of a voice.

Those men embody a pattern that I've anecdotally observed, including in myself: Immaturity and ignorance correlate with overconfidence in our own opinions, and with a will to impose those opinions on others. Ignorance, by the way, isn't just lack of knowledge, but a lack of awareness of what knowledge we do possess, or don't.

And we don't really know much yet about how people read and interpret visualizations. Robert Kosara (2016), a researcher at Observable, has said that professional advice in visualization is an empire built on sand. Here's Robert:

> Many of the supposed rules in visualization are tightly interwoven with aesthetics. It's easy to side with the idea of minimalist charts that lack the garish embellishments of infographics. Pie charts are easy to hate. Staggered animations and 45° line charts make intuitive sense. The danger of these seemingly obvious rules and facts is that they are deceptive in their beauty and simplicity. What if reality is more complicated and doesn't adhere to modernist design aesthetics? What if our perception and memory are messier and work better when there are more decorative elements to hang on to? What if there is no single rule that tells us what aspect ratio to pick? What if our existing visual representations don't mesh well with our ways of thinking about the data?

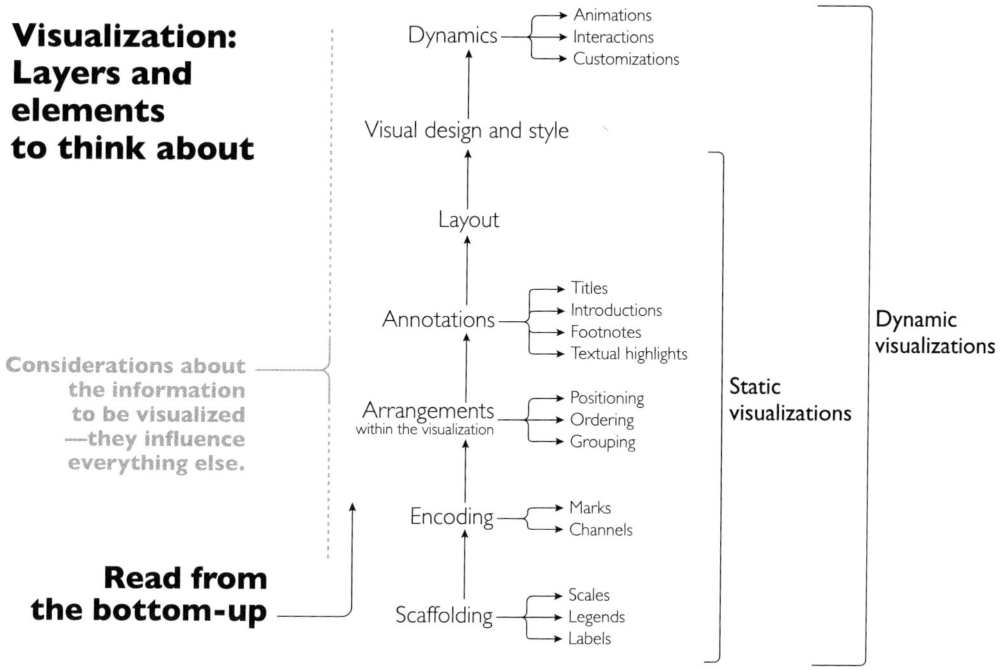

Figure E.2: A diagram that I often use in classes and workshops. It lists some elements in a visualization that we need to make deliberate choices about.

That said, and despite the gaps in our knowledge of what works in visualization—we *do* know a bit, but much remains to be studied—we designers need to keep getting our work done, don't we? Moreover, some of us also teach.

In Chapter 2 I gave you a hint of how I do both. Putting aside my anarchic leanings and sympathies, I teach in a rather structured way. The diagram on **Figure E.2**, listing many of the layers and elements in a graphic we need to make choices about, appears often in my classes and workshops. I use it, step by step, to walk students through my own reasoning process. If I ever write another book about visualization, an updated and more thorough version of it might become its index.

I believe that the designers you've met in this book, even the most heterodox among them, have a personal version of this schema in their minds. They know that choices in visualization should be based on the peculiarities of the data that we wish to represent, on the nature and purpose of the project we intend to design—visualizations can be exploratory, expositive, explanatory, artistic, emotive, prosaic, poetic, and more—and on many constraints related to intended audience, publishing platform, and so on.

You might remember that my personal approach—and I'd like to emphasize that it's *personal*; I don't claim that it's generalizable—is grounded on the notion that my role in the classroom isn't to teach *how to* make decisions in visualization design, but to demonstrate and exemplify how *I*, an individual, make decisions based on what I've observed in a career that spans many years, on my personal tastes, and on what I've learned from the limited empirical evidence we possess.

In Chapter 2 I referred to this process as an internal conversation that can become external if we share the reasons for our choices with other people. If you ever attend one of my classes, expect to be constantly asked to persuade me of the soundness of your visualizations by saying something like, "Here's what I've done, and here are the reasons for every decision I've made. Do they make sense? Do you find them convincing? Do you think that they'll work? If not, please tell me why, suggest alternatives, and explain to me the reasons behind them. I'm happy to change my mind."

If I could go back in time, this is what I'd encourage my geography teacher to do.

More than a decade has passed since the publication of *The Functional Art*, my first book in English. The worlds of data journalism, information design, and data visualization—my worlds—have changed substantially, and for the better. There are more people visiting them, more software tools and programming languages to use, more books, courses, and tutorials to learn from, more spaces, venues, conferences, and professional associations to interact with others and nurture friendships.

Things have changed, yes, and I've changed, but a handful of my core beliefs haven't. First, designing information is part science, part art; it belongs in STEM fields as much as it belongs in the humanities. That's why I found it unsurprising that many of the people I engaged with for this book have hybrid backgrounds in math, statistics, or engineering on the one hand, and in the arts, journalism, history, or philosophy on the other.

Second, visualization, like writing, responds to an instinctual desire to organize the chaotic complexity of reality, and to a longing for the joys of seeing and understanding better. I wish we talked more about pleasure as a motivating force; I've tried to do it in many of the conversations I had for *The Art of Insight*. This pleasure is first a personal one ("Now *I* see it!") but can become a shared one, as there's a lot of pleasure to be gained in helping others see better with us.

Third, reading and creating maps, charts, and diagrams is the way that I've always tried to grasp the world and interact with it. If designing information hadn't become a career for me, I'd have kept practicing it anyway. For some mysterious reason, it's central to who I am. I love it, and I've come to love those who love it as much as I do. We're in this together, and when the time comes to vanish, one can hope that it'll be many years from now! I shall wish to borrow Bertrand Russell's words from his 1956 essay "How to Grow Old":

> An individual human existence should be like a river: small at first, narrowly contained within its banks, and rushing passionately past rocks and over waterfalls. Gradually the river grows wider, the banks recede, the waters flow more quietly, and in the end, without any visible break, they become merged in the sea, and painlessly lose their individual being. The man who, in old age, can see his life in this way, will not suffer from the fear of death, since the things he cares for will continue. And if, with the decay of vitality, weariness increases, the thought of rest will not be unwelcome. I should wish to die while still at work, knowing that others will carry on what I can no longer do and content in the thought that what was possible has been done.

Good work can imbue a life with meaning. *Homo sapiens*, a being who learns and knows, is sometimes happier when acting as *Homo faber*, a being who makes. We're fleeting stardust specks in an immense universe but, through acts of creation that make our lives, and the lives of others, healthier, wiser, or happier, we can carve a tiny mark on it while defiantly whispering, "Here I stood."

Alex, my youngest son, who in the introduction to this book was curious about the meaning of life, has begun to grasp this simple, ordinary truth, and today he plays the piano and the bass, draws, and paints. What about visualization, you might wonder? Funny you should ask. He's not interested—yet. Time will tell.

One day I might introduce him to the Algerian-French writer Albert Camus. *The Art of Insight* begins with one of his quotes and, if you are familiar with his thinking, his presence should have been evident here and there. Camus was a humanist of profound decency who witnessed the clash between the totalizing narratives of his time, the early 20th century—fascism and communism in particular—and grew skeptical of them all.

To Camus, there's no idea, no matter how persuasive, elegant, or beautiful, that legitimizes the suffering or death of human beings. Moreover, whatever we devote our lives to, it better be done to the benefit of those who surround us, as the inescapable absurdity of human existence can be alleviated by sharing everyday joys, pleasures, and laughter with others.

In his early essay "Summer in Algiers" (1936), Camus, who loved to be alive in this world, and felt uneasy with those who are indifferent to its beauty, wrote, "Between this sky and the faces turned toward it there is nothing on which to hang a mythology, a literature, an ethic, or a religion." All that remains, he concluded, are "stones, flesh, stars, and those truths that the hand can touch."

So there it is, Alex. That's the magic.

Acknowledgments

This book exists thanks to my agent, David Fugate, and to the patience and generosity of Bill Falloon, Stacey Rivera, and the rest of the team at Wiley. Life has a knack for making the most careful plans crumble, so *The Art of Insight* sees the light of day two years later than it should have; at times I thought I would not be able to complete it but, luckily, here it is.

Thanks to my friends and colleagues at the University of Miami: at the School of Communication, my first home, Dean Karin Willis, Sallie Hughes, Kim Grinfeder, and Sam Terilli; at the Institute for Data Science and Computing—my second home—to Nick Tsinoremas, Eve Cruz, Helen Gynell, Mitsu Ogihara, Ben Kirtman, and Ken Goodman. Also thanks to friends at organizations I regularly work with, such as the Congressional Budget Office, McMaster-Carr, Google, Microsoft, the World Bank Poverty and Equity group, and so on.

Thanks to the Hurakan research group for so many hours discussing maps and graphs: Barbara Millet, Sharan Majumdar, Scot Evans, Brian McNoldy, and Kenny Broad.

Numerous friends read the manuscript of *The Art of Insight* in part or in its entirety, and kindly offered suggestions. In no particular order: Jen Christiansen, Catherine D'Ignazio, Nigel Holmes, Ken Field, RJ Andrews, Giorgia Lupi, Nick Desbarats, Nigel Hawtin, John Grimwade, Robert Grant, Paul Albert, Nick Cox, Moritz Stefaner, Steve Wexler, Bridget Cogley, Randy Krum, John Bailer, Nathan Yau, Isabel Meirelles, Claus Thorn Ekstrøm, Brent Dykes, and so many others. Thanks also to Tamara Munzner and Elliott Morsia, my co-editors at CRC Press's AK Peters Visualization book series.

Thanks to Hicham Bou Habib. He knows why. Stay well, friend.

Getting image permissions for a book like this is time-consuming, so thanks to some individuals and organizations that helped me with it: Marcelo Duhalde (*South China Morning Post*), Archie Tse (*The New York Times*), Chiqui Esteban (*The Washington Post*), Alan Smith (*Financial Times*), and Simon Scarr (*Reuters*).

Thanks to all my students, past, present, and future, but particularly to my PhD student Qian Ma, and to my spring of 2023 Data Visualization Studio Class, Carolina Sánchez, Daniela Rodríguez, William Pacetti, and Luís Ángeles. They all had to endure more than a few rants while I was putting the last touches on this book.

Bibliography

Abelson, R.P. (1995) *Statistics as Principled Argument*. New York: Psychology Press.

Battle-Baptiste, W., and Rusert, B. (eds.) (2018) *W.E.B. Du Bois's Data Portraits: Visualizing Black America,* New York: Princeton Architectural Press.

Bozóki, A. (2016) "Mainstreaming the far right: Cultural politics in Hungary," *Revue d'études comparatives Est-Ouest*, 47(4), December.

Bremer, N. and Wu, S. (2021) *Data Sketches*. Boca Raton, FL: CRC Press.

Broussard, M. (2018) *Artificial Unintelligence: How Computers Misunderstand the World.* Cambridge, MA: The MIT Press.

Camus, A. (1970) *Lyrical and Critical Essays*. New York, NY: Vintage Books.

Christiansen, J. (2023) *Building Science Graphics: An Illustrated Guide to Communicating Science through Diagrams and Visualizations.* Boca Raton, FL: CRC Press.

Csikszentmihalyi, M. (1990) *Flow: The Psychology of Optimal Experience*. New York: Harper Perennial.

Curzan, A. (2014) *Fixing English: Prescriptivism and Language History.* Cambridge, UK: Cambridge University Press.

D'Ignazio, C. and Klein, L. (2020) *Data Feminism*. Cambridge, MA: MIT Press.

D'Anieri, P. (2023) *Ukraine and Russia: From Civilized Divorce to Uncivil War*. Cambridge, UK: Cambridge University Press.

Elavsky, F., Bennett, C. and Moritz, D. (2022) "How accessible is my visualization? Evaluating visualization accessibility with Chartability," *Computer Graphics Forum*, 41, pp. 57–70. https://doi.org/10.1111/cgf.14522.

Elmqvist, N. (2023) "Visualization for the Blind," *ACM Interactions,* 30(1). doi: 10.1145/3571737. https://interactions.acm.org/archive/view/january-february-2023/visualization-for-the-blind.

Felton, N. (2016) *Photoviz: Visualizing Information Through Photography*. New York, NY: Gestalten.

Fragapane, F. (2018) "I'm a Visual Designer whose sight is not perfect anymore," Medium. https://medium.com/@frcfr/im-a-visual-designer-whose-sight-is-not-perfect-anymore-c6e7dfdd5461.

Fragapane, F. (2022) "On visualizing women's data and delegitimisation," Instagram. https://www.instagram.com/p/CmJUfVpsVI3/.

Friendly, M. (2008) "The Golden Age of Statistical Graphics," *Statistical Science*, 23(4), pp. 502–535. doi: 10.1214/08-STS268.

Goma Lanzón, J. (2019) *Imitación y Experiencia: Tetralogía de la Ejemplaridad*. Barcelona, Spain: Penguin Random House.

Grudin, R. (1990) *The Grace of Great Things: Creativity and Innovation*. Boston, MA: Ticknor & Fields.

Hadot, P. (2004) *What is Ancient Philosophy?* Cambridge, MA: Belknap Press.

Hacking, I. (1990) *The Taming of Chance*. Cambridge, UK: Cambridge University Press.

Holder, E. and Xiong, C. (2022) "Dispersion vs Disparity: Hiding Variability Can Encourage Stereotyping When Visualizing Social Outcomes," *IEEE Transactions on Visualization and Computer Graphics*, 29(1), pp. 624–634. doi: 10.1109/TVCG.2022.3209377.

Jacob, Mary Jane M. J. (2018) *Dewey for Artists*. Chicago, IL: The University of Chicago Press.

Jones, C. C. (2023) *Easy Beauty: A Memoir*. New York: Avid Reader Press.

Kosara, R. (2016) "An Empire Built On Sand: Reexamining What We Think We Know About Visualization." *BELIV '16: Proceedings of the Sixth Workshop on Beyond Time and Errors on Novel Evaluation Methods for Visualization,* October, pp. 162–168. https://doi.org/10.1145/2993901.2993909.

Krutch, J. W. (1953) *The Best of Two Worlds*. New York: William Sloane Associates.

Le Breton, D. (2022) *Marcher la vie : un art tranquille du bonheur*. Paris, France: Éditions Métailié.

Lupi, G. (2017) "Data Humanism: The Revolutionary Future of Data Visualization," *Print,* January 30. https://www.printmag.com/article/data-humanism-future-of-data-visualization/.

Macdonald, H. (2020) *Vesper Flights*. New York: Grove Press.

Makulec, A. (2020) "Ten Considerations Before You Create Another Chart About COVID-19," *Nightingale*. https://medium.com/nightingale/ten-considerations-before-you-create-another-chart-about-covid-19-27d3bd691be8.

May, T. (2019) *A Decent Life: Morality for the Rest of Us*. Chicago, IL: The University of Chicago Press.

Monteiro, M. (2019) *Ruined by Design: How Designers Destroyed the World, and What We Can Do to Fix It*. San Francisco CA: Mule Books.

Monteiro, M. (2020) *The Collected Angers: Essays About Design for an Unwilling Audience*. San Francisco CA: Mule Books.

Munzner, T. (2014) *Visualization Analysis and Design*. Boca Raton, FL: CRC Press.

Nagel, T. (1986) *The View From Nowhere*. New York: Oxford University Press.

Nisbett, R.E. and Ross, L. (1980) *Human inference: Strategies and shortcomings of social judgment*. Englewood Cliffs, NJ: Prentice-Hall.

Noble, S. U. (2018) *Algorithms of Oppression: How Search Engines Reinforce Racism*. New York: New York University Press.

Oakeshott, M. (1991) *Rationalism in Politics and Other Essays*. Carmel, Indiana: Liberty Fund.

O'Neil, Cathy (2016). *Weapons of Math Destruction: How Big Data Increases Inequality and Threatens Democracy*. New York: Broadway Books.

Palonen, E. (2017) "Building a New City through a New Discourse: Street Naming Revolutions in Budapest," in Rose-Redwood, R. et al. *The Political Life of Urban Streetscape: Naming, Politics, and Place*. New York, NY: Routledge.

Prado, L. G. (2021) *Crepúsculo en Budapest: Hungría en los tiempos de Orbán*. Madrid, Spain: Báltica Editorial.

Prado, L. G. (2022) *Vida en un clima iliberal*. Madrid, Spain: Alamut Bibliópolis.

Rendgen, S. (2019) *History of Information Graphics*. Cologne, Germany: Taschen.

Richards, N. (2023) *Questions in Dataviz: A Design-Driven Process for Data Visualisation*. Boca Raton, FL: CRC Press.

Rogers, S. (2012) "Anyone can do it. Data journalism is the new punk," *The Guardian,* May 24. https://www.theguardian.com/news/datablog/2012/may/24/data-journalism-punk.

Rothenstein, J. (2019) *Black Lives 1900: W.E.B. Du Bois at the Paris Exposition*. London, UK: Redstone Press.

Russell, B. (2013) *The Conquest of Happiness*. New York, NY: Liveright Publishing.

Sennett, R. (2008) *The Craftsman*. London, UK: Penguin Books.

Setlur, V. and Cogley, B. (2022) *Functional Aesthetics for Data Visualization*. Hoboken, NJ: John Wiley & Sons.

Slovic, P. and Slovic, S. (2015) *Numbers and Nerves: Information, Emotion, and Meaning in a World of Data*. Corvallis, OR: Oregon State University Press.

Slovic P., Västfjäll D., Erlandsson A., Gregory R. (2017) "Iconic photographs and the ebb and flow of empathic response to humanitarian disasters," Proceedings of the National Academy of Sciences, 114(4), pp. 640–644. doi: 10.1073/pnas.1613977114.

Tufte, E. R. (2001) *The Visual Display of Quantitative Information.* 2nd edition. Cheshire, CT: Graphics Press.

Vande Moere, A. and Purchase, H. (2011) "On the role of design in information visualization," *Information Visualization,* 10, pp. 356–371. doi: 10.1177/1473871611415996.

Index

C

D

E

H

I

J

K

N

O

P

Q

R

S

T

W

X

Y

Z